D1759999

Mortality and Immortality

RESEARCH SEMINAR IN ARCHAEOLOGY AND RELATED SUBJECTS

Since 1968, the Executive Committee of the Research Seminar in Archaeology and Related Subjects has sponsored seminars on themes of mutual interest to archaeologists and specialists in diverse fields in the social and natural sciences. Already, seminars dealing with domestication, settlement patterns, culture changes, prosimian biology, social evolution, and art and society have been organized and published. These volumes reflect the latest theoretical trends and research results in the rapidly changing areas of modern archaeology and connected subjects.

S. C. Humphreys and Helen King
Mortality and Immortality: the anthropology and archaeology of death, 1982

Mortality and Immortality: the anthropology and archaeology of death

*Proceedings of a meeting of the Research
Seminar in Archaeology and Related
Subjects held at the Institute of
Archaeology, London University, in June 1980*

edited by
S. C. HUMPHREYS AND HELEN KING
Departments of Anthropology and History
University College London

1981

ACADEMIC PRESS

A Subsidiary of Harcourt Brace Jovanovich, Publishers
LONDON NEW YORK TORONTO SYDNEY SAN FRANCISCO

Academic Press Inc. (London) Ltd
24–28 Oval Road
London NW1

US edition published by
Academic Press Inc.
111 Fifth Avenue,
New York, New York 10003

British Library Cataloguing in Publication Data

Mortality and immortality: the anthropology
and archaeology of death.
1. Death — Congresses
I. Humphreys, S. C.
II. King, H.
393   GT3150

ISBN 0-12-361550-X

LCCN 81-67910

Phototypeset by Dobbie Typesetting Service, Plymouth, Devon
Printed by T. J. Press (Padstow) Ltd., Padstow, Cornwall

Contributors

G. J. ARMELAGOS
Department of Anthropology. University of Massachusetts, Amherst, Massachusetts 01003, USA

N. BARLEY
Museum of Mankind, Burlington Gardens, London WIX 2EX, England

R. J. BERRY
Department of Zoology, University College London, Gower Street, London WC1E 6BT, England

M. BLOCH
Department of Anthropology, London School of Economics, Houghton Street, London, WC2A 2AE, England

E. CASSIN
Maison des Sciences de l'Homme, 54 Boulevard Raspail, Paris 75006, France

D. DE COPPET
CNRS, 44 Rue de la Tour, Paris 75014, France

T. CULLEN
Department of Archaeology, University of Indiana, Bloomington, Indiana 47401, USA

M. C. DA CUNHA
Department of Anthropology, Universidade Estadual de Campinas, Cidade Universitária Barão Geraldo, 13100 Campinas (São Paulo), Brazil

F. R. HODSON
Institute of Archaeology, University of London, Gordon Square, London WCIH OPY, England

S. C. HUMPHREYS
Departments of Anthropology and History, University College London, Gower Street, London WCIE 6BT, England

K. H. JACOBS
Department of Anthropology, University of Texas, Austin, Texas 78712, USA

T. W. JACOBSEN
Department of Archaeology, University of Indiana, Bloomington, Indiana 47401, USA

A. MACFARLANE
Department of Social Anthropology, University of Cambridge, Free School Lane, Cambridge CB2 3RF, England

D. L. MARTIN
Department of Anthropology, University of Massachusetts, Amherst, Massachusetts 01003, USA

T. MOLLESON
Department of Palaeontology, British Museum (Natural History), Cromwell Road, London SW7 5BD, England

S. F. MOORE
Department of Anthropology, Harvard University, Cambridge, Massachusetts 02138, USA

C. R. ORTON
Institute of Archaeology, University of London, Gordon Square, London WCIH OPY, England

P. RAHTZ
Department of Archaeology, University of York, Micklegate House, Micklegate, York YOI IJZ, England

A. STRATHERN
Department of Anthropology, University College London, Gower Street, London WCIE 6BT, England

R. THAPAR
Centre for Historical Studies, Jawaharlal Nehru University, New Mehrauli Road, New Delhi 110067, India

J.-P. VERNANT
Collège de France, Place Marcelin-Berthelot, Paris 75005, France

Preface

Many people helped to make the seminar at which these papers were presented an enjoyable and stimulating meeting. As well as thanking the contributors, I should particularly like to thank on their behalf and my own the Institute of Archaeology of the University of London for allowing us to hold the seminar on its premises; Phil Burnham, Mike Rowlands and Ian Glover of the Research Seminars Committee, and also Robert Garland and Amélie Kuhrt, for a great deal of help before and during the seminar; and finally my co-editor Helen King for doing most of the hard work in preparing the manuscript for the press. It should perhaps be made clear here that no systematic attempt has been made to incorporate the results of our discussions during the seminar into the text. Some contributors have rewritten or revised their papers since they were initially circulated, others have not. To ask everyone to do so would have delayed publication unduly.

July 1981   SALLY HUMPHREYS

Contents

Introduction: comparative perspectives on death

S. C. HUMPHREYS

In coming together as a group of archaeologists, physical and social anthropologists and historians to discuss research on death, we faced problems of comparison on two levels: comparison of the perspectives of different disciplines, and comparison of the practices and cultures of different societies. During our discussions it was, on the whole, the differences in research perspective and data which appeared most salient, and I shall begin this introduction with some brief remarks on these. But in retrospect, considering the papers in their final form, it appears to me that we missed many opportunities of reflecting on the differences between our own cultures and those of the other societies and periods discussed; and in the second part of my introduction I shall suggest some themes which it might have been interesting to pursue in more depth.

The disciplines represented here are limited, and the focus is emphatically on death as a social phenomenon. Even in the papers by physical anthropologists we are never very far from the social frame of reference. Animal and plant death is mentioned (with the exception of Berry's genetic studies and Molleson's introduction distinguishing human from animal death) only where certain animals or plants acquire a particular social or cultural significance which in some respects assimilates them to persons: leopards and cattle among the Dowayo (Barley), pigs for the 'Aré 'Aré (de Coppet, cf. also Strathern), a pet lamb in the Romano-British rural cemetery at Owslebury (Molleson), cedar trees in ancient Mesopotamia (Cassin). At the same time, however, this inclusion of selected animals and plants indicates

1

that death is not defined in religious terms as the separation of the human spirit from the body. The first paper in the collection, by Theya Molleson, begins by distinguishing human responses to death from those of animals in terms of *ceremonial behaviour*; and what seems to me to characterise our approach to the archaeology and anthropology of death, in contradistinction from the traditional approaches inherited from the nineteenth century, is that we focus on this ceremonial behaviour and the discourses associated with it, and try to derive from them the functions they serve and the assumptions they presuppose, rather than trying to explain them by reference to some preconceived schema of beliefs concerning the after-life. With this shift, some of the themes traditionally prominent in the comparative study of death — the place of death in different religions and, more specifically, concepts of the soul and their implications for the conceptualisation of the personality, or the association of different fates in the after-life with moral conduct during life — have come to be neglected. The only paper here which focuses on eschatology (Cunha) looks at it from the point of view of the structural relationship between the society of the living and the world of the dead, in order to consider the social functions of and social constraints on eschatological speculations. We are looking at death as the removal of a social person from society, and in dealing with what happens after death most of us have unreflectingly adopted the perspective which Vernant has explicitly shown to be that of Greek epic poetry: it is the fate of socially significant aspects of the person (status, exploits, personal relationships) which matters. We did not invite a psychologist to join our discussions. Perhaps we should have.

Almost all those taking part in the seminar were used to working in more than one of the disciplinary frameworks represented, or collaborating across disciplinary boundaries. The archaeologists had close links with physical anthropology and history; the historians with archaeology, social anthropology and, in Macfarlane's case, demography; both social and physical anthropologists are concerned with historical developments over time, and Bloch's paper explicitly addresses from a social anthropologist's viewpoint the archaeologist's problem of trying to interpret material culture with inadequate information on culture and social structure. Nevertheless, it takes more than interpersonal contact and goodwill to solve the problems of inter-disciplinary research. For example, in excavation the physical anthropologist's needs are very different from those of the archaeologist oriented to the study of material culture, and they are unlikely to be satisfied at all adequately while most excavations are directed principally towards the recovery and dating of artefacts, as is still the case in too many areas. The physical anthropologist needs more graves dug than the student of pottery sequences, and is concerned with a far longer time-scale; evolutionary changes will rarely show up in the time-span covered by most excavations on a single site and where, as at Armelagos' Wadi Halfa or Jacobsen's Franchthi, a single site does produce material covering several millennia, the sample of graves excavated is usually too small to provide a secure statistical basis for conclusions. (Carlson, 1974, 1976, studied 240 crania from deposits stretching from *c.*3400 B.C. to *c.* A.D. 1100; his 1977 article compares these with 12 Mesolithic crania.) The same problem of sample size is faced by archaeologists who wish to use cemetery data as a basis for reconstructing stratification patterns, as is emphasised by Hodson and Orton. Again, social anthropologists raise questions about the spatial positioning of the dead in relation to the living (Cunha, this volume; cf. Ucko, 1969, Leach, 1977) which archaeologists could only begin to consider if they had far more complete data on the relations between settlements and cemetery sites than are usually available. The archaeologist's conception of an adequate sample and definition of the "site" as the unit of research are called into question by the perspectives of other disciplines.

Historians also have problems in adjusting their focus to that of the demographers, as Macfarlane's paper indicates. It would seem reasonable, *prima facie*, to expect the "demographic transition" which dramatically reduced infant and child mortality to have some effect on attitudes to the death of young children, as Lawrence Stone (1977) and others have argued. But the view that before this change parents refrained from directing too much emotion towards young children assumes a relation between emotion and expectations of stability in relationships which will not be accepted without question by a social historian or social anthropologist. It assumes, indeed, that the individual is free to manage his or her psychological economy in a way which will minimise the risks of severe trauma. Even commonsense or common experience might suggest that there is something wrong about this view. The meaning and intensity of emotional relationships is surely affected by the value placed on them by the actor's culture (which will not necessarily place a high value on the avoidance of all kinds of risk); and reactions to child death therefore have to be related to the status of children in the culture (which may involve considering the significance of future, as well as past, time: cf. Strathern's paper, on the Wiru), and to the meaning attached to intrafamilial relationships in general (a shift to a much greater expression of concern over child deaths took place in Athens in the late fifth–fourth century B.C. with no demographic change behind it, cf. Humphreys, 1980; note that the more or less contemporary Herodotus, I. 136–137, ascribes to the Persians the attitude which modern historians ascribe to the pre-bourgeois family). Again, one would expect severe epidemics to affect attitudes to death, and we do indeed have some striking accounts in historical sources of changes in attitudes *during* plagues (Thucydides; Lebrun, 1971; cf. Vanstiphout, 1980). But it is difficult to identify long-term results of such experiences with any confidence. (Note Rahtz's suggestion of a possible connection between the fourteenth-century plagues and the prominence of macabre themes in representations of death.)

Such interdisciplinary confrontations tend to leave archaeologists, in particular, feeling somewhat beleaguered: asked to expand their framework of reference in both space and time to impracticable dimensions, and at the same time warned — as Maurice Bloch warns them here — that if they try to interpret material culture without any data on ideology or any other source of information on social structure they are liable to jump to the wrong conclusions. Peter Ucko, one of the founders of this seminar series, already gave the same warning in a brilliant article (1969) which made several essential points: that a single cemetery site may well not contain a representative sample of the population using it from the point of view of sex, age, social status, cause of death or physical condition at the time of dying; that there is variation in the treatment of the dead within all cultures as well as between cultures; that burial practices are not necessarily stable or closely correlated with other aspects of social structure or beliefs (cf. Cunha's remarks in this volume on the instability of eschatology); that it is in the highest degree unlikely that any two societies will resemble each other sufficiently for an archaeologist or historian to be able to make direct inferences from ethnographic data to fill gaps in our knowledge of past societies.

Ucko nevertheless claimed that familiarity with ethnographic data was of the utmost value to the archaeologist or historian because it served to "widen the horizons of the interpreter"; and I turn now to consider the contribution which the perspectives on different societies collected here can make to such a widening of horizons. It is a commonplace of social anthropology that experience of other cultures is particularly valuable in relation to phenomena in which we have a deep emotional involvement and which our own culture (and others: Bloch, in press) tends to dignify by classing them as "natural"; and I shall try now not only to point out some of the more significant differences and resemblances between cultures which emerge from the papers collected here, but also to analyse the papers themselves as a discourse on death which can tell us something about the culture which produced them.

By way of preamble, it is worth remarking that the ideas current in different societies about the way other people dispose of their dead are in themselves an interesting topic for research. Ancient Greek ethnographers situate Greek funerary practices in the centre of a spectrum which ranges from the utter neglect practised by Persian magi who expose corpses to be mauled by dogs and vultures (Herodotus, I.14) to the over-incorporation of the dead into the world of the living practised on the one hand by the Egyptians (image of a corpse at symposia, Herodotus, II.78; necrophily, ibid. 89) and, at the other end of the evolutionary scale (cf. Rossellini and Said, 1978), by Indian tribes who eat their dead associates (*hoi malista homileontes* is the term used), the endophagy being sexual as well as social (ibid. III. 99). (Herodotus seems inclined to oppose the magi who expose corpses to ordinary Persians who cover them with wax—a practice analogous to Egyptian mummification, belonging to the "civilised" end of the evolutionary continuum—but is not sure of the facts: his Hellenised Persian informants may well have been inclined to reticence.) The works of early European travellers, missionaries and anthropologists provide ample material for similar studies. The remark of R. Taggia quoted by Cunha, in which he unhesitatingly recognises among the Krahó the desire to pass eternity in the company of one's own kin which played such an important part in nineteenth-century European burial practices, is typical of the sympathetic form of ethnocentric distortion: the "others" are assumed to share "our" feelings. But the converse attitude of eagerness to swallow any story which heightened the contrast between the practices of "savages" and "civilised peoples" was equally common, especially of course in the form of stories about cannibalism. The effects of these western attitudes on colonial administration also require study (cf. Strathern).

We may now be able to see more clearly the motes in the eyes of earlier researchers and the biases in the legacy they have left to us; but how far can we go towards detecting the beams which distort our own vision? What do the areas of concentration and neglect in this volume suggest?

Many of the contributors seem to share a feeling that death confronts human beings with an awareness of their own transience, to which they react with attempts to salvage out of this disturbing experience some residue to which permanence can be attributed. Tombs, and especially tomb monuments, are one of the main ways of doing this in western

culture, and this is one reason why so much research into death is
concerned with tombs. Funerals are thought of as ephemeral
phenomena and therefore receive less attention; but Strathern's and
de Coppet's papers on Melanesia reveal a different perspective in
which funerary exchanges lead on to further exchanges and thus
constitute a basis for the incorporation of the dead into a processual,
rather than static, immortality. Tomb monuments in western culture
— and in the Indian hero-stones discussed by Romila Thapar —
individualise those they commemorate; and most contributions here
betray traces of the Greek attitude sharply delineated by Vernant, in
which life is associated with individuality, and death threatens to put
an end to differentiation unless the dead person is rescued from the
finality of death by preservation of the memory of him or her as an
individual. Western culture does its best to hold off the idea of death as
indifferentiation. Archaeologists try to use grave-goods and skeletal data
to reconstruct as many of the individual features of the dead as
possible; even the physical anthropologists' current concern with the
survival of genes (which, viewed in comparative perspective as an
ideology of death — and what alternatives does our culture now offer?
— seems distinctly bizarre) may be seen as related to interest in the
transmission of individualising features from generation to generation
(in contrast to an earlier focus on the stability of racial types). Other
cultures seem particularly striking when they reverse this perspective:
the Merina who crunch up the bones of the dead all together in order to
make the tomb into an ideal representation of group unity (Bloch); the
Krahó who think that the images of the dead lack the individualising
ties created by affinity and become steadily less differentiated until they
end as stocks and stones (Cunha). It is remarkable to find the Greek
model of the commemoration of heroic individuality turning up here
both in India (Thapar) and in Melanesia (Strathern: commemoration
of prominent men in exchange cycles). Only de Coppet's paper seems
to escape entirely from the tendency to discuss the fate of the dead in
terms of the survival or non-survival of residues of the individual — a
significant exception in view of the constant emphasis of de Coppet's
teacher Louis Dumont on the distortions which the influence of
individualism is likely to introduce in the study of non-modern
civilisations (cf. e.g. Dumont, 1975).

    Another feature of the majority of the papers in this collection which
seems diagnostic of our own culture is that death is treated as something which happens to others. Only Vernant looks at death from the
point of view of the man who confronts it. Martyrdom is barely
mentioned. We seem reluctant even to look at the possibility that there

may be a wide variety of attitudes towards the prospect of one's own death — with the suffering, or release from suffering, which it may bring — and that these need research.

Besides revealing such aspects of our attitudes to death, the seminar papers and the discussions which took place implicitly demarcated antitheses in our ways of perceiving and classifying the world which underlay our difficulties in communicating between the different disciplinary subcultures represented: the oppositions between "nature" and "culture" and between "things", "persons", and the shared beliefs and interactions which make up society. We failed to develop any general comparative discussion about views on the causes of death, for example, and this was surely due at least in part to a feeling of incompatibility between the explanations of death put forward by scientific medicine and beliefs such as those of the 'Aré'Aré, who divide deaths into those caused by human killers and those caused by ancestral spirits. But we ought to have been alerted by Berry's remark that human biologists do not know what causes ageing and death to the realisation that the concept of "natural death" — if by this one means a death resulting from the operation of normal processes rather than from their breakdown — has as precarious a status in western medicine as it has in those cultures which ascribe all deaths to witchcraft, but nevertheless show less concern to find the witch in the case of the deaths of the very old. Medical explanations of death, though couched in a "natural" idiom, still seek to apportion blame (to one organ rather than another); and they can easily be combined with moral judgments. Nowadays we are all warned of the mortal dangers of smoking, drinking, over-eating and taking too little exercise; in Victorian novels young ladies died of a "decline" brought on by falling in love with an unsuitable man, or of infectious diseases caught by showing too much zeal in visiting the poor.

Reluctance to integrate "natural" and "social" factors in the study of society is also responsible for noticeable omissions and distortions in many social anthropologists' and social historians' studies of social structure. Because they look for normal and typical patterns of social relationships and have tended, at least until very recently, to regard early death as abnormal and "accidental" even in those societies where it is statistically frequent, there is a marked bias towards the description of social structure as if each actor lived to a ripe age. Orphans, widows (see, however, Pitt-Rivers, 1977) and widowers, second marriages and step-relationships, the childless, are seldom mentioned (as are the disabled and the chronically sick). Most of the categories listed here are, of course, commoner in monogamous situations; but even in "polygynous societies" not every man can afford several wives, and variations in family size can still be very significant. Sally Falk Moore points out in her paper that the implications of an inheritance rule which favours eldest and youngest sons and leaves their intermediate siblings to seek new land for themselves may be radically affected by demographic change. If, as Bourdieu (1977) recommends, we should move from the construction of normative models of social structure to the study of the manifestation of dispositions shaped by social experience in actors' strategies, then the incidence of death is a situational factor which will have to be given serious consideration. If historians must learn to think in terms of the aggregate effects of demographic patterns—as they have recently been doing (Macfarlane)—social anthropologists need to integrate the time dimension and an awareness of the significance of particular historical events (such as a death) into their analysis of even short-term situations.

Between social anthropologists, or historians, and archaeologists the conceptual barrier is based on the antithesis between "things" and the meanings people attach to them. It is all too easy for social anthropologists to produce examples of burial forms or artefact patterns of which the archaeologist would never guess the meaning without help from ethnographic or written sources; and it is attractive to some archaeologists, in response, to look for a solution in stressing the materiality of their data, in associating themselves with "science" rather than with history, in seeking ways of "making the facts speak for themselves". Insofar as archaeological studies in the past have too often relied on unquestioned and ethnocentric assumptions about the relation between beliefs and behaviour, rather than studying the material record thoroughly, and with a full awareness of the possible range of variations which it might reveal, this movement is of course fully justified; but it still conceals unscrutinised assumptions about the place of "things" in culture which need discussion. The question of the relations between persons and things is one of the areas where the attitudes of western culture are most often taken for granted. Strathern and de Coppet have difficulty here in finding a language in which to express the Melanesian view that both things and persons are manifestations of sets of social relationships, or that "it is the person who is the prime form of movable property" (Strathern). By contrast, we can see that western archaeologists make a more direct connection between persons and things: they see things as *belonging to* persons, as property and above all as symbols of personal status and (for certain categories of objects thought to have had emotional significance to the dead) residues of personal life-histories. It is because children in

Western society do not own property, except for toys, and have no achieved status, that the discovery of children with rich grave-goods becomes problematic. To take the use of things as symbolising status as something to be demonstrated for each culture, rather than as a quasi-universal phenomenon, would immediately indicate a further direction for research which oddly enough seems to have been little exploited by archaeologists concerned with the social significance of grave-goods: it becomes obvious that iconographic evidence for the differentiation of social statuses by dress, possessions and other uses of material objects should be sought and compared with the assemblages found in tombs of the same culture. Such a perspective would also show clearly the value, emphasized by Rahtz, of studying the material culture of societies and periods for which written sources (or ethnographic data) are also available.

The fact that archaeologists tend to pay particular attention to signs of social stratification or ranking in their attempts to deduce social status from grave-goods or the forms of tombs and monuments (sex, age and other criteria of status differentiation have been less thoroughly researched and are often integrated into models of social stratification) no doubt reflects the preoccupations of modern society. (We had hoped to include in the seminar an archaeological paper on kin groupings in tombs, but unfortunately it was not ready in time.) It is important to be aware of other potential bases for differential treatment of the dead. Archaic Greeks and medieval Indians (Thapar) paid greater attention to those whose manner of death conferred a retrospective glory on their lives; heroes often belonged to an upper stratum of society, a warrior group, but not everyone in this stratum became a hero. Implicitly, it is far too often assumed that the expenditure of wealth and effort on the burial and commemoration of the dead comes from the estate or the kin of the dead person, and that these resources are directly correlated with his or her status in society. But this need not be the case. Where funerals are celebrated or monuments are set up by groups based on some criterion which cuts across lines of economic stratification (as for example in the commemoration of saints and martyrs by a religious congregation) this assumption breaks down.

It is an obvious ethnocentric mistake to assume that the behaviour evoked by death is to be seen solely as a reaction to the disruptions of social and emotional equilibrium caused by a particular decease. Death provides occasions and materials for a symbolic discourse on life — through the different treatments accorded to those whose lives have ended in different ways and at different stages of development, through theories about what happens in the after-life, through the symbols used in funerary rites or eschatology to express the contrast between life and death. From this point of view one of the obvious lacunae of this volume is the absence of any systematic consideration of conceptions of sexuality and procreation in relation to conceptions of death, although the subject is touched on in the papers of Barley and Cassin.

Even in the small sample of cultures studied here, the recurrence of the same symbols may appear noteworthy: an association of water in general, or moving water in particular, with life and of dryness, solidity and stillness with death; an association of differentiation with life, as already noted above, and of lack of differentiation with death. Does this recurrence suggest the existence of a set of ''natural symbols'' particularly apt for the contrast between life and death, which might provide a lead in interpreting the symbolism found in archaeological data? Unfortunately, closer examination of the examples cited here seems discouraging. The association between water or wetness and life seems obvious enough. But while the Dowayo (Barley) associate wetness with nature and fertility and (relative) dryness with culture and with death (and regard flowing water as ''drier'' than still water), the situation for the Krahó (Cunha) is much more complex. Moving water is associated with life and ''ripening'', the latter association being connected with the fact that the fruits of the *buriti* palm have to be soaked in water for several days to make them edible (Cunha, 1973); still water is associated with death and changelessness. Yet for the Timbira in general dryness is associated with life and culture, wetness with nature and death (ibid.). Finally, for the Merina (Bloch), water from special sources blown by an elder or a king carries the blessing of life and fertility. In the first case we seem to be dealing with a theory which asserts a ''natural'' causal connection between fluids and fertility (with explicit reference to rain and bodily fluids), in the second case with an analogical relation between the pairs moving water/still water and life/death, and also with an analogy drawn from the use of water in the cultural processing of food, and in the third case with water as a fluid medium which can absorb and transmit intangible forces derived from contact with spirits, ancestors, elders or kings. Are we justified in saying that ''the same'' symbol is present in all three cases? But again, is it justifiable to try to distinguish between causal theories, analogy or metaphor and what we might be inclined to call magical operations? Do the differences in the underlying models matter, except from our parochial viewpoint?

Again, the idea that the dead — or at least some of them — lose their individuality is present in Merina, Krahó, Dowayo and ancient Greek thought; but its implications are very different in each case. For Greek aristocrats the thought of the anonymity and lack of individuality of the unremembered dead was terrifying; for the Krahó the solidarity of the kin group among the *mekarõ* is ambiguous, both ideal and unrealisable, negatively marked by the fact that the dead progress on through further stages of loss of personal identity until they become stocks and stones; for the Merina the union of skeletons crushed together in family tombs provides an ideal representation of the society of the living as it is supposed to be, only kings being allowed to retain their individuality; for the Dowayo the lack of differentiation of the dead seems to be related to their association with a generic control over fertility which benefits groups rather than individuals. More detailed ethnography would be needed in order to work such comparisons out more fully, and there are certainly problems here on which it would be interesting to collect more comparative data. But it is clear that the comparison will have to deal not with discrete "symbols" or even symbolic oppositions, but with complex combinations of social experience, practical observation, speculation and metaphor for which the notion of "natural symbols" may provide a heuristically fruitful starting point, but not a ready-made blueprint. (It may be noted here that death itself provides "natural symbols" used in other *rites de passage* and elsewhere, in ways which need to be studied.)

While the possibility of comparative generalisation is not explicitly ruled out by any of the contributors to this volume, there is a tendency to be content with the more modest aim of formulating research schedules for collecting data on which such generalisations might eventually be based (cf. especially the papers by Jacobsen and Cullen, Rahtz, Macfarlane and Humphreys). However, a consensus also seems to emerge from several papers that if fruitful generalisations are to be produced, comparative studies must be based on a more historical approach than has been common in anthropological studies until recently. There is convergence here between Berry's demand for more historical studies of the genetic patterns found in particular localities; Sally Falk Moore's insistence that inheritance laws change their significance according to the demographic and economic context in which they are operated; Romila Thapar's demonstration that the functions of a single type of grave monument, and the status and structure of the groups concerned with erecting and tending it, can change over time; Maurice Bloch's hope that a wide-ranging study of changes in material culture over time could tell archaeologists more about the relations between material culture and social structure than analyses concentrated within a limited period; and Manuela da Cunha's search for a theory of "speech forms" rather than of "grammar", i.e. an analysis of symbolic communication which shows its relation to the context in which it is produced. Bourdieu's focus on "strategy" rather than "rules" (1977) leads in the same direction: to a view that even within a single society and period situations do not reproduce themselves exactly. It is because death both emphasizes the impermanence and unrepeatability of social experience and calls forth attempts to preserve or re-create some aspects of it in permanent form that it offers a particularly stimulating focus for reflections on the paradoxical mixture of the transient and the permanent which constitutes society.

References

BLOCH, M. (1971). "Placing the Dead". Seminar Press, London and New York.

BLOCH, M. (in press). Death, women and power. *In* "Death and the Re-generation of Life" (J. Parry and M. Bloch, eds). University Press, Cambridge.

BOURDIEU, P. (1977). "Outline of a Theory of Practice". Cambridge University Press, Cambridge. (Original French edition, Droz, Geneva, 1972.)

CARLSON, D. S. (1974). Temporal variation in prehistoric Nubian crania. Ph.D. Dissertation, University of Massachusetts, Amherst, Massachusetts.

CARLSON, D. S. (1976). Temporal variation in prehistoric Nubian crania. *American Journal of Physical Anthropology*, **45**, 467–484.

CARLSON, D. S. and VAN GERVEN, D. P. (1977). Masticatory function and post-Pleistocene evolution in Nubia. *American Journal of Physical Anthropology*, **46**, 495–506.

CUNHA, M. C. da (1973). Logique du mythe et de l'action. Le mouvement messianique canela de 1963. *L'Homme*, **13** (4), 5–35.

DUMONT, L. (1975). On the comparative understanding of non-modern civilisations. *Daedalus*, **104** (2), 153–172.

HUMPHREYS, S. C. (1980). Family tombs and tomb cult in ancient Athens: tradition or traditionalism? *Journal of Hellenic Studies*, **100**, 96–126.

LEACH, E. R. (1977). A view from the bridge. *In* "Archaeology and anthro-pology: areas of mutual interest" (M. Spriggs, ed.), pp.161–176. British Archaeological Reports Supplementary Series 19.

LEBRUN, F. (1971). "Les Hommes et la mort en Anjou aux XVIIe et XVIIIe siècles. Essai de démographie et de psychologie historiques". Mouton, Paris/Hague.

PITT-RIVERS, J. (1977). "The Fate of Shechem or the Politics of Sex". Cambridge University Press, Cambridge.

ROSSELLINI, M. and SAID, S. (1978). Usages de femmes et autres nomoi chez les "sauvages" d'Hérodote: essai de leçon structurale. *Annali della Scuola Normale, Pisa* (ser. 3), **8**, 949–1005.

STONE, L. (1977). "The Family, Sex and Marriage in England 1500–1800". Weidenfeld and Nicholson, London.

UCKO, P. J. (1969). Ethnography and the archaeological interpretation of funerary remains. *World Archaeology*, **1**, 262–277.

VANSTIPHOUT, H. L. J. (1980). The death of an era: the great mortality in the Sumerian city laments. *In* "Death in Mesopotamia" (B. Alster, ed.), pp. 83–89. Akademisk forlag, Copenhagen.

The Archaeology and Anthropology of Death: what the bones tell us

THEYA MOLLESON

Introduction

Along with large brains, toolmaking and language, the deliberate inhumation of the dead is a unique human characteristic. Badgers are known to earth up the part of a sett where a badger has died; other animals will remove dead bodies from their immediate living area but these activities hardly constitute the ceremonial associated with human death.

Our closest living relatives, the chimpanzee and gorilla, respond to death in the troupe in limited ways although there does seem to be an appreciation of death. Jane Goodall has recorded the responses to a number of deaths in the chimpanzee group she studied at Gombe, Tanzania. The mother, called Olly, was concerned for her baby when it was sick and in pain but her attitude changed when the baby died, although she did hang on to the body for a day or two.

The day following the death Olly arrived in camp with the corpse of her infant slung over her shoulder. Olly seemed dazed, she looked neither to right nor left, she ignored the female chimpanzees and baboons who came to stare . . . The following afternoon Olly and Gilka [her daughter] arrived in camp without the body.

In another case Merlin, the orphaned three-year-old, pined and eventually died for want of the comfort he depended on from his dead mother (van Lawick-Goodall, 1971). But that is not to say he mourned for her.

A chimpanzee that has been killed by other chimpanzees may be eaten but there is no evidence that this is other than opportunist carnivore activity. There is no indication here of sacrifice or ritual eating. However it does seem that the place where a chimpanzee has last been seen alive might acquire a significance. "For nearly six months he [Humphrey] returned again and again to the place where Gregor had spent the last days of his life . . ." (van Lawick-Goodall, 1971.)

The origins of burial

It is of interest therefore to seek out the earliest evidence that we have for this human activity. The australopithecines are the earliest undisputed close relatives of our own lineage, becoming extinct at least 1·0 million years ago. Their fossilised remains have been found, fragmented, in caves in South Africa. In all probability they are the remains of leopard dinners that fell, unmourned, into the mouth of the underground cavern (Brain, 1970).

The *Homo erectus* occupants of a vast cave at Choukoutien near Peking about half a million years ago may have practised cannibalism. The fragmented skull and jaw bones and a few other bones with damaged ends have been found in the cave deposits together with broken animal bones that probably were used for food. But we have absolutely no evidence as to the context of thought or ritual in which any eating of the dead might have occurred.

At Ngandong, in deposits probably over 100 000 years old, on the Solo River, Java, 11 skull vaults were found, most lacking the base. Many have suggested (e.g. Howells, 1959) that here is evidence that the Solo people had gouged out and eaten the brains of their fellow men and women, although today it is the *top* of the skull that the people of Gunung Mulu break open when they want to eat the brain of a monkey or other animal.

Our first real evidence that people held the dead, and therefore death, with any special regard comes with the earliest evidence for burial of the dead. This characteristically human practice appears to have been initiated by the neandertals of north-west Europe about 70 000 years ago. At Le Moustier in France the burial of a child was found in a cave associated with tools of Mousterian type. A similar burial in a cave at Teshik Tash, Uzbekistan, also features a child. The body was surrounded by mountain goat horns, particularly large ones, held in place by stones and the whole covered over with earth. Finally a small fire was burned near the burial spot (Movius, 1953). The body in spite of the careful burial was disturbed and the bones chewed by a hyaena. It is possible to infer from the nature of the burial that it was accompanied by some form of ceremony in which a number of people took part.

The part that ceremony plays in a society today is very often a cohesive one in which roles and obligations are reaffirmed. The rite brings together a group of people varying from the family for a birth, to the community for a death. The *rites de passage* welcome and declare a new member at the point of transition. There is a sense of ownership or property. The newborn belongs to the family — now recognised as an entity; on his marriage he belongs to the community; on his death the community bids him farewell while declaring he was one of theirs. The action reinforces the group and reaffirms reciprocal obligations.

Thus the advent of ceremonial in the human life-style may have had far-reaching repercussions on the social organisation of society and the hold society might have had on its members. Evidence for burials may be our first archaeological evidence for ceremony and the first sign that early hominid groups had extended beyond the strict limits of the family to a larger entity — a community of unrelated people.

The habit of burying the dead spread through Europe. Often the evidence is to be found in caves. Yet there may have been open interments not preserved from this time. And buried bones have become an important testimony of early man.

If the reason why the Solo skulls have been damaged is associated with necrophagia it could indicate an attitude to the dead that is reminiscent of some neandertal burial practices found in Europe. At Monte Circeo in Italy we even have a fairly close parallel. The skulls in the cave are surrounded by a circle of stones, though again the evidence for removal of the brain is circumstantial. The base of a skull is easily damaged, particularly if handled during ritual. But the evidence for ritual remains. And we can take it that from the time of the Last Ice Age man had acquired attitudes and a social organisation of a sophistication that included particular treatment of his dead.

These attitudes to the dead included not only those too young to hunt as at Le Moustier, La Ferrassie and Teshik Tash but also those killed in accidents as at Shanidar in Iraq. Here on more than one occasion several people were killed by rock falls in their rock-shelter home. Their survivors who continued to live in the rock-shelter accorded those killed some kind of attention, probably in the form of funeral feasts. They also placed bunches of aromatic and colourful flowers on the bodies of other members of the group who died and were buried in the rock-shelter (Solecki, 1971).

Rock-shelters and caves were the repositories for the dead throughout the Last Ice Age. Often the bones indicate careful interment, although at other times the bones are fragmented and disarticulated, forming part of the rubble fill of the cave. Some, of course, could have entered the cave with the other soil deposits, during a storm, as hill-wash brought into the cave. The human bones could have been washed out of other deposits or burials on the surface.

In Britain, Upper Palaeolithic burials of the Later Pleistocene present a conflicting picture, from orderly burial as at Paviland, Gower, and Gough's Cave, Cheddar, Mendips, to charnel house at Aveline's Hole, also in the Mendips (Molleson, 1977). At Paviland a man (called "The Red Lady") was buried in a shallow pit — it may be that the soil was frozen, for the ice-front was not far away (Molleson, 1976). There were two slabs of rock near the body and a mammoth skull near the head. The underlying sediments had been disturbed and tools of more than one culture seemed to be mixed up. The deposits appeared to have been reworked before the man came to be buried in the cave with such care. This gap in time between the use of the cave as a tomb and its former use as a habitation would seem to be confirmed by the radio-carbon dating of the skeleton (16 500 bc. BM — 374) which is about 9000 years younger than the date (about 25/26 000 bc, BM — 1367) obtained on a *Bos primigenius* bone chosen at random from the underlying deposit (Molleson and Burleigh, 1978).

It is as though the cave had been used for burial long after it had ceased to be used for habitation. At the time of the inhumation the cave would have been some distance from the sea owing to the lowered sea-levels during the Ice Age. Yet the dead man had come from the sea, for there was a cache of periwinkle shells associated with the skeleton — placed where a man's trouser pocket would be (Buckland, 1823). We can speculate that the cave had been chosen for burial because it held some significance for the people. Alternatively it was merely a handy place to bury someone who met his death while out hunting.

There may be a similar use of Gough's cave. Here the Cheddar Man skeleton, dated 7000 bc (BM — 525), seems to be younger than the Creswellian culture in the underlying deposit; a reindeer antler has been dated to 8970 bc (Q — 1581). On the other hand Aveline's Hole, near Cheddar, contained a large number of bones, some associated as skeletons but most at least partially disarticulated. Dates (6000 bc) from the cave do not indicate whether this site was used intensively for a short period, mass death or sacrifice, or sporadically as for the disposal of the body of a member of a nearby community every few years. The last explanation seems the most probable in view of the varying condition of the bones from intact skeletons to fragments.

At the end of the Last Ice Age, with rising sea-levels, we lose track of most of the burials that must have taken place in Britain during Mesolithic times, unless a single arm bone and a motley collection of skulls found usually in river-beds is representative of a burial rite favoured by the Mesolithic people. Certainly they seem to have been river people, arriving by water and taking much of their sustenance from the coast, rivers and lakes which abounded in Europe at that time. Mesolithic camping sites were frequently in river valleys close to the water's edge (Wymer, 1977). It would not be surprising therefore if the Mesolithic people did dispose of their dead to the water.

During Neolithic times we find the first structures specifically constructed for containing the dead. At least 229 long barrows were constructed in England mostly in the south between 3500 bc and 2000 bc. They contain an estimated 1500 to 3000 burials and average 6 or 7 individuals per barrow. The burials occur in varying states of articulation and may thus be assumed to represent people whose deaths occurred over a span of time, and it is likely that the building of a long barrow was the terminal stage in a funerary ritual which lasted over an extended period (Atkinson, 1968).

From Neolithic times in Europe at least, the role that death plays in the life of the individual appears to change. Populations were on the whole more settled and buried their dead in fixed places or, if not, they failed to do so for a reason that in itself has a significance. Thus our interpretation of the bones can go beyond the mere evidence for burial and although site, method and form of burial remain important guides to death in the past we can add a closer look at the bones for an insight into the causes of death and the attitudes to death in prehistoric to historic times.

Age at death and mortality rate

If we look at the Lankhills data (Clarke, G., 1979) we can get an impression of mortality rates and vulnerable ages for death. The sample, 473 skeletons, can be divided into eight classes according to estimated age at death (Fig. 1). The adult classes can be further divided according to sex but include one class of adults who could not be aged.

The histograms show the numbers in each class. There are peaks for childhood deaths and young adults and a noticeably low mortality for young adolescents. This low mortality is consistent with a constant death-rate and is maintained for youths in the late adolescent/young adult period, but there is a marked early increase in female mortality during this period. Of course this sex difference might reflect a failure to identify correctly the sex of the younger skeletons, but it is more likely to reflect the high mortality of women during childbirth. Very few women in particular appear to have lived more than thirty-five years, but I suspect that in this last age group women may be under-represented (the rugosity of an old skeleton can mistakenly be taken to indicate a male) for there are only 73 women in the whole sample whilst there are 113 men. However, it is probably worth pointing out that female skeletons are more difficult to sex, and may be over-represented in the "unsexed" class.

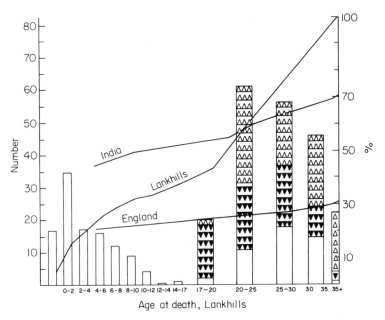

Fig. 1. Apparent mortality rate in a Romano-British population from Lankhills. The histograms (and left axis) show the number of dead, in each age group, in the Lankhills cemetery. Blank columns = unsexed skeletons, solid triangles = females, open triangles = males. The cumulative curves (and right axis) show the percentage dead. The curve for Lankhills is unlike the curves for India or England (after Pearl, 1940). At Lankhills infant and child deaths are probably considerably under-represented while the age at death of the adult skeletons has probably been under-estimated in some cases.

Neonate skeletons are undoubtedly under-represented, either because they decayed *in situ* or because they were buried elsewhere, and a neonate mortality of 30 to 40% is much more likely than the apparent 4% in the cemetery. Bearing this in mind, together with the fact that many infant deaths may also not be represented, the cumulative curve can only give an indication of mortality rates but it does show that at least 40% of those born did not survive childhood and that the average age at death was about 24 years. The mortality rate after a rapid increase at the end of adolescence remains constant, but high. Very few survived their early thirties. The shape of this curve is similar to survival curves obtained for non-industrial societies but is much steeper. Why the mortality rate for archaeological societies should be so much higher than it is for present-day societies that also lack advances in hygiene and medicine I do not understand. It is possible that present methods of determining age at death may be under-scoring. There is some indication that under-scoring may be the case at Winchester where excavations on the Cathedral Green have unearthed an unduly large number of undoubted cases of Paget's disease. This is a disease of unknown aetiology which causes gross thickening of the skull and long-bones in old age. Its incidence in a modern population is very low, and we would not expect to find many cases in a population of the size of Winchester during Medieval times.

Death from "natural causes"

It is possible to arrive at some idea of the population size from the number of burials found in a burial ground as Atkinson (1968) has shown for the Neolithic, Collis (1977b) for the Romano-British settlement at Owslebury and C. Green (1977) for the Dorchester cemetery, among others. Further estimations of age at death give some indication of living conditions and life stresses.

It is difficult to determine infant mortality rates for several reasons. The dead child was often not buried in the community cemetery but rather under the floor of the dwelling as at Frilford (Collis, 1977a), in a nearby ditch as at Owslebury (Collis, 1977b) or to the side of the main cemetery. The bodies of infants can easily be missed during incomplete excavation of a site, especially in those cases where children, dying before they could toddle or talk, were buried in another part of the cemetery (Collis, 1977b). Or, being fragile, they may be destroyed by erosion in the soil.

Where excavation has revealed a large number of infant burials infant mortality can be shown to have been as high as 30%, rising on occasions to as much as 60% (Collis, 1977b). This last figure may require an explanation of other than natural causes, and infanticide during hard times has been suggested. It is, however, worth recalling the time in St Kilda, Outer Hebrides, when a large number of babies died of tetanus administered unwittingly by the midwife when she applied contaminated fulmar oil and donkey dung mixture to the umbilicus of the newborn babe (Gibson, 1928). Such disasters are not recorded on the bone.

The hazards of weaning, dysentery and gastroenteritis, to judge from the number of burials of young children, were a major cause of death in 2–4 year olds. An indication of those that survived severe illness at this time may be found in the number of adults with evidence for major arrest in growth on their teeth. Hypoplastic lines on incisors and canines and disrupted cusp patterns on third molars are the permanent marks of a hiatus in growth at the time when that part of the tooth was being formed. A survey of the Poundbury teeth for hypoplasia has revealed a 38% frequency of hypoplasia on the permanent canines (Joyce Smith, in preparation). This arrest in growth of the teeth would have occurred as a result of severe illness during infancy. For every child that survived there must have been a number who died. Schulz and McHenry (1975) have shown from the frequency of hypoplastic lines on teeth that the most vulnerable age in Californian Indians was 4–5 years. This could be the age of weaning.

Life expectancy at birth would not have been high, perhaps even as low as 20 years (compared to 35 years today for a non-industrial society). After childhood this figure might have risen to 30 or so although high mortality figures for women in their early twenties does suggest that many did not survive childbirth. However those that did survive may have lived to a considerable age. Thus the mortality curve is not simple but has peaks at birth, early childhood, early 20s and old age; and figures giving the average age at death may not be representative of the age when most people actually died. When the life expectancy in a static population is 20 years, for example, about half the deaths occur before age five, a quarter after 50, and only about 6·5% occur in the 10-year span centred on the mean age at death (Coale, 1974).

Determination of age at death is fraught with uncertainties. In the growing skeleton, stage of epiphyseal closure and dental eruption is a reasonable guide to skeletal, if not chronological, age. In the adult a consensus of cranial suture closure, dental attrition and arthritic lipping is used as a guide in estimation of age. Rates of change of any of these characters varies with race and environment. The introduction of stoneground flours with the addition of grit to the flour to aid the grinding process greatly increased rates of dental attrition in populations from Neolithic times. Teeth could be worn out and edentulous mouths become a characteristic of modern man (our own species as distinct from fossil species). However the first people to live longer than their teeth seem to have been the neandertals. The australopithecines died before their teeth wore out as did the *Homo erectus* people. Heavy tooth wear and antemortem loss, indicating old age and an abrasive diet, is apparent in the neandertals. The old man at La Chapelle-aux-Saints had lost many of his teeth before he died. The teeth of the Gibraltar neandertal show heavy wear that occurred so rapidly that secondary dentine did not have time to form and the pulp cavities are exposed.

Death in old age, the only natural death, remains rare until comparatively recent times, though I suspect it may be more common than many archaeologists have been led to believe. And further work might need to be done on a more accurate ageing of skeletal material.

The mortality curves for most non-industrial societies after a high neonate mortality show a fairly constant rate of death from infancy to the eighties. This pattern we can assume would describe death rates in cultures represented by archaeological cemetery material. The rate itself and thus the steepness of the curve would doubtless have varied in different cultures and at different times. Atkinson, for example, has assumed a death rate of 40 per 1000 for Neolithic Britons (Atkinson, 1968). This rate decreases as we approach more recent times and the advent of better hygiene and improved sanitary conditions. Since the industrial revolution, improved nutrition and medical knowledge have also contributed to the reduced death rate in all except the very old, so that present-day mortality curves for industrial societies more nearly approach a rectangular form with most deaths occurring in old age.

The number of skeletons we find in a graveyard also reflects the birth rate in the community. And to get an idea of mortality in ancient times we really need to know the size of the community we are dealing with. Details of death rate, birth rate and settlement size are still very vague but there is no doubt of a dramatic change in all of these quantities since the introduction of agriculture and sedentary residence patterns in the last ten thousand years.

Death from disease

Not many of the epidemic diseases which can kill in vast numbers leave their marks on bone. The plague and cholera pits of London and elsewhere, containing sometimes hundreds of bodies, are identified rather from documentary evidence. Many of these diseases depend on overcrowding and impoverished standards of health and hygiene to be really effective scourges of the population and such conditions did not exist until the development of towns. Other killing diseases with similar environmental associations, such as tuberculosis, can leave a fairly characteristic mark on the bones. We do not find much evidence of this disease in Britain until medieval times and its presence in Egypt indicated by Morse *et al.* (1964) has recently been questioned (Price and Molleson, in press).

Leprosy is one disease that has fairly characteristic features that make its diagnosis at least in the later stages fairly certain. It is a disease whose history is difficult to document for other reasons. The disease was so disfiguring that victims from biblical times were outcasts in life—excluded from contact with their fellows. And in death as in life victims of leprosy were often isolated, buried in separate graveyards —sometimes cemeteries attached to the leper colony. Thus it was something of a surprise to find at least one case at Poundbury (Reader, 1974) from the fourth century A.D. Leper colonies did not exist in England until late Saxon or early Medieval times. The Lazar house on the island of Tean in the Isles of Scilly has been dated to the seventh century (Howe, 1976) but was not necessarily built to house only lepers since the word was generic in meaning and applied to any "poor and diseased person".

Nutritional diseases affect mostly the growing young and it is an imbalance in the diet that affects bone growth rather than starvation. Certainly children and adults alike must have died of starvation in the past but anthropologists would be hard put to it to identify bones of the victims of starvation. On the other hand lack of calcium, vitamin D, vitamin C, and iron do mark living bone and scoring the skeletal stigmata of these deficiency diseases should give us some idea of the toll they might have taken in the past. Rickets is rare in pre-medieval times when most people lived in rural conditions with access to fresh food. There are, however, several possible cases from Poundbury from the fourth century A.D. Unfortunately active rickets, scurvy and such diseases are difficult to diagnose in even microscopic sections of bone. Bone has a fairly limited response to interference in its growth and death from one cause can look much like death from another.

Natural selection

Eventually the anthropologist will look for evidence of selection by death in past populations. Since Darwin suggested that natural selection might be the mechanism by which evolution took place (Darwin, 1859) "survival of the fittest" has been implicit in much biological theory. Evidence for the early death of the genetically unfit is to be found occasionally on the malformed bones of youngsters who died before reaching maturity. Such congenital anomalies have only been recorded from post-Neolithic populations. Indeed there is little evidence that the physically handicapped survived at all before the emergence of modern man, although a possible healed fracture of an australopithecine femur from Koobi Fora (KNMER 739 *in* Leakey and Leakey, 1978) and a healed severe injury to the elbow of one of the Shanidar individuals (Solecki, 1971) are examples of just a couple of exceptions. However these are exceptions of a kind that occur in wild animals and there is no evidence at this early date for the succouring of invalids by family or community.

Perhaps the collection of pathological bones from Nubia (Reisner, 1910) provides the best evidence for survival or not of the congenitally abnormal. Cases of metabolic abnormalities including hydrocephalus, premature suture closure, and osteogenesis imperfecta were all collected and have recently been reviewed by Price and Molleson (in press). These diseases, however, are not all necessarily genetic as distinct from congenital in origin and anyway have an extremely low incidence in any population.

Attempts to detect micro-evolutionary trends have been made with varying degrees of success (Brothwell, 1965; Berry and Berry, 1972; and Musgrave and Evans, 1979). Thus there is a trend towards loss of third molars with the doubtful selective advantages of avoiding death from impacted wisdom teeth and saving of calcium in the formation of teeth. Similarly a comparison of the incidence figures for frontal sinus agenesis indicates a reduction of the incidence from Neolithic to modern times (Molleson and Brown, in press). It would be altogether too facile to suggest that advances in medicine have altered the mortality rate for sinusitis. Presumably other factors, such as genetic drift, are manifest in these and the variation of other non-metric variables in different populations. Berry has discussed the value of morphometrics and non-metric variant incidences for providing genetical information from skeletons (Berry, 1979).

The incidence of non-metric congenital anomalies, including such variables as metopism, wormian bones, undeveloped teeth, if distributed unevenly in a population, could be a means of estimating family relationships. Work on this kind of data has rarely been performed with cemetery material. At Poundbury there is already some evidence that the occurrence of the metopic suture is not evenly distributed among the burials; there are groups of skeletons in certain parts of the cemetery which have a much higher frequency of metopism than would be expected from the overall incidence in the population.

Violent Death

Fatal injury is not easy to recognise in skeletal material since most injury involving bone only leaves its mark when the individual has survived and the bone healed. But for every one who survives there must have been several who died and we can take the evidence for healed injuries in a population as some kind of measure of the deaths from violent causes in a population.

The circumstances of the discovery of the skeleton will sometimes indicate the possibility that the individual had met with an accident. The discovery of two or three skeletons of neandertals beneath a mass of rock debris at Shanidar suggested that they may have been the victims of huge rock falls during earthquakes (Solecki, 1971). Several of the skeletons attributed to the Mesolithic in Holland and Norway were probably the victims of drowning. The skeleton of an adult male was found in undisturbed marine clay at Bleivik in Norway. There was no burial pit and the individual was in a primary position so had apparently been drowned (Newell et al., 1979) although it is possible the man died "at sea" and was given a seaman's burial. The cranium found in a peat bog at Ravstrup, Denmark, was also that of a drowning victim, as was the skeleton found in lake beds at Koelbjerg, Denmark. It has also been suggested that two skeletons found in shell bank deposits at Stangenäs, Sweden, were the remains of victims of drowning, washed up on a beach and then covered by gravel from a beach wall.

It is only from Neolithic times that we can be really certain of killings and death in warfare. Neolithic missile points embedded in a contemporary skeleton from Fengate, Peterborough, may illustrate their effectiveness as weapons (Pryor, 1976) although of course the man could have been killed during a hunting accident, especially in view of the fact that there is a virtual absence from this time of defended sites or other skeletons with evidence of wounds. By Saxon times, however, skeletons with healed injuries of the kind that could be sustained in warfare are not uncommon.

The skeleton dated A.D. 635 at Maiden Castle was the object of a detailed study by Brothwell (1971) who came to the conclusion that it had been the subject of severe mutilation by a reasonably large metal weapon. The injuries seem most likely to have been received about the time of death and a number in the head region could have killed the individual. The distribution of the injuries suggests that the majority may have been intentionally directed at certain parts of the body as a definite policy of dismemberment. Why this should have been done remains a puzzle. There appears to be no satisfactory literature to suggest that such dismemberment was an official mode of execution during the Anglo-Saxon period.

Punishment by death

At Sewerby, Yorks., a contorted prone burial above a richly furnished supine burial of sixth-century date suggests sacrifice of a living serving woman to her dead mistress (Rahtz, 1960). But it has also been suggested that she was buried alive as a punishment — perhaps for the murder of the other woman (Hirst, in preparation, discusses evidence for this).

At Worthy Park, Kingsworthy, there are two burials in which the body is lying prone (face down); one is a woman in her late twenties, the other an adolescent girl of about 16 years. The girl's wrists are crossed, her heels together and her limbs may have been bound when she was put in the grave. Both are single inhumations (Hawkes and Wells, 1975).

There may be other cases of live burial either as a punishment or as a sacrifice attending the death of a more important figure. Sue Hirst (in preparation) discusses the evidence for ritual killing in the light of the Sewerby skeletons.

The executioners' pits sampled by Wood Jones and George Reisner during rescue excavations in Nubia (Reisner, 1910) provide evidence of a large number of hanged, speared and decapitated criminals who received mass burial and evidently were not claimed by their families for ritual interment. The evidence for capital punishment, though, comes from the archaeologists rather than the anthropologist, since none of the skulls in the Nubian Pathology Collection shows even cut marks on the vertebrae. Some of the skulls however did show a crack at the base of the skull which Wood Jones considered to be the result of hanging (Reisner, 1910: 73). The position of the two executioners' trenches, inside the Roman camp, suggested that the executions took place in Roman times, as a result of the revolts and troubles known to have occurred in that period.

Careful study of the bones by Robin Watt has revealed possible evidence for similar execution practices in the Romano-British site at Lankhills, Winchester. There were cut marks on the third or fourth neck vertebra of several skeletons, in particular nos 427, 441 and 445; the last two were female. In each case, and for several other skeletons not showing cut marks, the skull had been placed in a non-anatomical position — at the feet or between the legs (Clarke, G., 1979). On the other hand the exactness of the cut between the third and fourth vertebrae is taken, by Robin Watt (ibid.), to indicate that the head was severed after death and the act may have been sacrificial. G. Clarke (1979) has reviewed the evidence for decapitation, either post- or ante-mortem, from other Romano-British sites. In the Thames Valley, at least, there appears to be a clear association between decapitation and prone burial during Romano-British times. At Radley the two treatments are accorded the one individual (Harmon, Molleson and Price, 1981).

Sacrifice

Once man had learnt to take the life of his fellow man, whether in warfare or as a means of punishment, the way was open for other ritualised killings.

The double burial at Sewerby, Yorkshire, has already been discussed as possibly representing a ritual murder but a more likely explanation of the prone skeleton above a richly furnished supine burial does seem to be the sacrifice of a living serving woman to her dead mistress (Rahtz, 1960; Hirst, in preparation).

There is documentary evidence that the Vikings sacrificed slaves to attend their masters in the after-life. An Arab historian, Ahmad Ibn Fadnlan, writing in 922, has left an elaborate account of a ship burial of one of the Slavic leaders. Ceremonies included the immolation of a slave girl and the burning of the ship and its contents on the banks of the Volga.

Thus the skeleton from a boat burial at Ballatear, Isle of Man, found with arms upraised and a roundel removed from the back of the skull by the slash blow of a heavy instrument, may be a sacrifice (Bersu and Wilson, 1966). The Vikings had little respect for the earlier burials at a site they had taken over. For example at Balladoole, also on the Isle of Man, they disturbed even recent burials, removing bones, hands and feet still articulated and spreading them out on the surface to the north of their cists. Whether the Viking use of the existing burial site was coincidence (as Megaw believed, cf. Bersu and Wilson, op. cit.) or a deliberate demonstration of their dominance over the indigenous population (as Bersu believed) the bones cannot tell us.

During the Shang period the ideological emphasis on the sacrificial slaughter of humans and animals is pervasive in the homes of both the living and the dead in China. The palatial houses are sometimes as large as 60 metres in length and are all built on tamped earth foundations with pillar bases of stone or bronze. During construction, the three sacrificial animals of the Shang, dog, sheep and ox, were interred in the foundations. Human guardians with daggers and shields of bronze were sacrificed and buried inside and outside the doors. The cult of sacrifice grew to momentous proportions: in the main compound of Hsiao T'un, there are 852 human victims, 18 sheep, 35 dogs and 15 horses (Treistman, 1975).

The mass sacrifice recalls the burial at Ur of a King attended by something like 65 presumed courtiers and servants. Death on such a scale must to some extent have been voluntary or the result of mass hypnosis of a kind recently achieved in Guyana by the American cult leader, Rev. Jones, and his nine hundred followers who took their own lives by drinking cyanide. Sir Leonard Woolley in his discussion of the tomb at Ur, noting the calm layout of the bodies with head-dress all in place, suggests that the victims walked to their places, took some kind of drug—opium or hashish would serve—and lay down in order (Woolley, 1938:36).

Ritualised use of the dead

It is on record that in 1872 when the Hooghly Bridge was being built across the Ganges the native population feared that, in order to placate the river, each structure would have to be founded on a layer of children's skulls. Frazer in the Golden Bough quotes examples of living people being built into the foundations of walls and gates to serve as guardian spirits; and throughout the world stories of human sacrifice are associated with bridges, to the erection of which the rivers are supposed to have an especial antipathy.

When the bridge gate at Bremen was demolished in the last century the skeleton of a child was found embedded in the foundations (Opie and Opie, 1975). There are several legends in which all attempts to build a bridge fail until a human, usually a child, has been immured in the foundations.

Perhaps too few bridges have been excavated to verify the factual basis for these legends but there are several instances of finding human skeletal material in the foundations of buildings. At Lowbury Hill, Berkshire, and at Springhead Temple IV, foundation sacrifices were made in the second and third centuries A.D., a rite which was found at Hod Hill, Dorset, in pre-Roman times. Two of the sacrificed babies at Springhead were decapitated although their heads were not deposited with the rest of the body (Penn, 1960; Macdonald, 1979).

In death as in life

As a generality those that have lived together are buried together whether in the local cemetery or more particularly in a family tomb. Exceptions underline the constancy of this practice.

A young sheep found buried in the cemetery at Owslebury had received a quasi-human burial—it even had a coin (Collis, 1977b). This treatment of an animal which we can suppose had lived as a pet lamb, because it had a healed fracture of a leg, contrasts with the discovery of the mummy of a human anencephalic body found in the catacombs of Hermopolis where the sacred ape and ibis were normally buried (Brothwell and Powers, 1968). On the other hand a grave (no. 400) at Lankhills contained no human bones but the skeleton of a dog had been placed in the carefully dug grave, probably on top of the empty coffin. G. Clarke (1979) suggests that the empty grave might be a cenotaph, erected to ward off the worst fate that anyone could suffer, to die without receiving a proper burial.

So perhaps Schopenhauer was right when he suggested (Midgley, 1978) that the purpose of anything was what came at the end of it and therefore that death was the purpose of life.

References

ATKINSON, R. J. C. (1968). Old mortality: some aspects of burial and population in Neolithic England. *In* "Studies in Ancient Europe" (J. M. Coles and D. D. A. Simpson, eds), pp. 83–93. Leicester University Press, Leicester.

BERRY, R. J. (1979). Section 1. Genes and skeletons, ancient and modern. *Journal of Human Evolution*, **8**, 669–677.

BERRY, A. C. and BERRY, R. J. (1972). Origins and relationships of the Ancient Egyptians. Based on a study of non-metrical variations in the skull. *Journal of Human Evolution*, **1**, 199–208.

BERSU, G. and WILSON, D. M. (1966). "Three Viking Graves in the Isle of Man". The Society for Medieval Archaeology Monograph Series, No. 1, London.

BRAIN, C. K. (1970). New finds at the Swartkrans Australopithecine site. *Nature*, **225**, 1112–1119.

BROTHWELL, D. R. (1965). Micro-evolution in man. *Science Journal*, **1**, 79–85.

BROTHWELL, D. R. (1971). Forensic aspects of the so-called Neolithic skeleton Q1 from Maiden Castle, Dorset. *World Archaeology*, **3**, 233–241.

BROTHWELL, D. R. and POWERS, R. (1968). Congenital malformations of the skeleton in earlier man. *In* "The Skeletal Biology of Earlier Human Populations" (D. R. Brothwell, ed.), pp. 173–203. Pergamon, London and Oxford.

BUCKLAND, W. (1823). "Reliquiae Diluvianae", pp. 82–98. John Murray, London.

CLARKE, G. (1979). "The Roman Cemetery at Lankhills". Winchester Studies No. 3, Pre-Roman and Roman Winchester Part 2, Clarendon Press, Oxford.

COALE, A. J. (1974). The history of the human population. *Scientific American*, Sept. 1974, 40–51.

COLLIS, J. (1977a). Pre-Roman burial rites in North-Western Europe. *In* 'Burial in the Roman World' (R. Reece, ed.), pp. 1–13. CBA Research Report No. 22. Council for British Archaeology, London.

COLLIS, J. (1977b). Owslebury (Hants) and the problem of burials on rural settlements. *In* "Burial in the Roman World" (R. Reece, ed.), pp. 26–34. CBA Research Report No. 22, Council for British Archaeology, London.

DARWIN, C. R. (1859). "The Origin of Species". John Murray, London.

GIBSON, G. (1928). The tragedy of St. Kilda. *Caledonian Medical Journal*, 50–62.

GREEN, C. (1977). The significance of plaster burials for the recognition of Christian cemeteries. *In* "Burial in the Roman World" (R. Reece, ed.). CBA Research Report No. 22, Council for British Archaeology, London.

HARMON, M., MOLLESON, T. I. and PRICE, J. L. (1981). Burials, bodies and beheadings in Romano-British and Anglo-Saxon cemeteries. *Bulletin of the British Museum (Natural History), Miscellanea*, **35**, part 3.

HAWKES, S. C. and WELLS, C. (1975). Crime and punishment in an Anglo-Saxon cemetery?'. *Antiquity*, **49**, 118–122.

HIRST, S. in preparation.

HOWE, G. M. (1976). "Man, Environment and Disease in Britain". Penguin Books, Harmondsworth.

HOWELLS, W. (1959). "Mankind in the Making". Pelican Books, Harmondsworth.

van LAWICK-GOODALL, J. (1971). "In the Shadow of Man". Collins, London.

LEAKEY, M. G. and LEAKEY, R. E. (1978). "The Fossil Hominids and an Introduction to Their Context 1968–1974". Koobi Fora Research Project, Vol. 1, Clarendon Press, Oxford.

MACDONALD, J. L. (1979). Religion. *In* "The Roman Cemetery at Lankhills" (G. Clarke, ed.), pp. 406–433. Clarendon Press, Oxford.

MIDGLEY, M. (1978). "Beast and Man: the Roots of Human Nature". Harvester Press, Hassocks, Sussex.

MOLLESON, T. I. (1976). Remains of Pleistocene Man in Paviland and Pontnewydd Caves, Wales. *Transactions of the British Cave Research Association*, **3**, 112–116.

MOLLESON, T. I. (1977). Skeletal remains of Man in the British Quaternary. *In* "British Quaternary Studies, Recent Advances" (F. W. Shotton, ed.), pp. 83–92. Clarendon Press, Oxford.

MOLLESON, T. I. and BROWN, W. A. B. (in press). Evidence for the heritability of frontal sinus size and shape.

MOLLESON, T. I. and BURLEIGH, R. (1978). A new date for Goat's Hole Cave. *Antiquity*, **52**, 143–145.

MORSE, D., BROTHWELL, D. R., and UCKO, P. J. (1964). Tuberculosis in Ancient Egypt. *American Review of Respiratory Diseases*, **90**, 524–41.

MOVIUS, H. V. (1953). The Mousterian Cave of Teshik Tash, South Eastern Uzbekistan, Central Asia. *Bulletin of the American School of Prehistoric Research*, **17**, 11–71.

MUSGRAVE, J. H. and EVANS, S. P. (1979). "By Strangers Honor'd: a statistical study of ancient crania from Crete, Mainland Greece, Cyprus, Israel, and Egypt". MS., Department of Anatomy, University of Bristol.

NEWELL, R. R., CONSTANDSE-WESTERMANN, T. S. and MEIKLEJOHN, C. (1979). The skeletal remains of Mesolithic Man in Western Europe: An evaluative catalogue. *Journal of Human Evolution*, **8**, 1–228.

OPIE, I. and P. (eds) (1975). "The Oxford Dictionary of Nursery Rhymes", pp. 275–276. Oxford University Press, Oxford.

PEARL, R. (1940). "Introduction to Medical Biometry and Statistics". Saunders, Philadelphia.

PENN, W. S. (1960). Springhead: Temples III & IV. *Archaeologia Cantiana*, **74**, 113–140.

PRICE, J. and MOLLESON, T. I. (in press).

PRYOR, F. (1976). A Neolithic multiple burial from Fengate, Peterborough. *Antiquity*, **50**, 232–233.

RAHTZ, P. (1960). Sewerby. *In* Medieval Britain in 1959 (D. M. Wilson and J. G. Hurst, eds). *Medieval Archaeology*, **4**, 134–165.

READER, R. (1974). New evidence for the antiquity of leprosy in early Britain. *Journal of Archaeological Science*, **1**, 205–207.

REISNER, G. A. (1910). "The Archaeological Survey of Nubia, Report for 1907–1908", Vol. 1. Archaeological Report, Ministry of Finance, Survey Dept., Egypt.

SCHULZ, P. D. and McHENRY, H. M. (1975). Age distribution of enamel hypoplasia in prehistoric California Indians. *Journal of Dental Research*, **54**, 913.

SOLECKI, R. S. (1971). "Shanidar, the Humanity of Neanderthal Man". Allen Lane, London.

TREISTMAN, J. (1975). The Far East. *In* "Varieties of Culture in the Old World" (R. Stigler, ed.), pp. 106–128. St. James Press, London, and St. Martin's Press, New York.

WOOLLEY, SIR CHARLES L. (1938). "Ur of the Chaldees". Pelican Books, Harmondsworth.

WYMER, J. J. (1977). The Archaeology of Man in the British Quaternary. *In* "British Quaternary Studies, Recent Advances" (F. W. Shotton, ed.), pp. 93–106. Clarendon Press, Oxford.

Death and Demography in Prehistoric Sudanese Nubia

GEORGE J. ARMELAGOS,
KENNETH H. JACOBS AND
DEBRA L. MARTIN

Death is the ultimate measure of maladaptation in biological populations. Individuals and populations are continuously challenged in their
ability to adjust to their environment and to changes which alter their
habitat. The success of individuals or populations is reflected in their
ability to survive and reproduce. Maladaptation is signalled by
retardation in growth, a rise in the frequency and severity of disease
and, ultimately, in death. It is ironic that analysis of death and disease
in prehistoric skeletons provides the data which allows us to reconstruct
how the populations lived.

Skeletal analyses from Egypt and the Sudan have played an
important role in interpreting cultural developments in the area. The
excellent preservation of abundant skeletal material was an important
factor in their use. Carlson and Van Gerven (1979) note:

Throughout history, Nubia has been a land between — a connecting link between sub-
Saharan Africa and the Mediterranean. Scholarly recognition of that fact has led to one
irresistible conclusion: the driving force behind Nubian history has been the movement
of people and the diffusion of cultural traditions. In that, Nubia provided a natural
laboratory for Graebner's "Methode der Ethnologie" (1911). An archaeological
chronology should, if the diffusionist were correct, bring into focus the historical
connection between sub-Saharan and Mediterranean cultural traditions. According to
the diffusionist position, study of Nubian skeletal remains should provide a biological
basis for reconstructing the migration of ancient races through the Nile Valley as an
integral part of the diffusion process.

In this paper, we will review the traditional use of racial analysis of skeletons for reconstructing culture history and their potential for understanding the biological and cultural adaptation of prehistoric populations.

Human skeletal remains have played an integral role in the reconstruction of Nile River Valley population history since the middle of the last century (Morton, S. G., 1844). As might be expected given the culture-historical paradigm of that earlier era (MacGaffey, 1966), paleoanthropological studies soon developed a singular focus on the description of racial history in that region (Van Gerven *et al.*, 1973). In Sudanese Nubia especially, skeletal variation through time came to be attributed to the cyclical resurgence of one or another racial group.

The basis for this sort of interpretation was provided in studies by Batrawi (1935, 1945, 1946), Elliot-Smith and Wood-Jones (1910), and Morant (1925). In short, two racial types were thought to have been indigenous to the Nile River valley; a Lower Egyptian, or Caucasoid type; and an Upper Egyptian, or Negroid type (Morant, 1925). From the historian's perspective, periods of cultural growth and decline in Sudanese Nubia were assumed to correspond to periods of greater and lesser Caucasoid influence in the region (MacGaffey, 1966). The major goal of skeletal analysis thus became the search for "Negroid elements" in the remains of each of the cultural periods (Van Gerven *et al.*, 1973).

While the later researchers analysing Sudanese Nubian skeletal populations shed the racist notions that racial composition was responsible for the advance and decline of Nubia, Nubian skeletal biology continued to be dominated by questions of the precise time and extent of Negroid admixture during Nubian history. Burnor and Harris (1967) proposed a very early date for Caucasoid-Negroid admixture in this region. They suggest that prior to 14 000 B.P., the dominant peoples of the Mediterranean coast and the Nile River valley were Negroids similar to extant Khoisan speakers in South Africa. Following 14 000 B.P., however, these groups were displaced by immigrating Caucasoids, who inhabited the Nile Valley and have since remained racially stable.

Strouhal has sought to document later occurrences of Negroid incursion into Nubia. In his analysis of 177 Badarian crania, deriving from the earliest Upper Egyptian settled farming/pastorialism horizon (*c.* 4000 B.C.), he concludes that there is a clear mixture of Europoid and Negroid features (Strouhal, 1971a). He reaches similar conclusions through an analysis of intermediate C-group materials (Strouhal, 1971c), and much later Meroitic/X-group crania (1971b). He thus sees

Nubian population history as an "undulating" phenomenon, due largely to the "influence of a foreign element, which was predominantly Negroid" (Strouhal, 1976: 140). In its broad outline, this conclusion is supported by Dzierzykray-Rogalski (1977), Crichton (1966), and Billy (1976).

Recent studies have cast considerable doubt on our ability to invoke the waxing and waning of Caucasoid and Negroid genes in order to explain the biological transformation of Nubian populations (Greene, 1979). For example, Greene (1966) has analysed 16 discrete dental traits in Meroitic, X-group, and Christian populations. His analysis demonstrates no significant shifts in the frequency of these genetic features such as would be expected if there had been extensive gene flow. He further noted the similarity between the Mesolithic and later groups in the presence and frequency of several discrete traits, suggesting an even longer period of biological continuity in the Nubian corridor (Greene, 1966). Through an analysis of discrete cranial traits, Berry et al. (1967) and Berry and Berry (1973) have reached similar conclusions. Yet while there is seemingly sound evidence for genetic continuity through several thousand years of Nubian populations, there is nonetheless compelling evidence for concomitant morphological changes, especially in the cranio-facial complex.

The populations used in the study of the evolutionary changes in cranio-facial morphology include over 1000 burials from prehistoric Sudanese Nubian sites from the Wadi Halfa area associated with Mesolithic (10 000 B.C.), A-group (3400–2400 B.C.), C-group (2400–100 B.C.), Meroitic (350 B.C.–A.D. 350), X-group (A.D. 350–550) and Christian (A.D. 550–1400) periods. The Mesolithic populations relied on the exploitation of large game, fishing and collecting seeds. The A-group through C-group represents a transition from gathering and hunting to primary food production while the Meroitic, X-group and Christian groups subsisted on intensive agriculture (Adams, W. Y., 1967, 1970, 1977).

Nubian Mesolithic populations are characterized by robust crania, typically with large brow ridges, large flattened faces and bun-shaped occiputs (Greene and Armelagos, 1972). The dentition is similarly large and morphologically complex (Greene et al., 1967). Changes in later Nubian populations involve a progressive decrease in the robusticity of the entire cranio-facial complex, a rotation of the mid-face and lower face to a position more inferior to the cranial vault, and a relative increase in cranial height, with a decrease in cranial length (see Fig. 1) (Carlson, 1974, 1976a, b; Carlson and Van Gerven, 1977; Van Gerven et al., 1977).

Two alternative models have been proposed to explain these morphological changes. Carlson (1976b) and Carlson and Van Gerven (1977) have developed the "masticatory function hypothesis" wherein dietary changes from the Mesolithic through the Christian periods

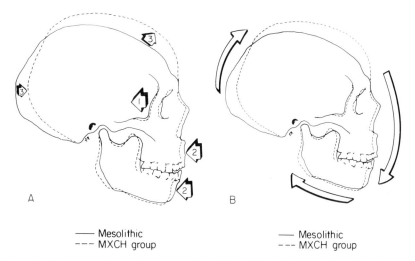

———— Mesolithic
–––– MXCH group

———— Mesolithic
–––– MXCH group

Fig. 1. A. Summary of cranial changes from Mesolithic to MXCh. 1, reduction in size of masticatory muscles; 2, reduction in size of lower face and jaw; 3, reduction in cranial length and increase in cranial height. (Modified from Carlson and Van Gerven 1977: 502.) B. Cranial rotation, by which the face is located more inferioposteriorly (modified from Carlson and Van Gerven, 1977: 502).

would produce a decrease in muscular stress on the jaws and teeth. They suggest that reduced neuromuscular activity would have decreased the mechanical stimulation of periosteal membranes, resulting in a lesser cranio-facial robusticity. Furthermore, changes in maxillo-mandibular growth patterns would lead to a smaller, more inferioposteriorly located mid-face and lower face, and a more globular vault with a more acute basicranial flexure (Fig. 2).

The "dental reduction hypothesis" was proposed by Greene and Armelagos (1972). They suggest that dietary changes involving a reduction in attrition rate and an increase in cariogenic foods would have precipitated selection for smaller, morphologically less complex teeth. The development of smaller teeth would in turn have led to a reduction in the facial architecture, with the same compensatory changes in the cranial vault and base as those predicted by the alternative hypothesis.

The attribution of changes in cranial morphology to alteration of subsistence patterns represents a biocultural approach that goes far beyond the static studies based on racial typology. Biocultural studies emphasise the interaction of environmental, cultural, and biological factors in the processes by which human populations attempt to maintain an adaptive equilibrium. One model describing the interaction of

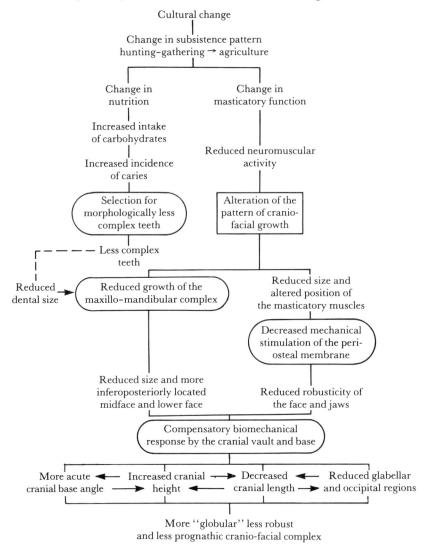

FIG. 2. Alternative pathways producing cranio-facial change from Mesolithic through Christian periods in Nubia. *Right:* the masticatory-functional hypothesis. *Left:* the dental reduction hypothesis. (Modified from Carlson and Van Gerven, 1979: 575.)

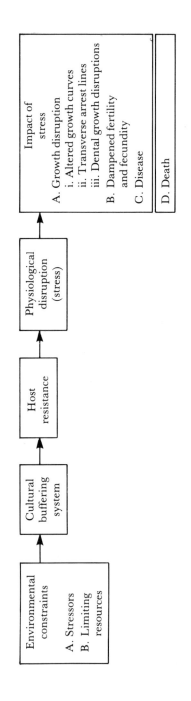

Fig. 3. Simplified diagram of model relating environmental constraints and stressors to skeletally observable stress indicators in prehistoric populations.

these variables has recently been developed by Goodman and Armelagos (1980; Huss-Ashmore, Goodman, and Armelagos, in press) (Fig. 3).

The environment is seen to impose various constraints on a human population. These constraints may arise from limitations of essential resources or from other, more specific stressors (insults) that may disrupt an individual's or group's equilibrium state. While cultural systems function largely to buffer the effect of these environmental constraints and stressors, many cultural features may themselves act as stressors, thus increasing the stress load on the population. For example, subsistence changes associated with agricultural intensification often led to an increase in nutritional deficiencies and diet/disease synergism in prehistoric populations (Lallo *et al.*, 1977; Mensforth *et al.*, 1978; Huss-Ashmore *et al.*, 1981).

The impact of a potential stressor on an individual is mediated by a variety of host resistance factors. The general health of the individual and the characteristics of the target organ can influence the magnitude of the physiological disruption (the stress) caused by a given stressor. When stress occurs, it is best measured by the resulting disruptions in growth, decrease in fertility and fecundity, increase in disease, and (ultimately) death.

Our objective is to use the evidence from growth and development, disease patterns and mortality to infer biocultural adaptation of the group. As Ackerknecht (1953) has stated:

> The pathology of a society reflects its general conditions and growth and offers, therefore, valuable clues to an understanding of the total society.

In this sense, the pattern of pathology may reveal the effects of the pattern of adaptation which are not apparent from the archaeological record.

The success of the analysis of the disease patterns of prehistoric Nubians is due in part to the excellent preservation of the skeletal remains. The preservation of skin, hair and bone is excellent. For example, there is evidence of parasitic infestation (*Pediculus humanus capitis*) in 40% of hair samples from one population. In addition, there was one instance each of decorative scarification, tattooing and ear piercing.

There is also evidence of pathological conditions which are very rare in archaeological populations. The occurrence of hydrocephalus, Legg–Calve–Perthes disease, hyperostosis frontalis, a case of sarcoma, carcinoma, osteochondromas and endochondromas have been found in the series of prehistoric Nubian skeletons. As Strouhal (1976) notes, instances of malignant tumours are infrequent in prehistory. The existence of these conditions in archaeological populations should dispel the notion that tumours are diseases of modern civilization.

The discovery of a hydrocephalus child in one of our Nubian sites (X-group) reveals a great deal about the society's attitude about illness. The hydrocephalic child's cranium was nearly 2000 cm^3 (the adult average is 1300 cm^3) and there is evidence that the child's locomotor abilities were impaired. The width of the long bones of the leg indicate that the child was not ambulatory and had to be carried from place to place. The child lived to its 10th year—a survival comparable to modern medicine prior to the development of surgical techniques to remedy the hydrocephalus. The Nubians obviously were able to provide the care necessary for the survival of an individual who was seriously handicapped.

We have selected three conditions which we believe illustrate the richness of demographic analysis for understanding the biocultural adaptation of a group: trauma, nutritional deficiencies, and infectious lesions.

Trauma

The incidence of traumatic lesions provides a broad index of another form of stress in culture. It is possible to determine traumas which result from aggression and those that are the result of accidental falls. For example, some fractures of the radius (Colles Fracture) and sometimes the ulna (bones of the forearm) occur when the individual trips and the arm is extended to break the fall. The fracture usually occurs near the region of the wrist. Fractures of both bones of the forearm most commonly occur when individuals raise the arm to protect themselves from a blow. The "parry fracture", as this trauma is known, is an index of strife in a group. The frequency of Colles fracture is an index of clumsiness.

It is difficult to distinguish intentional cranial injuries from accidental trauma; however, the location of many cranial injuries suggests purposeful intent. A fracture on the left parietal bone would most likely result from a blow administered by a right-handed individual.

In the Nubian samples, the frequency of traumatic lesions of the cranium was as follows: Meroitic 14·2%, X-group 13·2%; Christian 13·4%. In the combined sample, 56·1% were male while 42·9% were female ($n = 30$). The postcranial trauma shows variation in frequency. The Meroitic group had 5·6%, the X-group had 3·1% and the Christians showed 11·3% with postcranial injuries. Of the twelve individuals with postcranial injuries in the combined sample, ten (83%) were males and two (17%) were females. The two females were Christians who displayed multiple injuries. Although generalisation from such a small sample must be made with care, it is interesting to note that there is an increase in both aggressive and accidental trauma during the Christian period.

Nutritional deficiency

The determination of nutritional status of prehistoric populations has been an extremely complex problem for prehistorians. Early studies attempted to uncover instances of specific nutritional deficiencies. For example, there have been studies which survey the occurrence of scurvy (Vitamin C deficiency) and rickets (Vitamin D deficiency), with little success. Steinbock (1976: 322) states:

It should be emphasized that malnutrition is rarely selective for only one vital component. Malnutrition (including mal-absorption and excessive loss of nutrients) is always multiple, resulting in deficiencies of several or many nutrients to varying degrees.

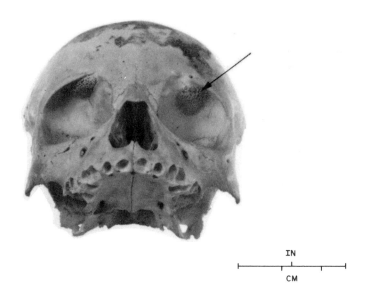

IN

CM

Fig. 4. Porotic hyperostosis in a Nubian juvenile.

Carlson *et al.* (1974) had some success in demonstrating that pre-historic Nubians were suffering from iron deficiency anaemia. Using porotic hyperostosis (Fig. 4) as an indicator of iron deficiency, Carlson and co-workers found that 25% of the Nubians showed evidence of porotic hyperostosis. While porotic hyperostosis can result from a number of anaemias, the restricted location of the lesion (on the superior border of the orbits) and the relatively mild manifestation of the condition supports a nutritional cause (Hengen, 1971). In addition, the high frequency (32%) among the youngest segment (0–6 years) of the population supports the contention. The Sudanese Nubian's reliance on cereal grains such as millet and sorghum which are poor sources of iron contributed to the iron deficiency anaemia.

The demonstration that Nubians were experiencing nutritional deficiencies required systematic analysis of a number of stress indicators. Martin and Armelagos (1979), and Huss-Ashmore (1978) used growth and development, juvenile osteoporosis and premature osteoporosis to show that the Nubians were suffering dietary deficiencies.

Osteoporosis is a form of bone pathology characterised by a decrease in bone mass as a response to a variety of stresses. Bone growth and maintenance is very sensitive to a variety of factors such as nutritional adequacy, biomechanical stress, and disease states (Frost, 1966). While this condition is generally thought to be related to the ageing process, its occurrence has also been noted in both juveniles (Garn, 1970) and young adult females (Martin and Armelagos, 1979). Regardless of the age or sex class affected, osteoporosis represents a biological response to stress, and has been a useful tool for studying the health dynamics of a population.

There are several reasons for biological anthropologists to investigate this condition. Osteoporosis remains one of the most crucial clinical problems in elderly humans, and especially in post-menopausal females. Osteoporosis contributes significantly to the death and disability rates in most contemporary populations as the underlying cause of fractures, breaks, and shattered bones, as well as costing hundreds of millions of dollars in medical costs to the elderly (Marx, 1980).

Archaeological skeletal populations have an advantage of being relatively complete samples of individuals of both sexes and varying ages allowing for a population analysis which emphasises variation. Archaeological specimens can be examined at various sites on different bones, whereas autopsy and biopsy material cannot.

An examination of the pattern of long bone growth in the juvenile portion of the Nubian population indicates the possibility of nutritional stress during early childhood. Juvenile osteoporosis has been observed to result from protein-energy malnutrition in modern studies (Garn *et al.*, 1966). Length and width of the long bones as a function of age was determined for Nubian children (Huss-Ashmore, 1978). While the actual length of long bones is not particularly sensitive to stress, growth in thickness (or cortical width) is. The comparison of cortical thickness with total midshaft diameter indicates growth retardation (Fig. 5). Cortical thickness not only fails to increase, but shows evidence of an actual decrease after age ten.

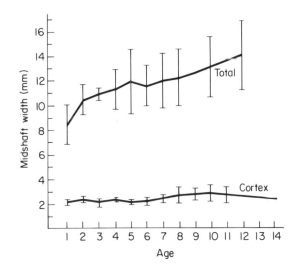

FIG. 5. Growth in femorial midshaft diameters in Nubian juveniles.

Further analysis at a microscopic level reveals that histological processes are responding to stress in very definite patterns. It is evident from a microscopic analysis of thin sections from Nubian juvenile bone that more bone is being resorbed than is being laid down (Fig. 6). The presence of large and very active resorption spaces indicate that these individuals are experiencing problems with normal bone maintenance. A comparison of a bone section of an osteoporotic juvenile with a healthy individual reveals a difference in the amount and kind of bone present. Bone in normal growth and development shows regular but small resorption spaces with rapid mineralisation as well-maintained units of bone (Fig. 6). One factor for this decrease in bone mass can be due to an adaptive biological response to a nutritional stress. A recycling of stored nutrients may be taking place in order to divert

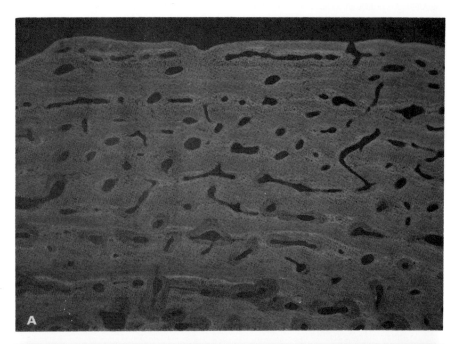

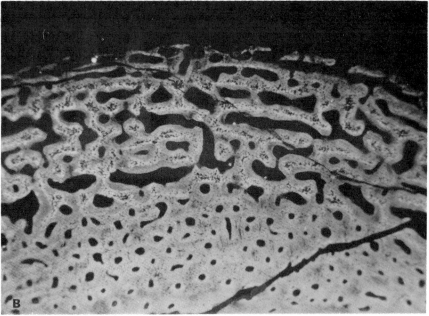

Fig. 6A. Thin section of bone from a healthy juvenile. B. Thin section of bone from an osteoporotic juvenile.

essential minerals and nutrients to other body systems in times of stress. The result is that bone length is maintained at the expense of bone width.

Evidence also exists for premature osteoporosis in young adult females in the Nubian population. While rates of loss vary between individuals, modern studies have relied primarily on older segments of the population who are the most severely affected by age-related osteoporosis. In contrast to what is known from clinical studies, archaeological studies have established that bone loss begins earlier than comparable changes in contemporary populations. Specifically for the Nubian group, there was a definite and continual loss of cortical bone (as measured by the percentage of cortical bone) in females following the twentieth year, and continuing throughout life (Fig. 7). Because of the early age of onset and distinctive pattern of bone loss, factors other than ageing processes appear to be affecting bone loss in the female segment of the population. Males do not exhibit significant changes and wide variability in bone maintenance, but rather a slow decline from middle adulthood to the older age periods. The male pattern of bone loss is very similar to that of males in modern populations.

A preliminary microscopic analysis was undertaken to investigate the underlying histological processes which influence the occurrence of

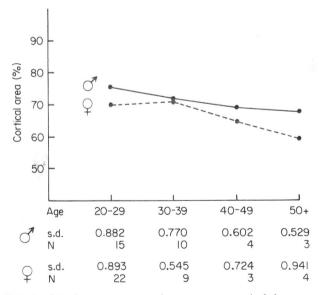

FIG. 7. Relationship between age and percentage cortical bone. s.d., standard deviation; N, sample size.

osteoporosis. Two separate processes at the histological level appear to be at work affecting the total amount of bone present in these adults. First, young females exhibit bones which are extremely porotic due to the increase in resorption activity similar to that seen in juveniles. Secondly, the bone which is present is not as well mineralised, suggesting a slowing down in the forming and maintenance of bone.

The finding of such evidence of stress during the peak reproductive period suggests the possibility that nutritional and physiological factors are involved. While bone is deposited during pregnancy, it is resorbed during prolonged lactation (Garn, 1970). Females who are lactating can be deprived of 300 mg of calcium and 500 calories per day. Multiparous females are especially at risk, since their reserves of nutrients are likely to become depleted, with resultant bone loss and poor maintenance.

The analysis of premature osteoporosis illustrates the influence of demographic profiles on the disease pattern. The onset of premature osteoporosis in children and young adult females reflects the high fertility rates in the agricultural population. Early weaning of children and prolonged lactation in young adult females are critical factors in producing nutritional deficiency in these segments of the population.

While we have not discussed the pattern of senile osteoporosis in the Nubian population, it is also influenced by the mortality pattern of the population. The loss of bone in the adult Nubians begins earlier and loss is greater than in modern populations. Bone loss in a 51-year-old Nubian female is as great as loss which occurs in a 60-year-old female from modern populations. Yet the Nubian females never experience the pathological fractures so common in osteoporotic females in modern populations. Only 1% of Nubians reach their 50th year while 90% of contemporary Americans reach this plateau. In modern America, nearly a quarter of the population is still alive at their 85th year, a period in which continued osteoporotic bone loss often results in pathological fractures.

The demonstration of nutritional stress is difficult. The approach in which single stress indicators are used as evidence of nutritional deficiency is often ambiguous. In the Nubian example, it was necessary to use a number of indicators (porotic hyperostosis, growth retardation in long bone width, juvenile osteoporosis and premature osteoporosis in young adult females) to demonstrate indisputable evidence of nutritional deficiencies. Finally, a consideration of nutritional deficiencies in conjunction with demographic analysis and the archaeological reconstruction provides a more complete perspective on diet in prehistory.

Infectious lesions

The frequency of infectious lesions often increases in populations undergoing stress. Changes in subsistence patterns in prehistoric populations from the Illinois River valley showed an increase in infectious lesions from 27% to 87% during a 350-year period. In addition, there was evidence of a synergistic relationship between infectious lesions and nutritional deficiencies. Individuals with both conditions show more serious manifestations of each. In fact, in those American Indian groups, the occurrence of infectious lesions seemed to predispose the group to nutritional deficiencies (Lallo et al., 1977).

The occurrence of infectious lesions is extremely low in the Nubian population. For example, among the Meroitic population only 6·6% of the individuals show evidence of infectious lesions. Two of these are cases of sinus infection, one instance of Brodie's Abscess (an infection which is walled off and contains sterile pus) and one case of a localized periosteal reaction.

In the X-group population, 12% ($n = 172$) show evidence of infection. Of those with infections, 76% are localized. There are only four instances of more general periosteal reaction. This pattern is similar to that found among the combined Christian sample (sites 6G8 and 6B13) in which there were 3 (15%) cases of localized infections ($n = 20$) and no instances of more general infection.

The low rate of infectious lesions might be explained by evidence that prehistoric Nubians were ingesting tetracycline — a broad spectrum antibiotic. Examination of femoral cortical bone from X-group skeletons shows a pattern of fluorescence which indicates tetracycline use, 1400 years before the medical discovery of the substance (Bassett et al., 1980). Soon after the discovery of tetracyclines in the 1950s, it was learned that their use stained calcifying tissue such as bone and teeth and caused it to fluoresce. Since the tetracyclines can stain or label only actively calcifying tissues, the administration of the substance has been used to measure the amount of bone forming during the period in which the substance is metabolised. For example, tetracyclines administered at two-week intervals would indicate the amount of calcified tissue formed during that period.

A sample of 15 X-group individuals showed the distinctive yellow-green fluorescence at the 490 nm wavelength which characterises the tetracyclines. While post-mortem mould infestation can result in the production of fluorescing substances, the preservation and patterning of fluorescence suggests in vivo deposits. (Fig. 8).

In the Nubian material there is a distinct pattern of fluorescence within individual osteons (the bone-forming units) and between osteons (labelling only the osteons that were in the process of mineralising when the tetracyclines were ingested). The fluorophors (the substances that cause the fluorescence) are deposited only on actively mineralising surfaces.

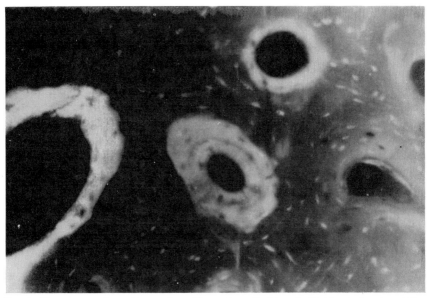

FIG. 8. Fluorescence in a thin section of bone from Prehistoric Nubia, indicative of the presence of tetracyclines.

The existence of tetracyclines in a ''pre-antibiotic population'' raises questions about the source of the substance. Bassett *et al.* (1980) hypothesise that grain stored in mud bins provided the environmental conditions for the growth of streptomycetes, mould-like bacteria that produce tetracyclines. The streptomycetes usually grow slowly except in a very dry, warm, alkaline environment. The faster growing bacteria which are the usual source of food contamination thrive on acid, moist and moderate temperature environments. Streptomycetes are ubiquitous in Egypt and Nubia comprising 60–70% of the desert soils.

Bassett *et al.* (1980) suggest that grains, wheat, barley and millet stored in mud bins provide nutrients and environmental conditions that favour the growth of streptomycetes. While the streptomycetes would be considered a contaminant (it has a bitter taste), the grain would have been consumed during periods of food shortage.

The amount of tetracyclines ingested has not been determined, but preliminary analyses suggest therapeutic levels. The use of tetracycline has broad implications for nutrition, health–disease, demography and the evolution of resistance factors (r-factors) in "pre-antibiotic" populations.

Mortality

The most basic information provided by a prehistoric skeletal sample concerns the age at death of the individuals. The use of life tables has proved to be the most effective means of quantitatively analysing this mortality data (Swedlund and Armelagos, 1969; Weiss, 1973; J. Moore *et al.*, 1975).

A life table consists of several columns of calculations, each representing a population attribute that is a direct function of the mortality data for the population in question (Swedlund and Armelagos, 1969). Given the nature of skeletal ageing techniques, age intervals are usually broader than those used for living populations (although cf. Lovejoy *et al.*, 1977). The more significant calculations include survivorship (l_x), probability of dying (q_x) and life expectancy (e_x^o).

Angel (1969) has criticised the use of life tables, largely on the grounds that pre- and post-burial processes differentially remove infant skeletons from a cemetery sample. This under-enumeration of infants, he feels, negates the significance of any life table calculations. Using a simulation approach, Moore *et al.* (1975) have effectively rejected this contention. They demonstrate that the effects of infant under-enumeration, especially on life-expectancy estimates, are not evident except in the under-enumerated age interval.

The utility of life tables has been ably demonstrated in Sudanese Nubia, where it has been possible to analyse the interaction of cultural systems and mortality on three distinct levels: the effects of growth and decline of a Christian era village on mortality patterns; the impact of intra-village status differences on mortality rates; and changes in mortality produced by the Meroitic/X-group/Christian traditions in a circumscribed geographic region.

Village growth and decline

The island of Meinarti is located in the second cataract of the Nile and was occupied continuously between A.D. 200 and A.D. 1300 (Adams, W. Y., 1964, 1965, 1967). Within the excavated area, numerous macrostrata were observed. The focus of our study was a village of the Christian period which was associated with a large cemetery. According to W. Y. Adams (1967), Levels 9–7 (A.D. 1050–1150) indicate a period of village stability, cultural growth, and security while Level 6–4 (A.D. 1150–1300) shows a decline in the village development.

Life tables were constructed for a skeletal sample derived from a cemetery spanning Levels 9–4 (Swedlund and Armelagos, 1969; S. Green *et al.*, 1974). A comparison of the data for Levels 9–7 and 6–4 demonstrates the impact of the decline on the mortality pattern of the group. At every age, there is at least a two-year difference in mortality (Fig. 9). At birth, in life expectancy of the population inhabiting the village during the period of growth. At age ten, the difference has decreased to 3·5 years and at age 20 and 30 there is still a 2·4-year difference in life expectancy.

Status

In addition to these longer-term mortality trends, a clear and significant association of status and differential mortality has been demonstrated in Levels 9–7 (Green *et al.*, 1974). The operating assumption in this analysis was that presence of a burial superstructure was an indication of increased individual status. This is not unlikely, since the association of mortuary practices and status is well-supported in the archaeological/ ethnographic (Brown, J. A. 1971) and historical records (Meinardus, 1970).

Three factors were found to be closely associated with the probability

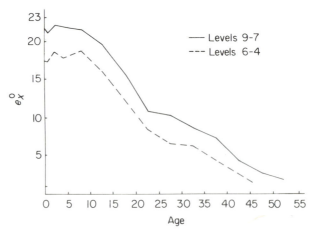

FIG. 9. Curves of life expectancy for Levels 9–7 and 6–4 at Meinarti.

of being buried with a superstructure. First, the greater the age at death, the greater the probability of an associated superstructure. Second, males were disproportionately represented in the group found associated with superstructures. Finally, as can be observed in the survivorship curves of those found with and those found without burial superstructures, the former group had a significantly higher life expectancy in all age intervals (Fig. 10). Despite the positive association of increased age, male sex, and probability of a superstructure, this differential mortality cannot be totally explained in these terms.

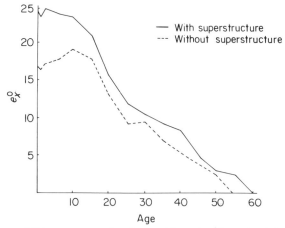

FIG. 10. Curves of life expectancy for those with and without burial superstructures at Meinarti.

For example, 47% of all adults and 33% of all adult males were *not* found with superstructures. It seems highly likely that those individuals who, because of their high status, were buried with superstructures, also enjoyed, because of that same status, an increased survivorship (S. Green *et al.*, 1974).

Inter-group differences in mortality

The analysis of Nubian development has always assumed that the Meroitic period represented the pinnacle of Nubian culture. The break-up of the Meroitic kingdom and establishment of local X-group populations was considered as indisputable evidence of serious decline in cultural development. Even with the rise of Christianity which unified Nubia and which was centred in the Wadi Halfa area, it was never considered to equal the Meroitic advancement.

The analysis of mortality profiles of the Meroitic, X-group and Christian cemeteries discloses some interesting results (Fig. 11). Age specific life expectancies of the Meroitic and X-group populations are very similar while life expectancy in the Christian sample was greater. Although samples of additional material are needed to evaluate these

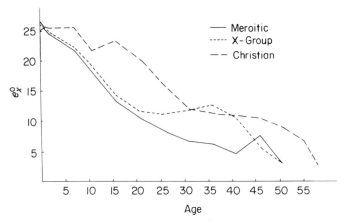

FIG. 11. Curves of life expectancy for Meroitic, X-Group, and Christian samples from Sudanese Nubia.

preliminary results, they do suggest that *in the Wadi Halfa area*, the break-up of the Meroitic kingdom did not result in a decline in life expectancy. In fact, the X-group population experienced some improvement in life expectancy in early adulthood. On the other hand, the Christians show a greater life expectancy at almost every age. These results suggest that while the Meroitic kingdom may represent the most significant political development in prehistoric Sudan, the Wadi Halfa populations may not have benefited from this advancement. The re-unification of Nubia under Christianity, however, did result in a considerable improvement in life expectancy.

Conclusions

The old adage that "Dead men tell no tales" is obviously false in the face of modern techniques of skeletal biology. The remains of dead men and women provide valuable information on how people lived and died. The analysis of skeletal material has moved beyond the descriptive characterization of skeletal remains which relied on racial typology to reconstruct culture history. Modern techniques allow us to demonstrate how changes in subsistence patterns can explain the evolutionary changes in facial morphology. Furthermore, the analysis of demographic information on the rates of migration, fertility and morbidity provide information on the groups' population structure.

The analysis of prehistoric Sudanese Nubian demography illustrates its potential for understanding the biocultural adaptation of earlier populations. The interrelationship of biological and cultural aspects of adaptation allow the anthropologist an opportunity to infer the success of the group in adjusting to its environment. In this way, biological indicators of stress can be used to infer cultural adaptation. Conversely, cultural evidence of stress could be used to predict the impact of stressors on biological systems. The use of cultural and biological features of adaptation provides the holistic approach which characterizes anthropology.

We support Saul Jarcho's observation (1966) that anthropologists have in the past approached skeletal material as if they were governed by the advice of St. Paul when he wrote to the Colossians about "the shew of wisdom in neglecting the body". However, Jarcho says:

[It is] now opportune . . . to take action by a different principle. Let us cease to be Colossians. Let us instead remember Paul's message to the Corinthians: "For the trumpet shall sound, and the dead shall be raised incorruptible."

References

ACKERKNECHT, E. H. (1953). Palaeopathology. In "Anthropology Today" (A. L. Kroeber, ed.), pp. 120-126. University of Chicago, Chicago.

ADAMS, W. Y. (1964). Post-pharaonic Nubia in the light of archaeology, 1. Journal of Egyptian Archaeology, 50, 102-120.

ADAMS, W. Y. (1965). Sudan Antiquities Service Excavation at Meinarti, 1963-4. Kush, 13, 148-176.

ADAMS, W. Y. (1967). Continuity and change in Nubian culture history. Sudan Notes and Records, 48, 1-32.

ADAMS, W. Y. (1970). A reappraisal of Nubian culture history. Orientalia, 39, 269-279.

ADAMS, W. Y. (1977). "Nubia: Corridor to Africa". Allen Lane, London.

ANGEL, J. L. (1969). The basis of palaeodemography. American Journal of Physical Anthropology, 30, 427-437.

ARMELAGOS, G. J. (1969). Disease in ancient Nubia. Science, 163, 255-259.

ARMELAGOS, G. J., MIELKE, J. H., OWEN, K. H., VAN GERVEN, D. P., DEWEY, J. R. and MAHLER, P. E. (1972). Bone growth and development in prehistoric populations from Sudanese Nubia. Journal of Human Evolution, 1, 89-119.

ARMELAGOS, G. J., GOODMAN, A., and BICKERTON, S. (1980). Determining nutritional and infectious disease stress in prehistoric populations. *American Journal of Physical Anthropology*, **52**, 201.

BASSETT, E. J., KEITH, M. S., ARMELAGOS, G. J., MARTIN, D. L. and VILLANUEVA, A. R. (1980). Tetracycline-labeled human bone from ancient Sudanese Nubia (A.D. 350). *Science*, **209**, 1532–1534.

BATRAWI, A. M. (1935). "Report on the Human Remains". Mission Archéologique de Nubie, 1929–34. Government Press, Cairo.

BATRAWI, A. M. (1945). The racial history of Egypt and Nubia, Part 1. *Journal of the Royal Anthropological Institute*, **75**, 81–101.

BATRAWI, A. M. (1946). The racial history of Egypt and Nubia, Part 2. *Journal of the Royal Anthropological Institute*, **76**, 131–156.

BERRY, A. C., BERRY, R. J., and UCKO, P. J. (1967). Genetical change in ancient Egypt. *Man*, **2**, 551–568.

BERRY, A. C. and BERRY, R. J. (1973). Origins and relations of the ancient Egyptians. *In* "Population Biology of Ancient Egyptians" (D. R. Brothwell and B. A. Chiarelli, eds), pp. 200–208. Academic Press, London and New York.

BILLY, G. (1976). La population de la forteresse de Mirgissa, and Affinités morphologiques de la population de Mirgissa. *In* "Mirgissa III. Les Nécropoles" (J. Vercoutter, ed.), pp. 7–55 and 97–140.

BROWN, J. A. (ed.) (1971). "Approaches to the Social Dimensions of Mortuary Practices". Memoirs of the Society for American Archaeology, No. 25. Society for American Archaeology, Washington.

BURNOR, D. T. and HARRIS, J. E. (1967). Racial continuity in Lower Nubia: 12,000 to the present. *Proceedings of the Indiana Academy of Science*, **77**, 113–121.

CARLSON, D. S. (1976a). Temporal variation in prehistoric Nubian crania. *American Journal of Physical Anthropology*, **45**, 467–484.

CARLSON, D. S. (1976b). Patterns of morphological variation in the human midface and upper face. *In* "Factors Affecting the Growth of the Midface" (J. A. McNamara, ed.), pp. 277–299. Center for Human Growth and Development Cranio-facial Growth Series Monographs, No. 6. Ann Arbor, Michigan.

CARLSON, D. S. and VAN GERVEN, D. P. (1977). Masticatory function and post-pleistocene evolution in Nubia. *American Journal of Physical Anthropology*, **46**, 495–506.

CARLSON, D. S. and VAN GERVEN, D. P. (1979). Diffusion, biological determinism and biocultural adaptation in the Nubian Corridor. *American Anthropologist*, **81**, 561–580.

CARLSON, D. S., VAN GERVEN, D. P. and ARMELAGOS, G. J. (1974). Factors influencing the etiology of cribra orbitalia in prehistoric Nubia. *Journal of Human Evolution*, **3**, 405–410.

CRICHTON, J. M. (1966). A multiple discriminant analysis of Egyptian and African Negro crania. *Papers of the Peabody Museum of Archaeology and Ethnology*, **57**, 45–67.

DZIERZYKRAY-ROGALSKI, T. (1977). Neolithic skeletons from Kadero, Sudan. *Current Anthropology*, **18**, (3), 585–586.

ELLIOT-SMITH, G. and WOOD-JONES, F. (1910). Reports on the human remains. *In* "Archaeological Survey of Nubia. Report for 1907–8". Egyptian Survey Department, Government Press, Cairo.

FROST, H. M. (1966). Morphometry of bone in paleopathology. *In* Symposium on Human Palaeopathology, Washington D.C. 1965. Human Palaeopathology; Proceedings" (S. Jarcho, ed.), pp. 131–150. Yale University Press, New Haven.

GARN, S. M. (1970). "The Earlier Gain and Later Loss of Cortical Bone in Nutritional Perspective". C. C. Thomas, Springfield, Illinois.

GARN, S. M., ROHMANN, C. G., and GUZMAN, M. A. (1966). Malnutrition and skeletal development in the preschool child. *In* "Preschool Child Malnutrition". National Academy of Sciences, National Research Council, Washington, D.C.

GOODMAN, A. H. and ARMELAGOS, G. J. (1980). The chronology of enamel hypoplastic growth disruptions in prehistoric, historic and modern populations (abstract). *American Journal of Physical Anthropology*, **52**, (2), 231.

GRAEBNER, F. (1911). "Methode der Ethnologie". C. Winter, Heidelberg.

GREEN, S. GREEN, S., and ARMELAGOS, G. J. (1974). Settlement and mortality of the Christian site (1050 A.D. – 1300 A.D.) of Meinarti, Sudan. *Journal of Human Evolution*, **3**, 297–311.

GREENE, D. L. (1966). Dentition and the biological relationships of some Meroitic, X-group and Christian populations from Wadi Halfa, Sudan. *Kush*, **14**, 284–288.

GREENE, D. L. (1979). A critique of methods used to reconstruct racial and population affinity in the Nile Valley. Paper presented at the Second International Congress of Egyptologists, Grenoble, France.

GREENE, D. L., EWING, G. H., and ARMELAGOS, G. J. (1967). Dentition of a Mesolithic population from Wadi Halfa, Sudan. *American Journal of Physical Anthropology*, **27**, 41–55.

GREENE, D. L. and ARMELAGOS, G. J. (1972). The Wadi Halfa Mesolithic population. Research Report No. 11. Department of Anthropology, University of Massachusetts, Amherst, Massachusetts.

HENGEN, O. P. (1971). Cribra orbitalia: pathogenesis and probable etiology. *Homo*, **22**, 57–75.

HUSS-ASHMORE, R. (1978). Nutritional determination in skeletal populations. *American Journal of Physical Anthropology*, **48**, 407.

HUSS-ASHMORE, R., GOODMAN, A. H., and ARMELAGOS, G. J. (in press). Nutritional inferences from paleopathology. *In* "Advances in Archaeological Method and Theory" (M. B. Schiffer, ed.), Vol. 5. Academic Press, New York and London.

JARCHO, S. (ed.). (1966). "Symposium on Human Palaeopathology, Washington D.C. 1965. Human Palaeopathology; Proceedings". Yale University Press, New Haven.

LALLO, J. W., ARMELAGOS, G. J., and MENSFORTH, R. P. (1977). The role of diet, disease and physiology in the origin of porotic hyperostosis. *Human Biology*, **49**, 471–483.

LOVEJOY, C. O., MEINDL, R. S., PRYZBECK, T. R., BARTON, T. S., HEIPLE, K. G., and KOTTING, D. (1977). Paleodemography of the Libben Site, Ottawa County, Ohio. *Science*, **198**, 291–293.

MACGAFFEY, W. (1966). Concepts of race in the historiography of Northeast Africa. *Journal of African History*, **7**, 1–17.

MARTIN, D. L. and ARMELAGOS, G. J. (1979). Morphometrics of compact bone: an example from Sudanese Nubia. *American Journal of Physical Anthropology*, **51**, 571–578.

MARX, J. L. (1980). Osteoporosis: New help for thinning bones. *Science*, **207**, 628–630.

MEINARDUS, O. F. A. (1970). "Christian Egypt: Faith and Life". American University Press, Cairo.

MENSFORTH, R. P., LOVEJOY, C. O., LALLO, J. W., and ARMELAGOS, G. J. (1978). The role of constitutional factors, diet, and infectious disease in the etiology of porotic hyperstosis and periosteal reactions in prehistoric infants and children. *Medical Anthropology*, **1**, 1–57.

MOORE, J., SWEDLUND, A. C., and ARMELAGOS, G. J. (1975). The use of life tables in paleodemography. *In* "Population Studies in Archaeology and Biological Anthropology: a Symposium" (A. C. Swedlund, ed.), pp. 57–70. Memoirs of the Society for American Archaeology No. 30, Washington.

MORANT, G. M. (1925). A study of Egyptian craniology from prehistoric to Roman times. *Biometrika*, **17**, 1–52.

MORTON, S. G. (1844). "Crania Aegyptiaca". J. Penington, Philadelphia.

RUDNEY, J. D. (1979). An evaluation of pathological bands in tooth enamel as indicators of developmental stress. *American Journal of Physical Anthropology*, **50**, 477.

STEINBOCK, R. T. (1976). "Palaeopathological Diagnosis and Interpretation". C. C. Thomas, Springfield.

STROUHAL, E. (1971a). Anthropometric and functional evidence of heterosis from Egyptian Nubia". *Human Biology*, **43**, 271–287.

STROUHAL, E. (1971b). A contribution to the anthropology of the Nubian X-group. *In* "Anthropological Congress Dedicated to Ales Hrdlica", pp. 541–547. Humpolec, Praha.

STROUHAL, E. (1971c). Evidence of the early penetration of negroes into prehistoric Egypt. *Journal of African History*, **12**, 1–9.

STROUHAL, E. (1976). Tumors in the remains of ancient Egyptians. *American Journal of Physical Anthropology*, **45**, 613–620.

SWEDLUND, A. and ARMELAGOS, G. J. (1969). Une recherche en paléo-démographie: la Nubie soudanaise. *Annales: Économies, Sociétés, Civilisations*, **24**, 1287–1298.

VAN GERVEN, D. P., CARLSON, D. S., and ARMELAGOS, G. J. (1973). Racial history and biocultural adaptation of Nubian archaeological populations. *Journal of African History*, **14**, 555–564.

VAN GERVEN, D. P., ARMELAGOS, G. J., and ROHR, A. (1977). Continuity and change in cranial morphology of three Nubian archaeological populations. *Man* (n.s.), **12**, 270–277.

WEISS, K. A. (1973). "Demographic Models for Anthropology". Memoirs of the Society for American Archaeology, No. 27, Washington.

Note
The original excavation and analysis of the Sudanese Nubian material were supported by grants GS7, GS286 and GS557 from the National Science Foundation. Subsequent analyses were supported by NIH grant NIH-I-R01-02771-01. The analysis of tetracycline was partially funded by University of Massachusetts biomedical research support grant RR07048.

The Genetics of Death —
Mortal, Morbid and Selfish Genes

R. J. BERRY

Life is a predicament which precedes death.

Henry James

Introduction

Death may follow violence or accident, or it may result from an intrinsic failure of the body after infection (or parasite attack), constitutional upset, or simply "old age". Intrinsic causes have almost certainly shaped the pattern of death in all communities at all times except when death results from extreme physical hazard or war; even accident is liable to penalise the innately clumsy or short-sighted, and starvation affects some genetic types before others (Coleman, D. L. 1978). In the words of Richard Dawkins (1976) we are survival machines shaped and modified by multitudinous environments to live long enough to hand on our genes to another generation. This essay is concerned with the past and continuing interactions between nature and nurture that show forth in disease and death, whether as stark statistics or as the personal triumphs and tragedies which are hidden by the brutal simplicities of the demographer (Knudson, 1977).

Before considering the forms which these interactions may take, it is, however, necessary to recognise that the final cause of death may be very different from the predisposing cause. This is particularly important when we are concerned with genetical influences on death. Even a simple dominantly-inherited disease like Huntington's chorea where a single gene produces cerebral degeneration over a 10–15-year

59

period with mental deterioration and characteristic involuntary movements (many female sufferers were burnt as witches in past centuries: Critchley, 1934) is grossly under-recorded on death certificates. In 1977 only 106 deaths in England and Wales were attributed to this cause although a simple calculation based on the incidence and progression of the disease shows that there must have been at least 300. Presumably the ''missing'' 200 deaths were attributed to intervening or associated conditions such as pneumonia, cardiovascular disease, or subdural haematoma (Scoones, 1980). In conditions where the link between proximate and ultimate cause is less direct, the predisposing cause may never enter the formal statistics.

Senile changes and senility

Consideration of the link between death and its causes prompts the apparently trite question: What causes ageing and death? The answer to this is far from obvious. The first attempt at explanation was by August Weismann (1891). He believed that organisms ''wear out'' like machines, but that there is a specific death mechanism designed by natural selection to eliminate the old and deteriorated members of a population. His view is usually discounted. It seems intuitively obvious that selection pressures must decline with age and the end of the reproductive period. Pearl (1922) believed ''no more perverse extension of the theory of natural selection than this was ever made''. Comfort (1956) goes so far as to argue that ''senescence is outside the developmental programme that concerns natural selection . . . almost no wild organisms ever attain the senile stage''. However Williams (1957) has pointed out that Comfort confuses the process of ageing with the state of senility. As he says, ''No one would consider a man in his thirties senile, yet, according to athletic records and life tables, senescence is rampant during this decade. Surely this part of the human life-cycle concerns natural selection. The rate of senescence, as measured by life tables, is known to be subject to genetic variation. It is inconceivable in modern evolutionary theory that senescence, such as operates in man between ages thirty and forty, is selectively irrelevant.'' Williams believes ''natural selection will frequently maximise vigor in youth at the expense of vigor later on and thereby produce a declining vigor (senescence) during adult life''.

The difficulty about such arguments is that the causes of ageing are still very poorly known (Sacher, 1977). Genetical analysis in animals has shown that it is a multi-event phenomenon and that genetical variance for longevity exists in all organisms looked at (Curtis, 1971;

TABLE 1
Mean longevity in years (after Deevey, 1960)

Neanderthal	29·4	Classical Rome	32
Upper Palaeolithic	32·4	England 1276	48
Mesolithic	31·5	England 1376–1400	38
Neolithic Anatolia	38·2	USA 1900–1902	61·5
Classical Greece	35	USA 1950	70

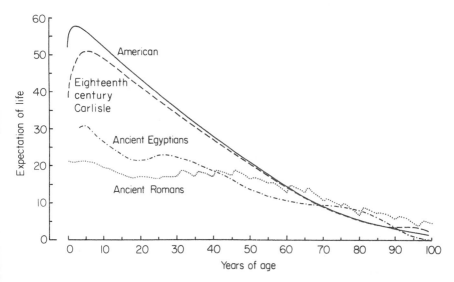

FIG. 1. Expectation of life at different ages in various populations determined actuarially: ancient Romans (data of Macdonell, 1913), ancient Egyptians (Pearson, 1902), Carlisle in the eighteenth century, and white North Americans in 1910 (Glover, 1916; Pearl, 1922).

Rose and Charlesworth, 1980; Bellamy, 1981), but the direct analysis of ageing processes in man has not revealed any unequivocal evidence of inherited differences which would be available for selection (Cohen, 1964). Although mean longevity has increased dramatically since prehistoric times, this has been almost exclusively as a result of both early and adult mortality with little change in total life-span (Fries, 1980) (Fig. 1, Table 1). As far as man is concerned, the most promising approach seems likely to be the dissection of life-table factors by investigating the influence of specific mortality factors (such as cardiovascular disease) in different families (e.g. Hammond et al., 1971; Nam et al., 1978; Robertson and Cumming, 1979; Berry, 1979a).

Genetic load

In the discussion that follows, we shall be concerned with the factors that affect the presence of genetic variation in populations, and especially those that affect the likelihood of death. However, before beginning a systematic description of genetical influences on death, it is necessary to point out that the persisting idea of virtually all inherited variation being detrimental to its carrier is both wrong and still responsible for a great deal of confusion.

The simplest form of this argument was put forward by H. J. Muller (1950). He was a *Drosophila* laboratory geneticist and regarded man as little more than an overgrown fruitfly. He had observed many times the effect of ionising radiation in inducing deleterious mutations in his fly cultures, to the extent that even apparently recessive conditions affect heterozygotes unfavourably. On average, such heterozygotes have their fitness lowered by 2½ %. If one extends this argument to man and assumes that there is a 2½ % detriment to a carrier for every heterozygous locus, such alleles would persist for an average of 40 generations before being eliminated by natural selection.

Now if the number of genes in man is 5000 and if the mutation rate/gene/generation is 1 in 50 000, then the average number of detrimental genes in the heterozygous state per individual = 2 (because we have 2 chromosome sets) × number of loci × mutation rate × persistence = 8.

This crude estimate is supported by studies in which the frequencies of death and inherited disease in the children of cousins has been compared with that in the children of unrelated parents (Table 2). If it is assumed that all the excess abnormality in cousin marriages is due to rare alleles becoming homozygous, it is possible to calculate the average number of deleterious recessives we carry. Most such estimates indicate a figure of three to five per person.

Returning to Muller's argument, he maintained that the mean fitness in man is reduced by (8 × 2½ % =) 20% as compared to the maximum fitness of a person carrying no mutants. He called this the *genetic load*. It means that the average number of surviving children born to a couple is only 80% of those that might have been, and hence at least 2·5 children per couple must be conceived if the population size is to remain constant.

Muller believed that this genetic load was effectively the result of recurrent mutation. It follows that if the mutation rate is doubled, only 60% of the children conceived would survive. This would mean that each couple would conceive 2·5 children, but only produce 1·5 living adults for the next breeding generation. The population would not replace itself, and would rapidly become extinct.

TABLE 2
Effects of inbreeding (after United Nations, 1962)

| | % frequency among | |
	First cousins	Controls
USA		
Infant and juvenile death	22·9	16·0
Death under 20 years	16·8	1·6
Miscarriage	14·5	12·9
Still birth; neonatal death	3·3	3·0
Abnormality	6·2	9·8
France		
Still birth	4·1	2·1
Infant death	8·9	4·5
Death from 1 to 30 years	11·7	5·9
Abnormality[a]	16·2	4·3
Japan		
Stillbirth; neonatal death	4·5	3·3
Infant death	6·6	4·7
Juvenile death	11·7	5·5
Abnormality[a]	1·4	1·0

[a] Some overlap with previous categories.

This argument attained the status of a prophecy, but it involved two fallacies. Family size is limited by many factors, of which the least important in most communities is the possibility of only siring 2·5 children. Much more far-reaching, however, is Muller's assumption that most genetical disease is the result of recurrent mutation. For example, stabilising selection when the extreme expressions of a trait have a lower fitness than the mean is common. The simplest genetical mechanism for producing stabilising selection is where the heterozygote is favoured over the two homozygotes for a unifactorial or the multiple homozygotes for a multigenically determined condition. An example of the latter is birth weight, which is clearly affected by stabilising selection, particularly in primitive communities where perinatal care is not developed: light and heavy babies have a higher chance of death than those of mean weight, with the result that those of average weight will survive and in due course pass on their "average weight" genes to their own children (Karn and Penrose, 1951; Van Valen and Mellin, 1967) (Fig. 2).

In situations like this some genotypes will be less fit than others, and therefore impose a load upon the population. This is a *segregational* load in contrast to the *mutational* load emphasised by Muller. About half the zygotes formed in human populations fail to survive and reproduce in the next generation, even under the best medical conditions. It has been suggested that half this failure is due to stabilising selection (Penrose, 1955).

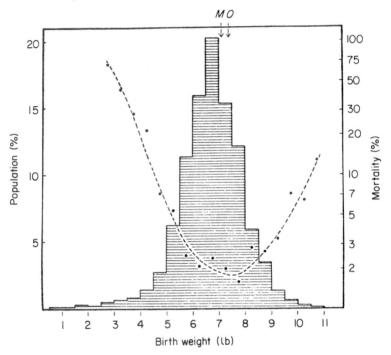

FIG. 2. The distribution of birth weight among 13 730 children born in London between 1935 and 1946, also the weight of 614 still-born or dead by 28 days. *M* is the mean birth weight, *O* is the birth weight associated with the lowest mortality (and hence the optimum weight). (From Mather, 1964, after Karn and Penrose, 1951).

There are other components of the total genetic load. J. B. S. Haldane (1957) called attention to the *substitutional* load, which he described as the "cost" of natural selection. This occurs whenever one allele spreads in a population. The allele that is being replaced will confer a lower fitness on its carriers than the allele that is spreading. If the allele spreads to fixation (i.e. if the former allele is completely eliminated in a population whose size remains constant), the number of individuals that die through natural selection will be equal to nearly two-thirds of those alive in any one generation. The advantage produced by the new allele does not matter: an allele that spreads rapidly (i.e. has a high selective advantage) will be responsible for a higher proportion of selective deaths in fewer generations than an allele spreading more slowly. Clearly, however, a population can only tolerate a limited number of substitutions going on at the same time, or too many individuals will be dying to maintain a viable population. Haldane calculated that one allele will be substituted every 30 generations on average, and supported this conclusion by deductions about the rate of evolutionary change in fossil lineages.

The implication from this argument is that there is an upper limit to the amount of variation that can be tolerated. This can be illustrated by considering a population segregating for both sickle cell (S) and normal (A) haemoglobin, producing a segregational load. A typical situation in Central Africa where cerebral malaria is endemic would be a frequency of the sickle cell allele of just under 30%. The relative fitnesses of the three genotypes can be ascertained by comparing the number of children born to each. Then:

	AA	AS	SS
Fitness (f)	0·8	1·0	0·5
Proportion of each genotype (r)	0·51	0·41	0·08
Proportion of population dying from genetical causes $(r(1-f))$	0·10	0	0·04

Hence $(0·10 + 0·04 =)$ 14% of the population die from causes which would not be present if every individual possessed the optimum genotype (AS).

The average fitness of a population like this will be $(1 - 0·14 =)0·86$. If the population were to support 10 such polymorphisms, the average fitness would be $(0·86)^{10}$ or about 0·15. This means that only one zygote in seven would survive to become a reproductively effective member of the population. The human species could just about survive in a precarious way, provided that most of the genetical loss took place before implantation. If selection acted later, an intolerable amount of available pregnancy time would be wasted.

Muller's genetic load ideas were originally put forward in the context of the hazards of atomic radiation. They acquired poignancy when electrophoresis began to be applied to proteins and enzymes on a population scale and it was shown that virtually every species (including man) had segregating alleles at one quarter to one third of all loci, and any individual was heterozygous at between five and fifteen per cent of his total genes (Harris, H., 1966; Selander and Kaufman, 1973; Nevo, 1978). According to theory this should have led to extinction, whereas extinction of whole species is clearly not a common event. This is not the place to review the selectionist-neutralist controversy of the early 1970s. Suffice it to say that it is now generally accepted that most of the inherited variation revealed by electrophoresis is believed to be biologically significant in particular environments (i.e. not neutral), and that it is probably maintained by a balance of inconstant selective forces (Harris, H., 1971; Berry, 1977; Clarke, B. C., 1979).

The change from the picture of a mainly invariable population type which reigned from Linnaeus to Muller, to that of a population composed of a collection of effectively unique genomes has still not been absorbed by most population workers. The genetical heterogeneity which we now know to characterise virtually all populations means that genetical adjustment by natural selection is the normal situation (Berry, 1980); this is very different from the ponderous ideas of gene spread and decay predicted by classical concepts of population genetics, and enshrined in Muller's load and Haldane's cost. Some of the implications of this revised view are set out in the following sections.

Biological death and genetical death

All too often natural selection is assumed to involve the death of individuals. Osborn (1960) spelt this out explicitly: "In the past, natural selection operated mainly through deaths. Obviously we are not going to return to that method if we can help it." This is too simplistic a view. A dead person cannot reproduce, but even a living person may not transmit his or her genes because of some inherited condition: achondroplasic dwarfs only have one-fifth of the number of children produced by normal people although their actual fertility is unimpaired; neurofibromatosis causes skin blemishes—the fitness of affected men is reduced to 41·3% of normal, but of affected women only to 74·8%. Conversely the death of a child from a genetical cause may be "over-compensated" by the parents having more children to replace the dead one. This was first suggested by R. A. Fisher (1930) as an explanation for the maintenance of Rhesus negative alleles (haplotypes) in the population, since every time a baby dies from haemolytic disease due to Rhesus incompatibility one negative and one positive allele is lost. Since negative alleles are less common than positive ones, the effect should be a fall in negative frequency. A number of studies have shown that families which lose a child through haemolytic disease (but not other causes) have more subsequent children than control families (Reed, 1971; Vogel and Knox, 1975). Consequently it is necessary to distinguish biological death in the normal sense from genetical death, which describes a failure to transmit a particular trait. Genetical death may take place in a single generation (where a phenotype is lethal or infertile) or be spread over several generations.

Nevertheless, there are obviously strong links between biological death and genetical death. Virtually all deaths from intrinsic causes involve genes (*vide supra*), and the genetical component of death is currently increasing as the chances of dying from infection, trauma, etc. are reduced. Nevertheless genetical factors may be involved in deaths at any age, with the likelihood that the genetical composition of the population is changed thereby, i.e. that natural selection is operating.

Early death

Between a third and a half of zygotes fail to survive to birth. Most of this loss occurs in the first two months of gestation; indeed the greatest amount takes place before implantation. Around a third of early spontaneous abortions involve chromosomally abnormal conceptuses. The frequency of chromosomal abnormalities at this period is about sixty times greater than at birth, showing the selective elimination of these anomalies. Not surprisingly the survival of different chromosomal variants differs widely: the single most common defect in early abortions is XO (*c*.20%), but fewer than 3% survive to term; in contrast trisomy-21 (Down's syndrome) is less commonly aborted (although all trisomies except those of chromosome 13, 18 and 21 are completely eliminated), and *c*.30% survive to be born normally. One in six of abortuses with normal karyotypes have congenital malformations.

Antigenic incompatibility gives rise to an unknown amount of early selective death. Waterhouse and Hogben (1947) found a 20·6% deficiency of blood group A children from A♂ × O♀ matings as compared with the reciprocal O♂ × A♀. Although their work has been criticised for combining probably heterogeneous data, the results have, in essence, been confirmed by further studies. For example N. E. Morton *et al.* (1966) reported significant deficiencies associated with A_1 incompatibility but not A_2 or B in a Brazilian population with high fecundity and high infant mortality.

Other possible examples of early selection are an unexplained excess fertility of women negative for the $Kell_1$ blood group (Reed *et al.*, 1964) and a higher proportion than expected of MN children (Morton and Chung, 1959). However it is impossible to distinguish between prezygotic selection and a combination of incompatibility selection and excess heterozygous viability, so the exact causes of these segregational upsets are still unsolved (Hiraizumi, 1964).

Adult death

A useful distinction about natural selection has been made by Wallace (1975) in distinguishing "hard selection" where survival is prevented by physiological or developmental incompetence, from "soft selection" which acts with varying intensity depending on density and other ecological variables. The spontaneous elimination of chromosomally abnormal foetuses can be regarded as the operation of hard selection, whereas the effects of infectious diseases and other agents which act intermittently and with varying consequences may produce soft selection.

Haldane (1949) was the first to develop the argument that the present distribution of human genes is largely a legacy from the epidemic diseases of the past. He based this belief on the distribution of certain alleles which broadly paralleled that of fatal or debilitating diseases. The best example of this is, of course, the relationship between various haemoglobinopathies (notably sickle cell) and falciparum malaria, the most commonly fatal malaria of childhood (Allison, 1954; Livingstone, 1965). Haldane also suggested that thalassemia might be a mechanism of protecting multiparous women on poor diets from chronic anaemia, since heterozygotes for this disease accumulate iron. However thalassemia and glucose-6-phosphate dehydrogenase deficiency are now both thought also to protect against severe malaria (Siniscalco et al., 1961; Luzzatto et al., 1969).

Before Haldane developed his ideas, Ford (1942) had suggested that the common blood groups should be regarded as stable polymorphisms and urged that associations should be sought between blood groups and specific diseases. The first of these was found by Aird et al. (1953), who showed that duodenal ulceration is 40% commoner in blood group O people than in other of the ABO types. Other associations have followed (e.g. A and stomach cancer, pernicious anaemia, and cancer of the pancreas: Clarke, C. A., 1961; Tyrrell et al., 1968), but the selective differences produced by these links are small and cannot in themselves explain the observed polymorphisms. More recently, a range of much stronger associations between haplotypes of the major histocompatibility locus (HLA) and a series of diseases has been uncovered (Bodmer et al., 1978). However virtually all these involve degenerative conditions of old age (multiple sclerosis, ankylosing spondylitis, etc.), and hence are relatively unimportant from the point of view of selection.

Of more significance is the discovery that severe and fatal smallpox was much commoner in Indians of groups A and AB than in their sibs of groups B and O (Vogel and Chakravartti, 1966; Bernhard, 1966). In laboratory studies, F. Vogel *et al.* (1960) found that an antigen produced by the plague organism *Pasteurella pestis* cross-reacts with the *H* antigen produced by group O people. They suggest that O is frequent only in areas where there have been no major epidemics of plague.

The evidence in man for inherited susceptibility to killing diseases is still fragmentary, but there is sufficient to be certain that the genetical composition of a population before and after an epidemic is likely to be different, i.e. the disease is acting as a selective agent. The difficulty of collecting hard evidence on the subject can be illustrated by the effects of myxomatosis in rabbits. When the virus first spread across Britain in 1953, 99% of an estimated 60 to 100 million animals in the country were killed. Most of the survivors had contracted the disease but recovered. There are now regular small epidemics but the proportion of survivors has increased every time — partially due to changes in the virus itself, and partially due to a decreasing susceptibility in the rabbits infected. For some years, epidemiologists denied that there had been an increase in innate resistance to the disease, but artificial infection of rabbits at an age when any maternal immunity has disappeared has produced a general acceptance that this has happened (Burnet and White, 1972). It is rare for explosive pandemics of human disease to occur, but when they do (as when plague spread through Europe, smallpox was taken to South America and the Pacific by the Spaniards, or in the 1919 influenza epidemic: Creighton, 1891–4; Zinsser, 1935; McNeill, 1977) it must be accepted that the chances of death or survival would almost certainly be influenced by genetic factors. Blackwell (1981) has reviewed an impressive volume of evidence for inherited resistence to parasites and other pathogens in house mice.

Changing causes

A major error of theoreticians is to assume that selective forces are unvarying in direction and strength. A moment's reflection shows that this cannot be: selection is a response to environmental pressure, and varies as much as the environment. Myopia is presumably a grave disadvantage to a Stone Age hunter, but of little importance to modern man, particularly if he is fitted with correcting lenses; sickle cell trait has no advantage to the descendants of the Africans taken as slaves to the malaria-free environment of North America, and seems to be declining in frequency there; the inherited porphyria carried by 5000 white South Africans was of no consequence until the use of barbiturates rendered them liable to fatal paralysis with a therapeutic dose (Dean, 1963); genes which confer resistance to smallpox are redundant since the virus has been exterminated. Even apparent hard selection can be avoided or reduced, as in the case of dietary, surgical or replacement therapy in phenylketonuria, galactosaemia, pyloric stenosis, haemophilia, and diabetes mellitus. These are potentially killing diseases which can be treated by means of procedures which amount to specific environmental changes. All these are examples involving pathological conditions of varying severity, but highlight the dynamic nature of the genetical composition of any population. A major factor in human evolution has been the establishment of new colonies by small groups of founders, exposing new gene combinations to new environments. These genetical bottle-necks involve repeated stochastic changes in gene frequencies. Indeed, the founder effect is the most powerful method there is of changing gene frequencies. Natural selection acting on a variable gene pool is superimposed on this chance diversity, and results in a rapid and probably precise genetical adjustment. The resulting heterogeneity in space makes it extremely difficult to disentangle directed processes in time (Berry, 1978).

When we attempt to identify how we adapted to past environments, we can do little more than speculate. It is possible to know something about the causes of death in earlier populations and living primitive communities, but it is virtually impossible to discover how pathogens have changed in response to new challenges posed to them by host adaptation (Flor, 1956; Clarke, B. C., 1976, 1979). For example, 15 to 20 species of malaria infect present-day wild-living primates, but only four are normally found in man although apes can be infected with human strains and vice versa (Bruce-Chwatt, 1965). The spread of *HbS* and other inherited "anti-malarial" devices is probably fairly recent in human history. The main host of sleeping sickness in Africa is the mosquito *Anopheles gambiae* which is a "weed species" thriving in the open spaces made by man in the tropical jungle.

Transfers of parasite from one host to a new one continue to occur. For example, rinderpest invaded Africa in 1891, killing up to 90% of domestic cattle and wild antelopes, but failed to establish itself and become endemic. It disappeared after a few years, presumably from lack of susceptible surviving ungulates to infect. In 1959 a new human disease called O'nyong nyong fever appeared in Uganda, probably as a result of a virus previously confined to monkeys. The disease spread rapidly and widely, but like rinderpest, failed to establish itself, and disappeared. Ten years later another and much more serious fever was found at Lassa in Nigeria. By 1973 it was identified as a normal pathogen of rodents, which enabled appropriate preventive measures to be taken (Fuller, 1974). Another rodent pathogen which has waxed and waned in human populations is plague. This was rampant in early Christian times (Procopius recorded that it killed 10 000 people daily for four months when it first reached Constantinople), but was unrecorded in Europe from 767 to 1346. When it was reintroduced (most likely by Mongol invaders over the Eurasian steppes disturbing the ecological balance between man, rat, flea, and pathogen) it remained endemic until the nineteenth century. In England it reduced the population by two fifths (from 3·7 in 1348 to 2·2 million in 1377), and depressed population growth for a further 150 years (Russell, 1958). The effect in continental Europe was probably similar.

To return to the transition of man and the apes, De Beer (1958) has argued that the key factor was a spectacular change in growth rates, so that man is really an ape with a greatly extended immature stage. On this view human adults are really sexually mature children with the body proportions of a young person. One consequence of this idea is that skull ossification would be delayed allowing the brain to grow to a larger size than if it were contained in a firm bony case. Whilst it is true that the difference in brain size between *Australopithecus* and modern man is one of the most rapid of known evolutionary changes, it can be argued that it only represents a selection pressure of 0·04% per generation over half a million years (Cavalli-Sforza and Bodmer, 1971), which is very small when compared with many observed selections in the wild (Berry, 1971), although selection would have been more intense if it took place in less than the total time. When we come to the meaning of the differences between human races, we are in the realm of speculation — such as the possibility that dark skin may protect against tumours induced by ultraviolet radiation. It has also been argued that the observed decrease in weight-to-surface ratio between populations living in cold climates and those in hot ones is an adaptation to help temperature regulation (Schreider, 1964). The honest answer is that we do not know how much of racial differentiation is adaptive, and how much due to chance. Furthermore we can only guess about the selective effects of the neolithic revolution with its increase in population and close association with resident populations of animals, or of urbanisation, or of industrialisation — or indeed of the psychosocial or sociogenetic phase of evolution that Julian Huxley and C. H. Waddington believe we have entered.

Nevertheless, it is reasonable (and testable) to look on human history as a continuing interplay between a series of genetically determined reacting systems and a series of environments of varied stability; the fact of our continued survival means we can be regarded as successful "survival machines". It would be wrong to think of ourselves as being elevated into a situation where natural selection is no longer operating; western man now faces an environment where crowding, noise, obesity, stress-induced hypertension, chemical carcinogenesis, etc. are producing an environment unlike any he has experienced before, but which is no less of a genetical challenge (Dubos, 1965, 1973). Medicine and welfare generally have not abolished natural selection; they have merely changed those traits which are adaptive.

The genetics of death

So far we have considered the effect of genes on death. The genetical variation we have reviewed has largely been that which predisposes its carriers to illness of varying severity—although by the nature of the variation we can look at it from the point of view of predisposing to life and health. However, we have dealt exclusively with physiological and pathological processes. There is another side to man's survival, and that is his capacity to behave towards himself and members of his group in such a way that his genes are handed on to the next generation at least as frequently on average as those of others. There is a problem here, in that behaviour which benefits the individual is usually "selfish". The classical expression is that of J. B. S. Haldane (1955), who pointed out that if he dived into a stream to save a drowning child (which would be a *good* action for the community), he would be increasing his chance of death, and decreasing his chance of passing on any genes he had for unselfish behaviour (assuming that such genes exist). In contrast a selfish character who watched the child drown would have a higher fitness, and his "selfish genes" would spread at the expense of any altruistic alleles. The difficulty is that altruistic behaviour undoubtedly exists, and attempts to explain it through "group selection" inevitably founder since it is individuals who survive and breed. The solution to this paradox was pointed out by Haldane himself, that if the drowning child and his rescuer are related, altruistic behaviour can evolve if the risk to the genes carried by the rescuer is more than outweighed by the genes "saved". Maynard Smith (1964) has called this process "kin selection", producing "the evolution of characteristics such as self-sacrificing behaviour which favour the survival of close relatives of the affected individual". Hamilton (1964, 1975) has formalised kin selection by defining a trait called "inclusive fitness" which adds the investment an individual has in his own genes to those he shares with his living relatives. He has shown mathematically that natural selection will tend to maximise this inclusive measure in the same way as it maximises individual fitness; selection will favour the activities of an individual which benefit his relatives and repress those which harm them.

It is worth noting in passing that the evolution of altruism in the above sense is not a base for ethics as sought by humanists from Herbert Spencer onwards. The recognition of goodness as good seems to be a property of man which qualitatively separates him from his closest ancestors, and cannot be derived from the evolutionary process (Thorpe, 1961).

In the final analysis there is no such thing as a gene for behaviour. Genes control the structure of proteins — they are concerned primarily with chemistry rather than psychology. Yet we make a major mistake if we reduce our genetical makeup to molecular lottery: man is more than the sum of his genes and it is not enough to understand the chemical nature of genes, the segregation and transmission of inherited traits, mutation, and the forces that change gene frequencies; we still need to investigate the occurrence and operation of inherited factors in individual cases.

Local causes of death may be purely environmentally determined — as on the Hebridean island of St. Kilda where the custom of putting pony dung and fulmar oil on the cord of newborn infants used to lead to most of them dying of tetanus 8 days later, or among the Fore people of Papua New Guinea where the disease of CNS degeneration known as kuru was spread by cannibalism — an ironic discovery since a complex genetic hypothesis had been erected to explain transmission through the female line with varying ages of onset (the responsibility for eating the brains of dead people rested largely with the women, who passed tit-bits to young children) (Bennett et al., 1959; Mathews, 1976). Inherited causes of death are usually recognised because of vertical transmission in families: the Talmud gives dispensation for boys not to be circumcised who are the children of "bleeders" (i.e. haemophiliacs), and extended this to sons of all sisters of the mother, but not sons of the father's sibs; the South Atlantic island of Tristan da Cunha has the highest frequency in the world of a recessively inherited blindness (retinitis pigmentosa) through the chance misfortune of one of the original 15 founders of the community carrying a mutant gene, and the population clearly appreciates the dangers of inbreeding (Sorsby, 1963; Roberts, D. F., 1971). In other situations the relation between genes and death are more debatable: multiple sclerosis almost certainly has a genetic basis, although its distribution is correlated with a cold temperate climate and it seems to be precipitated by a viral infection, probably around the time of puberty (Berry, 1969; Kurtzke and Hyllested, 1978). Death is a cue to geneticists: What caused it? Did it involve inherited factors? What are the distribution of these in time and space? What is the relationship between physical, behavioural and cultural factors?

The studies carried out on the Hebridean island of Barra are an object lesson on how intellectual excitement and useful results can blend together. Barra is the southernmost inhabited island of the Outer Hebrides, with a population of 1232 in 1972. The island doctor diagnosed a rare form of anaemia in a 5-year-old girl, and then found that ten out of 18 deaths in her relatives whose cause he could determine were due to carcinoma of various organs (Hill, 1976). This led to a detailed demographic and historical survey of the population, involving karyotypic and allozymic characterisation of every inhabitant (Morton *et al.*, 1976; Dick and Izatt, 1978). Genes, geography, history and culture very often meet in death. Where they do, we can learn about them all (Berry, 1979b; May and Anderson, 1979).

References

AIRD, I., BENTALL, H. H. and ROBERTS, J. A. F. (1953). A relationship between cancer of stomach and the ABO blood groups. *British Medical Journal*, i, 799–801.

ALLISON, A. C. (1954). Notes on sickle-cell polymorphism. *Annals of Human Genetics*, **19**, 39–57.

BELLAMY, D. (1981). Ageing: with particular reference to the use of the house mouse as a mammalian model. In "Biology of the House Mouse" (R. J. Berry, ed.), pp.267–300. Academic Press, London and New York.

BENNETT, J. H., RHODES, F. A. and ROBSON, H. N. (1959). A possible genetic basis for kuru. *American Journal of Human Genetics*, **11**, 169–187.

BERNHARD, W. (1966). Über die Beziehung zwischen ABO-blutgruppen und Pockensterblichkeit in Indien und Pakistan. *Homo*, **17**, 111–118.

BERRY, R. J. (1969). Genetical factors in the aetiology of multiple sclerosis. *Acta neurologica scandinavica*, **45**, 459–483.

BERRY, R. J. (1971). Conservation aspects of the genetical constitution of populations. In "The Scientific Management of Animal and Plant Communities for Conservation" (E. Duffey and A. S. Watt, eds), pp. 177–206. Blackwell, Oxford.

BERRY, R. J. (1977). "Inheritance and Natural History". Collins New Naturalist, London.

BERRY, R. J. (1978). Genetic variation in wild house mice: where natural selection and history meet. *American Scientist*, **66**, 52–60.

BERRY, R. J. (1979a). Genetical factors in animal population dynamics. In "Population Dynamics" (R. M. Anderson, L. R. Taylor and B. D. Turner, eds), pp. 53–80. Blackwell, Oxford.

BERRY, R. J. (1979b). The Outer Hebrides: where genes and geography meet. *Proceedings of the Royal Society of Edinburgh*, **77B**, 21–43.

BERRY, R. J. (1980). Genes, pollution, and monitoring. *In* "Biological Effects of Marine Pollution and the Problems of Monitoring" (A. D. McIntyre and J. B. Pearce, eds). *Conseil Permanent International pour l'Exploration de la Mer Rapports et Procès-Verbaux des Réunions*, **179**, 253–257.

BLACKWELL, J. M. (1981). The role of the house mouse in disease and zoonoses. *In* "Biology and the House Mouse" (R. J. Berry, ed.), pp.591–616. Academic Press, London and New York.

BODMER, W. F., JONES, E. A., BARNSTAPLE, C. J. and BODMER, J. G. (1978). Genetics of HLA: the major human histocompatibility system. *Proceedings of the Royal Society of London B*, **202**, 93–116.

BRUCE-CHWATT, L. J. (1965). Paleogenesis and paleoepidemiology of primate malaria. *World Health Organisation Bulletin*, **32**, 363–387.

BURNET, M. and WHITE, D. O. (1972). "Natural History of Infectious Disease", 4th edition. University Press, Cambridge.

CAVALLI-SFORZA, L. L. and BODMER, W. F. (1971). "The Genetics of Human Populations". Freeman, San Francisco.

CLARKE, B. C. (1976). The ecological genetics of host–parasite relationships. *In* "Genetic Aspects of Host–Parasite Relationships" (A. E. R. Taylor and R. Muller, eds), pp. 87–103. Blackwell, Oxford.

CLARKE, B. C. (1979). The evolution of genetic diversity. *Proceedings of the Royal Society of London B* **205**, 453–474.

CLARKE, C. A. (1961). Blood groups and disease. *Progress in Medical Genetics*, **1**, 81–119.

COHEN, B. H. (1964). Family patterns of mortality and life span. *Quarterly Review of Biology*, **39**, 130–181.

COLEMAN, D. L. (1978). Diabetes and obesity — thrifty mutants? *Nutrition Reviews* **36**, 129–132.

COMFORT, A. (1956). "The Biology of Senescence". Rinehart, New York.

CREIGHTON, C. (1891-4). "A History of Epidemics in Britain" (2 volumes). University Press, Cambridge.

CRITCHLEY, M. (1934). Huntington's Chorea and East Anglia. *Journal of State Medicine*, **42**, 575–587.

CURTIS, H. J. (1971). Genetic factors in ageing. *Advances in Genetics*, **16**, 305–324.

DAWKINS, R. (1976). "The Selfish Gene". University Press, Oxford.

DEAN, G. (1963). "The Porphyrias". Pitman Medical, London.

DE BEER, G. R. (1958). "Embryos and Ancestors", 3rd edition. Clarendon Press, Oxford.

DEEVEY, E. S. (1960). The human population. *Scientific American*, **203** (3), 194–204.

DICK, H. M. and IZATT, M. M. (1978). HLA antigens and IgG allotypes on the Island of Barra (Outer Hebrides). *Annals of Human Biology*, **5**, 441–451.

DUBOS, R. (1965). "Man Adapting". Yale University Press, New Haven.

DUBOS, R. (1973). "A God Within". Angus & Robertson, London and Sydney.

FISHER, R. A. (1930). "The Genetical Theory of Natural Selection". Clarendon Press, Oxford.

FLOR, H. H. (1956). The complementary genic systems in flax and flax rust. *Advances in Genetics*, **8**, 29–54.

FORD, E. B. (1942). "Genetics for Medical Students". Methuen, London.

FRIES, J. F. (1980). Aging, natural death and the compression of mortality. *New England Journal of Medicine*, **303**, 130–135.

FULLER, J. G. (1974). "Fever! The Hunt for a New Killer Virus". Dutton, New York.

GLOVER, J. W. (1916). "United States Life Tables, 1910". Bureau of the Census, Washington.

HALDANE, J. B. S. (1949). Disease and evolution. *Ricerca Scientifica, Supplement*, **19**, 68–76.

HALDANE, J. B. S. (1955). Population genetics. *New Biology*, **18**, 34–51.

HALDANE, J. B. S. (1957). The cost of natural selection. *Journal of Genetics*, **55**, 511–524.

HAMILTON, W. D. (1964). The genetical evolution of social behavior. *Journal of Theoretical Biology*, **7**, 1–16, 17–52.

HAMILTON, W. D. (1975). Innate social aptitudes of man: an approach from evolutionary genetics. *In* "Biosocial Anthropology" (R. Fox, ed.), pp. 133–155. Malaby Press, London.

HAMMOND, E. C., GARFINKEL, L. and SEIDMAN, H. (1971). Longevity of parents and grandparents in relation to coronary heart disease and associated variables. *Circulation*, **43**, 31–44.

HARRIS, H. (1966). Enzyme polymorphisms in man. *Proceedings of the Royal Society of London B*, **164**, 298–310.

HARRIS, H. (1971). Annotation: polymorphism and protein evolution. The neutral-mutation-random drift hypothesis. *Journal of Medical Genetics*, **8**, 444–452.

HILL, R. D. (1976). Familial cancer on a Scottish island. *British Medical Journal*, ii, 401–402.

HIRAIZUMI, Y. (1964). Prezygotic selection as a factor in the maintenance of variability. *Cold Spring Harbor Symposia on Quantitative Biology*, **29**, 51–60.

KARN, M. N. and PENROSE, L. S. (1951). Birth weight and gestation time in relation to maternal age, parity and infant survival. *Annals of Eugenics*, **16**, 147–164.

KNUDSON, A. G. (1977). Genetics and etiology of human cancer. *Advances in Human Genetics*, **8**, 1–66.

KURTZKE, J. F. and HYLLESTED, K. (1978). Multiple sclerosis in the Faroe Islands: I. Clinical and epidemiological features. *Annals of Neurology*, **5**, 6–21.

LIVINGSTONE, F. B. (1965). The distribution of the abnormal hemoglobin genes and their significance for human evolution. *Evolution*, **18**, 685–699.

LUZZATTO, L., USANGA, E. A. and REDDY, S. (1969). Glucose-6-phosphate dehydrogenase deficient red cells: resistance to infection by malarial parasites. *Science (New York)*, **164**, 839–842.

MACDONELL, W. R. (1913). On the expectation of life in ancient Rome, and in the provinces of Hispania and Lusitania, and Africa. *Biometrika*, **9**, 366–380.

MCNEILL, W. H. (1977). "Plagues and Peoples". Blackwell, Oxford.

MATHER, K. (1964). "Human Diversity". Oliver & Boyd, Edinburgh and London.

MATHEWS, J. D. (1976). Kuru as an epidemic disease. *In* "Essays on Kuru" (R. W. Hornabrook, ed.), pp. 83–104. Classey, Faringdon.

MAY, R. M. and ANDERSON, R. M. (1979). Population biology of infectious diseases. *Nature, London*, **280**, 361–367; 455–461.

MAYNARD SMITH, J. (1964). Group selection and kin selection. *Nature, London*, **201**, 1145–1147.

MORTON, N. E. and CHUNG, C. S. (1959). Are the MN blood groups maintained by selection? *American Journal of Human Genetics*, **11**, 237–251.

MORTON, N. E., KRIEGER, H. and MI, M. P. (1966). Natural selection on polymorphisms in northeastern Brazil. *American Journal of Human Genetics*, **18**, 153–171.

MORTON, N. E., SMITH, C., HILL, R. D., FRACKIEWICZ, A., LAW, P. and YEE, S. (1976). Population structure of Barra (Outer Hebrides). *Annals of Human Genetics*, **39**, 339–352.

MULLER, H. J. (1950). Our load of mutations. *American Journal of Human Genetics*, **2**, 111–176.

NAM, C. B., WEATHERBY, N. L. and OCKAY, K. A. (1978). Causes of death which contribute to the mortality crossover effect. *Social Biology*, **25**, 306–314.

NEVO, E. (1978). Genetic variation in natural populations: pattern and theory. *Theoretical Population Biology*, **13**, 121–177.

OSBORN, F. (1960). A return to the principles of natural selection. *Eugenics Quarterly*, **7**, 204–211.

PEARL, R. (1922). "The Biology of Death". Lippincott, Philadelphia and London.

PEARSON, K. (1902). On the change in expectation of life in man during a period of *circa* 2000 years. *Biometrika*, **1**, 261–264.

PENROSE, L. S. (1955). Evidence of heterosis in man. *Proceedings of the Royal Society of London B.* **144**, 203–213.

REED, T. E. (1971). Does reproductive compensation occur? An analysis of Rh data. *American Journal of Human Genetics*, **23**, 215–224.

REED, T. E., GERSHOWITZ, H., SONI, A. and NAPIER, J. (1964). A search for natural selection in six blood group systems and ABH secretion. *American Journal of Human Genetics*, **16**, 161–179.

ROBERTS, D. F. (1971). The demography of Tristan da Cunha. *Population Studies*, **25**, 465–479.

ROBERTSON, F. W. and CUMMING, A. M. (1979). Genetic and environmental variation in serum lipoproteins in relation to coronary heart disease. *Journal of Medical Genetics*, **16**, 85–100.

ROSE, M. and CHARLESWORTH, B. (1980). A test of evolutionary theories of senescence. *Nature, London*, **287**, 140–142.

RUSSELL, J. C. (1958). Late ancient and medieval population. *Transactions of the American Philosophical Society* (new series), **48** (3), 1–152.

SACHER, G. A. (1977). Life table modification and life prolongation. *In* "Handbook of the Biology of Ageing" (C. E. Finch and L. Hayflick, eds), pp. 582–638. Van Nostrand, New York.

SCHREIDER, E. (1964). Ecological rules, body-heat regulation, and human evolution. *Evolution*, **18**, 1–9.

SCOONES, T. (1980). "Huntington's Chorea". Office of Health Economics, London.

SELANDER, R. K. and KAUFMAN, D. W. (1973). Genic variability and strategies of adaptation in animals. *Proceedings of the National Academy of Sciences of the United States of America*, **70**, 1875–1877.

SINISCALCO, M., BERNINI, L., LATTE, B. and MOTULSKY, A. G. (1961). Favism and thalassaemia in Sardinia and their relationship to malaria. *Nature, London*, **190**, 1179–1180.

SORSBY, A. (1963). Retinitis pigmentosa in Tristan da Cunha islanders. *Transactions of the Royal Society of Tropical Medicine and Hygiene*, **57**, 15–18.

THORPE, W. H. (1961). "Biology, Psychology and Belief". University Press, Cambridge.

TYRRELL, D. A. J., SPARROW, P. and BEARE, A. S. (1968). Relation between blood groups and resistance to infection with influenza and some picorna-viruses. *Nature, London* **220**, 819–820.

UNITED NATIONS. (1962). Report of the Scientific Committee on the effects of atomic radiation. *General Assembly official Records 17th Session*, Supplement Number 16 (A/5216).

VAN VALEN, L. and MELLIN, G. W. (1967). Selection in natural populations. 7. New York babies. *Annals of Human Genetics*, **31**, 109–127.

VOGEL, F. and CHAKRAVARTTI, M. R. (1966). ABO blood groups and smallpox in a rural population of West Bengal and Bihar (India). *Humangenetik*, **3**, 166–180.

VOGEL, F., PETTENKOFFER, H. J. and HELMBOLD, W. (1960). Über die Populationsgenetik der ABO-Blutgruppen. *Acta genetica*, **10**, 267–294.

VOGEL, H. P. and KNOX, E. G. (1975). Reproductive patterns after stillbirth and early infant death. *Journal of Biosocial Science*, **7**, 103–111.

WALLACE, B. (1975). Hard and soft selection revisited. *Evolution*, **29**, 465–473.

WATERHOUSE, J. A. H. and HOGBEN, L. (1947). Incompatibility of mother and foetus with respect to iso-agglutinogen A and its antibody. *British Journal of Preventive and Social Medicine*, **1**, 1–17.

WEISMANN, A. (1891). "Essays on Heredity". Clarendon Press, Oxford.

WILLIAMS, G. C. (1957). Pleiotropy, natural selection, and the evolution of senescence. *Evolution*, **11**, 398–411.

ZINSSER, H. (1935). "Rats, Lice and History". Routledge, London.

A Consideration of
Mortuary Practices in Neolithic Greece:
burials from Franchthi Cave*

T. W. JACOBSEN AND TRACEY CULLEN

The last decade of archaeological research has witnessed an increasing concern for the systematic study of prehistoric human burial practices, with particular emphasis on the elucidation of patterns of socio-economic organisation. Unfortunately, however, little attention has been given to that dimension of human behaviour by researchers interested in prehistoric Greece. It is, therefore, the primary objective of this paper to consider the social and, to a lesser extent, economic implications of Greek Neolithic mortuary data in an initial attempt to formulate an interpretative framework for the future study of such remains. Although allusions to burial customs throughout Greece will be made, the data from the site of Franchthi Cave in the Argolid will serve as our major focus.

It will be assumed in this paper that mortuary data represent a structural embodiment of social, economic, technological and religious behaviour as well as reflections of human values and attitudes. The suitability of archaeological mortuary data for use in the pursuit of explicitly anthropological goals is an issue of debate (e.g. Ucko, 1969; Binford, 1971; Leach, 1977). The complex interface of ceremonial behaviour and religious beliefs which may lie between the social system and the material funerary remains is difficult to identify and certainly

*The authors would like to thank the following for their useful comments on this paper: Dr J. L. Angel, Dr Maurice Bloch, Ms Sharon DeHoff, Mr Michael Fotiadis, Ms S. C. Humphreys, and Dr K. D. Vitelli. Financial support for much of the research and writing of this paper was provided by a grant from the National Endowment for the Humanities, Washington, D.C.

requires caution in interpretation. Nevertheless, recent ethnographic studies support a correlation between mortuary variability, in archaeological terms, and social differentiation (Saxe, 1970; Binford, 1971). These studies have shown that the number of social dimensions (age, sex, occupational role, lineage membership, etc.) symbolised in mortuary ritual generally varies in accordance with the complexity and degree of differentiation of a society. To the extent, therefore, that the present holds explanatory value for our understanding of the past, and vice versa, the archaeologist's role in the investigation of the social correlates of mortuary data is of importance.

The different perspectives from which the archaeologist and the social anthropologist view mortuary data necessitate different research foci and strategies. The focus of the social anthropologist is upon the living members of a society, their interactions and reactions to death; the archaeologist, limited to a dependence upon material remains, can only focus upon the dead themselves, their treatment and the circumstances of their interment. The attempt to elucidate concepts of death and structural categories of thought of prehistoric societies is of critical importance in the study of mortuary data (Leach, 1977). It must be noted, however, that while such objectives are practicable in investigating the nature of human experience among living groups, they are not attainable at this point in time by the archaeologist concerned with behavioural variability, cultural processes, and testable models and hypotheses designed to facilitate his research.

Consequently, archaeologists have focused upon the nature of mortuary ritual as a reflection of the social status of the deceased, thus attempting to determine the degree of hierarchy present in a society. The theoretical basis for such a correlation lies in Hertz's observation (1907) that, among some societies, the intensity of emotion expressed by the living at death will vary with the status of the dead. Binford (1971) has further suggested that the death of a high-ranking individual will necessarily disrupt the workings of a community more than that of an individual of lesser rank due to the greater number of social and economic ties which are abruptly cut. Finally, Tainter (1975, 1978) has successfully tested the correlation between the degree of community disruption (and the associated rank of the deceased) and the amount of energy expended on the attendant mortuary ritual. The importance of energy expenditure as an interpretative framework for the analysis of Greek Neolithic burial practices lies in the utilisation of several components of the data base: the interment facility, disposal of the corpse, and the grave goods (Tainter, 1978).

The problems in viewing Greek Neolithic funerary remains from a socio-economic perspective are formidable. Problems of sample size and incomplete study and publication of the material prohibit the application of statistical or formal analyses.[1] Limited horizontal exposure at most sites and the interference of disturbed contexts and poor preservation further reduce the sample size. Perhaps the most serious obstacle, however, is the neglect of many archaeologists working in Greece to collect and record their data in a manner amenable to sociological analysis. Too often, burial practices have been isolated from their cultural contexts, viewed as a static category of form and content merely to be described and catalogued. Considerable variability in the formal aspects of mortuary practices in Neolithic Greece should not be surprising in view of the time span (c. 3000 years) and the regional and, presumably, organisational diversities underlying the adaptive strategies of the various communities. A meaningful assessment of this variability depends upon our ability to look beyond the economic and technological dimensions of subsistence (which have dominated Aegean archaeological studies in recent years) and consider the organisational principles of a given community.

To this end, it is worthwhile to examine the mortuary sample from Franchthi within the wider context of prehistoric Greek burial customs in an attempt to understand the place of death and ritual in the Neolithic period and to determine what, if anything, can be learned of the organisational complexity of the society from such data.

Franchthi Cave

The prehistoric site on the headland of Franchthi lies along the coast near the southern tip of the Argolid peninsula in eastern Peloponnesos (Jacobsen, 1969, 1973a,b, 1976, 1979, 1981). It consists of a large cave, now partially collapsed and filled to a great extent with breakdown from the roof, and an attendant open settlement (Fig. 1). Excavation in the cave revealed evidence of human occupation from the later Palaeolithic through the end of the Greek Neolithic, c. 25 000 B.P. to c. 5000 B.P., as measured by nearly 60 radiocarbon determinations. The open settlement of built stone structures (hereafter termed "Paralia" because of its location along the modern shoreline) was first established near the beginning of the Neolithic (c. 8000 B.P.) and, apart from a brief hiatus around 6000 B.P., was occupied until the end of the Neolithic. There is no evidence of pre-Neolithic activity on Paralia, and both cave and open site seem to have been abandoned at the same time, c. 5000 B.P.

The earliest indications of formal human burial practices at Franchthi belong to Mesolithic levels, dated *c.* 10 000 to *c.* 8000 B.P. The inhabitants of the site at that time were certainly engaged in hunting—red deer was the dominant quarry—and gathering, although it is not yet clear whether oats and barley were also being cultivated. Fishing, especially for tunny, became an important subsistence strategy in the Upper Mesolithic (roughly the ninth millennium B.P..). Although seasonal occupation of the site seems likely, we cannot as yet document it satisfactorily.

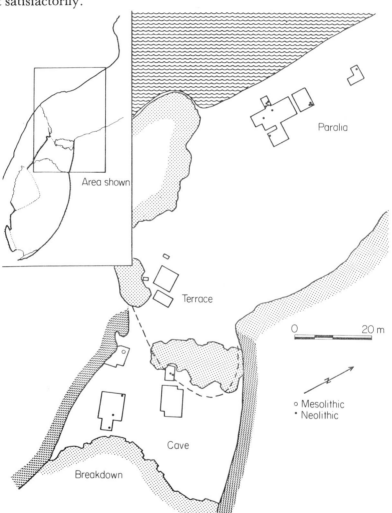

FIG. 1. Plan of the Franchthi Cave excavations showing the locations of the Mesolithic and Neolithic burials.

Neolithic activity at Franchthi covered a span of some 3000 radio-carbon years and has been divided into the following periods in accordance with the generally accepted sequence for Greece (Weinberg, 1970; Renfrew, 1972): Early Neolithic (E.N.), Middle Neolithic (M.N.), Late Neolithic (L.N.) and Final Neolithic (F.N.). While mixed farming based on the standard eastern Mediterranean domesti-cates — sheep (dominant), goats, pigs, cattle, cereals (wheats and barley) and legumes — seems to have been the primary subsistence activity of the probably more numerous inhabitants of the site at this time,[2] there is reason to believe that the relationship of agriculture to animal husbandry varied through time. It is possible, for example, that seasonal pastoralism (transhumance), which may have been a component of the local economy throughout the Neolithic, became a more significant subsistence strategy during L.N. (Jacobsen, 1978). Although, in general, an increased degree of sedentism may perhaps be assumed from the shift to agriculture, we cannot document adequately the existence of a permanent, year-round settlement at Franchthi in the Neolithic.

The material assemblage of Neolithic Franchthi is generally quite typical of this cultural stage in Greece and, for that matter, most of the eastern Mediterranean. Ceramics and lithics (especially flaked stone tools of flint/chert and obsidian) are the largest categories of artefactual remains, and they are of types which eventually came to be shared over a large part of eastern Peloponnesos. Most of the raw materials were available locally but obsidian, already present in pre-Neolithic levels, must have been procured by direct or indirect exchange from its source(s) on the Aegean island of Melos. Other exotic materials, such as marble and andesite, may have come from sources closer to the site. It is clear, in any case, that contacts with neighbouring regions were established at an early date and, with time, came to be increasingly active.

In view of the above, many archaeologists (e.g. Flannery, 1972a; Milisauskas, 1978) would regard the remains from Franchthi as typical of those expected from a ''band'' society of hunters and gatherers which was eventually transformed into a ''tribal'' society of Neolithic agriculturalists (Service, 1971), status distinctions being based primarily upon criteria of age, sex, and individual achievement (''egalitarian''). One cannot always correlate particular subsistence strategies with types of social systems, nor should we necessarily expect the Greek data to conform to a single evolutionary trajectory. Never-theless, given this shift in subsistence practices with the likelihood of increased sedentism and population (and the attendant social implications), and the documented complexity of social organisation in the Greek Bronze Age (Renfrew, 1972), one might reasonably expect to find evidence of increasing social differentiation in the Neolithic. One form such evidence could take in the archaeological record would be an increased elaboration of mortuary ritual and attention to the dead. At the same time, an increase in the number of social distinctions among the living should be paralleled by increased variation in the treatment of the dead. With these possibilities in mind, let us examine the mortuary data from Franchthi.

Franchthi mortuary data

The funerary remains from Franchthi may be divided into two categories: "proper" burials (in which most or all of the human skeleton is preserved in varying degrees of articulation), and bone scatter. Excavations at Franchthi have produced 18 burials (only 17 if 61–62 *Fr* is regarded as a double burial; see below), identified by the *Fr* numbers assigned them by J. L. Angel in his preliminary study of the material. The state of preservation of these burials varies considerably in accordance with the age and sex of the deceased, the circumstances of interment, and the depth of the overlying deposits. Table 1 lists the Franchthi burials according to ten selected variables: location (cave or Paralia), date, grave form (where blank, the excavators were unable to identify the outlines of a pit with certainty), type of interment (primary or secondary), orientation (body axis and facial orientation), position (flexure and position of body), age (a simplification of Angel's initial groupings of the material), sex, grave goods and associated features.

The sample of bone scatter consists of over 100 individual pieces (given 90 *Fr* numbers), representing nearly all parts of the human anatomy: fragments of skull, teeth, and post-cranial members. This information is not included in Table 1; apart from the difficulty of comparing dissimilar remains (i.e. scatter versus formal burials), the bones themselves have yet to be studied in detail. Relevant information obtained from preliminary analyses pertaining to the age and sex of the individuals will be included when available.

Proper burials and bone scatter were found both inside the cave and on Paralia (Fig. 1). All periods represented at Franchthi have provided evidence, albeit meagre, for the treatment of the dead. The pre-Neolithic sample from the cave itself consists of a small number of isolated bones and teeth and a single Mesolithic burial of an adult male. The early and middle phases of the Neolithic provide the most evidence of burial and bone scatter, while the later phases are less well represented.

TABLE 1
Franchthi cave burial data

Fr Number	Location	Date	Grave form	Interment	Orientation [a] Body	Face	Position	Age	Sex	Grave goods	Associated features
1	Cave	Meso	Pit	Prim	N-S	E	SFl, back	A(25)	M		Rock cover
11	Cave	EN	Pit?	Prim	N-S		SFl, L. side	C (5-6)	F?		Stone pillow
12	Cave	EN	Pit	Prim	N-S	E	Fl, back	C (8)	M?		
18	Par	MN?	Pit?	Sec	NW-SE		Fl, R. side	A (33)	F		Stones
19	Par	FN	Pit?	Sec				A (28?)	F?	Spindle whorl	
31	Cave	EN/MN		Sec?	SE-NW	NE?	Stomach	A(17)	F	Rubbing stone	Wall
48	Cave	EN	Pit (L?)	Prim	S-N	E	SFl, L. side	I	F?	Half pot, marble bowl	Capstone
59	Par	MN	Pit	Sec	Fl		Fl	A (39)	F	Pot, bone tools, obsidian tools	Wall
61	Par	FN		Sec				A	F		
62	Par	FN		Sec				A	M		
63	Par	FN		Sec	SE-NW		Side	A (28)	F	Pot	
66	Cave	EN	Pit	Prim	SW-NE	NW	SFl	I	M?		Capstone
69	Par	FN	Pit?	Sec?				C (>7)	M?		
103	Par	EN	Pit (L)	Prim	NW-SE	SW	SFl, L. side	I (Foet?)	F?		Capstones (2)
104	Par	EN	Pit	Prim?	S-N		R. side	I	M?		
105	Par	EN	Pit (L)	Prim?	SW-NE	S?	SFl, L. side	I	M?		Capstone
106	Par	EN	Pit	Sec?	NE-SW	SE	SFl? L. side	I	M?		Capstone?
115	Par	FN		Sec?				C (8)			

[a] Head position second. *Abbreviations*: Par = paralia; Pit (L) = lined pit; Prim = primary; Sec = secondary; SFl = semi-flexed; Fl = flexed; A = adult (16 +); C = child (1–15); I = infant (0–1); foet = foetus.

Most burials are individual inhumations in simple pits. The one complete burial from the Mesolithic, perhaps the best preserved example from the site, seems to have been interred in a shallow depression and the body covered with a layer of stones (Jacobsen, 1969). Neolithic burial pits are usually smaller, occasionally lined with unworked stones and covered with slabs of stone.

Although individual inhumation appears to have been the rule, 62 *Fr* (a young adult male) and 61 *Fr* (an adult female) may represent a double burial of F.N. date from Paralia. The two bodies appear to have been buried in close juxtaposition and may have been simultaneous secondary burials. Although the presence of skeletons of opposite sex and comparable ages in double burials has sometimes been interpreted as evidence for conjugal pairs (Saxe, 1971; van de Velde, 1979), such an interpretation in this case can only be accepted with the greatest caution.

Interment was of two types: primary and secondary. Primary burial is a one-stage process and, since it may have taken place soon after death, will normally be reflected by a virtually complete and articulated skeleton. Our use of the term "secondary", on the other hand, indicates that ultimate burial was the last of (at least) a two-stage process in which the initial stage may have been exposure of the corpse or temporary burial. Secondary burial, then, entails a lapse of time between death and final burial and is often reflected archaeologically by an incomplete skeleton whose parts are found at least partially disarticulated. The possible natural or cultural transformation of the mortuary remains necessarily complicates the distinction between secondary and disturbed primary burials. In some cases the lack of articulation or unusual posture may be due solely to later disturbances (for which there is some evidence from Paralia). The uncertainty of these cases (31 *Fr*, 69 *Fr*, 106 *Fr*, 115 *Fr*) is noted in Table 1.

Although there may be no chronological significance to the distinctions between interment types (*pace* Weinberg, 1970), it is interesting to note that the practice of primary burial is restricted to the E.N. at Franchthi, and is apparently the common form of interment for the very young.[3] Secondary burial, on the other hand, appears to have been the regular practice for the disposal of adults. Two children (69 *Fr* and 115 *Fr*) may have received secondary burial during F.N., but the possibility that they are disturbed primary burials cannot be excluded. The small sample, however, and the discovery of only infants and children in E.N. levels (receiving primary burial)[4] and predominantly adolescents and adults in later levels (receiving secondary burial) discourage any firm conclusions about the chronological or social significance of interment types.

Orientation of the skeleton was sometimes difficult to discern because of the nature of interment (e.g. 59 *Fr*, a secondary burial of an adult female wedged almost vertically into a small pit). In cases where orientation could be reasonably established, the axis of the body was normally aligned roughly north–south. This consistency of alignment is striking and may indicate deliberate positioning of the dead. The ethnographic record (e.g. van Gennep, 1909; Ucko, 1969) offers a multitude of possible explanations underlying patterns of orientation and, more recently, archaeological studies have linked skeletal orientation with the season of interment (Gruber, 1971; Saxe, 1971). The Franchthi sample, however, is too small to warrant similar analysis. Beyond this, there was no apparent regularity in orientation at Franchthi. The heads were oriented either to the north or to the south and faced in no consistent direction.

The majority of our skeletons were laid out in flexed or semi-flexed postures. Most were on their sides, but there is no obvious significance attached to the left or right side. The most unusual burial posture was that of 31 *Fr*, a young adult female, who was found on her stomach with arms extended, the lower half of her body entirely missing. In addition, the upper skeleton appears to have been deliberately disarticulated, the spinal column having been separated from the rib cage and removed (Jacobsen, 1973a; Angel, 1973a). The deviant posture and condition of this burial suggest a range of possible explanations, depending upon the nature of interment: sacrifice, punishment by death, deliberate disturbance by later cave occupants, etc. (cf. Molleson, this volume).

An attempt to determine whether the age and sex structure represented by the Franchthi burials comprises a representative or a selected part of the larger population was, again, discouraged by the size of the sample. The Neolithic remains, excluding bone scatter, consist of eight adults (16 + years), six infants (0–1) and four children (1–15). As indicated above, a distinction in interment types appears to have been made in accordance with age classes.

Distinctions according to sex are also suggested by the data. In the first place, there are more females represented in our sample (proper burials and scatter) than males. If all sexable human bones are combined, the male to female ratio is 25:39, or 61% female. One might even expect that the percentage represents a conservative estimate (Shennan, 1975). The proper burial sample includes only one adult male skeleton from the Neolithic and that (62 *Fr*) possibly part of a double burial with a female. Although there might be a temptation to interpret the numerical dominance of females in our small sample as a reflection of polygynous marriage practices (cf. Shennan, 1975), it is safer to hypothesize that, in terms of the location of burials, adult males merely received different treatment from females. Consideration should therefore be given to risks associated with possible male roles (hunter, herder, mariner, etc.), under which conditions death (and burial?) could well have occurred away from the settlement.

Of the 17 (or 18) proper burials at Franchthi, only five clearly contained grave goods.[5] With the exception of the infant, 48 *Fr*, only female adults appear to have received offerings. The goods are generally utilitarian in character: clay pots were found in three of the five graves while the other objects (a spindle whorl, a rubbing stone, a small marble bowl, a set of bone points and a set of obsidian tools) were each found in a single grave. The largest concentration of grave goods, 11 items in all, was found with the tightly flexed burial of an older woman from Paralia (59 *Fr*).

Little can be said about other features associated with these burials. There seems to be no particular correlation between burials with grave goods and unusual associated features. The young woman, 31 *Fr*, was buried inside an apparent windbreak across the mouth of the cave (Jacobsen, 1973a) and the female burial from Paralia, 59 *Fr*, was located at the base of a wall of uncertain purpose, possibly a terrace or retaining wall of the settlement. Capstones are a reasonably common feature in Neolithic burial pits, and the stone scatter over the Mesolithic burial may have served the same purpose. There is a single instance of a skull of an E.N. child burial from the cave (11 *Fr*) found resting on a ''pillow'' of pebbles, a practice known both ethnographically (Wace and Thompson, 1914) and archaeologically (e.g. Coleman, J. E., 1977) from elsewhere in Greece.

Discussion

Although the circumstances leading to the creation and distribution of bone scatter at archaeological sites are difficult to assess, careful attention must be given to this component of mortuary samples. Bone scatter such as that at Franchthi has also been reported from other Greek Neolithic sites, e.g. Lerna in the Argolid (Angel, 1971) and Nea Nikomedeia in Macedonia (Rodden, 1962). Although it is possible that this phenomenon indicates ''that little heed was taken in the disposal of the dead'' (Rodden, 1962), other explanations may also be offered. Bone scatter may represent a ''sowing'' or ''planting'' of human parts possibly in accordance with a fertility ritual (Angel, personal communication), abandonment or exposure of the corpse, cannibalism

(Brothwell, 1961; Ucko, 1969), a special funerary ritual entailing the deliberate destruction of the integrity of the corpse (Bloch, 1971), the disturbance of secondary burials or primary burials by natural (e.g. erosion, burrowing animals) or human agency (e.g. pits, building or levelling activities). Scattered bone may also reflect selected portions of extramural secondary burials brought by the living into the settlement area as a focus for ceremony or remembrance (Brothwell, 1961). A deposit of several partially articulated phalanges, with no evidence of other parts of the skeleton, in association with one of the walls on Paralia, may support this interpretation. The varying frequency of scattered bone through time, the relative proportions of different parts of the skeleton represented, and the dominance of female adults in the sample provide interesting avenues for further research. The present paper, however, will focus on information provided by the Franchthi burials themselves.

Very little is as yet known about pre-Neolithic mortuary practices in Greece. The entire sample consists of a possible Neanderthal skull from Petralona Cave in Macedonia (Hourmouziadis, 1973), a few enigmatic remains, dated to the Middle and Upper Palaeolithic, from Tsouka Cave (Mt Pelion) and open sites along the Peneios River in Thessaly (Angel, 1966), and the Mesolithic burials from Maroula, Kythnos (Honea, 1975, in press; cf. Cherry, 1979) and Franchthi (Jacobsen, 1969; Angel, 1969).

The picture for Neolithic Greece is clearer but, in spite of data from some 25–30 sites,[6] it is still very incomplete and the total sample is relatively small. Allowing a margin of error for poor preservation and for incomplete study and publication, the Neolithic sample from Greece is no more than 250–300 individuals, and nearly half of the sample is derived from the sites of Kephala and Nea Nikomedeia. The rarity of excavated skeletal remains from Greece thus deserves comment.

Part of the explanation undoubtedly lies in the limited horizontal exposure of Neolithic sites by excavators and the difficulties in the preservation and discovery of burial forms not characterised by monumentality and material display. Although the Neolithic Greek dead may lie undiscovered in cemeteries or in the unexposed areas of habitation sites, it is quite possible that some of the dead did not receive formal burial.

Disposal of the dead in cemeteries (i.e. discrete areas specifically for burial of the deceased, usually, but not necessarily, apart from the domestic area of the living) does not appear to have been commonly practiced in Neolithic Greece, in contrast with the situation in the

Early Bronze Age (Renfrew, 1972). Although rare, a few Neolithic cemeteries have been identified; generally, they are quite small and have been assigned to the end of the period.[7] Despite intensive survey of the area, a Neolithic cemetery has not been located in the vicinity of Franchthi Cave.

Monumentality and conspicuous display in interment practices have been discussed in terms of organised cooperative effort (Renfrew, 1973) and energy expenditure, measured in man-hours of labour as well as by the requirements of skill and labour (Piggott, 1973; Tainter, 1978). Monumental tombs provide, in addition to homage to the dead, visible assertions of the power and/or wealth of the surviving family (Fleming, 1973). It has further been suggested that megalithic tombs, as well as the presence of a formal cemetery, function as territorial foci, symbols of community identity and cohesion and visible references to ancestral authority (Bloch, 1971; Flannery, 1972a,b; Kinnes, 1975). Finally, Saxe (1970) has proposed that formally structured cemeteries are present to the degree that authority is linked to the practice of lineal descent in a given community.

In light of the above, the apparent *absence* of emphasis on the visibility of the dead in Neolithic Greece is of considerable interest. Elaborate mortuary rituals may well have occurred; if so, and if they took the form of clan gatherings, feast and sacrifice, dance, the exchange or deposition of perishable gifts, few traces will remain in the archaeological record (cf. Strathern, this volume). Graves may have been marked, as perhaps in the multiple interments of the Kephala cemetery, but the choice of perishable markers (if such was the case) suggests that a permanent material reference to one's ancestors, not only for the present generation but for future generations as well, was not of utmost importance. There is no evidence from Franchthi that graves were marked. Although negative evidence in part, the unmarked, intramural burials with relatively little indication of ritual elaboration or excessive expenditure of time and labour, viewed in conjunction with the apparent absence of a cemetery, may indicate that authority was personally attributed rather than vested in corporate descent groups at Franchthi.

Although, in general, there may be an increased attention to mortuary ritual through the Neolithic, it would be premature to explain this in strictly evolutionary terms. Evidence of ritual in the burials from E.N. Prodromos (Thessaly) and L.N. Alepotrypa Cave (Mani) is relevant in this respect. Two or three successive deposits of disarticulated bones, mainly skulls and long bones, were discovered beneath a house floor at Prodromos, suggesting the practice of excarnation and selective reburial. It appears from the published drawing (Hourmouziadis, 1971: fig. 1) that the mandibles were deliberately separated from the skulls. A similar case was reported from Alepotrypa Cave (Papathanasopoulos, 1971; Lambert, N., 1972b). It consisted of a concentration of 15 skulls as well as a few assorted bones and, again, the mandibles had been removed from the skulls. A few of the skulls were given further emphasis, set apart and encircled with stones, near a paved area with traces of burning.

Similar evidence of deliberate dismemberment of the corpse may be indicated by the burial of the young woman (31 *Fr*) at Franchthi. While the burials from Alepotrypa and Prodromos may have served to affirm the collectivity and unity of a clan or sodality, the unique circumstances of the Franchthi burial, with the attendant suggestion of violence, probably indicate a different function.

Although primary inhumation in pits within the settlement area seems to be the most common practice in Neolithic Greece, evidence for secondary burial of adults[8] and cremation[9] has also been reported. The presence of both primary and secondary forms of interment at a single site has been attributed by some to varying locations of death, i.e. those who died on the trail received delayed burial, the assumption being that the community practised a mobile economy (Mellaart, 1975).[10] A range of practical considerations (place and season of death, topography, soil conditions, climate, etc.) undoubtedly affect the choice of interment form. The possible correlation, however, of age and form of interment at Franchthi may indicate more complex factors underlying the choice of primary or secondary burial.

The practice of secondary burial may be viewed in terms of energy expenditure, the time and effort required for the disposal of the corpse and the contingent potential of rallying resources and kin for the final ceremony clearly being greater than that required for primary burial. If the Franchthi burials are ranked according to apparent energy expenditure—those characterised by secondary burial, grave goods and associated features listed first, simple primary burial with no associations last—the sample divides into two groups according to age, adults generally receiving more attention than infants and children.

A discussion of secondary burial is necessarily incomplete without mention of the work of Hertz (1907) and van Gennep (1909) and their views of death and funerary ritual as a social process of transformation, characterised by the tripartite structure of all rites of passage (separation/transition/incorporation). Based on his work on Borneo, Hertz postulated that the stages of burial, exhumation, and reburial parallel the journey and evolving status of the soul as well as the stages of pollution and gradual reintegration of the mourners into society. It must be emphasised, however, that the practice of secondary burial need not imply a belief in the soul nor its journey to an afterworld. In any case, this is a difficult area to explore archaeologically.

Van Gennep (1909), in stressing the autonomy of the transitional phase of rites of passage, noted that the length of the period of mourning is dependent upon the intensity of ties of the living to the dead and the relative social rank of the dead. The archaeological implications of this statement are considerable. If one assumes that the period between first and second burial (or the time of exposure) corresponds with the mourning period of the survivors (in the most general sense), then the degree of articulation should vary inversely with the status of the deceased.

Unfortunately, the difficulties of determining the length of the transitional period from the degree of articulation exhibited by the skeleton may be insurmountable. Although the extent of disarticulation might be expected to correspond roughly with the length of the mourning period, one must also consider the potential effects of the following variables (Angel, personal communication):

1. The age of the dead individual: infants and children will decay more rapidly, create less stench and leave fewer archaeological traces than adults.
2. The treatment of the body during the interim period: exposure of the corpse entails a more rapid decay and greater stench than burial. The discovery of partial skeletons and toothmarks on the bones might suggest that bodies were exposed, rather than buried, probably at some distance from the settlement.
3. The season of death: the rate of decomposition will depend upon the humidity, temperature and intensity of sunlight; in this connection, independent evidence of seasonal occupation of a site would be relevant.
4. The soil conditions: the acidity and moisture of the soil will affect the rate of decay if the body is buried.

Determination of the length of the interim period is further discouraged by the possibility of the mummification of ligaments, under which circumstances the bones could be held in loose articulation for as long as several years.

Leach (1977) is also concerned with the liminal aspect of mortuary rites, arguing that an understanding of the choice of location for the graves of the dead will elucidate the structure of thought implicit in the practices of a society.[11] The decision to bury the dead intramurally rather than in a well-marked cemetery may reflect a less rigid boundary between the places of the living and the dead. The proximity of the dead at Franchthi (as at most Greek Neolithic sites) may suggest that they functioned primarily in a sphere of personal memory, with little apparent need to stress status distinctions or ancestral authority with material display. On the other hand, the formal separation of the dead from the living and the emphasis on permanence implicit in the concept of a cemetery are echoed in the practice of secondary burial by the separation of flesh from bone.

As indicated above (p. 91), adults at Franchthi generally received more mortuary attention than young individuals. The burial of a two-week-old baby (48 *Fr*) represents a notable exception to this pattern. The infant, carefully laid out in a flexed position, received primary burial in a lined pit with a capstone. Half of a ceramic vessel and a small marble bowl were associated with the skeleton. The inclusion of a marble bowl, a prestigious item more commonly linked with Bronze Age burials, is unusual in itself. The association of such a find with an infant burial is unique in the Greek Neolithic.[12]

Special funerary treatment of infants has often been interpreted as evidence for a hierarchical social system, the child being ascribed or inheriting a status which it could not have yet earned in a system of ranking based primarily on age, sex and individual merit (Saxe, 1970; Wright, 1978). Unequal access to resources, the basis of differential wealth and, presumably, power, is commonly believed to be reflected in the pattern of distribution of grave goods. The uniqueness of 48 *Fr*, however, not only at Franchthi but in the Neolithic Greek mortuary sample as a whole, necessitates that caution be exercised in drawing conclusions about the nature of ranking at Franchthi. Indeed, it has recently been suggested that "the presence of richly accompanied child or infant burials" is not by itself an adequate test for the existence of ranking in early societies (Peebles and Kus, 1977). In the absence of independent evidence of ranking, we must consider untestable psychological factors such as parental grief or aborted expectations as equally plausible explanations of this unusual phenomenon.

In evaluating the significance of grave offerings, one must beware of assuming the goods were former possessions of the dead (Renfrew, 1972) or necessarily reflect the relative affluence of the society (Coleman, J. E., 1977).[13] The decision of a society to transform its material wealth into a mortuary context may be made independently of the level of affluence of that society. The social selection of goods, however, will reflect the value systems of a community as they pertain to different statuses and roles of the deceased. The relative value of grave goods presumably depends upon a number of factors: the function of the object (primarily in a utilitarian or ceremonial context), the raw material used in manufacture, that material's availability, the amount of labour and craftsmanship expended in creating the object and, more difficult to discern from the archaeological record, the personal associations of an object (Winters, 1968).

The majority of the grave goods from Franchthi and other Greek Neolithic sites are of a utilitarian character (ceramic vessels, stone and bone tools, spindle whorls, etc.), equipment appropriate to occupational roles in the domestic sphere. The Franchthi offerings, on the whole, appear to be linked with community and family roles expectable of women in a non-industrial society. Interestingly, an examination of the bones in some cases corroborates this impression.[14]

Notably rare in the Franchthi mortuary assemblage (as well as in other Neolithic Greek assemblages) is evidence of grave goods which may have functioned in a ceremonial context, ornaments which define and reinforce individual status, or symbolic "badges" of office. Such evidence (the use of ochre, beads and pendants, stylised figurines, etc.) does occur in Neolithic *habitation* deposits, in greater numbers than in Mesolithic contexts, perhaps indicating an increased need to reinforce structural societal divisions overtly through the use of material status markers in life if not, apparently, in death.

The objects associated with 48 *Fr* may indicate ritual activity. The marble bowl (its diminutive size indicating forethought in the choice of an appropriate offering for an infant?) and the pot were both incomplete, suggesting the possibility of deliberate breakage.[15] This practice may have served a variety of functions, the symbol of the loss of a life, the result of a ritual toast, or a deterrent of evil spirits (Grinsell, 1961).

With the exception of the obsidian implements (59 *Fr*) and possibly the marble vessel (48 *Fr*), the materials employed in grave goods at Franchthi were obtainable locally and in common use at the site. Although the procurement of obsidian from its source(s) on the island of Melos represented a certain amount of enterprise and risk, the increasing exploitation of that material from the Palaeolithic (attaining about 75% in M.N. and nearly 100% in F.N. of all chipped stone tools) suggests that it was not, at least through most of the Neolithic, a particularly valuable commodity. Such may not have been the case for marble, which is considerably rarer at Franchthi.

Although many of the grave goods represent considerable skill and patience in manufacture, none is of exceptional virtuosity or unparalleled by examples from habitation levels. The fine carinated bowl associated with 59 *Fr* was broken, and attempts to mend it had been made in antiquity, perhaps indicating a personal value exceeding the vessel's intrinsic worth.

Mortuary ritual serves to emphasise the cohesion and continuity of the social order, to reaffirm relationships among the living and to resolve the dissonance created by the unpredictable loss of a community member (Malinowski, 1925). The formality and abstract nature of ritual, its essential symbolising character, act to legitimise and reinforce the existing system of social differentiation, whether articulated along lines of age, sex, personal achievement, lineage or sodality membership. Material (i.e. clearly visible) expressions of ritual behaviour, from the use of ornament and ochre to the ceremonial display of a skull, may be of particular importance in legitimising systems in which power is ascribed or denied at birth. It seems reasonable, therefore, to assume that the degree to which a society exhibits ritual behaviour may be correlated with the degree of its institutionalised hierarchy (Bloch, 1977). In general, the few burials documented from the 3000 years of the Greek Neolithic show relatively little evidence of elaborate ritual behaviour.

The evidence from Franchthi suggests little social stratification, distinctions in mortuary ritual primarily being made in accordance with age and sex and, possibly, occupational roles. The presence of secondary burials may reflect the need to transform the corpse into a more permanent form (cf. Humphreys, this volume). The notable lack, however, of ostentation and monumentality in the Franchthi burials, together with the presence of scattered human bone, may indicate that the physical integrity of the dead was relatively unimportant to the living.

Although it is of critical importance to evalutate funerary data in conjunction with other cultural and environmental variables, our grasp of population parameters, settlement patterns and degree of sedentism of occupation during the Neolithic at Franchthi is unfortunately adequate for little more than speculation. We have noted the possibility of an increasing reliance upon transhumant pastoralism as the Neolithic progressed. One factor which could have contributed to that situation was a rise in sea level (Van Andel *et al.*, 1980) which would have gradually usurped the old coastal plain and caused a blockage in the major nearby stream. A rising sea level may also have led to a more intensive exploitation of resources in the immediate neighbourhood of the site. Both possibilities would have had significant implications for the treatment of the dead. Increased mobility and dependence on pastoralism during L.N. may have resulted in burial away from the base camp. Intensified exploitation of nearby resources, on the other hand, may have contributed to an enhanced sense of territorialism and community identity, evidence of which might lie in the eventual discovery of a cemetery near the site. Although the absence of burials in L.N. levels at Franchthi is undoubtedly linked with poor representation in general of this period, the possibility of changing disposal practices and attitudes toward the dead should not be discounted, particularly in view of developments elsewhere in Greece at that time.

Viewing the Neolithic of Greece as a whole, we may suggest increasing attention to mortuary ritual through time, as indicated by the increased frequency of secondary burial and cremation, and the inclusion of grave goods, a concern with the special treatment of skulls, and the establishment of formal cemeteries. Although the small sample from Franchthi lends some support to this impression, our data correspond in a general way with expectations generated by a tribal model of society. There is little evidence of institutionalised hierarchy. To the extent that one may judge from present archaeological evidence, the process of death in Neolithic Greece, and associated mourning and ritual, would appear to have ended with final burial, the dead not having been required to serve further purposes for the living.

Notes

1. For an excellent review of various quantitative approaches to the study of mortuary data, see Tainter (1978).
2. The question of the population of Franchthi at any given time is extremely difficult to answer. There are too many uncontrolled variables at present to permit an accurate estimate, but the innovations in the archaeological record and the physical expansion of the site at the beginning of the Neolithic combine to suggest a noteworthy increase in numbers of people at that time. It is likely that further investigation of the offshore area adjacent to Paralia, begun in 1979 (cf. Van Andel et al., 1980) and planned to continue in 1981, will provide additional clarification of the Neolithic boundaries of the site. For the present, we have no reason to disagree with Milisauskas' (1978) estimate that the Neolithic sites of southeastern Europe rarely exceeded 200 in population (Jacobsen, 1981).
3. One possible exception, 106 Fr, has been designated a secondary burial only because of the unnatural orientation of its head: although the body faces to the west, the skull has been turned 180° to face southeast. The orientation could be the result of tectonic displacement and the burial actually primary.

4. Although only infant and child *burials* were discovered in E.N. levels, adults are represented in the bone scatter from this period.
5. This is perhaps a conservative estimate. Items such as individual potsherds, animal bones, pebbles and shell (especially terrestrial molluscs) were excluded from consideration as grave goods. The vague pit outlines and the ubiquitous occurrence of these items throughout the site necessitate caution in their attribution as grave gifts. It may, of course, prove useful to reconsider such finds upon further examination of the material.
6. In addition to the burials from Franchthi Cave, mortuary remains have been reported from aceramic Neolithic levels at Knossos; E.N. levels at Souphli (Gallis, 1975, 1979), Sesklo (Orlandos, 1977), Argissa, Prodromos, Lerna, Kefalovryso, Ayios Petros (Halonnesos), Nea Nikomedeia and Nemea (?); M.N. levels from Dimini (Mycenaean?), Ayioryitika, Chaeronea, Cave of Pan, Lerna and Prosymna; L.N./F.N. levels from Prosymna, Elateia, Alepotrypa Cave, Rachmani, Servia, Tsangli, Athenian Agora, Kitsos Cave (Lambert, N., 1969, 1970, 1971, 1972a), Souphli, Kephala (Coleman, J. E., 1977), Lerna, Rhodochori Cave in Macedonia (?) (Rodden, 1964), and Plateia Magoula (Gallis, 1975, 1979). For other references, see Weinberg (1970) and Hourmouziadis (1973).
7. The F.N. site of Kephala on Keos is the clearest example of a Neolithic cemetery, with more than 30 built stone graves, some covered with stone platforms. Other examples, less well documented, may include Souphli, Prosymna, and Plateia Magoula.
8. Secondary burial has been reported from the following sites: Prodromos, Ayioryitika, Prosymna, Alepotrypa Cave, and Servia (?).
9. Cremation has been reported from the following sites: Souphli (E.N. and L.N.), Prosymna (?), Servia (?), Plateia Magoula, and Kitsos Cave.
10. Since there is reason to believe that transhumance was practised to some extent at Franchthi (and perhaps elsewhere in Greece) during the Neolithic, the question of transhumant burial practices is of some interest to us. Unfortunately, little has been written on the subject. Hole (1978) has suggested that the burial places of mobile pastoralists in the Middle East are often found scattered along their migrational routes, whether associated with camp sites or not, but he also notes (personal communication) that pastoralists in Iran today are usually buried quickly because of Islamic law. Leshnik (1972) has observed among the pastoral nomads of India the existence of major (''primary'') cemeteries at each end of their migration routes and intermediate (''secondary'') cemeteries along those routes. An awareness of such practices, as he points out, can explain ''the presence of multiple cemeteries, some of which may be quite small, in remote places''.
11. Maurice Bloch (personal communication) rightly cautions against necessarily interpreting the locality of the dead as straightforward evidence of separation. Meaningful boundaries may be employed which leave no archaeological trace; note, for example, the custom in parts of

New Guinea in which a plant symbolic of territorial boundaries is planted on the grave (Rappaport, 1967).

12. A marble vessel was found in each of two graves (20 and 34) at Kephala. Neither, however, was associated with an infant burial (Coleman, J. E., 1977).

13. For ethnographic examples which demonstrate the need for caution, see Winters (1968) and Ucko (1969).

14. For example, J. L. Angel (personal communication) has observed that the tooth wear of 59 *Fr* (whose grave contained a complete clay pot, six bone points, and four obsidian tools) indicates "thread-biting, spindle-holding and other industrial usage as in spinning, weaving, etc.", adding that the "breakdown of neck intervertebral surfaces and of the right thumb metacarpophalangeal joint and stress on hand tendon-sheaths and anterior deltoid origins fit such activities as pot-making."

15. Ritual breakage has also been suggested in association with the recently discovered cremations from Souphli (Gallis, 1979). The practice is known in Greece today as well. Nicholas Gavrielides (personal communication) has observed ritual breakage at a funeral in Fourni, a village not far from Franchthi. The Vlachs of northern Greece break a glass on the spot where the body was laid out for viewing (Wace and Thompson, 1914). The villagers of the Zaghori smash a jug at the gate of the courtyard "to prevent the dead taking anything else with him from the house and to break the power of Charon" (ibid.). Ritual activity is also indicated by the presence of small, crudely made vessels in the graves from Plateia Magoula, items not paralleled in habitation deposits and possibly created expressly for funerary purposes at the time of cremation (Gallis, 1975, 1979).

References

ANGEL, J. L. (1966). Effects of human biological factors in development of civilization. *Year Book of the American Philosophical Society*, 315–317.

ANGEL, J. L. (1969). Human skeletal material from Franchthi Cave. Appendix II. *In* T. W. Jacobsen (1969), pp. 380–381.

ANGEL, J. L. (1971). "The People of Lerna: Analysis of a Prehistoric Aegean Population". Smithsonian Institution Press, Washington, D.C.

ANGEL, J. L. (1973a). Neolithic human remains. *In* T. W. Jacobsen, 1973b, pp. 277–282.

ANGEL, J. L. (1973b). Early Neolithic people of Nea Nikomedeia. *In* "Die Anfänge des Neolithikums vom Orient bis Nordeuropa", Teil VIIIa. 1, pp. 103–112. Institut für Ur- und Frühgeschichte der Universität zu Köln.

BINFORD, L. R. (1971). Mortuary practices: their study and their potential. *In* "Approaches to the Social Dimensions of Mortuary Practices" (J. A. Brown, ed.), *Memoirs of the Society for American Archaeology*, **25**, 6-29.

BLOCH, M. (1971). "Placing the Dead: Tombs, Ancestral Villages and Kinship Organization in Madagascar". Seminar Press, London and New York.

BLOCH, M. (1977). The past and the present in the present. *Man*, **12**, 278-292.

BROTHWELL, D. R. (1961). Cannibalism in early Britain. *Antiquity*, **35**, 304-307.

CHERRY, J. (1979). Four problems in Cycladic prehistory. *In* "Papers in Cycladic Prehistory" (J. Cherry and J. Davis, eds), pp. 22-47. Monograph XIV, Institute of Archaeology, Los Angeles.

COLEMAN, J. E. (1977). "Kephala: a Late Neolithic Settlement and Cemetery". American School of Classical Studies, Princeton.

FLANNERY, K. (1972a). The cultural evolution of civilizations. *Annual Review of Ecological Systems*, **3**, 399-426.

FLANNERY, K. (1972b). The origins of the village as a settlement type in Mesoamerica and the Near East: a comparative study. *In* "Man, Settlement and Urbanism" (P. J. Ucko, R. Tringham, G. W. Dimbleby, eds), pp. 23-53. Duckworth, London.

FLEMING, A. (1973). Tombs for the living. *Man*, **8**, 177-193.

GALLIS, C. J. (1975). Kauseis nekron apo ten Archaioteran Neolithiken epochen eis ten Thessalian. *Athens Annals of Archaeology*, **8**, 241-258.

GALLIS, C. J. (1979). Cremation burials from the early Neolithic in Thessaly. *In* "La Thessalie". Actes de la Table-Ronde, 21-24 Juillet 1975, Lyon. Collection de la Maison de l'Orient Méditerranéen No. 6. Série archéologique 5.

GRINSELL, L. V. (1961). The breaking of objects as a funerary rite. *Folk-lore*, **72**, 475-491.

GRUBER, J. W. (1971). Patterning in death in a late prehistoric village in Pennsylvania. *American Antiquity*, **36**, 64-76.

HERTZ, R. (1907). Contribution à une étude sur la représentation collective de la mort. *L'Année sociologique*, **10**, 48-137. English edition: "Death and The Right Hand" (R. and C. Needham, translators). Free Press, New York, 1960.

HOLE, F. (1978). Pastoral nomadism in western Iran. *In* "Explorations in ethnoarchaeology" (R. A. Gould, ed.), pp. 127-167. University of New Mexico Press, Albuquerque.

HONEA, K. (1975). Prehistoric remains on the island of Kythnos. *American Journal of Archaeology*, **79**, 277-279.

HONEA, K. (in press). Mesolithic settlement of the Greek Cyclades Islands. *In* "Actes, IXième Congrès International des Sciences Préhistoriques et Protohistoriques". Nice, France.

HOURMOUZIADIS, G. (1971). Two new early Neolithic sites in Western Thessaly (in Greek). *Athens Annals of Archaeology*, **4**, 164-175.

HOURMOUZIADIS, G. (1973). Burial customs. In "Neolithic Greece" (D. R. Theocharis, ed.), pp. 201–212. National Bank of Greece, Athens.

JACOBSEN, T. W. (1969). Excavations at Porto Cheli and vicinity, preliminary report, II: the Franchthi Cave, 1967–1968. Hesperia, 38, 343–381.

JACOBSEN, T. W. (1973a). Excavation in the Franchthi Cave, 1969–1971, part I. Hesperia, 42, 45–88.

JACOBSEN, T. W. (1973b). Excavations in the Franchthi Cave, 1969–1971, part II. Hesperia, 42, 253–283.

JACOBSEN, T. W. (1976). 17 000 years of Greek prehistory. Scientific American, 234 (6), 76–87.

JACOBSEN, T. W. (1978). Transhumance as a mechanism of exchange in Neolithic Greece. Abstracts, The Archaeological Institute of America, 3, 47.

JACOBSEN, T. W. (1979). Excavations at Franchthi Cave, 1973–1974. Archaiologikon Deltion, 29 B, 268–282.

JACOBSEN, T. W. (1981). Franchthi Cave and the beginning of settled village life in Greece. Hesperia, 50.

KINNIS, I. (1975). Monumental function in British Neolithic burial practices. World Archaeology, 7, 16–29.

LAMBERT, N. (1969). Grotte de Kitsos. Bulletin de correspondance hellénique, 93, 956–966.

LAMBERT, N. (1970). Grotte de Kitsos (Laurion). Bulletin de correspondance hellénique, 94, 755–764.

LAMBERT, N. (1971). Grotte de Kitsos (Laurion). Bulletin de correspondance hellénique, 95, 703–735.

LAMBERT, N. (1972a). Grotte de Kitsos (Laurion). Bulletin de correspondance hellénique, 96, 817–844.

LAMBERT, N. (1972b). Grotte d'Alépotrypa (Magne). Bulletin de correspondance hellénique, 96, 845–871.

LEACH, E. (1977). A view from the bridge. In "Archaeology and anthropology: areas of mutual interest" (M. Spriggs, ed.) pp. 161–176. British Archaeological Reports, Supplementary Series 19.

LESHNIK, L. S. (1972). Pastoral nomadism in the archaeology of India and Pakistan. World Archaeology, 4, 150–166.

MALINOWSKI, B. (1925). Magic, science and religion. In "Magic, Science and Religion and Other Essays", pp. 17–92. Doubleday, Garden City, N.Y., 1954.

MELLAART, J. (1975). "The Neolithic of the Near East". Thames and Hudson, London.

MILISAUSKAS, S. (1978). "European Prehistory". Academic Press, New York and London.

ORLANDOS, A. K. (1977). Sesklo. To Ergon tés en Athenais Archaiologikés Etaireias, 88–93.

PAPATHANASOPOULOS, G. A. (1971). Spelaia Dirou, 1971. Athens Annals of Archaeology, 4, 289–303.

PEEBLES, C. S. and KUS, S. M. (1977). Some archaeological correlates of ranked societies. American Antiquity, 42, 421–448.

PIGGOTT, S. (1973). The Dalladies long barrow: NE Scotland. Antiquity, 47, 32–36.

RAPPAPORT, R. A. (1967). "Pigs for the Ancestors". Yale University Press, New Haven.

RENFREW, C. (1972). "The Emergence of Civilisation". Methuen, London.

RENFREW, C. (1973). Monuments, mobilization and social organization in Neolithic Wessex. In "The Explanation of Culture Change: Models in Prehistory" (C. Renfrew, ed.), pp. 539-558. Duckworth, London.

RODDEN, R. J. (1962). Excavations at the early Neolithic site at Nea Nikomedeia, Greek Macedonia (1961 season). *Proceedings of the Prehistoric Society*, **28**, 267-288.

RODDEN, R. J. (1964). Recent discoveries from prehistoric Macedonia: an interim report. *Balkan Studies*, **5**, 109-124.

SAXE, A. A. (1970). Social dimensions of mortuary practices. Ph.D. dissertation, University of Michigan. University Microfilms, Ann Arbor.

SAXE, A. A. (1971). Social dimensions of mortuary practices in a Mesolithic population from Wadi Halfa, Sudan. In "Approaches to the Social Dimensions of Mortuary Practices" (J. A. Brown, ed.), pp. 39-57. *Memoirs of the Society for American Archaeology* **25**. Society for American Archaeology, Washington.

SERVICE, E. R. (1971). "Primitive Social Organization", 2nd edition. Random House, New York.

SHENNAN, S. (1975). The social organization at Branč. *Antiquity*, **49**, 279-288.

TAINTER, J. A. (1975). Social inference and mortuary practices: an experiment in numerical classification. *World Archaeology*, **7**, 1-15.

TAINTER, J. A. (1978). Mortuary practices and the study of prehistoric social systems. In "Advances in Archaeological Method and Theory" (M. Schiffer, ed.), vol. 1, pp. 105-141. Academic Press, New York and London.

UCKO, P. J. (1969). Ethnography and archaeological interpretation of funerary remains. *World Archaeology* **1**, 262-280.

VAN ANDEL, Tj. H., JACOBSEN, T. W., JOLLY, J. B. and LIANOS, N. (1980). The Quaternary history of the coastal zone near Franchthi Cave, southern Argolid, Greece. *Journal of Field Archaeology*, **7**, 389-402.

VAN DE VELDE, P. (1979). The social anthropology of a Neolithic cemetery in the Netherlands. *Current Anthropology*, **20**, 37-58.

VAN GENNEP, A. (1909). "Les Rites de passage". Emile Nourry, Paris.

WACE, A. J. B. and THOMPSON, M. S. (1914). "The Nomads of the Balkans". Methuen, London.

WEINBERG, S. S. (1970). The Stone Age in the Aegean. In "Cambridge Ancient History", third edition, vol. 1, part 1, pp. 557-618. Cambridge University Press, Cambridge.

WINTERS, H. D. (1968). Value systems and trade cycles of the Late Archaic in the midwest. In "New Perspectives in Archaeology" (S. R. and L. R. Binford, eds), pp. 175-221. Aldine Publishing Co., Chicago.

WRIGHT, G. A. (1978). Social differentiation in the early Natufian. In "Social Archaeology" (C. L. Redman *et al.*, eds), pp. 201-223. Academic Press, New York and London.

Rank and Class: interpreting the evidence from prehistoric cemeteries*

C. R. ORTON AND F. R. HODSON

In a number of recent studies, archaeologists have attempted to determine the status of individuals in a prehistoric society from their graves. The evidence cited may be the scale of grave structures, the nature and quantity of grave goods and the location of graves within a cemetery or landscape.

In treating this evidence a variety of qualitative arguments are often combined to provide the interpretation: graves are classified into groups and a rank or status attributed to each group. Thus Frankenstein and Rowlands (1978: 84 ff.) have suggested five political levels for south-west Germany in the Iron Age (paramount chief, vassal chief, sub-chief, minor chief and general low status). Their arguments cite not only the quantity but the function of grave goods and the geographical location of graves. Peebles and Kus (1977) assembled similar wide-ranging evidence in their classification and interpretation of rank in the Moundville cemetery.

However, other archaeologists have employed what is, on the face of it, more direct and objective, fully quantified evidence in such contexts: a single numerical index is devised that is intended to reflect wealth and/or status and that may be calculated for all burials under consideration. The distribution of values of this index is plotted as a histogram which is then used to distinguish rank or classes within the society. Figures 1(a) and 2(a) are histograms of this type, taken from well-known studies on Bronze Age Europe. The intention of this

*This work is supported by a grant from the Science Research Council.

103

present paper is to discuss some of the statistical problems that arise
when this quantitative approach is followed, and these two diagrams
will serve as a starting point.

Figure 1(a) comes from an investigation by Randsborg (1974) of
"mortuary wealth" within different groups of graves in prehistoric
northern Europe. Randsborg takes the weight of bronze grave goods as
an index of wealth and studies this index for the different archaeological
groups (in this instance, Fig. 1(a), for male graves without gold objects

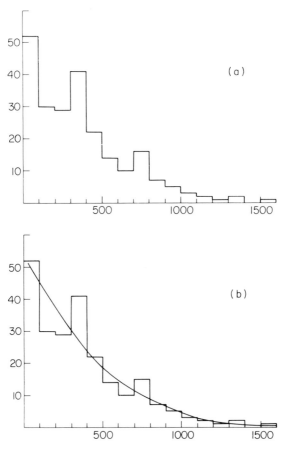

FIG. 1. Weight in grams of bronze grave goods. Male graves without gold of the
Northern Bronze Age Period II, after Randsborg (1974). (a) The raw data (see Table
3, column "n"). (b) A simple empirical distribution superimposed on (a) (see Table 3,
column "$\hat{n}_e$").

from Bronze Age period II). He points to three peaks in the distribution and suggests that they represent "heterogeneity within the population of mortuary wealth" although he adds that "it does not seem possible — so far — to separate these groups by means of independent information" (1974: 49).

Shennan (1975) follows a similar approach, although her wealth index is more ambitious, admitting different weighting for different raw materials and for the estimated time taken to produce finished objects. Her distribution of such wealth scores for the graves at Brančx, an early Bronze Age cemetery in Czechoslovakia, is reproduced as Fig. 2(a). Shennan points to an apparent discontinuity in the distribution: "The histogram shows a marked break between those graves that have less than 10 points and those that have 10 or more, which have therefore been defined here as rich." (1975:284.)

Similar, although more extreme, claims are made and a similar index is presupposed by Tainter and Cordy (1977). They suggest seven

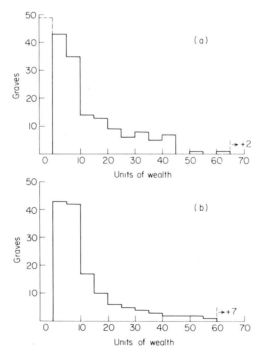

Fig. 2. Wealth scores for graves at Brančx after Shennan (1975). (a) The raw data (see Table 2, column "n"). (b) A Pareto distribution fitted to these data (see Table 2, column "$\hat{n}_2$").

distinct rank levels within 117 burials of the Kaloko cemetery, Hawaii, and cite as evidence a measure of "labour expenditure" calculated from "the volume of stone in the structure and the extensiveness of stone facing about the periphery of the monument". However, histograms of these values are not given.

One of the authors has published a preliminary study of the Hallstatt cemetery where a crude status index is derived by simply counting the number of distinct functional types appearing in graves (Hodson, 1977). Histograms of these counts were used to compare major groups of graves, for instance cremations with inhumations.

In each of these case studies, the wealth or status index proposed could be criticised and the superficial objectivity questioned. However, a more pressing problem concerns the interpretation of such histograms, irrespective of the individual index from which they derive. To revert to the Branč diagram and its interpretation (Fig. 2(a)), is the drop in the count of graves above and below the score of 10 units really the main feature and sufficient evidence to divide the graves into two major groups? Is it more striking than, say, the drop after 45 units, or than the existence of the few graves with more than 85 units? Before discontinuity or irregularity may be accepted, some expected or null distribution is really needed as a basis for comparison, whether by eye or by more formal tests. But it is not too clear just what kind of distribution could be accepted as null in this context.

We can approach the question of criteria for a suitable null distribution by supposing that the individuals in a population can be assigned to "states" (for example, in Fig. 2 the values 0, 1–5, 6–10, 11–15, etc. of the wealth scores can be treated as "states"). Over time, an individual may move from one state to another: the wealth score of a burial is simply the state in which that individual died. It should be noted that "states" as used here refers to the value of goods that would be buried with an individual, and not to the sum total of his wealth. The implication behind discontinuities seems to be that they represent barriers to movement from one state to another (whether upwards or downwards): a suitable null distribution should therefore reflect a situation in which there are no such barriers. Such a situation can be modelled by a simple Markov chain (accounts of which can be found in many textbooks on Probability Theory or Stochastic Processes, e.g. Feller, 1957: 338–396; Cox and Miller, 1965: 76–145), in which a transition matrix specifies the probability that an individual moves from one state to another in a given period of time (say one year). If we assume that the probabilities of change are independent of the original state of the individual, then in time the distribution of the population settles down into an equilibrium distribution, in which the proportion of the population in each state remains the same, although individuals may move freely from one state to another. It can be shown that under these and other more technical assumptions, the distribution takes the form known as a Pareto distribution, expressed mathematically by the cumulative distribution function:

$$F(x) = 1 - \left(\frac{a}{x}\right)^{\theta}, x \geq a > 0, \theta > 0$$

(Champernowne, 1973: 250–254)

The Pareto distribution has been used extensively in studies of present-day distribution of income (e.g. by Champernowne, 1973), and it was this aspect which first drew our attention to it. However, claims for its suitability as a null distribution rest on its Markovian properties, and not on the possibility of analogies between present-day income and prehistoric wealth.

Before comparing this distribution with archaeological examples, we should note that it does not allow us to consider burials with zero wealth (i.e. burials for which $x = 0$) because there cannot be a zero divisor in the formula. The expedient of adding an arbitrary constant to all values of x is not permissible in this situation because it would affect the shape, as well as the location, of the distribution. There are archaeological reasons too for not treating zero values as part of the general distribution: it could be argued that they differ from the others qualitatively and not just quantitatively, and it would be impossible to refute this argument on statistical grounds. Also, we should be aware of the possibility that the life-time of individuals may not be long enough for time equilibrium to be reached, and that very high scores may therefore be absent. In statistical terms, we anticipate that an observed distribution may be truncated.

A Pareto distribution can be fitted to data in many ways (Champernowne, 1973: 216), no one of which is the "best" for all possible situations: the method used here is to estimate a by the lowest observed value, and to use the UMVUE (uniformly minimum-variance unbiased estimator) for θ, given by

$$\theta = (n - 1)/\left(\sum_{i}^{n} \ln x_i - n \ln \hat{a}\right),$$

where there are n observations $x_i, \ldots, x_n$ (Patel et al., 1976: 173). For grouped data (e.g. those of Fig. 2) the approach is slightly different, as the mid-point value of each group (e.g. 3 of 1–5, 8 of 6–10) is used to stand for the group as a whole. If the number of groups is k, and there are n_j observations in the jth group, of which the mid-point is y_j, then

$$\text{and} \qquad \begin{aligned} \hat{a} &= y_1 \\ \hat{\theta} &= (n-1)/(\sum_{k}^{k} n_j \ln y_j - n\ln\hat{a}). \end{aligned}$$

In either case, the fitted Pareto distribution is given by

$$\hat{F}(x) = 1 - \left(\frac{\hat{a}}{x}\right)^{\hat{\theta}}.$$

Clearly, we cannot expect the data to fit a theoretical distribution exactly. Two courses are open to us: we can either treat our material as a population in which case the distribution will not (in general) be Pareto, and there is no more to say statistically, although we can consider informally whether the discrepancy is likely to be of practical, as opposed to statistical, significance. More fruitfully, perhaps, we can consider our material as a sample from a population (giving careful thought as to what that population might be), and use a goodness-of-fit test to assess whether the distribution of the population could reasonably be Pareto. This approach allows us to generalise about the population.

The fit between the observed and theoretical distributions is examined here by the use of the Kolmogorov–Smirnov test in preference to the more widely used, but less sensitive and more problem-prone, chi-squared test. (Accounts of the chi-squared test can be found in many statistical textbooks; for a detailed exposition see Cochran (1952). The Kolmogorov–Smirnov test is more commonly found in texts on non-parametric statistics: a detailed account is given by Darling (1957). The two approaches are compared briefly by Lindgren (1960: 304). Experience suggests that the Kolmogorov–Smirnov test is perhaps more useful when looking for systematic but relatively small deviations, and the chi-squared test preferable when looking for isolated aberrant values). The Kolmogorov–Smirnov statistic D_n is the greatest difference between the observed distribution $F_n(x)$ and the theoretical distribution $\hat{F}(x)$,

i.e. $$D_n = \sup_{x} | F_n(x) - \hat{F}(x) |.$$

If the data are grouped, then a slightly smaller value of D_n may be obtained: in practice this is not usually serious. Tables showing the values of D_n at various levels of significance have been published (Massey, 1951; Birnbaum, 1952).

As a first basis for comparison, an ostensibly straightforward archaeological example based on a large sample would seem appropriate,

TABLE 1
Functional types in graves at Hallstatt (see Fig. 3)

x	n	$F_n(x)$	$\hat{F}_1(x)$	$\hat{n}_1$	$\hat{F}_2(x)$	$\hat{n}_2$
1	212			}437		}454
2	220	0·584	0·590		0·613	
3	138	0·770	0·756	122	0·785	127
4	82	0·881	0·832	57	0·864	58
5	41	0·936	0·874	31	0·908	33
6	25	0·970	0·900	19	0·935	20
7	9	0·982	0·918	13	0·952	13
8	6	0·991	0·931	10	0·968	11
9	3	0·995	0·941	7	0·977	7
10	2	0·997	0·948	6	0·985	6
11	0	0·997	0·954	4	0·991	4
12	1	0·999	0·959	4	0·996	4
13	1	1·000	0·963	3	1·000	3
Total	740	—	—	713		740

Note: 79 graves containing no functional types are omitted from this Table.

and the data presented in Table 1 and Fig. 3(a) will serve. These are derived by taking out of the first main series of approximately 1000 graves from Hallstatt valid single graves and by simply counting the number of distinct functional types that occur per grave (cf. Hodson, 1977). Only if these ostensibly innocuous data fit the proposed distribution would it seem worth proceeding to the more "irregular" data discussed above.

The first attempt to fit a Pareto distribution, using the method described above, gave values of:

$$\hat{a} = 1, \ \hat{\theta} = 1\cdot2854$$

The resulting theoretical distribution is shown as $\hat{F}_1(x)$ and $\hat{n}_1$ in Table 1. It can be seen that

$$D_n = 0\cdot070,$$

this value being attained when $x = 6$. A difference of this size is statistically significant at the 1% level (i.e. if the observations really were a sample from a population which had the theoretical distribution $\hat{F}_1(x)$, there would be less than one chance in 100 of observing a discrepancy as large as this). Examination of the figures, however, suggests that the large "truncation" may be partly responsible — the theoretical distribution predicts twenty-seven graves with more than thirteen functional types, the largest number actually observed. If the theoretical distribution is simply truncated at this point and redistributed over the lower values, we obtain the second theoretical distribution, $\hat{F}_2(x)$ and $\hat{n}_2$, shown in Table 1 and Fig. 3(b). Comparison with $F_n(x)$ gives a new value of

$$D_n = 0 \cdot 035,$$

still attained when $x = 6$. This is not significant at the 20% level (i.e. there is a greater than 1 in 5 chance of observing a discrepancy at least as large as this), indicating an adequate if not particularly good fit of the data to the model. A more sophisticated way of estimating θ for a truncated distribution might produce a better fit, but since we have an adequate one there seems little point in trying. Also, we should remember that adjusting the theoretical distribution on the basis of the sample tends to improve the fit (Lindgren, 1960: 304).

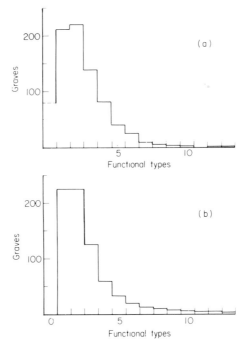

FIG. 3. Functional types in graves at Hallstatt (the Ramsauer series). (a) The raw data (see Table 1, column "n"). (b) a Pareto distribution fitted to these data (see Table 1, column "$\hat{n}_2$").

Having established the potential of the Pareto distribution for summarising a large body of apparently well-behaved data, we can now turn to the more contentious examples.

Applying the formulae for grouped data to the material from Branč, we obtain the values

$$\hat{a} = 3, \; \hat{\theta} = 0\cdot825,$$

immediately suggesting the need for truncation, since if $\hat{\theta} < 1$, the mean of an untruncated distribution is infinite (Patel *et al.*, 1976: 34). The fit of the data is mediocre (see $\hat{F}_1(x)$ and $\hat{n}_1$ in Table 2), with

$$D_n = 0\cdot096$$

occurring at $x = 15$. This value is significant at about the 15% level.

TABLE 2

Wealth scores for graves at Branč (after Shennan, 1975, see Fig. 2)

x	n	$F_n(x)$	$\hat{F}_1(x)$	$\hat{n}_1$	$\hat{F}_2(x)$	$\hat{n}_2$
1–5	43	0·299	0·344	50	0·301	43
6–10	35	0·542	0·630	41	0·588	42
11–15	14	0·639	0·735	15	0·708	17
16–20	13	0·729	0·791	8	0·777	10
21–25	9	0·792	0·826	5	0·822	6
26–30	6	0·833	0·850	3	0·856	5
31–35	8	0·899	0·868	3	0·881	4
36–40	5	0·924	0·882	2	0·901	3
41–45	7	0·972	0·893	2	0·918	2
46–50	0	0·972	0·902	1	0·932	2
51–55	1	0·979	0·909	1	0·943	2
56–60	0	0·979	0·916	1	0·953	1
61–65	1	0·986	0·921	1		⎫
66–90	1	0·993	0·940	4		⎬ 7
91–100	1	1·000	0·945	1	1·000	⎭
Total	144	—	—	138		144

Note: 49 graves with zero wealth score are omitted from this Table.

Simple truncation does not help in this case, since most of the redistributed values go to the first three cells, 1–5, 6–10 and 11–15, where the theoretical values are already greater than the observed. An adjustment to θ is needed, and a guessed value of

$$\hat{\theta} = 0\cdot6$$

gives the distribution shown as $\hat{F}_2(x)$ and $\hat{n}_2$ in Table 2 and shown in Fig. 2(b). The test-statistic D_n is reduced to $0\cdot069$ (still occurring at $x = 15$), which is not significant at the 20% level. A simple search procedure could probably produce a better fit, but there seems little point in doing so as we already have an adequate fit and, again, we run the risk of overfitting. On this evidence, there is really no statistical case for dividing the graves into two groups above and below the score of 10 (or indeed any other score).

In contrast to the previous example, Randsborg's data (Fig. 1 and Table 3) cannot be fitted to a Pareto distribution. Straightforward application of the formulae for grouped data gives

$$\hat{a} = 50, \; \hat{\theta} = 0\cdot6286,$$

leading to the distribution $\hat{F}_1(x)$, shown in Table 3, which is an extremely bad fit. Truncation does not help, and although decreasing the value of θ gives a marginally better fit, it is clear that the problem is the relative "flatness" of the observed distribution over the range 0–400, which is impossible to fit to a Pareto distribution.

However, it *is* possible to fit a simple empirical (hand-drawn) distri-

TABLE 3
Weight of bronze grave goods, North Europe (after Randsborg, 1974, see Fig. 1)

x	n	$F(x)$	$\hat{F}_1(x)$	$\hat{n}_1$	$\hat{F}_e(x)$	$\hat{n}_e$
0–100	52	0·222	0·353	83	0·209	49
101–200	30	0·350	0·582	53	0·385	41
201–300	29	0·474	0·676	22	0·530	34
301–400	41	0·650	0·729	13	0·645	27
401–500	22	0·744	0·765	8	0·735	21
501–600	14	0·803	0·790	6	0·806	16½
601–700	10	0·846	0·810	4	0·861	13
701–800	15	0·910	0·825	4	0·904	10
801–900	7	0·940			0·936	7½
901–1000	5	0·962			0·959	5½
1001–1100	3	0·974			0·974	3½
1101–1200	2	0·983			0·985	2½
1201–1300	1	0·987			0·991	1½
1301–1400	2	0·996			0·996	1
1401–1500	0	0·996			0·998	}1
1501–1600	1	1·000			1·000	
Total	234	—	—		—	

bution to the data using frequencies rather than cumulative densities (Fig. 1(b) and $\hat{F}_e(x)$, $\hat{n}_e$ in Table 3). This distribution has a Kolmogorov-Smirnov statistic of

$$D_n = 0.056,$$

which is not significant at the 20% level, and a chi-squared statistic of 14·85, which with ten degrees of freedom is not significant at the 10% level (it seems more relevant to use the chi-squared test here, because of the apparent peaks in the distribution). We can conclude that, from a statistical point of view, there is no need to look for archaeological meaning in the peaks observed in the distribution—they could plausibly be the result of sampling from a smooth, unimodal distribution.

In both cases, then, the subjective division of graves into groups by examination of the histogram is not supported statistically. This does not mean that groupings do not exist, but that the evidence is not strong enough to demonstrate them convincingly. One reason is the small size of the samples—if the patterns found by Randsborg and by Shennan were repeated on samples the size of that from Hallstatt (740 instead of 234 and 144 graves respectively), the deviations from the theoretical distributions would be statistically significant.

What more general conclusions can we draw from these results? Mainly, that it is extremely difficult to demonstrate division or groupings of graves simply from histograms of wealth scores, and that very large samples of graves are needed. Divisions may be claimed on the evidence of either (case 1) a sudden fall in a generally slowly falling distribution (e.g. Shennan's claim for Branč, see p. 105) or (case 2) a "break", or zero value, in a histogram). A study of the properties of the Kolmogorov–Smirnov statistic, as applied to histograms (Orton, unpublished), shows that even under very favourable circumstances the smallest number N of graves within which a division into c groups or classes can possibly be statistically significant is given by the approximate formulae:

$$N = (4Kc(c-1))^2 \text{ — case 1}$$

$$\text{and } N = 2K(2c-1) \text{ — case 2}$$

(provided that the "breaks" in the histogram are no wider than the adjoining blocks of non-zero values), where K is a constant depending on the chosen level of significance. For example, at the 10% level the value of K is $1 \cdot 22$, giving values of:

		case 1	case 2	
N	$\doteq$	100	50	when $c = 2$
N	$\doteq$	900	150	when $c = 3$
and N	$\doteq$	3500	300	when $c = 4$

These formulae are derived under artificially favourable conditions (favourable, that is, to the detection of divisions) and in most realistic situations the minimum sample size might be two or three times greater than shown here. In practice this means that there is no point in looking for a division into a number c of groups or classes unless the sample size N is greater than that given by the appropriate formula, because even if a division were apparently found, it would be almost impossible for it to be statistically significant.

Conclusion

Division of graves into groups or classes purely by examination of a histogram of wealth scores (however devised) is more difficult than it appears, and very large samples are required. In none of the examples given is a division found to be statistically significant. Arguments for such divisions would have to be based on more evidence than a simple histogram of wealth scores.

References

BIRNBAUM, Z. W. (1952). Numerical tabulation of the distribution of Kolmogorov's statistic for finite sample size. *Journal of the American Statistical Association*, **47**, 425–41.

CHAMPERNOWNE, D. G. (1973). "The Distribution of Income between Persons". Cambridge University Press, Cambridge.

COCHRAN, W. G. (1952). The χ^2 test of goodness of fit. *Annals of Mathematical Statistics*, **23**, 315–45.

COX, D. R. and MILLER, H. D. (1965). "The Theory of Stochastic Processes". Methuen, London.

DARLING, D. A. (1957). The Kolmogorov–Smirnov, Cramer-von Mises tests. *Annals of Mathematical Statistics*, **28**, 823–838.

FELLER, W. (1957) (2nd edition). "An Introduction to Probability Theory and Its Applications", vol. 1. John Wiley, New York.

FRANKENSTEIN, S. and ROWLANDS, M. J. (1978). The internal structure and regional context of Early Iron Age society in south-western Germany. *University of London Bulletin of the Institute of Archaeology*, **15**, 73–112.

HODSON, F. R. (1977). Quantifying Hallstatt: some initial results. *American Antiquity*, **42**(3), 394–412.

LINDGREN, B. W. (1960). "Statistical Theory". Macmillan, New York.

MASSEY, F. J. Jr. (1951) The Kolmogorov–Smirnov test for goodness of fit. *Journal of the American Statistical Association*, **46**, 68–78.

PATEL, J. K., KAPADIA, C. H. and OWEN, D. B. (1976). "Handbook of Statistical Distributions". Marcel Dekker, New York.

PEEBLES, C. S. and KUS, S. M. (1977). Some archaeological correlates of ranked societies. *American Antiquity*, **42**(3), 421–448.

RANDSBORG, K. (1974). Social stratification in Early Bronze Age Denmark. *Praehistorische Zeitschrift*, **49**, 38–61.

SHENNAN, S. (1975). The social organization at Branč. *Antiquity*, **49**, 279–288.

TAINTER, J. A. and CORDY, R. H. (1977). An archaeological analysis of social ranking and residence groups in prehistoric Hawaii. *World Archaeology* **9**(1), 95–112.

Artefacts of Christian Death

PHILIP RAHTZ

The interest of archaeologists in the dead of northern Europe has, until recently, been largely restricted to pre-Christian graves. There was, firstly, the reluctance to disturb the mortal remains of those whose religion we at least nominally share, the Christian dead. Secondly, there was the assumption that graves were interesting only if they contained grave-goods, a practice which in England was largely abandoned by the eighth century. There were exceptions, the notable one being the archetypal Early Christian St Cuthbert (Battiscombe, 1956) but the objects in his grave were studied largely from an art-historical viewpoint. Since they were in a demonstrably Christian context, it was assumed that their function and symbolism was not in doubt, any more than that of the objects added to the shrine in later centuries.

The Christian dead are now being studied in the same way as those of other religions. Archaeologists have, in recent years, begun to excavate Christian cemeteries on a large scale, using the same methods as those established for the earlier pagan dead. We may cite here the extensive excavations of urban cemeteries at Winchester (Kjølbye-Biddle, 1976), London (Hobley, personal communication), and York (Dawes and Magilton, 1980); those of monastic sites such as Hereford (Shoesmith, 1981) and Bordesley Abbey (Rahtz and Hirst, 1976); and of rural communities such as Wharram Percy (Hurst, ed., forthcoming). Grave-goods are certainly rare, but the cemeteries have begun to yield valuable data on the surprising range of mortuary practice in Christian contexts — gypsum and charcoal burials, varying body disposition, and a wide variety of grave-structures and body-containers. There is also demographic and palaeopathological information, and even some data possibly relevant to ethnic origins; the last is an interesting study in relation to social mobility, and genetic resistance to the perils of plague or urban life. Social differences are visible only in the upper echelons of society, and notably in the location of the graves of the secular or monastic aristocracy in relation to key areas in the ritual nucleus of the church.

This paper is not, however, concerned with the archaeology of the medieval and later Christian dead below the ground, but principally with the associated above-ground artefacts, those that are, in fact, available to an anthropologist who is not a digger. The relationship of the symbolism of grave-goods to that of these visible artefacts will be briefly explored, but most of the paper will be a descriptive catalogue of sources. Grave memorials will be especially considered, but such exotica as biers, hearses and undertakers' yards are also included. The material deserves serious analytical study by anthropologists as well as by archaeologists.

Many explanations have been given for the virtual extinction of grave-goods in the eighth century and later, which need not be dwelt on here (cf. Rahtz et al., eds, 1980). One should, however, be considered: that the wealth that had formerly been "conspicuously wasted" or "economically sterilised" in the grave,[1] was now given instead to the Church, in the same way as the end of the resource-expenditure on the Anglo-Saxon barrow coincides with the rise in church-building (cf. Shephard, 1979a,b).

We are familiar with the memorials of the secular aristocracy where wealth is expended, if not in the grave, then in the more permanent and conspicuous above-ground monument of stone or brass. The same objects are displayed—sword, shield, helmet, armour—fossilised in stone, metal or wood, or funerary versions hung up above the tomb. This is an often arrogant and permanent display of wealth, compared with that seen only on the occasion of the funeral, as at Sutton Hoo. More significant, however, is the symbolism of the memorials of the aristocracy of the Church itself. These are the elaborate effigies of archbishops, bishops and other dignitaries, such as that of Archbishop Walter de Gray at York. He is shown with his robes and accoutrements of office, in an architectural setting, in a great tomb-effigy, visible to all since the thirteenth century (Ramm, 1971). Yet beneath this, painted in colour on the lid of the coffin itself, was a further depiction of his earthly dignity. This can have been seen by only a relatively small number of people in the thirteenth century, in the period between the interment of the body and the completion and erection of the effigy stone. The link between the symbolism of these three- and two-dimensional representations is made in this case quite explicit by the fact that inside the coffin the skeleton of Walter de Gray was found with some of those same attributes as grave-goods: again a very short-lived exhibition of "conspicuous waste".

Similarly, at a lower level in the ecclesiastical hierarchy, the parish priest is depicted on gravestones and brasses with his hands in the position of prayer, and holding a chalice, indicating his status and function in society. The same image is found *in* his grave, the arm position and the chalice, with a paten (Fig. 1); but now, unlike the regalia of the Archbishop, they are token "models" of base metal, made especially for funerary purposes, and not those used in church, which passed to his successor.

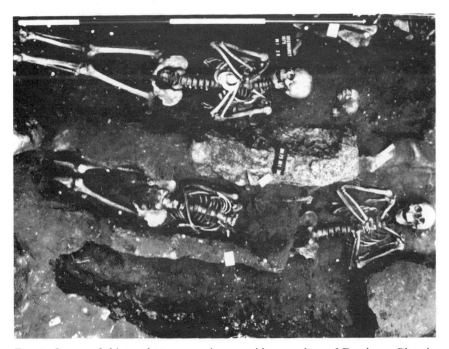

FIG. 1. Graves of thirteenth-century priests outside west door of Deerhurst Church, Gloucestershire, England (excavation by author, 1976).

Early medieval paintings (e.g. Boase, 1972: Plates 15 and 17) depict the horrors of Hell and the fate of the selected dead, but not the terrors of death itself or of bodily corruption. This appears only later, notably in the later fourteenth to fifteenth centuries, and it is tempting to relate this to the mid-fourteenth century plagues (cf. Boase, 1972: 98), when death became as usual as life, rather than the atypical or unnatural event often encountered by anthropologists. This is, however, probably an over-simplification — many other factors are present. Consciousness of bodily decay and corruption, contrasting with temporal magnificence, is shown commonly in the numerous depictions of the Three Dead and Three Living, and of the Dance of Death (Boase, 1972: 104–106), and very neatly in the double tier effigy tombs of the later Middle Ages, the upper emphasising the dignity of life and the lower the reality of the wasted cadaver at the time of death (Boase, 1972: Plate 109). This symbolism is also found on memorial brasses (info. Peter Newton).

The Christian graveyards of the Middle Ages had been in use for a length of time of up to 700 years by the late fourteenth century. They also represent a denser population than that of earlier centuries. The graves are, moreover, in a space constrained by rural or, more especially, urban development, in a defined graveyard. Multiple burial in the same place, or cyclically over the graveyard, became the norm. Every inhumation was the occasion for the exhumation of earlier dead, who may have been buried within living memory.[2] Accordingly, the art of the fifteenth century now depicts charnel as the inevitable accompaniment of death, itself now in a grisly guise (e.g. Boase, 1972: Plate 102). The gravedigger Robert Scarlett (the mode of his profession closely allied to that of the archaeologist) died in 1594 aged 98; he had buried Katherine of Aragon and Mary, Queen of Scots; he was famous, so we find him depicted in a painting displayed in Peterborough Cathedral (Fig. 2). Not only is he shown with his attributes of pick, shovel and keys, but also with a skull. In a painting of a funeral scene of the mid-fifteenth century, it is the grave-digger with his attributes and charnel who fulfils the role of *memento mori* in contrast to the pomp of the funeral procession (Boase, 1972: Plate 96).

From the sixteenth century onwards, death symbolism on memorials is frequent, though not universal, and can take many forms. Common are the symbols of death and the grave-digger, sometimes hung on ribbons in the side panels. In the famous Brouncker monument in Oxford of the middle of the seventeenth century, the sole symbol of death is a skull which separates husband and wife in death, but at the same time unites them in their pensive sorrow (Fig. 3). The monument of Viscount Campden and his wife at Chipping Campden is moving away from crude artefactual symbolism towards a more theatrical depiction of the tomb itself (Fig. 4). The husband and wife are dressed in their shrouds in their vault as if saying goodbye to their friends at a final pre-death party. But the stone doors never close (though they could—they are on proper hinges), and the loving couple have now been frozen at their pre-death party for three centuries.

The culmination of the theatrical expression of the horror of death as a winged skeleton, and its role as a grim warning against temporal pride, is the Bernini monument of the 1670s in St Peter's. Gilded, Death pushes his way through a doorway under a great marble carpet,

FIG. 2. Robert Scarlett, grave-digger of Peterborough Cathedral, England, who died in 1594, aged 98. From a painting displayed in the Cathedral.

flattening his wings as he does so, and shakes the powerful symbol of
the hour-glass at the temporal pomp of Pope Alexander VII above
(Fig. 5) (see also Hibbard, 1965: 215). The same scene is echoed a
century later on the Nightingale monument (1761, by Roubiliac) in
Westminster Abbey; here Death is the attacker, casting the fatal dart

FIG. 3. Memorial of Sir William Brouncker and his wife, died 1645 and 1649; in Christ
Church Cathedral, Oxford, England.

whose flight the husband is powerless to avert (Pevsner, 1957: 388–389 and Plate 78). This is a world far removed from that of the magnificent memorial (by Wyatt) in St George's Chapel, Windsor, to Princess Charlotte, who died in 1817 in childbirth. The horror of death is sublimated to the shrouded body, with the master-touch of the hand falling outside the drapery (Pevsner, 1966, 278–279 and Plate 32).

FIG. 4. Monument of Viscount Campden (died 1642) and his wife by Joshua Marshall, erected 1664; Chipping Campden Church, Gloucestershire, England.

The exhibition of the dead themselves, in contrast to stone depictions of them, has not been fashionable in England. There is a remarkable example in Assisi, of St Clare (d. 1253). In the 1930s she was a leathery cadaver set on a platform surrounded by a sunken area into which the

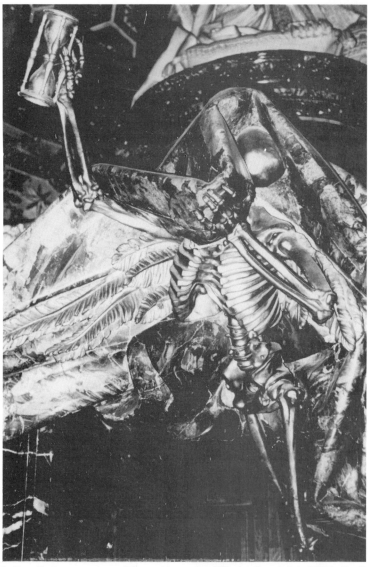

FIG. 5. Detail of monument of Pope Alexander VII, by Bernini (c.1671), St. Peter's, Rome, Italy.

faithful threw offerings. Since then, the saint has been de-fleshed and set behind glass in an open coffin for pilgrims to see and photograph (Fig. 6). She is holding a book in her wired fingers, and is dressed in fine muslins, which are renewed at frequent intervals by the enclosed nuns of the Order. The only Englishman never to have been buried is Jeremy Bentham, whose corpse (albeit with a new wax head) resides in a closet in University College, London. He is still, on occasions, wheeled into meetings, and recorded in Minutes as "present, but not voting".

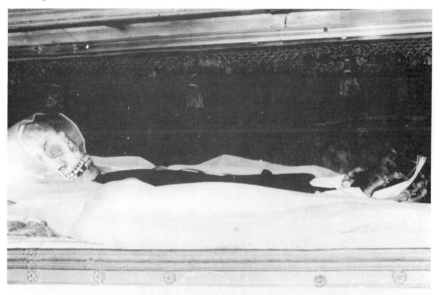

Fig. 6. Shrine of St Clare. Church of S. Chiara, Assisi, Italy, 1976.

The most neglected source of evidence for this theme is that of the exterior memorials in graveyards which become common in the late seventeenth century. They are of especial interest to anthropologists because they extend the range of memorial symbolism below the aristocratic level to that of the middle class, or that small percentage of the population who could afford a stone. This source may be, in some aspects, enlarged to a wider social sample by the associated written sources discussed by Alan Macfarlane (this volume). There are upwards of five million stones in Britain alone, which are, however, being steadily eroded by time and vandalism, in some cases encouraged by parish or diocesan "clearance" schemes (Jones, J., 1979). They display a vast variety of symbolism. The memorials themselves are often anthropomorphic, a set of head, body, and foot stones with the added symbolism of the "body" being in coffin-shape (Fig. 7). Pictorial symbolism develops on the upper and side borders. Deaths-heads and other grim images change gradually into cherubs during the eighteenth century; they occasionally combined symbolism with an

FIG. 7. Grave memorial of Denis Jones, died 1819; churchyard of Devils Bridge, Dyfed, Wales.

idealised portraiture (Figs 8 and 9). The process of transition from "death" to "soul" symbol has been extensively studied in America, together with other facets of grave memorial archaeology (Ludwig, 1966; see also refs in Jones, J., 1979). Later, in the eighteenth and nineteenth centuries, there are willows, urns and pictorial elements such as that of Father Time, through the magnificence of the early nineteenth-century pictorial stones (e.g. Fig. 10) down to the derived and degenerate horrors of more recent times.

There is comparable evidence in other countries. Of particular interest in the context of the 1980 seminar are the Mediterranean "cities of the dead" (Fig. 11), where paved streets and sidewalks are flanked by miniaturised apartment blocks, each "residential" unit being a coffin container. In the cities of the dead there are social distinctions, the rich having large separate mausolea. To the city come the living and quiet guests, usually on Sundays, as part of a social as well as a ritual circuit. Trees grow in open areas, and outside the "apartments" are hung flowers like those on the balconies of the living; there are often photographs of the dead, fossilising their pre-death appearance. These have not become popular in England, but they are clearly going to be of great interest not only to future social but also to physical anthropologists, in their direct association with skeletal remains. They may seem to British eyes to denigrate the dignity of the dead to a commonplace level, an immortality less evocative in the event than the simple name, age and date of death of the ordinary grave-stone.

FIG. 8. Gravestone of Lussod Watkin, died 1797, and sisters; churchyard of Llywel, Powys, Wales.

Conspicuous display is also seen in the offerings placed on modern graves. In England these are usually fresh flowers; the memory of relatives' and friends' offerings fades naturally with time. They are eventually thrown by the gardener onto the churchyard midden. This is usually over the churchyard wall; it is a valuable future (if not present) source for the artefacts of mortuary practice.

In France, however, the offerings are more lasting; multiple beaded wire wreaths, plastic flowers, and metal and stone plaques abound (Fig. 12); and in recent years, fresh flowers sealed in transparent plastic, like salad in aspic jelly. Even the smallest of these costs the

FIG. 9. Gravestone of Nicholas and Susannah Lane, died 1774 and 1742; churchyard of Castle Morton, Hereford/Worcestershire, England.

FIG. 10. Gravestone of Thomas Willis, died 1820; churchyard of Bitton, Avon, England.

equivalent of £30 to £40 in the lavish "pompe funèbre" shops, which are significantly so numerous and prominent in French towns. This is the living speaking to the living of the quantification of their mourning. Included in these offerings from relatives, friends and workmates are also souvenirs from shrines visited (presumably by the deceased), such

FIG. 11. Cemetery at Andraitx, Majorca, Balearic Islands, 1980.

as Lourdes. These are a valuable record to the anthropologist of the catchment area of such important religious centres. In France there are also displays of bodily remains, which may have a long life. A coil of hair of a young girl of *c.*130 years ago, kept behind glass (Fig. 13), reminds us of the potency of hair cut from the deceased as a source of continuing power in the houses in the medieval village of Montaillou (Le Roy Ladurie, 1980: 31 f.).

Other memorials record the occasion rather than depict symbolism such as those that record catastrophe—the St Mawgan frozen boat's crew (Fig. 14), or the well-known Bromsgrove railway accident stones (one is in Morley, 1971, Plate 60).

The parallel printed pictorial sources are, of course, as numerous in recent centuries as is the written evidence. Some seem to have escaped wide notice or critical analysis. Broadsides advertise mourning (e.g. Ludwig, 1966, Plate 156), and the entire range of symbolism seen on

FIG. 12. Grave in churchyard of Trois Eglises, Poitou, France.

grave memorials—charnel bones, grave-digger's pick and shovel, winged hour-glass, together with a shroud, remind the recipient about the attendant horrors of death. Modern death notices are more sober. In England they are put in newspapers, but in the eastern Mediterranean they are posted round the streets, announcing not only the death but the location of the funeral. The pictorial element in these is often a standard printer's block which is as romantically archaic as the "In Memoriam" verses in our newspapers.

Fig. 13. Grave reliquary set in gravestone behind glass, c.A.D. 1850; churchyard of Trois Eglises, Poitou, France.

Also neglected is the major pictorial source of Funeral Invitations, of which the best collection for England is in the John Johnson Collection in the Bodleian. These have an even wider range of death symbols, often with a theatrical frame. Depicted also on these are very useful pictures of funerals, a subject dearer to the hearts of anthropologists than its relatively mundane end-product, the grave. They extend through the eighteenth and nineteenth centuries with appropriate changes of decoration, sentiment and symbol (cf. Morley, 1971, Plates 7 and 9); Morley also describes a wide range of comparative material of the nineteenth century, such as drawings, paintings, ceramics, samplers, memorial cards, mourning ear trumpet and handkerchief,

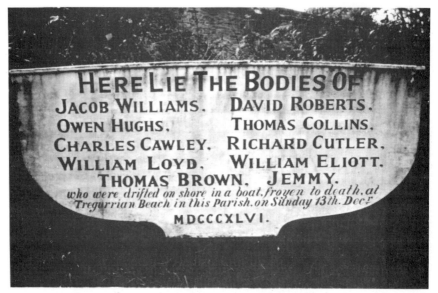

FIG. 14. Wooden memorial (renewed) to a boat's crew, died at sea 1846; churchyard of St Mawgan, Cornwall, England, 1974.

FIG. 15. Hearse, late nineteenth century, displayed on roadside near Brecon, Powys, Wales, 1975.

Fig. 16. Hearse, Salamanca, Spain, 1977.

Fig. 17. Monumental mason's display yard, Ribe, Denmark, 1964.

hatchments, jewellery, clothes, funeral equipment, undertakers' accounts and cartoons.

Some physical trappings of past days survive such as the bier (usually lying unused in the dark tower) and the hearse. Nineteenth-century examples (Fig. 15, cf. also Morley, 1971, Plates 52–55) are conspicuous in their detail, drawing attention to their unique function while modern ones (Fig. 16) would pass for three-door hatchbacks with exceptional driver visibility and cubic capacity of the boot.

The funeral industry has been studied adequately only for the USA, in the immortal works of Evelyn Waugh (1948) and Jessica Mitford (1963). In this country undertakers are remarkably reticent when they are approached by students for details of their business. We can observe only their uninspiring public front. At Ribe a more pleasant range of stones is available to the Danish public, many of which echo the prolific megalithic tombs of Jutland (Fig. 17). They are set out here, inviting death to take place, so that the emptiness of their surfaces may be filled.

Finally, to return to our starting-point below the ground, a class of material may be considered which will be available for study only when

Fig. 18. Coffin plaque; St Mary-le-Port Church, Bristol, England, 1962. (Author's excavation.)

comparatively recent cemeteries are dug. These are coffin-fittings — handles and plaques. Those that do turn up (Fig. 18) do so often in uncontrolled excavations where churchyards are bulldozed away, or where modern graves are sacrificed to reach more interesting ones below. They reflect a range of symbolism similar to that on memorials, but were, of course, seen only for a brief period before and during the funeral, like grave-goods.

The artefacts of Christian death are numerous, both below and above the ground. The former are unlikely to be available for study in the foreseeable future. The latter are seemingly inexhaustible in quantity, but are subject to steady erosion by aerial agents of weather and polluting air, and by the destructive needs of a changing society. Replacements are mundane, and the increasing incidence of cremation decreases the likelihood of their survival as a means of commemorating or marking the dead. This paper, it is hoped, will have indicated something of the range of sources for the study of the Christian dead, and its potential for anthropological research.

Notes

1. cf. the closing lines of *Beowulf* "the gold in the ground as "unavailable" to men as it had been before" (the Old English word is not really to be translated as "useless" as, e.g. in the Penguin translation but rather as removed from circulation — info. S. J. Bradley).
2. cf. Hamlet's boyhood friend Yorick, whose skull was disinterred during the digging of Ophelia's grave, and identified by the grave-digger (*Hamlet*, Act V, Scene 1).

References

BATTISCOMBE, C. F. (1956). "The Relics of St Cuthbert". Oxford University Press, Oxford.

BOASE, T. S. R. (1972). "Death in the Middle Ages". Thames and Hudson, London.

DAWES, J. D. and MAGILTON, J. K. (1980). "The Cemetery of St Helen-on-the-Walls". Council for British Archaeology, London.

HIBBARD, H. (1965). "Bernini". Penguin, Harmondsworth.

HURST, J. G. (ed.) (forthcoming). "Wharram Percy: the Church of St Martin". Monograph of the Society for Medieval Archaeology, London.

JONES, J. (1979). "How to Record Graveyards" (second edition). Council for British Archaeology and *Rescue*, Hertford.

KJØLBYE-BIDDLE, B. (1976). A Cathedral cemetery: problems in excavation and interpretation. *World Archaeology*, **7**, 87–108.

LE ROY LADURIE, E. (1980). "Montaillou". Penguin, Harmondsworth.

LUDWIG, A. I. (1966). "Graven Images". Wesleyan University Press, Middletown, Connecticut.

MITFORD, J. (1963). "The American Way of Death". Penguin, Harmondsworth.

MORLEY, J. (1971). "Death, Heaven, and the Victorians". Studio Vista, London.

PEVSNER, N. (1957). "London, Vol. 1: The Cities of London and Westminster" (Buildings of England). Penguin, Harmondsworth.

PEVSNER, N. (1966). "Berkshire" (Buildings of England). Penguin, Harmondsworth.

RAHTZ, P. A. and HIRST, S. M. (1976). "Bordesley Abbey; Redditch, Hereford-Worcs; 1st report on excavations 1969–73". British Archaeological Reports British Series 23, Oxford.

RAHTZ, P. A., DICKINSON, T. M. and WATTS, L. (eds) (1980). "Anglo-Saxon Cemeteries". British Archaeological Reports British Series 82, Oxford.

RAMM, H. G. (1971). The Tombs of Walter de Gray and Godfrey de Ludham. *Archaeologia*, **103**, 101–147.

SHEPHARD, J. F. (1979a). Anglo-Saxon barrows of the late sixth and seventh centuries A.D. Unpublished Ph.D. Thesis, University of Cambridge.

SHEPHARD, J. F. (1979b). The social identity of the individual in isolated barrows and barrow cemeteries in Anglo-Saxon England. *In* "Space, Hierarchy and Society: Interdisciplinary Studies in Social Area Analysis" (B. C. Burnham and J. Kingsbury, eds), pp. 47–79. British Archaeological Reports Supplementary Series 59, Oxford.

SHOESMITH, R. (1981). "Hereford City Excavations, Vol. 1. Excavation at Castle Green". Council for British Archaeology, London.

WAUGH, E. (1948). "The Loved One". Chapman and Hall, London.

Tombs and States

MAURICE BLOCH

In this paper I want to consider the relationship between social organisation and certain critical aspects of material culture in the evolution of states in Madagascar. In particular I want to look at tombs and coffins, since they are the most important artefacts of most Malagasy peoples. The two peoples I shall look at are the Merina in the centre of Madagascar and the Sakalava of the West Coast. These offer the two best examples of state formation in Madagascar. They also contrast fundamentally in a number of interesting and revealing ways.

Merina tombs and states

The Merina, a group of people numbering about 1 000 000, have from our earliest records been grouped in a number of states. One state, however, is better documented than any other. This was the state which grew up towards the end of the eighteenth century and which, by the end of the nineteenth century, encompassed not only all the Merina but most of the people in Madagascar as well. The period of state formation which I shall be concerned with is that between approximately 1780 and 1850 when this Merina state underwent its most rapid expansion. During this period a particular dynasty of kings established itself in the capital, Tananarive, where they built a great palace and held ever more sumptuous ceremonies to match their growing political and military power.

In order to understand the significance of tombs for the Merina it is, however, better to start away from the capital, in the countryside. Merina country is hilly and most of the hillsides are covered in poor lateritic soil which can for the most part only support occasional and

137

unproductive agriculture. In contrast to these stand the very limited valley areas where the soil is rich and often marshy. These valley areas are often isolated one from another by expanses of semi-barren hillside, but they are the places where the population is concentrated. The Merina's main form of agriculture is irrigated rice agriculture and the Merina practise this in these rich valley bottoms, which they terrace. These areas of irrigated agriculture are fairly discrete one from another and they were associated with a social group living in one, or several, villages situated near the irrigated rice-fields. These groups I have called demes (Bloch, 1971: 46). Although these demes have a vague notion of common descent, the way members of demes stress their unity is rather in terms of the permanent association of their group with the irrigated lands which they consider they hold in common. This is true in that in theory only members of the deme own the land. This communality exists therefore only at one level. At another level, however, the lands of the deme are divided between individual owners and are inherited bilaterally. Although land is owned individually, the Merina say that as a whole the deme owns the total area of irrigated land because they will not allow outsiders to hold individual titles to the deme lands. They ensure this by marrying amongst themselves so that, although inheritance divides holdings and leads to the need for complicated adjustments, it does not lead to the alienation of rights beyond the group. The Merina stress again and again the need for the land to be kept within the deme and therefore the need for endogamy. Endogamy is closely associated with the notion of the keeping together of land, but it is seen as also being important for keeping together the deme. People are considered, like land, a common deme asset which should not be dispersed by marrying out. Because of the regrouping of land and the regrouping of people through endogamy the association of land and people is considered as eternal and takes on a mystical character.

If people stay together and keep the land together then they will receive the blessing of their common ancestors and any action which leads to this regrouping is a source of blessing. Blessing, however, takes on a material form. The Elders pass on the blessing from the ancestors to their descendants by blowing water onto them. This action of blowing on water, *tsodrano* or blessing, transmits the undivided power of land and people from generation to generation. It makes the members of the deme fruitful in every sense.

For the Merina, therefore, the regrouping of land and the regrouping of people are two sides of the same holy activity which leads to the canalisation of fertility and power to the members of the group.

The link between people and land, however, is not only expressed at a mystical level but also takes on a material form. This material form is the tombs of the members of the deme which are placed in the land of the deme. These tombs are extremely solid and permanent megalithic buildings. They are made of stone and nowadays of cement and the durability of their construction contrasts sharply with the impermanence of the dwellings of the living. In theory it is the most important duty of any Merina to ensure that he or she and other members of his deme will be physically regrouped in the familial tombs of the deme; in other words, all corpses of deme members must ultimately be brought to the tomb. If, as often happens, a member of the deme dies away from his ancestral land, his corpse will be brought back with great ceremony to the deme tombs. These ceremonies are called in Malagasy *famadihana*.

Famadihanas principally involve the regrouping of the corpses of the members of the deme but they also involve taking out the corpses of the dead in the tomb for a short time, dancing with them and putting them back (Bloch, 1971). One aspect of these *famadihanas*, which I have stressed in other publications, is that they emphasise the group against the individual dead. Ordinary Merina do not consider tombs as important because they contain specific people but because they contain undifferentiated, and often ground-up together, people; this is produced quite literally as a result of the dancing with the corpses of the members of the deme in the *famadihana*. This grinding together of the corpses, and the communal symbolism of the tomb, is the funerary equivalent of endogamy, and it is contrasted in much Merina ritual with division, which is seen as immoral. The main symbol of division, and indeed of individuality itself, is individual kinship ties. Regrouping of corpses in the tomb is the supreme act which leads to the blessing of the ancestors. As in marriage, it means that through the regrouped dead the group will continue undivided in its land; the material hinge of group and land is the tomb.

Every deme, therefore, had its tombs and these are, by and large, the same sort of massive megalithic edifices. There was in the past, however, some difference in tombs which reflected the differential rank of the deme, a rank really only manifested in court rituals. The higher ranked demes, sometimes called noble demes, which had such privileges as the right to speak first at the court, placed their tombs inside their villages, as opposed to placing them outside the village boundary as demes of a lower rank did. In this they partly reflected the situation which we shall see existed for the royal tomb. This distinction, however, had no implication for the tomb itself. The tombs of those demes which had the right to have their tomb within the village were no different from those of the demes which did not have the right. Some demes, however, those holding the very highest ranks, had yet a further privilege. They could build on top of the tomb a little model house. The symbolical significance of this is not clear to me but I suspect it is again an indirect reference to the royal tombs which, as we shall see, were actually inside the royal palace. We should, however, be very careful not to confuse differences of rank with differences of power. The ritual rank of demes did not correspond directly to the politico-economic role they had in the kingdom. It is interesting to note that it is only this ritual role which is reflected in the material culture (Bloch, 1977).

It is impossible here to give an account of the development of Merina states, but one or two points are worth noting. Merina history is characterised by the historical permanence of the demes which contrasts sharply with the impermanence of kingdoms and dynasties. One important reason seems to lie in the nature of the demes them-selves and of the agriculture they practised. These were such solidary groups that the central government was never entirely able to bend the demes to the royal will. The failure of the rulers in this respect comes from the fact that they could not afford to break up the communal organisation of the deme and replace it by the royal administration, because to do so would also mean destroying the organisation of irrigated agriculture on which the kingdom relied.

As a result, although the central government was always trying to integrate and absorb its constituent units, it never fully succeeded, and the kingdoms were somewhat precarious. What tended to happen was that a dynasty would set itself up in a capital and try to dominate the demes as best it could. The capitals were therefore rather temporary products of the demes based on transformations of the principles of the demes. This can be seen in the royal tombs.

The tombs of kings are in many ways similar to those of their subjects, only grander, but they are situated at the very heart of their kingdom, in the very centre of their capital, in the middle of the palace. Kings, however, are different from ordinary subjects in a number of other ways. While members of lowly demes symbolically dissolve their individuality within the groups, kings stress their differentiation from others and express their status not as members of a group but as successors of a line of particular individuals, the previous rulers. This contrast is clearly linked with the nature of kingship as an individual office, and it reflects itself both in funerary practices and in kingship. Kings, because of their uniqueness, cannot enter into alliances with others in their kingdom, as this would be tantamount to recognising that there are others like them. Endogamy is the opposite of what they want. As a result Merina kings did not properly marry anybody but only had concubines. Their heirs were, in theory at least, their sisters' sons, not the children they had procreated, since these were not their lawful children as they had not married the mothers. Kings were therefore single people, in all senses of the word; heirs of a particular line of other single people. As a result the kings' tombs do not contain groups of royals but single lines of royal successors whose individuality is greatly stressed. The legitimacy of a particular ruler depends on his ability to show that he is a successor of another particular named ruler. This individuality takes a material form in the tomb. In the tombs of commoners, bodies are not buried separately but are put side by side on stone shelves and as a result of various ritual practices soon become mingled one with another; the names of individuals are soon forgotten. Kings, by contrast, are buried in most extraordinarily elaborate individual coffins which ensure that their bones will never be mingled with those of others or dispersed. Royal tombs, therefore, contain a limited number of clearly individualised coffins of extreme splendour. It is not surprising, therefore, that *famadihana*, in the sense of taking out corpses and mingling them with others, is never done for kings; indeed, their corpses should never be moved. An eyewitness account of a royal funeral is given in "Voyages and Travels round the World" by D. Tyerman and G. Bennet (1841).

If in some ways royal tombs contrast quite sharply in their ideological representation with those of subjects, in another way royal tombs are represented as though they were the communal tombs of the whole kingdom. This is one aspect of a fairly general tendency by which the familial rituals of the king become state rituals in which all the subjects of the ruler are represented as his family. For example, the circumcision ritual, which for subjects is a matter of passing on blessings not only to the boys who are to be circumcised but also to the other members of the deme, becomes in the case of the royal circumcision an occasion when the king blesses *all* his subjects *as though* they were his family; and similarly the whole kingdom puts on mourning at the death of a king. This same element can also be shown in the most important royal ritual — the yearly ceremony of the royal bath. In this complex ritual the king opened the royal tomb of his predecessors and took a little of the soil from that tomb which he then mingled with water in which he took a bath. This water was then used by the king to bless all his assembled subjects in a manner reminiscent of the way an Elder passes on the blessing of the ancestors to the living members of the deme. In the case of the royal bath, however, the blessing of the ancestors which the king passes on is that of his specific ancestors and he passes it on to all his subjects who are then seen as his quasi-descendants.

This symbolism of the state as one large family of which the king is the father is of course quite common, and the use of the royal tomb to stand, if only for a moment, as the tomb of all the kingdom fits into this perspective well. It is, however, important to notice that among the Merina this idea is severely limited. It is limited because in many other contexts the distinction and discontinuity between different demes is stressed. The fact that demes are endogamous groups means that they cannot be linked one to another by kinship. The kingdom is therefore made up of separate kinship groups and there is a sharp kinship break between royals and subjects in the same way as there are sharp breaks among the subjects themselves. Among the Merina, therefore, this image of the kingdom as one large family is more or less limited to a few large state rituals. In the more common representation, the kingdom is seen as an agglomeration of separate and distinct demes each with its own territory. This distinctiveness of the demes, as we have just noted, is linked with the nature of the Merina kinship system but it is also linked with the nature of the type of agriculture which the Merina practise and the geographical environment in which they practise it. The demes indeed are distinct one from another in terms of locality and their members have to remain primarily united amongst themselves because of the necessity of agricultural cooperation involved in irrigation of a distinct territory. Geography and technology therefore lead, in the case of the Merina, to the distinctiveness of the demes; and this distinctiveness meant that as the Merina system expanded and became centralised it could nonetheless not absorb the demes into a larger entity or destroy their distinctiveness. This political problem of the distinctiveness of demes was very significant for the Merina kings, who seem to be endlessly caught between their attempts to enforce their authority and their concern to keep the demes going as social groups because, as social groups, they organised agricultural production. This politico-economic problem manifests itself in terms of tombs in that, as the kingdom evolved, the place, significance and material appearance of deme tombs did not diminish and was not replaced by the royal tomb, although this latter became ever more grandiose and important. This situation, as we shall see, contrasts sharply with the situation we find in Sakalava kingdoms.

Sakalava tombs and states

The other example I want to consider is that of the Sakalava peoples who live on the west coast of Madagascar and number considerably over a million. The people who are referred to by this term are in fact extremely varied both in their origin, their social organisation and their mode of livelihood. What links them together is that they all became, from a period from the sixteenth century to the nineteenth century, the subjects of a number of rulers who, though based in a great variety of localities, were all closely interrelated amongst themselves. In fact the best way of thinking of a Sakalava kingdom is as an area over which a new ruling dynasty is in the process of establishing itself. When this process is finished the kingdoms tend to collapse and to dissolve. The base of this domination was of course military and political. The ruler established his authority usually over varied groups of agriculturalists, pastoralists, hunters and gatherers and fishermen.

The big difference, however, between the Sakalava kingdom and the Merina kingdom was that the population of these kingdoms did not form discrete endogamous groups and indeed the basic kinship units often had strong exogamous tendencies. In any case there was never concern for keeping land within a fixed social group, and the type of agriculture which is associated with such concern among the Merina did not exist. This difference meant that kinship ties could be established through marriage between the various groups in the society, and a characteristic aspect of the domination of Sakalava rulers was the variety of kinship alliances that they formed with their subjects. These alliances, however, were of a very specific kind and all had the same effect; that is, of sucking up the population into the royal group. The first such strategy involved the royal group taking wives from a large number of subject groups. This gave high status to the wife-giving groups, but a status derived from their affinal links with the royal family. The men of the Sakalava royal family therefore married large numbers of women from a variety of subject groups and produced large numbers of children. These children belonged to the royal group. The women of the royal family did not marry but were impregnated by a type of male concubine, also from the subject groups. However, because this alliance was not marriage in the traditional Sakalava sense, the children of the women of the royal group did not belong to the group of their father but also belonged to the royal group, since their mother was their only legal parent. By this kind of marriage policy, within a very few generations the royal group had absorbed the whole population, although of course this only led to internal divisions within this group itself. In a sense one can see the process of centralisation of Sakalava kingdoms as the absorption and destruction of the kinship groups of the subjects by the royal group. This lack of integrity of the subject groups was not resisted, as it was in the case of the

Merina, because the Sakalava subject groups were not formed in the same cohesive, organic, continually regrouping and reforming units which characterised the Merina demes. Sakalava subject groups, although they differed among themselves considerably, were all wide open to what one might call kinship predation.

This kinship system is reflected in the nature of the tombs of the various groups of the Sakalava. The Sakalava rituals stress the impermanence of the tombs of the commoners, and how after a few generations they are abandoned either because the group moves away or because there is nobody any more to care for them (Baré, 1977: 88). The only distinction which can be seen in Sakalava tombs is that between those of higher-ranking groups of subjects, especially those groups of subjects which had achieved status by becoming wife-giving groups to the royals (J. Lombard, personal communication), and those from lower-ranking groups of subjects. The tombs of the higher-ranking subjects are much more decorated than those of the lower-ranking groups, because various forms of decoration were the privileges of the higher groups. These decorations include in some areas the famous and elaborate carvings of birds and of erotic subjects which are the delight of visitors to ethnographic museums throughout the world, not to mention thieving antique dealers.

In such a system it might be reasonable to expect that the royal tombs would be the grandest and most decorated of all. In fact the opposite turns out to be the case. The reason for this strange fact lies in the nature of Sakalava kingship. The Sakalava turned the royal tomb into a kind of auxiliary capital of the kingdom. Unlike the tombs of subjects, the tomb of kings is basically a village filled with living people. This manifests itself in the architecture of the village, which reflects the plan of a tomb, and in the fencing round the village which mirrors the perimeter fence of a Sakalava tomb. In some parts of the Sakalava territories the king is actually buried in a tomb inside the village which becomes a tomb within a tomb; in others he is buried elsewhere and only a reliquary for a few royal objects and bits of bones is inside the village. In some cases there is not even that. It is not, however, the things inside the tomb-village which are most important, but the people. The two most important categories of people inside the tomb-villages are, first, royal spirit mediums and, second, royal slaves and officials, whose main function is to look after them. What happens among the Sakalava at the death of a king is that, a little while after his burial, officers are sent out from the tomb-capital to go on the look-out for somebody showing signs of being possessed by the spirit of the ruler. When somebody shows signs of possession and makes claims to being possessed by the spirit of the king he is brought to the capital and, after a number of tests to check on his authenticity, the medium is housed in the capital and dressed in clothes and insignia referring to the person whose spirit he incarnates. At the death of this spirit medium another spirit medium will be sought who will be possessed by the spirit of the dead king and who will replace the previous medium. In other words, Sakalava kings never die, although the people who incarnate their spirits vary. As this process goes on through time, the whole line of previous rulers is represented by mediums who are grouped together at the capital. The whole royal genealogy is alive and kicking. Only certain relics such as fingernails of the corpses of the dead kings may be kept in a small house in a part of the tomb-capital.

What actually happens as Sakalava states grow is that an ever more important part of the population is in one way or another immured inside the tomb and this tomb-capital becomes the focus of religious and dynastic interest of the whole population as well as a source of ancestral blessing. In the same way as the royal family swallows up the families of the subjects, the tomb of the king grows as the tombs of the subjects are destroyed. When the king is not actually buried in the tomb-village, his place of burial is of little importance, and the actual tomb is modest compared with that of his subjects. In a sense the decaying bodies of kings are almost irrelevant to the system, while their living corpse, the spirit medium, is the focus. In terms of material culture, however, this presents a clear problem in that the material aspect of royal tombs is more humble than that of the humblest commoner and would therefore mislead future archaeologists. This is also the case when the king is buried in the tomb-village because, from their material appearance, these tomb-villages are only different from other villages in ways which appear very minor to the uninformed eye. In any case, how could an archaeologist ever decide that these peculiar villages were symbolic tombs?

What can we therefore say, in the light of these two examples, about the relationship between material culture and social organisation?

When we understand the nature of the symbolism of the two systems, we have little difficulty in understanding why these systems produce the material products that they do. It is as easy to see why the royal tombs of the Merina are richer than those of their subjects as it is easy to see why the royal tombs of the Sakalava are poorer. We can understand why there are coffins in royal tombs and why there are no coffins in the tombs of Merina subjects. We can understand why the most elaborate Sakalava tombs should be those of the middle ranks of society rather than the top or the bottom. On the other hand if we did not have knowledge of social organisation and symbolism at our disposal—in other words, if we, like archaeologists, had unearthed a prehistoric society—would we be able to read back from the nature of the material remains the type of social organisation which had existed? At first sight I think the answer must be no. However subtle archaeologists might be at interpreting material culture I do not think they could reconstruct the Sakalava system or could fail to be misled into thinking that the tombs of the wife-giving groups were those of the dominant social group.

This conclusion, however, is perhaps unnecessarily pessimistic. What I have stressed in this paper is how the rationality of the social system which produces material objects is to be seen in terms of the nature of the development of the two types of kingdom. Perhaps an archaeologist could observe the transformation of tombs among the Merina and the Sakalava and make use of his intuition to understand the geographical and technological constraints on the development of these kingdoms, and then might be able to piece the whole process together. It might be possible to deduce the integrity of Merina demes from the stability of the villages and the continuity of their agriculture. It might be possible to see the instability of Merina dynasties in the continual movement of capitals and royal tombs. It might be possible to explain this from general principles about the nature of this type of kingdom, and therefore to grasp the internal politico-economic dynamic of the Merina system. With such a perspective, the significance of the differing tombs might be approached. In a similar fashion, the dynamic forces governing the evolution of Sakalava kingdoms might be constructed and then *perhaps* the significance of the tomb-villages might be recognised by a sign such as the similarity in the style of fencing of tombs and tomb-villages. This, however, could only be done by an observation of the process of transformation over time, not from a study of either Merina or Sakalava kingdoms at a particular moment in time. This conclusion may be indicative perhaps of the way in which there is hope of making some sense of a society from its material culture. It is surely indicative of just how great and bewildering are the pitfalls.

References

BARÉ, J. F. (1977). "Pouvoir des vivants langage des morts". Maspero, Paris.

BLOCH, M. (1971). "Placing the Dead". Seminar Press, London and New York.

BLOCH, M. (1977). The disconnection between power and rank as a process: an outline of the development of kingdoms in central Madagascar. *In* "The Evolution of Social Systems" (J. Friedman and M. J. Rowlands, eds), pp. 303–340. Duckworth, London.

FEELY-HARNIK, G. (in press) Ritual and work in Madagascar. *Africa*.

TYERMAN, D. and BENNET, G. (1841). "Voyages and Travels round the World", 2nd edition. John Snow, London.

The Dowayo Dance of Death*

NIGEL BARLEY

Anthropologists have been interested in the phenomenon of secondary burial at least since Hertz (1907). This seminal work draws a number of conclusions that have informed study up to the present day. For present purposes, however, I wish to reduce these to three that I shall look at with reference to my own field data, drawn from the Dowayo people of North Cameroon.

Firstly, Hertz declares that the changes that the physical body undergoes are to be regarded as a change from wet to dry. (Apparent exceptions to the universality of the phenomenon such as cremation and mummification can thus be reduced merely to extreme forms.) Secondly, the stages of pollution and reintegration that the close relatives pass through are associated with the stages by which the newly dead are integrated into the habitations of the ancestors. Thirdly, the explanatory concept that structures this whole area is that of "spirit".

From wet to dry

The change from wet to dry is a very significant one in the articulation of Dowayo cultural symbolism. It has a twofold aspect. There is a major division of the year into wet and dry seasons and associated activities. There are also changes that occur in the lives of men and women.

It is clear from a number of ceremonies that I have analysed fully

*Fieldwork was conducted in North Cameroon from June 1977 to September 1978 and April 1979 to August 1979. Thanks are due to the Social Science Research Council for funding and to ONAREST Cameroon for permission to conduct research.

149

elsewhere (Barley, forthcoming) that we can often view a womb as ritually depicted by a water-jar. At conception, the man places the baby in the "water-jar" and it is nourished by the woman. Adultery and other forms of irregularity after conception cause miscarriage. The Dowayos phrase this as "the water goes away". Wetness is, then, associated with female fertility. Thus, only women should clean out still waterholes. A wet climate is held to be conducive to fertility. Whenever I mentioned to Dowayos that "in my own village" there was rainfall all the year round, they always assumed that this would mean that White Men had many children. The model is that children are undifferentiated as to wetness/dryness. Onset of menstruation involves a shift towards wetness. The most valued form of wetness is that of still water. Association with the implements of rain control or places where water flows strongly is dangerous to women and may lead to abortion or excessive menstrual flow.

As regards males the model is a little different. The same basic model is used to articulate human and agrarian fertility. The rain falls on the fields and makes them fertile, just as the sperm falls on the womb. It will come as no surprise to learn that it is the rain-chief, responsible for the alternation of the seasons, who is in charge of male fertility and has the remedies that cure male impotence. There is a particular spot at the base of his mountain where the water gushes out with an abundance of foam. No woman must ever see this on pain of death. Dowayos explain that it is like the glowing end of the penis-shaped bellows used by the endogamous blacksmith. This too is forbidden to women, as is the sight of the circumcised penis. A woman must never see her husband naked. Numerous other facts link and oppose the blacksmith and his wives (who make the water-jars and act as midwives) and the rain-chiefs. The two should never come together. The women's pots would burst, the rain-chief would die of a cough. Between the two, with all manner of regulations governing the exchange of women, food and water stands the ordinary Dowayo who is neither blacksmith nor rain-chief. But whereas ordinary Dowayos are polluting to rain-chiefs, blacksmiths are polluting to ordinary Dowayos. We can sum this up in a single analogical statement.

Rain-chief : Dowayo :: Dowayo : blacksmith

But concern with wet and dry does not end here. The major change in a man's life comes at circumcision. This, above all, is regarded as a change from wet to dry. Dowayos explicitly state that an uncircumcised boy is "wet" and smelly "like a woman". The very extreme form of circumcision practised by the Dowayos is held to make him clean and dry — wholly male.

The alternation of the seasons and the ritual of circumcision are deliberately collapsed together. The boys are cut at the height of the rainy season. It is believed that it will rain continuously for three days as the boys bleed. They are required to kneel, without shelter, for this period in swift-flowing water while a friend rubs gravel into their wounds. The process of healing is articulated along two axes, the return from nature to culture and the change from wet to relatively dry. The boys are gradually allowed to move away from the river as the seasonal rains diminish. Only on the actual day when the dry season is proclaimed by the rain-chief can they return to the village. This is marked by setting fire to the grass on a particular mountain called *Waaduufi* "the crown of the boy's head". On the same day, the hut in which the boys live is fired over their heads. Sometimes blazing grass is held over their heads as they return to the village.[1] Thus, we can see that while female maturity is modelled on still wetness, male maturity involves relative dryness and a wetness of moving water.

The interest of this ethnographic matter for the present paper lies in the fact that secondary burial, like the first, is expressed explicitly in the idiom of circumcision.

At death, a man's body is tied in a kneeling posture[2] and wrapped in woven cotton burial cloth, sheep and goat skins and finally cattle skins. He also wears a blue ("dark" in Dowayo colour terminology) robe and a white one, as does the boy about to be circumcised. The entire ceremony is very complex. Its principal feature, however, is that the body is treated as if it is being circumcised. It is jostled and threatened with knives, circumcision songs are sung, men cut at the same time as the deceased must be present. Cattle will be killed and the skins attached to the body. The head is covered with a goatskin.

The body is dragged outside the village and buried in a rock tomb. Some three weeks later, the tomb is opened and the head removed and examined for witchcraft. It is cleaned and placed in a pot in a tree. Fig. 1 represents the careers of a male and female skull.

Thus far, then, we can say that burial and removal of the head have been depicted in terms of circumcision. But circumcision is held to cause rainfall. What of head removal as circumcision? Here again, there is a link with rainfall. Rain-chiefs at Mango explicitly forbid the removal of their heads on the grounds that this would cause floods. They are replaced by small water-jars kept inside the village. The skull-house outside the village, where the heads of the long dead would normally be kept, contain the stones that cause the rain.

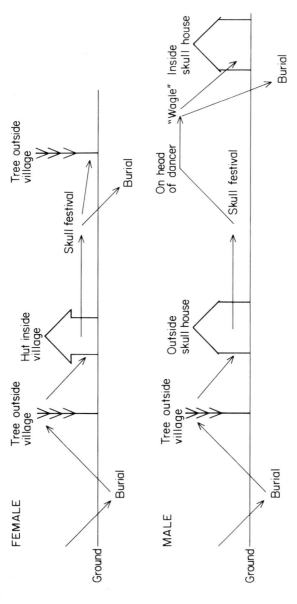

Fig. 1. The careers of a male and female skull.

At the other location where there are rain-chiefs, Kpan, heads are removed nowadays as an innovation of the grandfather of the present incumbent, but are immediately reburied lest there be a flood. They are buried on the mountain *Waaduufi*, on the top of which is a special stone. It was explained to me that, in the wars with the traditional enemy, the Fulani, were there ever a danger of the Dowayos being routed they would have retired up this mountain and the stone would have been moved to flood the world and kill everyone.

The "secondary burial" in Dowayoland, the skull-festival, is also phrased in terms of circumcision. The skulls are brought just outside the village and excrement is thrown on them. They are cleaned and dressed, again in a fashion that recalls the garb of candidates for circumcision. The bundle of skulls and wrapping is hefted on the head of a joking relative and danced into the village to be placed beside the skulls of sacrificed cattle. Only after this may they be placed in their final resting place, a skull-house or rock tomb outside the village. At the end of the ceremony, the man who has organised it declares, "I have circumcised these men." This ceremony may only take place in the rainy season. Normally, the rain-chief is required to be present. He will be paid money or offered beer to prevent downpours that disrupt the ceremony.

Relative dryness would seem then to be a desired attribute of the skulls; but we should note that offerings to the dead take a liquid form —moreover it is moving, flowing liquid—blood or fermenting beer. Total dryness would be dangerous. It would be a mark that descendants had not been making offerings. The result would be that the dead would refuse to enter into the wombs of women to be reincarnated as children.

Removal of heads and removal of foreskins both involve rainfall, then, and it is significant that the circumcision ceremonies themselves do not end with the re-entry of the boys to the village at the beginning of the dry season. The last part is usually carried out at the skull ceremony of a dead man. A significant part of the change from uncircumcised to circumcised is that the man may now enter the skull-house and have dealings with the ancestors. The first time that the boys enter the skull-house there is a fairly complex ceremonial, the details of which do not concern us here. The point is that this entry can only occur in the rainy season at the moment when the newly dead are allowed to enter the hut for the first time as ancestors. Both are then *relatively* dry with the wetness of rain or offerings.

The "drying" of the newly circumcised and their association with moving water are paralleled point by point with that of the new ancestors.

So much for men at secondary burial; what of women? The wrapping of women at death is an attenuated form of the male dressing. No cattle are killed and two robes are not used. No circumcision songs are sung. The principal feature of the operation is the hauling of the body from the village of the husband back to that of the parents. Similarly, at the skull-festival, women's heads are brought alongside the men's skulls and excrement is thrown on them, but they are then ignominiously dumped to one side. No one dances with them.

The structural replacement of the skull-festival for women is another ceremony where the dead woman's water-jar is wrapped as for circumcision and danced with back to her natal village. This only happens in the wet season. The jar is filled with fermenting beer and germinated millet is sprinkled on it by friends and relatives. The bubbling of the fermentation is held to be due to the spirit of the dead woman. Young women lick the outside of the jar as it froths over, "to become pregnant". Rainfall during this ceremony is held to be a mark of good fortune.

A full analysis of this ceremonial reveals an interesting paradox. I have stated that among the Mango rain-chiefs the human skull is replaced by a water-jar. But the skull-festival, like the jar-ceremony, is not celebrated here. If it *were* celebrated, then there is little doubt that it would be virtually identical with the jar-ceremony. Especially significant are certain irons attached to the pot and known as "the hands of the rain". These are morphologically identical with throwing irons and seem to be related with the ability of the rain-chief to throw lightning to kill his enemies. Also attached are broad hoe blades, the traditional payment to the rainchief for rainfall in time of need. The question then is, why should the rain-chief's skull ceremony be celebrated for a dead woman but not for the rain-chief?

The answer would seem to lie in notions of procreation. The women's jar ceremony is the occasion of an important change whereby women cease to be vessels of spirit, impregnated by others, and become themselves agents of impregnation. The relationship between rainfall and impregnation has been indicated above, the rain-chief being master of male fertility and procreative force. It is therefore quite appropriate that he should provide the idiom for the change from impregnated female to impregnating ancestor. Again an analogic statement formalises the relationship:

Female : ancestor : : male : rain-chief

Prohibitions on relatives of the dead

The relatives of the newly dead are subject to a number of prohibitions as shown in Fig. 2. Until a man has been buried his wife must sit, motionless, by the body. She may not enter the compounds of others or eat with them until the head of her husband has been removed. She must wear no ornaments until the bow of her husband has been fixed behind the skull-house, nor may she marry a close kinsman of her husband. Only after her husband's skull-festival may she dance or marry within her husband's kin group. The restrictions on a widower are as indicated. Similar restrictions, diminishing according to kinship distance, hold for close patrilineally related kinsmen.

The key would seem to be that the surviving relative may do nothing that the body, real or symbolic, has not done. When the jar of a woman has been decorated at the jar-ceremony (the ceremony is called "decoration") the son or husband may resume the use of rings and other body ornaments. Not until the jar has danced, may they dance.

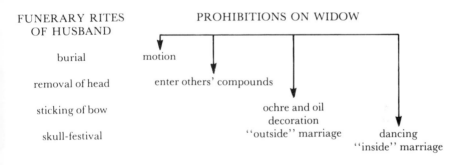

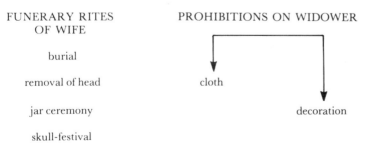

FIG. 2. Prohibitions on widows and widowers.

Once again, however, the idiom is that of circumcision. At the skull-festival of their husbands, the widows undergo a number of operations, all more or less explicit references to, and adaptations of, what happens to candidates at circumcision. The firing of the huts, the assembly at the circumcision grove, etc., are repeated. One significant difference is that the women are not, of course, circumcised (as we have seen, a very "wet" proceeding) but their vaginas are rubbed with a dried fish. Fish have notoriously feminine connotations in Dowayoland on account of their slipperiness and smell. The widows, having officially refrained from intercourse up to this point, are held to be particularly "dry".

Hereafter, they undergo the same processes of reintegration as the boys returning from circumcision in the bush, wear the same haircuts, sing the same songs. These are blatantly masculine in their content. The official version of what happens at circumcision is that the anus is blocked with cattle-hide so that the men never need to defecate again. In fact, the truth is common knowledge and the subject of much sly innuendo. Women and boys must not, however, ever reveal how much they know or they risk a beating. Between themselves, men never cease to refer to and joke about circumcision or excretion. The height of male wit is a loudly executed fart, a tacit allusion to the truth about circumcision. Several rituals involve similar actions. It is therefore tantamount to an act of transvestism when the widows sing, at the end of the skull-festival, "Hitherto, we have all slept together. Now I shall fart in my hut and you in yours." The same song is, in fact, sung by the boys at the end of the circumcision ceremony.

This identification between the women and the boys is doubly motivated. Firstly, the women are now returned to normal social life as are the boys returned from the bush. Secondly, they are reintegrated into the community as their erstwhile husbands are integrated into that of the ancestors.

The notion of "spirit"

Dowayos possess a term *looreyo* that can be rendered "soul" or "spirit". In our own language, these terms can be used to make a distinction between mass nouns and bounded nouns. Dowayos do not necessarily make this distinction. The only area in which they can present any sort of causal statement in terms of this explanatory concept is in the area of human mortality and reproduction. Even here, there are gaps. One might well expect that a patrilineal society, with belief in the reincarnation of souls and the possession of skull-houses, would develop the theory that the ancestral spirits actually constitute the bones of the foetus. Alas, they do not.

There are other areas of uncertainty. I have said that the spirit of a dead woman is held to be the cause of the fermentation of the beer in her water-jar during the jar-ceremony. But the spirit is also held to have returned to her native village with her body at the time of her funeral, and to inhere in her skull on the occasion of her skull-festival. There is not necessarily any contradiction in these separate beliefs. The spirit might be held to lead a peripatetic existence. It is clear, however, that Dowayos do not have any clear idea of the process by which a spirit can move from one place to another at various stages of the ritual. The post-mortuary ceremonies have a common theme — the change from differentiation to undifferentiation. Up till the skull-festival a man's skull retains its individuality. It is recognised by its kinsmen and called by name. Offerings are made to it separately. After the skull-festival, it is placed in a jar along with all the other skulls and offerings are simply made to all the skulls or even just flung onto the hut. It has returned to the ''pool''. The same happens to a woman's spirit after her jar-ceremony, with the result that Dowayos are extremely shifty and evasive when asked about the location of her spirit at the skull-festival. They reply with, ''We do not know. We have not seen'' — a standard answer to a culturally inappropriate question.

The same occurs in other areas that are structured by the same opposition between differentiated and undifferentiated (see Fig. 3).

	DIFFERENTIATED	UNDIFFERENTIATED
Human	skull in pot	stone or skull in skull-house
Cattle	skulls on ''shrine''	stones
Wild beasts	skulls on ''shrine''	stones
Millet	heads on ''shrine''	stones
Rain	local rain kit	stones or pots

FIG. 3. Opposition between differentiated and undifferentiated.

It will be seen that human fertility, like that of cattle, wild beasts and the fields, is maintained by a dual structure that also involves the rain. The skulls of sacrificed, individual cattle are displayed on a special ''shrine'' at the gate of the cattle park. This is called a *wagle*. Round the back of every rich man's compound, however, are certain stones ''from the ancestors'', buried and contained in a pot, that ensure the ongoing fertility of the cattle. The skulls slowly rot and disappear. The stones are permanent. Human skulls that rot before the celebration of the skull-festival or which cannot be recovered are simply replaced with a stone, which is deposited in the skull-house.

There is a "shrine" similar to the *wagle* for the heads of wild beasts except the leopard. The leopard's skull is treated as a human skull. The rain-chief is held to possess stones that control the reproduction of all *ferae*.

Millet is more complicated. A special class of male "true cultivators" thresh their millet in a ritual fashion that is a re-enactment of a myth which is entitled, "The beating to death of the old Fulani woman" and recounts the origin of circumcision. "Heads" (Dowayos use the same term) of millet are placed on the *wagle* and the skull-house at the end of each harvest. The Masters of the Earth also have stones that ensure the fertility of the fields.

Even rain is structured by a similar opposition between differentiated ("skull") and undifferentiated ("stone"). Both Mango and Kpan rain-chiefs have stones that are involved in the change from wet to dry and back again. Each, however, also has a portable rain-kit that allows him to cause a particular downpour at a specific time and place.

Dowayos are quite incapable of giving any account of whether or how spirits are involved in these various processes. Mechanistic thinking is not involved. We are simply in the presence of a single opposition that structures several domains simultaneously. It cannot, therefore, be claimed that an account of post-mortuary rites in terms of spirit gives an adequate picture of this area, though Dowayos will offer such an account of human affairs, albeit a fragmentary and incomplete one.

Conclusion

It is quite striking how well the statements of Hertz, written without benefit of fieldwork some seventy-five years ago, have stood the test of time. No anthropologist nowadays would expect such universal application of a simple model, opposing dry to wet, to hold. Yet in this particular case it fits fairly well—as I am sure it would for much of West Africa—albeit with a cross-cutting distinction between flowing and still wetness.

The identification of the surviving relatives and the cadaver may also be seen to account for a significant part of post-mortuary behaviour.

The notion of "spirit" is, indeed, invoked to account for the facts of human mortality and conception. We have seen, however, that the whole area is ordered by a more general structure (Fig. 3) that also reaches out to other sections of the symbolic system and that any complete account of the Dowayo notion of death must take this into account.

Notes

1. It should, however, be noted that the obsessive concern with "heads" of all kinds is a constant theme. The heads are shaved to resemble the pattern on the water-jar. The boys are given special knives with handles (in Dowayo "heads") made from the red head skin that develops in the male agama lizard on attainment of sexual maturity.
2. The left foot is placed over the right and the head is oriented towards the west. This is also the position adopted by the candidate for circumcision in the river.

References

BARLEY, N. (forthcoming). "Symbolic Structures of the Dowayos".

HERTZ, R. (1907). Contribution à une étude sur la représentation collective de la mort. *L'Année sociologique*, **10**, 48–137. English edition: "Death and The Right Hand" (R. and C. Needham, trans.), 1960, Cohen & West, London.

Eschatology Among the Krahó: reflection upon society, free field of fabulation*

MANUELA CARNEIRO DA CUNHA

(translated by S. C. HUMPHREYS)

This paper is a reflection on a previous analysis of Krahó[1] eschatology (Cunha, 1978), specifically on the limitations that this analysis contains. In it I interpreted Krahó eschatology as a speculation on society, a questioning of some of its basic premises. Krahó depict a harmonious after-life society, lacking all sources of conflict and disruption, which are attributed above all to affinity. Yet such a society appears as non-viable, condemned to stillness and involution. This appears as a demonstration *per absurdum* of the validity of living society.

I shall show in detail how I arrived at this conclusion, which I still hold to be correct. Yet my dissatisfaction arose from the feeling that such an account was highly reductionist, and could not explain the whole field. Whatever my inclination for more detailed structuralist analysis, there appeared to be no footing for it in Krahó eschatology. The diversity of versions seemed to be irreducible, except for a limited core. But this is not true of other fields such as mythology or even collective actions such as messianic movements with successive transformations, in which one may successfully account for each detail.

My suggestion is that this is a characteristic of the field itself. It seems that there are some *terrains vagues*, some no-man's-lands in which

*The author is most grateful to Mauro B. de Almeida of the University of Campinas for his very kind and helpful criticisms and suggestions.

imprecision is essential, as if in each society there were privileged *loci* for utopias, for fantasy. Eschatology, in societies that do not use it as a reward system or as a sanction for the living, could be seen as an example of such a relatively free domain of fabulation, regulated by a characteristically small number of rules. Therefore, structural or functional analyses can account only for this reduced core of structured relations between eschatology and society. Outside this core, analysis should rely more heavily on "speech forms" than on "grammar". This point has more general implications, for it implies that beliefs or symbolism can be distinguished into several fields which hold differential and non-equivalent relations to society.

The sources

There is little agreement, among the Krahó Indians, on detailed pictures of post-mortem existence, although, as we shall see, there are central and strong beliefs concerning the *mekarõ*. *Karõ* (collective *mekarõ*) is the word for the personal principle which endures after death. The *karõ* is therefore present also in living men, except for occasional absences during dreams or illness. Among the word's *denotata* we find the photograph, the reflection and any "bodily image". Yet the *karõ* is not just an image: it may assume a different aspect from the body it inhabits, and we may call it a "double" (cf. J.-P. Vernant, 1965), something which refers to an object without necessarily reflecting it.

Irreversible separation of the *karõ* from the body does not occur at the cessation of breath, but rather when the *karõ* accepts dead society, i.e. when he shares with the dead some food, corporal painting and log-racing.[2]

What, then, are the sources for eschatology? Several myths refer to the dead or to the transformations that follow death, but their authority is hardly ever invoked. Direct knowledge of the world of the dead is ascribed to a definite category of people, the *akrãgaikrit* (literally "light heads") who have personal experience of them. This category seems to include not only active shamans who are already in possession of recognised powers, but also potential shamans. The *karõ* of these people may have contacts with the dead, speak to them, go to their village and yet have enough power to return to the living.

Shamans are normally cited as authorities on the subject: they boast of extraordinary excursions and they are a source of fluent, but mostly impermanent, innovation in eschatology: for such innovations are not necessarily accepted and perpetuated in common belief. I wonder if acceptance is expected. Such innovations testify to the *de visu* knowledge which shamans are held to have of the dead, and therefore contribute to their prestige. In contrast to myths, these versions seem to be produced more or less *ad hoc* and not to emerge one from another. Their only consistent feature is a reduced core of shared beliefs, which I shall describe.

Dreams are another source of speculation, this time open to anyone. Since *karõ* means, among other things, an image, images seen in dreams are thought to be *mekarõ*. Therefore a Krahó may soundly infer from what he dreams a knowledge of the activities of the *mekarõ*.

Finally, there are also recurrent stories about meetings with *mekarõ*, in the forest or beside the river. This is always a personal experience, since the dead only show themselves to people who are alone. Such a vision may subsequently be more publicly discussed and compared with current ideas in order to reach conclusions about the real nature of the meeting.

Such a variety of sources, available to specialists (the shamans) as well as to non-specialists, generates a wide range of potential eschatological production. Since this production is apparently not meant to be codified into an orthodoxy, or even perpetuated, there seems to be little concern with control over it. The result is a typically unlimited and often self-contradictory corpus of representations. How are we then to analyse such a field? Before trying to proceed, it is time briefly to describe some general features of Krahó eschatology, distinguishing the level of more widely shared beliefs from that of more idiosyncratic versions.

The metamorphoses of the karõ

Detached from its corporeal basis, the *karõ* becomes a sort of freely floating image, in the sense that it appears no longer to be bound to reproduce the form of a specific body. This does not mean that it becomes immaterial, but that it can assume practically any aspect and undergo all manner of metamorphoses. The *mekarõ* are proteiform, it is said; they are also said to change their form according to the "stage" they have reached, for they are believed to be able to die several times and to take on successively first the forms of large animals, then of smaller and smaller animals (opinions vary on this point) and finally to end as stones, roots or tree-stumps—the list differing noticeably from one informant to another.

In a statement collected by Vilma Chiara from a shaman it is said that one individual may have many *mekarõ*, whose successive deaths correspond to changes in form. This shaman explains the stages of development of the *mekarõ*, in an original way, as follows:

I am alive, I have four *karõ*. When I die I shall be left with three. A year later another dies, I am left with two. The third *karõ* changes into a *po* (a type of deer). A hunter kills it, it will have wings, it changes into a *kokonré* (*koan* bird), at night it changes into a serpent. If someone kills it, it changes into a *vévé* (butterfly), when day comes, it changes into a tree-stump or a lizard; if an animal kills it, that's the end. If it stays in the village of the dead, it doesn't change. But the dead like to move around, so their *karõ* go through all their stages, and everything comes to an end.

V. Chiara, ms.

Among the animal forms which *mekarõ* adopt, some belong to game: the tapir, the deer, the armadillo. People will say that they are tasteless, or have a "nasty taste", or that they are stringy—but their flesh is edible. Only one shaman states that the flesh of the "peba" armadillo (*auxtet*), if it is the avatar of a *karõ*, is blue and causes colic. According to an informant of Melatti's (1970: 211) such flesh, if eaten by the kindred, would result in children resembling the dead: the *mekarõ*, he said, would be reincarnated in the children while in their mothers' wombs. This is the only mention of human reincarnation.

The *mekarõ* in whom there is most interest and those which may on occasion interact with the living, are those in the first "stage" of this series of metamorphoses, and it is with these that eschatological speculation principally concerns itself.

The spatial dimension of the dead

The spatial framework of the dead is the reverse and the complement of that of the living. The Krahó have often said to me, "The moon (*pëdlëre*) is the sun (*pëd*) of the *mekarõ*". The *mekarõ* like the shadiness of the forest and detest the plain or the cleared zone of vegetation at the foot of the hills which for the Krahó is the ideal form of landscape. The Krahó are even called by their Canela and Sherente neighbours *kenpokhrare* which means literally, "children of the cleared part of the hillside". The *mekarõ*, on the contrary, like dark and hidden places and winter days (i.e. days of rain) and fear the hot sun[3]; during the daytime, I have been told, they stay in their village, but during the night they wander in the forest. The Krahó say that when the *mekarõ* come to the village of the living they never haunt the central place of the village; some say that the farthest they venture is to the *krīkapé*, the circular path which runs in front of the houses, but according to the majority of informants they enter houses only "from behind", that is, by the door leading to the open countryside—which many houses lack, precisely in order to prevent their entry. Furthermore, this door may be called the *atëkrumpeharkwa*, which can be literally translated as "the door towards the direction of the dead".

In other words, either the dead are kept outside the social space of the village or they are confined to the domestic sphere. In both cases they are excluded from the society of the living, which is ideally conceptualised as ceremonial and has as its main theatre of action the central place of the village.

The opposition between the living and the dead

Departure to the world of the dead is a breaking-off of relations and almost like a betrayal: death is passage into the enemy camp. At the same time, the world of the dead is a mirror-image of that of the living. Thus a shaman said to me one day "The *mekarõ* call *us mekarõ*, they don't call themselves *mekarõ*; they are afraid of us."

What is significant is, of course, the relationship rather than the specific terms opposed. This appears clearly in Krahó cosmography. When the *mekarõ* are visualised as grouped in a village—which, as we shall see, is not always the case—the village is always situated in the west, due to the association already mentioned between on the one hand society, the interior and the east, and on the other hand the dead, the outside and the west. This is true for all Krahó *mekarõ*; however, the village of the dead contains no strangers.

If the new variable of the existence of strangers among the *mekarõ* is introduced, the geography changes: according to the headman of the village of Pedra Furada, the Krahó dead are located in the east whereas dead white men are to be found in the west. In this context what is important is the opposition between Krahó and foreigners, and their respective localisation carries the message that society in the true sense is found only among the Krahó (and therefore in the east), whereas foreigners are barbarians (and therefore in the west).

A similar logic can be perceived in data from the Shavante, another tribe of the same Gê linguistic stock. The eastern Shavante locate their dead in the west, but the western Shavante, who are organised into exogamous moieties, have a different system: each moiety locates its own dead in the east and those of the other moiety in the west (Maybury-Lewis, 1967: 292).

Kinship and the dead

It is his dead kin—especially his matrilateral kin—who gather round the sick Krahó to conduct him to the village of the dead. It is they, too, who try to keep him there, press him to accept food, to take part in "log races", to paint his body and cut his hair, all of which acts make it impossible for him to return to the village of the living. However, if one of these kinsmen strongly argues that the living (young children or aged parents) still need the support of the visitor to the village of the dead, he may be allowed to return to the world of the living. A dead mother is considered to be particularly anxious to keep her child with her, and the mediator who can put the case for the child's return to life — and will prevail if he has sufficient authority — is usually the *keti*.[4] We shall see below that the attitude attributed here to the category of kinsmen from which the name-giver is recruited is consistent with the functions of the naming system as guarantee of the self-reproduction of the Krahó social system.

The conception of the after-life as dominated by kinship is strikingly illustrated by the narrative of the first man to try to convert the Krahó, the Capuchin friar Rafael Taggia (or Tuggia), who in 1852 lamented the failure of his campaign for baptism, based on the promise (unpropitious, as it proved) that the souls of the baptised would go to heaven: "They thought that if they became Christians, they would no longer be able to go and dwell in the company of the dead kin whom they loved so much . . .' (Taggia, 1898: 123.)

This European perception of the situation, however, must not be allowed to distort the perspective: for the Krahó, the emphasis on kinship between the living and the dead is always subordinated to the primary opposition between the society of the dead and that of the living. The group of living kin stands in opposition to the group of dead kin, and funerary laments angrily express both the feeling of being abandoned by the dead and the desirability of breaking off relations with them. The living kin group has to defend itself against the attacks and enticements of the dead.

The Krahó thus share with the Shavante (Maybury-Lewis, 1967: 292) and with the distant, paradigmatic inhabitants of the Andaman Islands (Lévi-Strauss, 1967: 569–570) the conception of an after-life in which kin will be "on their own", the wheat and the tares finally separated.

The abolition of affinity: lack of paham

Among the dead there is no affinity. This principle underlies numerous statements, of which the most radical would be: "The dead have no brains: that's why they don't marry, although they 'work' (i.e. copulate). A man and his wife among the dead live together only for one night, then they separate. They know their brothers-in-law and fathers-in-law, but they no longer respect them.''

Other informants say that the *karõ* remarries after death, either attracting his spouse to the tomb or taking a new mate. But there appears never to be any question of alliance as the Krahó conceive of it, since there is no mention either of uxorilocality nor of the conventions of behaviour to affines which characterise it.

The point is summed up in the unanimous affirmation that the dead "don't think", "live just anyhow", or, in a word, are *pahamnõ*, shameless, lacking *paham*.[5] To be *pahamnõ* is to live in a disorganised way, to lack social norms. The "shameless" dead do not know how to behave, have no idea of etiquette, and above all do not recognise the fundamental principle of appropriate conduct towards affines.

The morphology of the village of the dead

The problem now is to systematise, in spatial terms, the cultural principles described above. This is a question which gives rise to endless speculation among the Krahó and has produced a large corpus of contradictory testimonies about the morphology of the village of the dead.

Some say that the *mekarõ* wander aimlessly in nuclear families, others that they live in villages. The former view seems to confirm the principle of the absence of affinity in the society of the dead, the latter to cast doubt on it. A further look at the spatial organisation of the village of the dead may clarify the question.

We have two fairly detailed statements on this topic, one from an old man and the other from a healer, and a comparison of these seems to me to bring out more clearly their common structural principles. But it must be noted that in doing this I only account for a small proportion of the two texts, and that only in a highly reductivist way. This inability to make full use in analysis of the richness of divergent statements is an important point to which I shall return.

According to Davi, the first informant,

The *mekarõ* do not live in a circular village, but instead, in a dark place in the forest . . . Their families are not located as they would be in a village: those who have no daughters live alone on the outskirts of the village, they move around all the time, they never rest. They have no central place in their village. It does not matter where they gather to sing. They don't sleep in their own houses, but in other people's. The *mekarõ* don't bathe, they only drink lots of water . . . they don't sing in the central place.

The second description, given to V. Chiara by a healer, mentions two villages. One is made of houses of *bacaba* straw round a lagoon in

which the *mekaro̅* swim all night (as we have seen, the night is their
"day", the period in which they are active). The stagnant water of this
lagoon brings forgetfulness: it is a tropical Lethe. "The karo̅ does not
bathe in the water outside, in running water, but only in still water".
During the day the *mekaro̅* move to the other village, and there they
sleep. "The *mekaro̅* have no central place or circular path in their
village; everything is privately owned, round the village there is
nothing but trees, lots of them. There is one road leading to a single
large field."

Note first of all that in both descriptions the village central place is
absent. In the first text, the houses evidently are not located in any
organised fashion, and this disorder is further reflected in the mention
of "sleeping in other people's houses". The non-existent central place
is replaced by a stream which runs on the inner side of the houses,
instead of running outside them as it does in the villages of the living.
The whole description is very reminiscent of the spatial disposition of
Krahó fields, and it should be stressed that going to live with one's
family in a hut in the fields is the only way of escaping from the social
life of the village, short of emigration.

In the second text the schema is duplicated: there are two villages
instead of one, and again neither has a central place. One village has
stagnant water at its centre, an inversion of the situation in the villages
of the living which have running water encircling them on the outside.
Both texts mention the fact that *mekaro̅* do not bathe in running water:
the significance of this will become evident later.

Finally, in the second text the village has a single communal field, as
if the whole village was a single unit of production as the domestic
group is in living society. This view of the village of the dead as a single
domestic group again, perhaps, derives from the domination of
consanguinity in the village of the *mekaro̅*.

In reality the villages of both descriptions are negations of the norms
of village life just as much as the statement that the dead wander
aimlessly; and more particularly they are negations of the norms of
affinity.

Dynamism and permanence

Informants are unanimous in stating that the *mekaro̅* have an abundant
ritual life. They are divided into moieties, they have *wïtï* (children
whose function is to represent the groups of men, women and boys, in
ritual), they have log races, they play their own kind of instrumental
music. Far from disappearing with the absence of the village central
place, activity in the ritual sphere is intensified.

Let us rapidly recapitulate the points so far established. The dead are an inverted image of the living: they live in the shade, the moon is their "sun", what is "outside" for the living is "inside" for them. Furthermore, they have no alliance: theirs is a world of pure kinship, the lost paradise of "being on our own". Finally, the ritual side of life is fully preserved among them. If the validity of these deductions is admitted, we can say that the relation of inversion or symmetry (in a broad sense) between the society of the living and that of the dead leaves the ritual sphere unaltered, heightens kinship and abolishes alliance.

In order to see what this means, we must look at the structure of Krahó society. It appears to be based on two partially contradictory systems.

Krahó marriage is structured neither by prescriptive nor by preferential rules. Chance and choice play a great part in it, and affinity is not inherited. These characteristics are consistent with the view of alliance as a disruptive factor: in the uxorilocal residence pattern, marriage swallows men up without guaranteeing the completion of the cycle of matrimonial exchange. The only mechanism which seems to offer compensation for the perpetual draining-off of men, and allow society to continue to reproduce itself, is the process of transmission of names, which is fundamental for the understanding of the Krahó social system.

The naming system ensures that men's names — which represent personal identity for the Krahó — are transmitted in such a way that they return to the house or residential segment from which they originated (see Melatti, 1970: 183–184). Women's names, on the contrary, which are preferentially transmitted from a kin category which includes FZ, circulate from house to house as men do, thus compensating for the immobility of women in this uxorilocal system.[6]

Thus the absence of marriage rules, which might be thought to lead to a sort of uncontrollable matrimonial haemorrhage, has its counter-weight in the naming system, which theoretically produces a stable and sure short-cycle reciprocity. We seem to have here a society whose stable, permanent base is not alliance, which is seen as a disruptive factor, but the transmission of names. It is this which provides the society with a model of itself as a static and unchanging entity.

This seems to me to explain the attitude of the *keti* when he restores his *itamtxua* (see note 4) to the society of the living: the story takes on the character of a parable about the importance of names for the permanence of society.

In Krahó terms, then, restriction to kinship and ritual activity crystallises society in its permanent aspect, in the forms which ensure its self-reproduction — and consequently represents a negation of the dynamic aspect incorporated in alliance.

This reduction of society to its static aspects runs through the physiology attributed to the *mekarõ* too: their gaze is fixed, their blood clotted — these being the elements associated with life and movement — and they have no flesh, only skin and bones. According to one informant, they have twittering voices like birds, they eat little and breathe shallowly. In general, their whole existence is attenuated: the water they drink is insipid, their food tasteless. Many say that they have no movement of their own, they are blown here and there by the wind.

We can now understand not only the mention of the stagnant water of the lagoon inside their village, but also why they do not bathe in running water; as I have tried to show elsewhere (Cunha, 1973), immersion in running water is thought of as a process of maturation, and forms the symbolic basis of initiation rites. The *mekarõ*, who lack all aspects of development, cannot mature and therefore avoid running water — in which, according to one informant, they would turn into fish. We can also now appreciate better the aptness of the term *karõ* as the Krahó translation of "photograph" and "picture". It appears to me to be associated with the static aspect of things, with an absence of process.

Thus the society of the *mekarõ* provides the society of the living with a reassuring picture of continuity; but it succeeds in doing this only by suppressing the disruptive and at the same time dynamic factor in the society of the living — alliance. The vision of continuity thus reveals itself as an illusion condemned by the price which has to be paid for it; for by excluding alliance the society of the *mekarõ* denies its own claim to be considered a society. And this is perhaps what the progressive involution of the dead means: a society without alliance is not viable, and so from being images of men the *mekarõ* turn into images of animals, until finally at the end of their metamorphoses they arrive at the permanence of stocks and stones — and, at the same time, the negation of all communal life. At the end of the analysis, therefore, eschatology appears not as a simple reflection of society — as has often been supposed — but as a reflection on its conditions of existence: a kind of proof by *reductio ad absurdum* of the truth of the premises on which the society of the living is based. Krahó eschatology contradicts these premises, but the society produced is not viable.

It might appear from this account that eschatology, even when it calls into question basic principles of the social system, is nevertheless profoundly conservative. I do not think that this is necessarily the case: a social movement, for example a millenarian cult, may deliberately adopt aims which it knows in advance are, in the long term, non-viable — as in Tolstoy's project for a perpetually chaste society, which would not be able to reproduce itself yet would fulfil the essential aim of harmonious coexistence.

Two questions arise out of this account. First, why is the analysis so impoverished and so reductionist, limited to the central core of a much larger field? Why did I have to abandon the hope of providing a structuralist explanation of each detail of divergent versions of the after-life? Why, at the same time, is the potency of the same method so much greater for myths as well as for, say, messianic movements? I was able, in an earlier work, to account for a messianic movement which arose in another Timbira tribe, the Canela, in 1963. It was not the absence of variations which made the task possible, for I considered successive transformations of the movement. But then, of course, there was much less multiplication of versions than here, since social acceptance of different versions and strong allegiance were indispensable for uniting the group around its prophetess (Cunha, 1973). Instead, in this case diverging versions do not necessarily demand public acceptance. Plausibility suffices. Yet this is not an explanation in itself but rather leads to the second question: Why is fabulation so much developed precisely in this field, and authority so weak to sanction it?

Krahó eschatology, it seems to me, must be seen as a domain in which fantasy is allowed to play very freely. The impossibility of accounting for every element of eschatological speculations in a structuralist analysis, therefore, would not be an indication of a deficiency but of a positive characteristic of this area of culture. In other words, eschatology in this society would be a privileged locus for socially encouraged creativity, unhampered by precise specifications. It would stand in contrast, then, to other more closely regulated domains, such as that of myth or of the ideology of social movements; these require social sanctioning and are therefore produced and validated under more rigorous conditions.

Utopias and "free zones"

Can this conception of eschatology be generalised? Yes and no. Eschatology is, of course, in all cultures a utopia in the literal, etymological sense: it portrays a society which exists nowhere. But this sense of "utopia" is different from that of Mannheim, who used the word to denote projects for change, for the society of the future. In any case, this non-existent world can have different functions. The after-life may function as a reward system which upholds moral norms by its judgments on conduct; it may, more simply, guarantee the continuity of hierarchy or of lineage distribution, the relation between social groups and territory, etc. In such cases it is doubtful whether eschatology can be characterised as a zone of free fantasy. We cannot therefore say that it is because the domain of eschatology is "more imaginary" than other domains that some societies handle it more casually.

One generalisation is perhaps possible: it seems that it is where societies sharply differentiate the living from the dead, stressing the rupture introduced by death rather than the continuity between the living and their ancestors — where the dead are "other", non-human, *par excellence* — that eschatology may become a free zone in which the imagination can take the bit between its teeth.

Krahó eschatology fits these conditions. Nevertheless it must be noted that the imagination seems to be given free rein only after the imposition of a preliminary condition: the society of the dead must be represented as non-viable. This seems to be the only hold which society has over its eschatology, which may explain why structural analysis can do no more than bring out principles which, however central, are somewhat general and do not serve to elucidate the whole richness of the material.

All this suggests that it is possible within the field of "collective representations" to distinguish different areas, or at least that different domains vary in their relation to society. Some symbolic domains seem to be subject to stricter social control than others: perhaps those which are more directly related to the reproduction of society? Yet this control over symbolic production does not exclude the possibility of semantic conflicts; however, in a strictly controlled and highly structured field the production of rival versions of, e.g. a myth, would be subject to strict rules of grammar, and this grammar could be deciphered in such a way that the place of each detail in the structure would be clear.

At the other end of the spectrum, however, we would find areas where speech-forms would be of prime importance, rather than the "grammar" of a symbolic language. Eschatology, in certain societies, would be one of these domains, linked to society only by a limited number of basic rules which make different representations intelligible but do not fully account for them. Hence the poverty of the analyses carried out in this field. This is not to say that we have to return to a view which finds the origins of representations in the individual, but only that greater emphasis and more consistent attention must be given, as Bakhtine (1977) has claimed, to speech forms (*énonciation*), and in particular to the specific refraction, shaped by situations of social conflict, which the individual's discourse imposes on collective representations. It is not a case of abandoning all hope of analysis, but of turning to an analysis of speech forms, which has still to be developed.

Notes

1. The Krahó Indians of northern Goiás, Brazil, belong to the Gê linguistic family and are closely related to the well-known Canela, Krĩkatí and Apinayé, as well as to the Shavante, Suyá and Kayapó groups.
2. Almost every day the Krahó perform relay races between two competing "teams", each carrying a section of the trunk of a palm-tree (*buriti*). Such races play a part in all rituals, with variations in the composition of the teams (according to different moiety systems) and in the shape and decoration of the logs. Log-racing, along with body decoration, is one of the major symbols of life in society (cf. Cunha, 1973).
3. This is why, according to one shaman, if a *karõ* is to be induced to return to the body it has abandoned, the corpse must be kept in the shade and never in full sunlight.
4. The *keti* is a kin category from which a boy's name-giver is selected: it includes, among others, MB, MF and FF. The reciprocal term is *itamxtua*.
5. *Paham* is a fundamental concept which has been studied by Roberto da Matta (1976), who emphasises for the Apinayé the aspect of "social distance" involved, and by Renate Viertler (1972: 35 ff.) who translates it, for the Bororo, as "shame".
6. It must, however, be noted that women's names have neither the importance nor the ritual significance of men's names. The ideal society of the Krahó is masculine and women only appear in it insofar as they are associated with masculine groups; this association is not reflected in their names, unlike the situation with regard to men's names.

References

BAKHTINE, M. (1977[1929]). "Le Marxisme et la philosophie du langage". Minuit, Paris.
CUNHA, M. CARNEIRO DA (1973). Logique du mythe et de l'action. Le mouvement messianique canela de 1963. *L'Homme*, **13** (4), 5–35.
CUNHA, M. CARNEIRO DA (1978). "Os Mortos e Os Outros. Uma análise do

sistema funerário e da noção de pessoa entre os índios Krahó". Hucitec, São Paulo.

Levi-Strauss, C. (1967). "Les Structures élémentaires de la parenté", 2nd edition. Mouton, Paris.

Matta, R. da (1976). "Um Mundo Dividido. O sistema social Apinayé". Vozes, Rio de Janeiro.

Maybury-Lewis, D. (1967). "Akwe-Shavante Society". Clarendon Press, Oxford.

Melatti, J. C. (1970). "O Sistema Social Krahó". Doctoral thesis, São Paulo University.

Taggia, Fr. R. (1898). Mapas dos Indios Cherentes e Chavantes na nova Povoacão de Thereza Christina no Rio Tocantins e dos Indios Charaõs na Aldeia de Pedro Alfonso nas Margens do mesmo Rio, ao norte da Provincia de Goyas. *Revista do Instituto Histórico e Geográfico do Brasil*, **19** (1st series, 6), 119–124.

Vernant, J.-P. (1965). Figuration de l'invisible et catégorie psychologique du double: le colossos. *In* "Mythe et pensée chez les Grecs" (J.-P. Vernant) pp. 251–264. Maspero, Paris.

Viertler, R. B. (1972). As Aldeias Bororo: alguns aspectos de sua organização social. Doctoral thesis, São Paulo University.

The Life-giving Death*

DANIEL DE COPPET

> Thus the tendency to exclude death from our calculations in life
> brings in its train many other renunciations and exclusions. Yet
> the motto of the Hanseatic League ran: *Navigare necesse est, vivere*
> *non necesse*. It is necessary to sail the seas, it is not necessary to
> live.
>
> Freud, vol. XIV, p. 291.

The data on which this paper is based come from a Melanesian society
called the 'Aré'Aré, living on the island of Malaita in the Solomon
Islands. Its object is to analyse a few points concerning the means by
which the society accommodates itself to death by changing death into
life again.

The analysis deliberately recalls the famous work of Robert Hertz
(1907), written at the British Museum Library. His conclusions may
be summarised as follows:

1. Death is not felt as an instantaneous destruction of an individual's
life.
2. Death is rather to be seen as a social event, the starting point of a
ceremonial process whereby the dead person becomes an ancestor.
3. Death is like an initiation into a social after-life, marking a kind of
rebirth.

One could add in the words of Robert Hertz himself: ''Death is not

*I should like to thank Dr Solange Faladé, Dr Cecile Barraud, Professor Louis Dumont,
Professor Andrew Strathern, Dr Hugo Zemp, Dr Raymond Jamous, André Iteaunu and
Dominique Casajus for their fruitful suggestions and comments at different stages of the paper.

originally conceived as a unique event without any analogue.'' (Hertz, 1907: 81.)

These conclusions open the way for a sociological analysis of death as a social phenomenon related to others such as initiation or marriage. But Hertz's analogy between death and other rituals indicates clearly the level at which he introduces the comparative analysis: a comparison should be made between these rituals in various societies, as they all seem analogous at the universal level of comparison. In the present paper, we wish to postpone that kind of comparison and try first to interrelate the different rituals performed in a given society so as to distinguish systems and sub-systems and to understand the society as a whole. As may be observed in Hertz's paper, if comparative analysis is introduced prematurely, before finding the interrelations between the rituals in the overall framework of the main values of a society, it will be difficult not to be overwhelmed by the perspective of our own individualistic and universalistic approach towards social phenomena. In that case, the comparison would inevitably centre on psychological issues or, even more misleadingly, concentrate on the different ways in which the individual's destiny is acted out at the levels of material operations or of mental logic.

Analysis of the different rituals and ceremonial feasts which take place in 'Aré'Aré society shows that the representation of death may be seen as the key point from which the different levels of social life can be articulated. The relations between the commoners on the one hand and the two kinds of big man on the other can be understood only if we relate these phenomena to the more powerful *rituology* of death. Here I should like to dispute the statement of Hertz that ''society imparts its own character of permanence to the individuals who compose it'' (ibid.: 77). We could say, regarding the 'Aré'Aré, that the society builds up its own character of permanence through the repeated dissolution *into* the ritual and exchange process of the main elements composing each individual.

The place of death in the 'Aré'Aré cosmos

According to the 'Aré'Aré, their first ancestors came into an already established world, whose three dividing elements were the land, the sea and the sky. All three elements were populated with animals. The Islands were covered with forest. When the primeval ancestors died, each was buried in a special grave on top of a different ridge and their descendants made their lives around these ancestral funeral sites. 'Aré'Aré land was thus covered by an extensive genealogical network of graves, each controlling the nearby land, and marking the land rights of all descendants, male as well as female. Not only was the land under the tight control of the ancestors, but so were the adjacent sea, the river-beds, the sub-soil and the sky over the mountain peaks. At the beginning of time these sites came under the control of wild animals like sharks, crocodiles, poisonous snakes and eagles, apparently similar to other members of their species, but in fact generated from the rotted fluids discharged by the corpses of the primeval ancestors. These fearful predatory ancestors extended their authority over a region surrounding their dwelling places. They are believed to control this area in two ways. First, they prevent wild animals similar to themselves from attacking the human descendants of the primeval ancestors. Second, they are supposed to sanction their living kindred if they breach any taboo, visiting them with illness or inducing wild animals to kill them in retaliation. Thus the ancestors control the surface area around the funeral sites and the depths of the sea, the sky and the earth. One must note that the predatory character of these ancestors should be distinguished from the savagery of their animal doubles.

All ancestors, the primeval ones with their avatars as well as the more recent ones, are the guardians of all taboos, and they impose illness or death on their living kin whenever one of these violates social norms.

Apart from the illnesses inflicted on the living by their ancestors to sanction their misconduct, there is a more dreadful kind of illness, mainly epidemic diseases, that can suddenly fall upon the whole 'Aré'Aré people. These epidemics come from the middle region of the sky and of the sea and are sent to 'Aré'Aré by *foreign spirits* living in these dangerous areas where clouds, rainbows, sun, moon and stars move about. These spirits have names and supposedly originate in other parts of the world, societies like Kwaio on Malaita, Birao on Guadalcanal or from more distant areas of "The-Eight-Isles-in-the-Sea" (the world). They behave mainly as enemies; they very seldom afford protection as the ancestors do, and no one can forecast their action or oppose their sudden attacks. They carry generic names which never refer to an individual being.

An important class of foreign spirits is called "biceps" or "avenging arm". Each such spirit is a kind of association or body incorporating the anger of the ancestors of a murdered person who was not avenged by his kin. In order to create such a body and to increase its anger, the murdered person has to invite his ancestors to drink his blood which will then change into the dreadful spirit. These "biceps" spirits live among other foreign spirits at the periphery of the world, encircling 'Aré'Aré society and inflicting epidemics.

In the world of 'Aré'Aré society, the centre of every piece of land is occupied by the authority of the ancestors, and the periphery of the world is inhabited by foreign spirits including the avenging ones which spring from the blood of unavenged victims. In such a situation, each member of the 'Aré'Aré population is under constant pressure from his ancestors, and the whole society is in danger of being attacked by foreign spirits sometimes called up by the unavenged. Obedience to all taboos is enforced by the internal law of the ancestors and potential enmity encircles the society in association with the unavenged. Death is everywhere, pervading the entire world, ''The-Eight-Isles-in-the-Sea'' (among which Malaita is the uncounted ninth island) and all its surroundings. Centre and periphery are densely peopled with death-giving creatures. There is menace to life at the centre as well as at the periphery.

It follows that 'Aré'Aré people are divided after death into two main categories: those *murdered* by the living and those *afflicted by illness and death given by their personal ancestors*. Each living adult is believed to be a combination of three different elements—the ''body'' (*rape*), the ''breath'' (*manomano*) and the ''image'' (*nunu*)—and it is of great interest to trace the transformations after death attributed to each of these elements. As we shall see, the *chains of transformations* are very different in the cases of ''murdered persons'' (*ráramua*) and of those ''killed'' by their ''ancestors'' (*hi'ona*).

The murdered who have been avenged have no ''breath''. Their ''bodies'' are not buried but left to rot in the forest or eaten, and it is believed that their ''image'' will never enter any real after-life. No funeral feast and no funeral cult will ever be offered to their ''image''. It may sometimes be heard crying in the forest, but it does no harm.

In the case of unavenged murder victims their ''breath'' will not disappear until it has been ''covered'' with the ''breath'' of a new victim, and if that hoped-for event is too long delayed, the victim's ''breath'' will try to change his blood into the ''biceps'' foreign spirit. The ''body'' and the ''image'' of an unavenged victim will have the same fate as an avenged victim.

The category of murdered persons also includes women who have died in childbirth, suicides and infants who die during the first forty days of life. Children who die before entering the years of discretion may fall into the same category, especially if their parents have concealed from each other sexual encounters that took place either before or after marriage.

With regard to the second category of dead, those seized and put to death by their own ancestors, two out of their three constitutive elements are dealt with by funerary rites. Their "bodies" are buried, exposed, cremated, or sunk at sea. Two or three years later a funeral feast honours the "image". But nothing is organised for the "breath", for it is said that it has disappeared at the time of death when the ancestors put an end to it by not liberating the "image". Young people who achieve no particular end in life such as marriage or some enterprise before death are not given a full funeral feast: they are the subject of a brief ritual in which money[1] is offered to the grave-digger by the family and placed on a mat lying on the ground. It is believed that after this ritual the deceased's "image" disappears, and no second funeral will be offered.

For adults, the second funeral feast allows the "image" to become a fully recognised ancestor sharing with others in a lengthy after-life. This continues as long as offerings are made and information is given regularly to the ancestor through various rituals. After two generations, no further ritual is offered directly to him, but rather he is honoured through the intermediary of more recent ancestors. Thereafter, if his name is not further recalled, an ancestor will leave his funeral site for the small island of Marapa in the Marau Sound at the eastern end of Guadalcanal. There he will live in a sort of mirage with many other ancestors. Much later, he will leave them permanently and slip away to the mythical island called Lost-forever before disappearing to the "above" which lies beyond the realm of the foreign spirits already mentioned. Some say that on the last island, if one were to break a stone or cut a tree, blood would run out if a murdered person were present within it, whereas in the case of a natural death pus would be found. These statements suggest that the two categories of dead people inhabit the same Lost-forever Island but again manifest themselves in two quite different ways.

In this part of Melanesia, what we may call subsistence[2] or, in a more radical way, survival seems to be the main task of a society: it is achieved through the everlasting *work of mourning*. Everyday life, peace, fecundity and prosperity are entirely dependent upon the proper mourning of the dead. The harvest, the fish catch, seduction in love, a successful journey through the forest or on the sea, the moving sound of Pan-pipe or slit-drum, the magnificence of the feasts, all depend on the constant flow of mourning work.

The work of mourning for the victims of murder

A settlement can only be had by murdering "in return" the murderer or someone related to him. In the case of a murder victim there is no "image" to be cared for, just a corpse to be dealt with. More important is his "breath": it will be a dangerous threat to his relatives until it has been avenged and thus neutralised. The second murdered person will extinguish the anger of the first and "replace the (first) man's breath". In such a series of murders, how can the "breath" of the last murdered person be replaced? Simply by a gift of *money* offered to his relatives.

In such a system killing is like stealing the job of the victim's ancestors, but with the peculiar consequence that the victim will have no "image" and will never become an ancestor. It is intervening outside one's own kindred, and more powerfully than ancestors usually do, when they inflict death and at the same time open the way for the birth of a new ancestor.

It must be stressed that in this system, the murder in revenge may be carried out either directly by a relative of the victim or by a third party in response to the price which the victim's relatives have placed on the head of the murderer and his relatives.

In cases where a third party commits the second murder, a feast will be organised by the family of the first victim to honour the second murderer and the blood-money called "nine" will be handed over to him. The result will be to ensure a state of peace between the first two groups with the help of a third partner who later on will have to defend himself against the retaliation carried out by the first murderer or his group. The logic of the system implies that even where both groups have suffered an equal number of losses peace is not possible, for the last victim's "breath" is still to be "replaced".

The last victim's relatives may end the sequence by accepting money for his "breath", but this response demonstrates clearly their inferiority. The strongest response is to demand that the opposing group choose and kill one of its own members and thereafter hand over his body. Soon after this, the people who have received the body will offer a feast and the blood-money ("nine") will be given to them. A long-lasting peace will thus be established between the two parties.

These examples show that in order to replace the "breath" of a murdered person, one has to take someone's life in exchange or else to ask the opposing party for a corpse that will be replaced finally by blood-money. The second case is illustrated graphically in Fig. 1.

These exchanges show several remarkable features which may be something of a shock to the Western way of thinking:

1. It would seem to a Westerner that an equal balance has been achieved when the B's give back the money which initiated the

dialogue (one victim on each side and the money returned). In fact, since the last victim is still left "uncovered", the sequence cannot yet be considered concluded.

2. The last victim is an A killed by the A's and chosen because he or, more frequently, she has broken a taboo some time before. In this case the victim's fate was already decided and was simply waiting to be sealed on the first occasion which might arise. This makes it clear that the "breath" of someone who has broken a taboo can be replaced by money without any loss of prestige by the receiving group.

3. To kill a person from one's own kin (only if he or she has breached a taboo) is in fact acting exactly like one's own ancestors when they

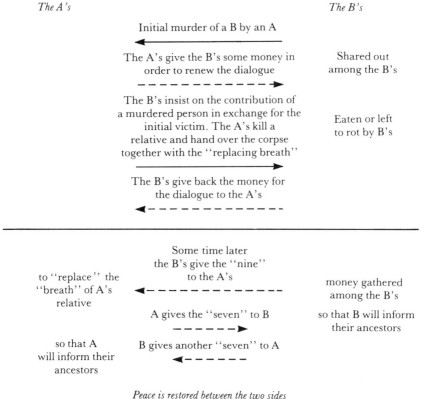

FIG. 1. Replacing the "breath" of a murdered person. The "nine" is quite a large sum: the "seven" only 7 beads. A is the "murderer", *namo*, B the peace-master, *aaraha*.

put to death any of their living relatives. Here one must note the superior value (with regard to the ancestors) of *killing one's own kin* compared with ordinary killing.

4. The killing of a (guilty) person chosen from one's own kin gives the opportunity to restore peace with an enemy. The initial murderer receives an important sum of money from the opposing group for the handing over of the corpse of a relative. Only in this way may peace leading to friendly exchanges, marriages etc., be re-established.[3]

5. In this case, where the first group has killed one of its own members, money has the power to "replace" the victim's "breath", as another killing normally would, and to change the level of exchanges radically from war to peace.

We see here how the *work of mourning* is carried out in the case of a series of murder victims and how it becomes possible to interrupt such a series and to re-establish prosperity.

The work of mourning for the dead seized by their ancestors

When someone is not murdered, it is considered that he dies as the result either of an epidemic due to foreign spirits, or of an illness due to his personal ancestors being infuriated by the many grievances they have against him. In the latter case it is believed that his ancestors keep his "image" away from his "body" and his "breath"; if no ritual treatment is successfully performed to bring back his "image", then he dies.

After death the "breath" is said to have stopped, in contrast to the fate of a murdered "breath", which struggles for revenge. During the first funeral[4] the "body" and the "image" of the dead person have to be cared for by the grave-digger chosen by the family as a partner in the many funeral rituals to follow. The "body" has to be buried and the grave-digger must ensure that the "image" has also entered the grave where it will be less of a threat for all the living relatives. One or two years later, a second funeral feast is given to the deceased in order to transform his "image" into one of the many ancestors.

During this second funeral feast, two ceremonial groups combine their efforts to ensure complete success. On one side stand the family of the deceased, "the roots of the feast"; on the other, the group of people who follow the grave-digger[5], "the handling people". The grave-digger is chosen by the dead person's family at the time of burial from among the friends or the affines of the deceased. The family group is responsible for the building of the ceremonial platform in the middle of the village, constructed especially for the occasion by the two groups. The platform, whatever shape it takes, permits three levels to be distinguished: the earth which is beneath it, the platform itself and a beam which is constructed horizontally above it (Fig. 2).

For several days, during the period between sunrise and sunset, two principal movements of money can be observed taking place at the same time, one ascending, the other descending. We shall deal first with the latter.

a. *Mourning through the descending money*
In this section we discuss the money which is handed over to the grave-digger standing at the foot of the platform. The money is called "stop quarrelling" and is offered by the dead person's family, who sit on the floor of the platform (see Fig. 2). The grave-digger keeps this money; it is never returned to the dead person's family. The "stop quarrelling" money is said to be paid for the funeral services rendered by the grave-digger, starting with the burial and ending with the completion of the second funeral feast, which frees the "image" for full ancestorship. The grave-digger carries out a number of important acts among which is the contribution of the great number of pigs, coconuts and taros

FIG. 2. Ceremonial platform for the funeral feast of Waiparo in August 1964. Here the descending money is offered to Aliki Non'ohimae, the leader of the Maasina Ruru movement.

which his group must bring to the second funeral feast. A roughly equal number of offerings of the same sort is given by the dead person's family. All the pigs will be killed; the pork and most of the vegetable food will be cooked and distributed to the entire assembly, some of whose members will partake of it. The exchanges performed in relationship with the descending money are summarised in Fig. 3.

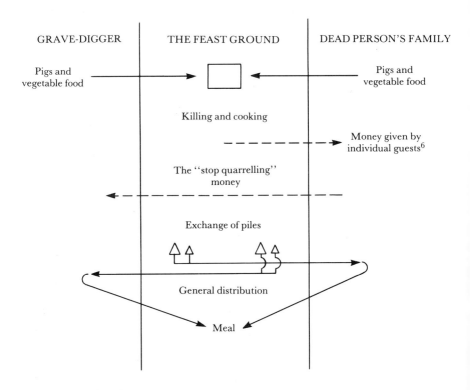

FIG. 3. Exchanges related to the descending money.

In contrast to the case in which a murdered person is to be mourned, here the two sides come together to build a village for the feast, to which they bring their pigs and their cultivated plants. They kill the pigs, then cook the meat and distribute all of it. The mourning of a deceased person cannot be effective without this exact combination, whereby the dead person seems to be reconstituted in all his elements.

Some of the different phases of the second funeral feast may be analysed as follows:

1. Pigs are put to death by both sides. These domesticated animals have been fed like children; ancestors, we know, bring death to their offspring. The analogy here is clear since the pig-killing at the funeral feast is similar to the settlement in the case of a murder, where the murderer's group brings the body of one of its own relatives in order to "replace" the "breath" of the previous victim. The difference lies in the fact that many pigs are killed here (not just one person), and they are gathered from both sides.

2. The payment of the "stop quarrelling" money to the grave-digger can be seen as "replacing" the breath of his pigs. While all animals have a "body", most of them have also a "breath", especially pigs. The "stop quarrelling" money is comparable to the "nine" handed over to the murderer at the blood-money feast, since both payments "replace breath" — human or animal — and ensure peace. The pigs brought to the feast by the family of the dead person have their "breath replaced" by the money offered by some of the guests who attend the feast (cf. note 6).

3. Towards the end of the funeral feast each side makes a big pile of some of the food which has previously been cooked. Although each of the two groups makes its own pile, the food incorporated in each pile is drawn from the common stock composed of the offerings to the feast brought by both groups. Each of these piles is made of taros and coconuts — some of them to be replanted, others to be eaten — together with taro puddings, pork meat and a piece of money. Each big pile is accompanied by a small one made of taros without their stems, i.e. unfit for replanting, some taro puddings cooked without coconut and a small amount of money. These two small piles are exchanged and then offered to all the women at the feast. Women are prohibited from eating the food in the two big piles and never eat pork at ceremonial feasts.[7] The two big piles are exchanged, and the two sides start to distribute all the food to the participants in the feast. The piles appear to reconstitute the dead person, one half coming from the grave-digger, the other from the relatives of the dead person.

The three main components of the big piles display the "body" (the taros and the coconuts), the "breath" (the pork), and the "image" (the money on top of the piles). In this rather theatrical way, the dead person's completeness manifests itself at another level of reality.

4. The distribution of pork and taro puddings goes on for many hours until each small piece has changed hands many times. Only the "body" and the "breath", represented respectively by the taro puddings and the pork, are shared. We may remember that when the body of a murdered person is offered to the opposing group the "breath" is not present, since it is seeking revenge elsewhere. Here the case is different, for the metaphorical sharing of the dead person comprises his "breath" and his "body". The money on top of the piles which represents the "image" is not further exchanged and distributed, because the ascending money (see below) brought to the feast deals with the entire "image" by transforming it into a full ancestor.

5. When all the pieces of food finally stop circulating, the men do not all start to eat their share, for some are prohibited from doing so: the affines of the dead person and his older relatives may not eat the food in question. Only younger relatives and unrelated men have the right to eat their share of the dead person's "body" and "breath".

This prohibition can be understood only if we recall the contexts in which certain beings fall into the same ritual category, in opposition to other beings in the contrasting category. In Fig. 4, which sets forth the relevant oppositions, it should be noted that the left-hand column incorporates the beings which may have *killed* really or symbolically *among their own relatives* and do not eat, while the right-hand column incorporates those which have not killed their own relatives and *have the right to eat*.

Figure 4 reveals not only a contrast but even more the hierarchical order (cf. Dumont, 1966) which pervades the whole society through the main opposition between *killing one's own people* and *eating* or *leaving to rot*. A puzzling detail — the fact that a murdered "body" can be equally eaten or left to rot, depending only on "personal preference" — may now be situated in the total value system.

b. *Mourning through the ascending money at the funeral feast*

This section deals with the money offered from the ground level by all persons attending the funeral feast. It is displayed on the upper beam of the platform; members of the dead person's family, standing on the wooden floor, tie it there above themselves. At the end of all celebrations (and also at sunset on each of the preceding feast days) the total amount of money tied to the upper beam is counted and loudly proclaimed. Finally it is given to the grave-digger, who will distribute it to all the people from his own group attending the feast. After another year or two the grave-digger will offer the small "return funeral feast" during which he stands on the floor of a small platform and receives back the money he had distributed at the end of the second funeral feast. Then he hands over this money to the dead person's family, who stand at the foot of the platform. This amount of money is equal to that

Among the supernatural beings

The ANCESTORS kill their descendants through illness	The FOREIGN SPIRITS kill people unrelated to them through epidemics

In a murder exchange

The "murderer" (*namo*) sometimes *kills among his own people*	The peace-master (*aaraha*) does not kill among his people; he *eats or leaves to rot* a relative of the murderer

At the second funeral feast with regard to the "body" and "breath"

The older male relatives and the male affines KILL THEIR OWN PEOPLE since they have killed their vegetable food and pigs to "replace" the "body" and the "breath" of a deceased relative and *do not eat*	The younger male relatives and the unrelated men DO EAT the vegetable food and the pork "replacing" the "body" and the "breath" of the person they have not killed

With regard to the "image"

	The "image" of the recently deceased person, represented by the ascending money, seems to *eat or let rot* older "images" (see below pp. 189–191).

At the peace-master's feast

	The "images" of the recently murdered persons, represented by the ascending money, seem to *eat or let rot* the "images" of former victims and at the same time the fame of the peace-master seems to *eat or let rot* the fame of former peace-masters.

FIG. 4. Ritual categories: *killing one's own people* versus *eating or leaving to rot*.

which was tied to the upper beam of the platform at the second funeral feast. Finally the dead person's family returns all these pieces of money to the persons who offered them at the second funeral feast. This is the conclusion of the funeral ceremonies.

The total amount of ascending money represents the most beautiful "image" of the dead person, built and displayed in his honour. It is the money collected from all persons attending the second funeral feast (members of both sides as well as other persons). All the participants in the second funeral feast either have mourned relatives at former funeral feasts or will mourn relatives at funeral feasts to come. The complete dead person's "image" is thus made out of pieces of money coming from all other ancestors' "images" displayed at one time or another at previous feasts.

The grave-digger has authority over the dead person's monetary "image", just as the ancestor has over the life and death of his living descendant. He manipulates the dead person's "image", just as he previously buried his "body". He keeps the monetary "image" and distributes it among his own people, who will have the use of it until the "return funeral feast". Then, at this feast, he reassembles the total amount of money which is then returned to all the participants[8] who offered it at the second funeral feast. At that time, the "image" becomes a full partner in ancestral life, i.e. an "image" which will push further into oblivion (*eat* or *leave to rot*) the "images" of earlier ancestors. This "push" repeated with every new funeral feast gives new ancestors the chance to flourish.

A few remarks should be made here about the special value of money in this social system. The different rituals so far analysed show that money can:

1. "replace" the vegetable food brought to the feast as an equivalent for the "body" of the dead person;
2. "replace" the "breath" of killed pigs or humans as in the cases of the "stop quarrelling" and the "nine";
3. represent the "images" of the dead when they become full ancestors.

As we can see, 'Aré'Aré money is a means of transforming certain things into others, but it is believed also that money manifests the might of the ancestors—more precisely, the power to *kill one's own people*. Consequently, it is very dangerous to hoard money; it must always circulate among people. The best way for someone to increase his social and monetary strength is for him to offer money for the upper beam at every funeral feast. As we have seen, this money will eventually be returned to him; in this way he may increase his monetary hoards without keeping money in his own possession. At the same time he honours many ancestors, pleases them by not hoarding, and regenerates their after-life. This again will lengthen his own life-time here and "above" and invigorate life all around him as well as enriching his own "image".

Money — the "nine", the "stop quarrelling" and other payments — is exchanged in order to "replace" the elements composing living creatures, especially human beings. These repeated "replacements" by money reactivate all exchanges and make possible the transformation of death into the life of new "bodies" and "breaths", which will again strengthen new "images" as we shall attempt to demonstrate below.

The reappearance of the murder victims' images at the peace-masters' feasts

We may now speculate about the whereabouts of murder victims' "images", supposedly lost, for we know quite well that their "bodies" have been *eaten* or *left to rot*, and that their "breaths" have been "replaced" by other "breaths" or by money. The resolution of this problem requires us to describe in some detail another 'Aré'Aré ritual: the big feast in honour of the peace-master.[9] During these feasts money ascends to the third level of a special platform. This money has been collected from the unmarried women by the bachelors during a flirtation campaign which lasts several months. These flirtations, carried on secretly in the forest, may come dangerously close to or sometimes even infringe certain taboos.

During the feast, which lasts one day, only men take part. The women watch the scene from the nearby village where they are protected from possible insults. Pan-pipe music is played, and there are coarse mimes, jokes and insults which may mock any participant in the feast and may be reciprocated without ending in a fight or a feud. At sunset the participants usually destroy the gardens of the peace-master and cut the heads off his coconuts with no opposition whatsoever. The only food consists of huge taro and coconut puddings, which are not cut into small pieces and distributed as at the funeral feast, but rather are pulled apart by the "nipping fingers" of everyone attending the feast.

Near the platform, wound in a spiral around the upper rung of a wide ladder, there is a display of coconuts and taros tied in a chain. The ladder with its load is called the "ladder of the victims' corpses". When, during the feast, another peace-master wants to proclaim his intention to start preparing for a future feast, he is offered one of these spirals displayed by the feast-giver. All the remaining spirals will be used to prepare the big puddings.

1. It is more than tempting to argue that the taro and coconut puddings, being torn apart in this way when they are eaten, and being made out of the plants which were previously displayed on the "ladder of the victims' corpses", represent the "bodies" of the victims *eaten* or *left to rot* during the peace-master's career. It must be noted that pork, which at the second funeral feast replaces the "breath" of a person who has been killed by his ancestors, is not eaten at the peace-master's feast: murder victims' "breaths" have either been "replaced" in a murder exchange, or changed with the help of the victim's blood into an avenging foreign spirit.

2. The fame of a peace-master depends on the amount of money collected among the unmarried women during the flirtation campaign previously mentioned. At the feast, on several occasions, some of this money is placed within a split bamboo stick shaped like a womb and is made to look like a foetus. All of the money collected (including the "foetuses") is carried up to the third level of the platform. In analysing this ritual, in which we are presented with a vivid image of miscarriages, we must recall that dead foetuses are considered "murdered persons". The feast itself cannot take place before the end of a flirtation campaign which lasts for eight periods of twenty-eight days, that is, less than the time for a normal gestation. The ritual in question represents, by a sort of mime, the "bodies" of the "murdered" foetuses, for the foetuses will never have an "image" to be converted into ascending money. So both foetuses and corpses (the taros and the coconuts wound around the rung of the ladder) are displayed at the scene of the feast.

3. The money which is all brought to the top of the platform represents the "images" of all the "murdered" persons who were old enough at the time they died to have an "image". In this way the fame of the peace-master is manifested by all the "images" of the victims killed during and in relation to his career.

In previous feasts of other peace-masters, the "images" of former victims have already made these other peace-masters famous. The present feast cuts to pieces (*eats* or *leaves to rot*) the monetary fame of these *big-men* and pushes them into oblivion, just as new murder victims eaten subsequently by the peace-master will *be added to* the collection of previous victims, that is will *eat them* or *leave them to rot*.

In the same way, when the total amount of money is proclaimed in honour of the peace-master at the feast, the bachelors will have their money returned to them and will later return most of it to the unmarried women. So the "name" of the peace-master will again be fragmented into the initial small pieces of money. This fragmentation means that the peace-master will be, as it were, *eaten* or *left to rot* by the peace-masters of the future, just as the "images" of the previous victims will be by the "images" of later victims.

Given this brief account of the peace-master's feast, it is now possible to identify the different victims represented by the ascending money. They all belong to the same class of "murdered" persons. During the feast all the flirtation money, either in the shape of dead foetuses or in another form, is brought to the top of the third level of the ceremonial platform where, as on the platform of the funeral feast, "images" are exhibited. Because the "images" of murdered people are "lost" and run senselessly through the forest, they can be scoffingly gathered together in this ceremony in the form of the many pieces of flirtation money offered by unmarried women to unmarried men during secret meetings in the thickets of the forest.

The peace-master's fame is displayed through this money which results from and represents a long series of transgressions: flirtations, matrimonial misconduct and other breaches of taboos either by men or by women. We may remember that the corpses received by a peace-master in satisfaction of his claim for revenge are the "bodies" of persons who have been convicted of violating some taboo. So the peace-master is in many ways locked into the structure of all ceremonial exchanges and at the same time tied to his counterpart the murderer. Even more, the famous feast which represents the peak of his career[10] brings to the centre of the stage, in a burlesque manner, the "forgotten" murdered. The fame of the peace-master is manifested by a complete display of all the "murdered dead".

While at the second funeral feast the descending money "replaces" the "body" and the "breath", and the ascending money is really the "image" of a new ancestor, the ascending money at the peace-master's feast, in mocking the errant condition of all the "images" of murdered persons, is complementary to the blood-money which deals with the "breath" of a murder victim (the "nine").

"Body", "breath" and "image"

Figure 5 summarises the different transformations after death of the three main elements which compose human adults. It shows that all three elements are in the end "replaced" by quite specific amounts of money, although certain of these elements have been metaphorically displayed and eaten before being replaced by money. This huge overall circulation of the three elements composing human adults turns into a self-feeding social process where nothing is ever lost and where death is the starting point of the long-lasting work of mourning, which ensures the "replacement" of all the elements. All exchanges take their place in chains of transformations which end up with money and nothing seems ever to be lost from the two 'Aré 'Aré sub-systems of replacement which follow either murder or normal death. However some murder victims whose "breaths" have not been "replaced" either by the "breath" of a "covering" victim or by the money of the "nine" will simply be expelled from 'Aré'Aré society. They fall out of the system and enter a quite different world, that of The-Eight-Isles-in-the-Sea, where peaceful or violent exchanges follow other rules which are enforced by foreign spirits populating the middle region of the universe and encircling mankind.

Nevertheless some of the murder victims, after giving up in despair their hope of being avenged by their living relatives, try to offer their blood to their ancestors who may eventually drink it and change it into a "biceps" foreign spirit. This spirit may then, through epidemics, take the lives of many people in an anonymous and vengeful gesture. In this case, the "image" of the first victim will be able to rejoin the overall circulation of the dead and, as such, re-enter the 'Aré'Aré system.

Chains of transformations

On the basis of Fig. 5, we may now draw a few conclusions concerning the way *things are tied together in chains*. For each of the three main elements composing a human adult chains may be observed, all of which eventually end in money. But if some of these indicate a quick replacement by money, others go a long way round before reaching that stage.

All "images" are directly changed into money and displayed at the third level of the different ceremonial platforms, but the treatment accorded to the "image" of a person who has died because of his ancestors is quite distinct from that accorded to the "image" of a person who has been murdered.

In the former case, the person's "image" is displayed only once, in full glory, at his second funeral feast. After that the beautiful monetary "image" is again fragmented into small pieces of money, which will play a part in other funeral feasts given for recently deceased persons.

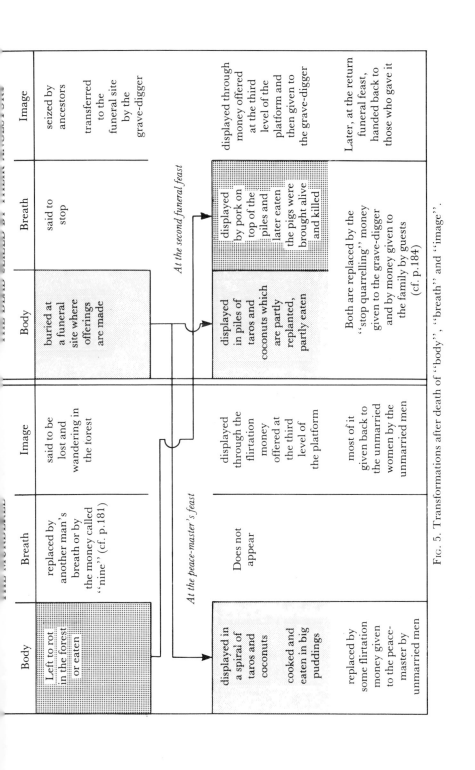

Fig. 5. Transformations after death of "body", "breath" and "image".

The "image" of the first person leaves the centre of the stage until the "return funeral feast" takes place and thereafter the small pieces of money again become anonymous. The dead person's "image" has become a full ancestor which depends exclusively on the care of its living kindred.

The new ancestor will be accessible to his living descendants at his funeral site where his skull is exposed in its little house. Here the "image", that is the ancestor, is firmly located. From this site he controls the everyday life of those of his descendants who are settled nearby. He may also grant them prosperity and bring them success in their gardening as well as in their fishing, in their marriages and in all their other activities. The new ancestor also controls the realm of the forest which surrounds him, in which region he will have a great influence on any pig raising which is carried out by his living relatives.

In contrast, the "images" of murdered persons follow chains which never lead to the exhibition of the "image" of an individual murdered person. These "images" do not celebrate their own good name; it is rather the peace-master's name which they build up. The chain that such an "image" follows does not last more than eight or nine months, from the time of a flirtation until the money is exhibited in the shape of an aborted foetus at the top of the platform. In this way the "images" of murdered persons are played with.

The two other elements of any human adult, the "body" and the "breath", follow chains which incorporate many different items before ending with money. The "breath" of a murdered person is the only exception since it is directly "replaced", either by another person's "breath", or by the blood-money (the "nine") offered to the murderer at the special feast. For this reason the "breaths" of murdered persons do not appear at the peace-master's feast.

The "body" of a person "killed" by his ancestors proceeds along a chain which may be divided analytically into the following stages:

1. Initially the "body" may be treated in one of several ways. It may be buried, either placed between the split halves of a sago-palm trunk or wrapped in pandanus leaves. It may be exposed either supported *above* the ground or placed in a canoe supported *above* the sea by the branches of a tree growing on a reef covered by the water at every high tide (Figs 6 and 7). Finally it may be immersed in the nearby sea, or cremated. In all the cases mentioned the deceased is assigned a funeral site located on the land. If the rotted fluids have gone into the sea (in the cases where the body is placed in a canoe or immersed), the deceased also has another funeral site located where a shark ancestor dwells, beneath the water near the shore (see

p. 177). The "image" of the deceased, which becomes an ancestor after the second funeral feast, will settle at his funeral site(s). Each funeral site controls the land or sea around it and all the gardens which may be cleared there or all the fishing done there. The rotted fluids or ashes go down and mix with the soil (or with the sea) near the future gardens (or sea-gardens) where the descendants of the deceased will harvest (or fish).[11] It is to be noted that in the case of burial or exposure, after a month has passed the skull of the deceased is separated from the corpse and brought to its land funeral site where it is given a small house or a shelter.

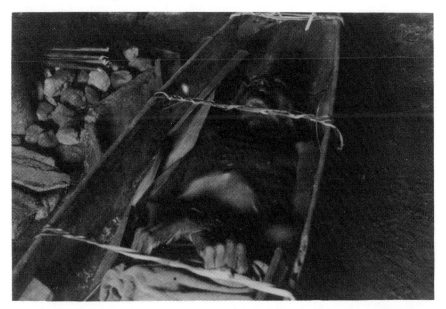

Fig. 6. Under the roof of his house the dead man is lying in his little canoe, before exposure on a nearby reef.

2. As the second step in the chain, the deceased's "body" is displayed at the second funeral feast in the forms of uncooked taros and coconuts and of two kinds of pudding, taro puddings for the women and taro and coconut puddings for those of the men who are permitted to eat. Some taros and coconuts will be replanted, the others are eaten.[12]

3. Finally all the vegetable food will be replaced by different amounts of money offered to the people who brought it to the feast.

The "bodies" of murdered persons follow a quite different chain:

1. Initially the "body" is either *eaten* or *left to rot* in the forest. The

choice between these two different possibilities is made by the murderer or in the relevant cases by the peace-master[13] in accord with their "individual" decision. From a structural point of view the two options are identical, and in both cases, the blood, the bones, the skull and the intestines of the victim are left uncooked in the forest (like the placenta after a successful birth). If the "body" is to be eaten, it is cut along the backbone, contrary to pigs which are cut first along the belly. The blood is not cooked and eaten as it is in the case of pigs, and while human bones are separated from the flesh and left in the forest, pig bones and flesh are cooked without being separated. These contrasted details show how differently killed pigs and murdered persons' "bodies" are treated, since they belong to

FIG. 7. The canoe with the dead man's body is exposed above the high tide level, between a few trees growing on a reef. A month later, the skull will be carried to the funeral site located on land.

two quite distinct chains. As in the case of bodies left to rot, the remains of bodies which have been eaten are not buried; they are left on the floor of the forest where pigs feed.[14]

2. The chain therefore leads to the forest and to the pigs which are raised there. Pigs are only killed and eaten in order to honour the ancestors, especially at the second funeral feast where they "replace" the "breath" of a dead person "killed" by his ancestors.

3. Finally, at the second funeral feast, pork is eaten by men and the pigs' "breaths" are "replaced" by money offered to those who brought their animals to the feast.

It must be noted that the chain followed by "bodies" after natural death leads to *gardening*, which produces taros and coconuts. This vegetable food will "replace" the "bodies" both of persons who have died naturally and of murder victims, respectively, at the funeral feast and at the peace-master's feast. It means that only those "bodies" to which a funeral site is given will take part in the replacement of all "bodies". On the other hand, only the "bodies" of murdered persons can help in the presentation at the second funeral feast of the "breath" of a person who has died a natural death, because it is they which lead to the pig raising activities which take place in the forest. These two contrasted chains recall the distinction already made between rotten fluids or pus on the one hand and blood on the other. We may remember also how the "body" is buried in the ground between the two split halves of a sago-palm trunk after the pulp has been removed; in 'Aré'Aré society, one of the principal foods given to pigs is the sago pulp removed by splitting open the trunk. But here the way in which the two halves of the palm are tied together, with the "body" protected between them, shows that the latter, unlike a murdered person's "body", is definitely *not to become pig food*.

In a diagram where arrows indicate the various transformations of the "bodies" we can observe:

A natural death leaves a "body" → to rot → gardening taros → eaten as "body" → money
A violent death leaves a "body" → to rot → forest pig raising → eaten as "breath" → money

These two series of transformations incorporate quite different events: first the rotting process, second the gardening and the pig raising, third and most crucial, the eating, and finally the money.

Not included in this diagram, but also of the greatest importance, is the transformation from life to death. It would have to be added to the beginning of these two chains as well as of the others which have already been discussed: in the two cases of natural death and death by murder, the 'Aré'Aré describe this transformation as "killing" either by living men or by ancestors.

Without needing to extend the analysis further, we find here again (see pp.186–187) the events which define the contrasted values of the society: *killing one's own people* and *eating* or *leaving to rot*.

'Aré'Aré values

In this paper, while discussing 'Aré'Aré ceremonial exchanges which carry out the *work of mourning* we have had to omit a discussion of many other important rituals such as those concerning birth, access to adulthood and marriage, where the different fates of men and women are sharply contrasted. It seems very likely that an analysis integrating an understanding of these different rites with the treatment of the death rites briefly sketched here would make possible a fuller understanding of the society as a whole. Here we refer to the programme set forth by Durkheim and Mauss in their "Essay on Primitive Classification":

> . . . if the totality of things is conceived as a single system, this is because society itself is conceived in the same way. It is a whole, or rather it is *the* unique whole to which everything is related. Thus logical hierarchy is only another aspect of social hierarchy, and the unity of knowledge is nothing else than the very unity of the collectivity, extended to the universe.
>
> (1903: 83–84)

If we accept that this quotation should be read without giving to the term "social hierarchy" the restricted meaning of social stratification, then the Melanesian case presented in this paper may fit into the Maussian model.

Every society possesses a different conception of what is real and what is not real and consequently develops a different and probably unique categorisation of its experience; how then can we understand another society by imposing on it the Western conception of reality and Western society's system of values?[15]

When we refer to a social phenomenon in another society as a "representation" of something we fall immediately into a trap, for in doing so we treat the phenomenon in question as "unreal" and thus accept the boundary which our own society has drawn between the "real" and the "unreal". More satisfactory comparative studies will not be possible until we learn to treat our own viewpoint as merely one among many and then go on to compare the different ways in which each society constructs its own system.

This Melanesian case shows how two different values, *killing one's own people* and *eating* or *leaving to rot* organize a hierarchical order (which is reversible at different levels of understanding as well as of practice).[16] In such a situation we must take into account that the society is not only made up of the living but also includes the dead who reveal the encompassing value to us.

If we make the assumption that the encompassing value for 'Aré'Aré society is *killing one's own people,* an act performed by ancestors and murderers, then the other value *eating* or *leaving to rot* seems an encompassed response (always provisional) on the part of the peace-masters and of the young people. Here again it is not possible to understand the murderers and the peace-masters separately, for they operate as parts of a single system. The fact that the world foreign to 'Aré'Aré society may only be reached through the falling out of the system of the "unreplaced victims" puts the *eating* and *leaving to rot* value at a more universal level, where the peace-masters and the younger people officiate but also fail: they have to be replaced by the might of the foreign spirits.

The life-giving death is certainly in full operation here, but through a very special "whole" that this paper leaves still to be fully constructed. To complete the discussion one would have to analyse the chains which lead back to human life. Not surprisingly the most important of these starts with money which, as we know, is at the end of the chains starting with death.

"Exchange theory" and the life-giving death

If we now touch briefly on how the analysis of 'Aré'Aré funeral exchanges sketched here can contribute to the criticism of "exchange theory", we must first recall some recent discussions of this subject. They all tend either to criticise the implications of the concept of reciprocity, or to extend the concept so as to include all "types of exchanges". The starting point of this recent research can be observed in Marshall Sahlins' reappraisal of the Polynesian *hau,* in which he explains, by referring to R. Firth's interpretation, the necessity of a third party in order to "show a turnover: the gift has had an issue; the recipient has used it to advantage" (1974: 160). The cycle which Sahlins describes when explaining the "true meaning" of the forest *hau* indicates how a chain ties together killings and offerings and thus maintains a regenerating flow of life through death between the forest and the society. This development leads Sahlins to question the relations between the different elements composing a Maori man (his *wairua,* his *hau* or his *mauri*) where the *hau* is identified with "the principle of fertility".

Further criticisms were to be found in Kapferer (1976) and in the series of recent articles published by Annette Weiner (1976, 1978, 1979, 1980). Both emphasise the need for transactional analysis to depart from its exclusive interest in individual decision-making and, as Kapferer writes, to concentrate more on "the processes of flow and feedback between the organizations and institutions in which individuals are active" (Kapferer, 1976: 16). A. Weiner, in an article entitled "Reproduction: a replacement for reciprocity" (1980), stresses the need to move beyond "the Western construct of linear sequences basically concerned with discrete acts of giving and receiving", and to give full attention to the building of a "model of reproduction" and to the analysis of the "process of regeneration" which she calls "replacement".[17]

Similarly, the present paper may be seen as leading us in the same direction as A. Weiner's recent important contributions, in the sense that it attempts to reduce the use of the concept of reciprocity at an empirical level of sociological analysis. While this concept retains all its value at a very abstract level, it provides no basis for the differentiation of the various types of exchanges observed in any specific society. Like the Maori case (Sahlins, 1974: ch.5), the 'Aré'Aré exchange system demonstrates the inadequacy of this over-estimated tool.

The concept of reciprocity, used at an empirical level of analysis, may be criticised for two fundamental reasons:

1. It separates the parties, who are considered to act in order to satisfy their personal needs and secondarily to maximise their gains with regard to each other, since they are *assumed* to participate in the same individualistic and egalitarian value system even if their shares of the "benefits" look rather unbalanced.
2. It posits in principle that each single exchange in a sequence can be understood alone by dividing time into periods during which the two partners accomplish only one act each, the first considered to be initial, the second to be final.[18]

On the contrary, exchanges are not a means employed to achieve individual goals, but rather the common task on which the society as a whole rests.

Consequently, as A. Weiner rightly points out, by emphasising individuals (or corporate groups understood as individualities), the reciprocity model adopts a basically Western framework of analysis.

In contrast with an analysis which posits reciprocity as the underlying principle for the understanding of all exchanges, we would like to stress:

1. The existence of a (sometimes invisible) *locus* [19] quite distinct from the parties involved, in which a hierarchical order of values prevails.
2. The chains of transformations associated with this *locus*, built up by the series of exchanges which follow socially defined channels and which incorporate the different procedures leading to the firm establishment and constant renewal of a *community*.

3. The fact that, by building these never-ending chains, the community works in obedience to the normative order which subordinates the living to the dead.

The chains incorporate various links which can equally well consist of objects, plants, animals, persons or elements of persons (living or dead). Specific actions — planting, animal raising, fishing, weather-making, and so forth — bring about the passage from one link to the next in a chain which eventually leads to the most important trans-formations: eating, killing, love-making and birth. Although some seem to have a beginning and a specified end, all are assumed to go on and on eternally as do time and society. Under these conditions, the exchanges which make up the chains are necessarily unbalanced, since it is the unequal and hierarchical nature of the exchanges which ensures the continuation of the chains. The principle underlying the chains and their construction is that any item appearing in one of them carries forward the item which precedes it, and has to be carried forward by another item. These successive prolongations ensure the continuation of the cycles of life-giving death.

Finally the chains are not so much invented as rather blindly and faithfully followed. This is the most important task to which all persons in a society must address themselves, because it is regarded by them as essential to the success of the overall social process which changes continuous decay and death into the emergence of life. It is not the life of the individuals or of the corporate groups which is at stake but the perpetuation of the community, which is seen as responsible for the "creation" of time and for the continuous resumption of life.

Notes

1. For details of the shell-money used in 'Aré'Aré society cf. Coppet, 1970.
2. Land is plentiful in the 'Aré'Aré region; the density of the population is low and each 'Aré'Aré has free access to the lands of both his parents. Land is not regarded as a commodity (cf. Coppet, 1976).
3. The position of inferiority in which the second group places itself by accepting a mere money payment frequently leads to a later renewal of the conflict.
4. The first funeral takes place two or three days after death. Then, a year or two later, the second funeral feast is given. Finally, the "return funeral feast" is offered after another one or two years' time.
5. Their group exists only for the purpose of the feast, was formed only for it and dissolves after it is over.

6. Certain persons who attend the feast act individually, presenting money offerings which are not considered to come from either of the two ceremonial groups. These persons may or may not in fact belong to one of these two groups. In most cases the money offered here is either a "returned" gift in relation to a former funeral feast, or will be returned at a future funeral feast.

7. Some women may eat pork together in a special hut, but this meal is never shared with men.

8. For these purposes, they are considered individual participants and not members of either of the two ceremonial groups.

9. People who by their acts bring peace and prosperity to their hamlet and the surrounding region are called *aaraha*, peace-masters. In many rituals the peace-master is ceremonially opposed to the murderer, although a peace-master may begin his career as a murderer. Some successful peace-masters may later be forced by the social structure to become murderers. (Cf. Coppet, 1973).

10. Some peace-masters never managed to give even one such feast. If a peace-master does give one it is unlikely that he will succeed in offering a second.

11. The products of the "gardens", plants or shellfish and fish are obtained by pulling them up and out of the surface (see Coppet, 1976). Fish and shellfish have "bodies" but no "breath" like taros, coconuts, etc.

12. This exchange of taros and coconuts which are to be replanted is a very important sign of mutual esteem and dedication.

13. When a murderer kills a person, he either brings back the body to his hamlet where he will decide if it is to be eaten or, more frequently, he leaves it on the spot. But when a murderer has killed a person from among his own kin he brings the corpse to the peace-master who will decide what to do with the body.

14. Pigs are raised near "pigs' houses" built in the forest. Fences which exclude the pigs are built around the village grounds and the gardens.

15. Which categorises observed social phenomena as "psychological", "political", "economic", "ideological", etc.

16. In certain rituals or situations the *killing one's own people* value may not have its usual encompassing position but rather may be subordinated to the *eating or leaving to rot* value.

17. The term "replacement" has frequently been used in the present paper as a translation of the 'Aré'Aré word *riki-sia*. However, the word "replacement" should not be understood here as "substitution", a notion which overstresses the individuality of a single object and thus again imposes a Western bias. The formula "chains of transformations" may express more adequately our idea.

18. Even if more than two acts are considered in a series, the reciprocity perspective leads us to search for an equal number of acts after which a fair balance is reached between the parties. It is assumed that at that point it will be possible to quantify the results and to compare the strategy of the two parties.

19. This term indicates that exchange relations cannot be defined either by reference to the parties or to the objects which circulate, or even by reference to them both. An exchange relation supposes the existence of a special "field" where all actions must conform to the contrasted values at work in the society.

In a sense "circulating connubium" (Wouden, 1935) and *échange généralisé* (Lévi-Strauss, 1967) are the first *loci* to have been identified. Both extend to the society as a whole and the "cycles" they deal with link groups (ultimately in an equal position with regard to each other). The cycles involve constantly repeated operations employing circulating objects all of the same sort.

The *chains* discussed in this paper link different transformations which tie together different objects, as well as elements of persons at different stages of their life and death, and in accordance with a special hierarchical order of values. The *échange généralisé* model is intended to operate at a universal level of understanding. The *chains* described here are only to be understood as specific to a given society taken as a whole. Only further research would reveal if other societies, especially in the Melanesian region, build similar chains which resume life through death.

References

COPPET, D. de (1970). 1, 4, 8; 9, 7. La Monnaie: présence des morts et mesure du temps. *L'Homme*, **10**, 17–39.

COPPET, D. de (1973). Premier troc, double illusion. *L'Homme*, **13**, 10–22.

COPPET, D. de (1976). Jardins de vie, jardins de mort en Mélanésie. *Traverses*, **5/6**, 166–177.

COPPET, D. de and ZEMP, H. (1978). " 'Aré'Aré, un peuple mélanésien et sa musique". Le Seuil, Paris.

DUMONT, L. (1966). "Homo Hierarchicus. Essai sur le système des castes". Gallimard, Paris.

DURKHEIM, E. and MAUSS, M. (1903). De quelques formes primitives de classification. *L'Année sociologique*, **6** (1901-2), 1–72. Page references to English edition, "Primitive Classification" (R. Needham, trans.), 1963, Cohen & West, London.

HERTZ, R. (1907). Contribution à une étude sur la représentation collective de la mort. *L'Année sociologique*, **10**, 48–137. Page references to English edition, "Death and The Right Hand" (R. and C. Needham, trans.), 1960, Cohen & West, London.

KAPFERER, B. (1976). "Transaction and Meaning; directions in the anthropology of exchange and symbolic behavior". Institute for the Study of Human Issues, Philadelphia.

LÉVI-STRAUSS, C. (1967). "Les Structures élémentaires de la parenté", 2nd edition. Mouton, Paris.

SAHLINS, M. (1974). "Stone Age Economics". Tavistock, London.

WEINER, A. B. (1976). "Women of Value, Men of Renown". University of Texas Press, Austin.
WEINER, A. B. (1978). The reproductive model in Trobriand society. *Mankind*, **11**, 175–186.
WEINER, A. B. (1979). Trobriand kinship from another view: the reproductive power of women and men. *Man*, **14**, 328–348.
WEINER, A. B. (1980). Reproduction: a replacement for reciprocity. *American Ethnologist*, **7**, 71–85.
WOUDEN, F. A. E. van (1935). "Sociale Structuurtypen in de Groote Oost". Ginsberg, Leiden. English edition, "Types of Social Structure in Eastern Indonesia" (R. Needham, trans.). Nijhoff, The Hague.

Death as Exchange:
two Melanesian cases

ANDREW STRATHERN

The regulative force in the reproductive and regenerative cycles
. . . occurs through death.

Death, then, represents an enormous loss, yet death constitutes
the major regenerating mechanism within the system.

A. Weiner, 1980: 81–82

1

In his elaborate analysis of mortuary customs among the LoDagaa of
Ghana, Goody includes a chapter on "income and outlay" (Goody,
1962: 156–82). He discusses voluntary and compulsory contributions
collected under a variety of rubrics, all within a matrix of kinship and
affinity and entitling contributors to shares in the meat of cows to be
sacrificed at a later stage of the funeral. Expenditures consist of cowrie
payments to the owners of xylophones and drums which are played,
and to the grave-diggers, any excess being saved to buy grave-cloths for
a future occasion. Careful rules determine how the flesh of cattle
sacrificed after the burial should be divided out. It is apparent that the
funeral is also an occasion of pooling, redistribution, and exchange.

For Melanesian societies the emphasis on prestations as a
concomitant of funerals is more striking. Not one paper, but several,
could be written on the topic. Why this difference, if it is real? I argue
that in Melanesian societies a more direct equation is made between
the person and movable wealth, and the problem set by death lies in

the necessary substitution and replacement of the person by means of gifts of wealth objects (cf. Weiner, 1980). These objects both ''oppose'' (cf. Wagner, 1967) the death of the person, and repair links between those connected with one another through that person. The process of replacement and repair may take some time. We are not, therefore, dealing with a single set of contributions and a single occasion of outlay, but with repetitive cycles of payments and returns made for them. The particular ways in which these cycles are constituted also tell us about differences between societies, although the basic ideas which underpin their activities may be very similar.

For the most part here, I shall follow through comparisons between two Highlands societies of Papua New Guinea with which I have been working since 1964, the Melpa and the Wiru. To date, contrasts have been established between these two in terms of ideas of sickness, the structure of exchange festivals, and the meaning of bridewealth and matrilateral payments. The question of exchanges at death is not separate from these themes, but integral with them, and consideration of it is therefore facilitated by drawing on ideas previously broached (e.g. A. J. Strathern, 1970, 1978, 1980; M. Strathern, n.d.).

From a sociological point of view, the result of the Melpa (Hagen) requirement to expend wealth at a person's death might be seen as an obviation of inheritance: not only have surviving co-residential kin lost the dead one, but they must also pay out valuables, so their depletion is doubled. But in fact this is a misleading perspective. They are actually using the occasion of death to reaffirm certain relationships of exchange. Further, they replace, by gifts to extra-clan kin, those aspects of the deceased person which tied him or her to their outside network, and simultaneously call in assistance from the same network. It is of interest, therefore, to see what kind of network is activated, given that a general rule reminiscent of that among the LoDagaa prevails: those who contribute to the funeral exchanges can attend the pig-killing which occurs at a later exchange, and they will be given pork; but anyone who has not been so involved would be ashamed to go (cf. Brown, P., 1961: 87). In other words, the funeral is an occasion when practical help is given and assessed, and those who do not help are signalling either a wish to drop out of the network or at least that the event is not one which carries priority for them. The death, then, actually stimulates and re-defines social relationships. It may generate new, or renewed, enmity also, since suspicions of sorcery commonly accompany a death, especially that of a big-man (political leader). The negative counterpart of payments to extra-group kin is the practice of seeking revenge for sorcery, by physical violence or counter-sorcery;

just as the items on which sorcery is carried out — fingernails, hair, exuviae, fragments of food — are the inverted counterparts of wealth objects which are used to pay compensation.

2

In Hagen there are two important phases of mourning: the first begins as soon as a death is made public and lasts until an initial cooking of food is completed, nowadays after about a week. It is during this time that kin and connections of all kinds should bring in gifts of food, sometimes small pigs, and nowadays cash. For a person of significance, and particularly when sorcery is suspected, the body is placed on a high trestle, suspended between two posts (*paka roromen*); mourners arrive covered in fresh yellow clay or ashes; and long speeches are made by orators of the deceased's clan. (These practices had largely been suppressed in 1964–5 when I began work, but throughout the 1970s they have been revived.) Before the body is buried, senior men kill a small pig or two at night, remove the bark belt and front apron, attach a vine to one of its fingers and call to the *min* or spirit of the dead asking it to give an indication of who did the killing. Putting names to it, and holding the vine, they wait to get an impression of the body jerking on it at a certain name. Any ''information'' thus ''obtained'' is kept a close secret, but steps to make counter-sorcery will be taken quickly.

Throughout this time, close kin arrive, weep, and sing songs of lament. For a big funeral, mourners circulate in a ring round the *paka* or stamp around the ceremonial ground. Women cry and sing most intensively and for the longest time, prolonging their tears throughout the period of the initial cooking of food. The crescendo of cries which accompany the departure of the body to its grave fades away only gradually, and the arrival of a new kinsman will occasion a fresh outburst. Hardest of all is if a son or daughter is away elsewhere and returns after the body is already nailed in the coffin. Sons are likely enough to throw themselves on the coffin and refuse to let it be buried for a while. The coffin itself is a Christian innovation, which was just becoming established in 1964. Previously bodies were wrapped in tree-bark bound with vines, and propped partly on branches and leaves till the flesh decomposed and bones could be taken as relics. The skull was the most important part for this purpose: a big-man's skull was taken and placed inside a small sacrificial house sheltered behind the living men's house (*wuö peng manga*). Sons made domestic sacrifices to it thereafter. No skulls are taken in this way now, though sacrifices certainly do continue: in other words, the disappearance of skull houses is because of mission influences but does not equate with the ending of sacrifices to ghosts. Any killing of pigs is also a sacrifice, if it is marked by thoughts in the mind of the killer, directed towards the ghosts and their power over health, fertility, and general well-being.

A person is supposed to pronounce last words (*könt ik, kant ik*) on the approach of death, giving kinsfolk an idea of how property should be distributed. In practice, if the person is old, little movable property remains (hence the fundamental change which the accumulation of cash up till death would make to this system). Their last wish is most likely directed towards the slaughter of a final pig from their herd, either to eat before they die or to be used at the funeral. A big pig may be saved until the next stage, which usually occurs more than a month (sometimes many months) later.

This is the *peng ndi kng* (head-hair pig). Frequently pigs are killed together for several persons who have died and a large collective distribution takes place. There are a number of different categories of recipients, while the responsibility for holding the occasion rests again on the group-mates of the deceased, if he was a man, or the husband's people, if it was a married woman who died. Timing depends on supplies of pigs, other commitments, agreed decisions by men of different sub-groups in the clan. Recipients are announced in terms of their tribe and clan affiliation, and the overall organisation of the event emphasises family and group identities; yet in many instances the true reason for presenting the pork is an individual link between the visitor(s) and the dead person's kin. In practice, also, there are several stages of distribution: (a) when pork and vegetables are removed from the earth-ovens, the man who has cooked the food makes an initial, private allocation to his family and other intimate guests; (b) sides of pork are laid in a house overnight and next day taken to a ceremonial ground for formal display and later division into pieces for giving to assembled visitors from many clans around; (c) recipients take their pork and re-divide parts of it for immediate consumption among themselves; (d) the rest they take home, usually re-cooking it before distributing it again.

This "imprinting" of group identities on the occasion of public presentation is significant, because it falls into line with what happens at times of bridewealth and *moka* exchange payments (on the latter see A. J. Strathern, 1971). Then, too, men appear in group formations, and pigs or pork are handed out in and to the names of clans, even if only a few members of the clans are participating. The usage shows how network relationships are assimilated into the actors' models of social structure: a death is structurally comparable to bridewealth or to a *moka*, because bridewealth is itself seen as a kind of indemnity for the "head" of the bride, and *moka* is often generated out of compensation payments for a killing (*wuö peng iti*, to make man-head).

3

Moka indicates the point about death and exchange in its sharpest form. Death releases exchange, compensation payments build up into alliance. This can happen in Hagen whether the death is due to violence or not. Regardless of the circumstances of death, a major payment at the time of the *peng ndi* should go to kinsfolk of the maternal clan of the deceased. There is a classic syndrome whereby at the funeral such kin mourn loudest, and threaten to destroy gardens or kill pigs in anger at the loss of their sister's son: the agnates must pay to appease them. In practice, they help with food at the first stage, and at the second receive a reward, along with other groups. One indigenous interpretation of the term *peng ndi* for this second stage is that it refers to the time of throwing away relics of the dead, including the wig of human hair which is traditional for men. It is worth recalling also, however, that a payment is made to maternal kin by the father of a child after its first hair-cutting, the head hair being seen as a sign of growth, facilitated by the goodwill of the mother and her people: this payment following birth is structurally correlative to the payment after death.

The point I wish to bring out here is that in either case such payments can also be converted into *moka*. This depends entirely on the wishes of those involved. During the period of pacification in the 1950s and 1960s, and before road accidents and tribal fighting began to generate new deaths and reasons for exchange, it became a popular option to use death payments to maternal kin as new beginning points for *moka*. In this guise they were taken out of the ordinary context of *peng ndi* cookings and described as *kik kapa roromen*, "they strike off the ashes" (from the body of the mourners), i.e. as payments to make the maternal kin stop their mourning and return to ordinary life. Any payment made under this rubric is intended in fact to issue in *moka*. During the deceased's lifetime certain exchanges may already have been built up between his agnates (or her husband's people) and the maternal kin; as a result of *kik kapa* these are augmented and extended. The present round of activities engaged in by a senior big-man in whose settlement I live, Ndamba, is intended precisely to orientate his sons towards future exchanges with his own maternal clansfolk, following his death. He thus clearly envisages his death as a means of strengthening, rather than weakening, exchange networks; but he is working hard to organise it that way before he dies, for his death would not *automatically* bring about such a result. (A culminating gift was made to his maternal kin in August 1980.)

Death by killing, however, sets a more peremptory question. Then payments must be made or revenge sought. And once the choice is made, either exchanges or revenges have to repeat themselves over time. There is an indigenous model of how *moka* starts, stressing that it may come from small initial payments after a death, building itself into escalating competitions. The process of making compensation payments is mapped onto *moka* as follows. In *moka* an initiatory or solicitory gift is followed by a reciprocal, but larger, main gift; in compensation the victim's side give a man-bone (*wuö-ombil*) gift to the killers, saying: "Here is the bone of the man you killed. You did not really eat him or enjoy anything, so here is a bone for you to have." The equation here between "bone" and "wealth" is clear, but the reference to eating needs a little clarification. The Melpa do not eat people: this is indeed the whole point of the saying. If you kill a pig, you can eat it, but not a man. The statement powerfully underplays, then, the significance of killing and the satisfaction which revenge is supposed to bring, referred to as "eating the man's liver". It invites, instead, the conversion of killing into exchange, victims into pigs, things which really can be eaten. The killers then respond by making the "man-head" payment (*wuö peng*). As the head is the most important bone in the body, so the man-head payment should exceed the bone payment. The head is the life value of the person. As I have noted, bridewealth is paid to "make the head of a woman", and the completion of any aimed-at figure in the price of a pig or a vehicle is also spoken of as "to kill the head of" the thing desired. The superiority of head over bone thus gives the blueprint for the excess of *moka* over the initiatory or "scraping" gift (*pek*) and the reason also for continuing the exchange relationship generated by the first pair of gifts. After this, the exchangers are able to "see a road" between themselves and to "make roads of pigs". The death is endlessly recapitulated in speeches and contrasted with the current good practice of making *moka*. At the same time the memory of the death, and therefore potential enmity, is kept alive; this in turn giving a neat reason for the repetition of gift-giving between the two sides and the competitive edge which informs such repetition and keeps it from becoming dull. In a sense, the original death turns into a kind of sacrifice, commemorated by both sides, as a reason for their present alliance, a negative image which supplies the reason why they must always make the effort towards positive friendship. In principle, such relations can continue indefinitely; in practice it will be interesting to see, for the major sets of exchanges between allies, whether shifts in reference to particular deaths as "charters" for action will be discernible between 1964, 1974 and perhaps 1984 when a main return for a large *moka* of 1974 is to be expected (A. J. Strathern, 1979: ch. 13).

4

There are no huge public prestations comparable to the *moka* among the Wiru; their particular bent has been to elaborate on and stress the individually based life-cycle payments as such. Payments for one's body or "skin" continue through life. A man should make them for his children to their mother's people, for otherwise the children will fall sick, perhaps die. The mother's brother in Wiru is a more stern character than in Melpa, although in both cases the uncle can exercise mystical powers. A Wiru uncle may spit on a sister's child and cause warts to grow, which can never be removed. He can send his *ipono* or spirit into the liver of the nephew or niece and eat it, causing wasting and death. In this regard, the Wiru ideas are close to those of the Daribi (Wagner, 1967). All the more reason, then, for ensuring that life-payments are indeed made. The mother's people, who have "borne" one (*opianango*), clearly also carry powers of death. It is as though in controlling birth they also are seen as controlling death, and hence the person's total lifespan, whereas the father is seen only as initiating the life of his children. To keep them alive, he must pay for the power of life, which is maternal.

The dogmas here are strong and impressive. Along with them, however, goes a variation in practice which is rather remarkable. One big-man I know simply refused to make child-payments for children by his first wife, in part to punish her, since he suspected she had killed some of her children at birth. This is an extreme case. More frequently, people choose *which* maternal kin to give to. Marriages are less clustered between friendly groups than in Hagen, and the unit of settlement is not the exogamous clan, but a locality of intermarrying small lineages loosely tied together by a "phratry" ideology. Some marriages, then, tie these lineages together, while in other cases women from distant places are married. Maternal kin may therefore be either very close or very distant, and in neither case does marriage contain the same ideal overlap between intergroup and interpersonal interests that it does in Hagen. In these circumstances, people show a strong preference for finding classificatory or "once-removed" maternal kin to exchange with from within their own locality. This can be done easily enough, by giving to the mother's kin of a lineage brother or to one's father's mother's, or (less often) mother's mother's people, for example. The lack of concern about distant kin may have to do with the idea that *ipono* only attack those nearby; it may also be influenced by the fact that with these distant kin one is less likely to fall into a quarrel, so one does not in practice have to appease them. In the past, a simpler explanation held: distant maternal kin would be in enemy territory and could not be visited at all.

It is at times of pig-kills that life-cycle payments are pre-eminently made. The basic pattern is that those who are paying for "skin" give shell valuables, especially pearl shells (in Wiru, these traditional valuables are retained, though cash is also now used). Those receiving shells return whole ribcages of pork. Perishable wealth which builds up substance or skin is thus returned for permanent wealth objects which "replace" or are "instead of" or "for" that skin. Therefore, at a pig-kill, some ribcages are given to those who gave shells much earlier; some new shell gifts are brought by affines who wish to receive pork; the killers also themselves give away some shells, to ensure return gifts of pork later. These highly significant gifts are all made on an inter-personal basis, without any group "imprinting" in the Hagen fashion. Other gifts, of legs of pork, may carry significance in terms of intergroup alliance or hostility, but they are not based on the combination of compensation + competition which characterises *moka*. Only in relation to death do we find a certain parallelism emerging between the two systems.

Two categories of prestation are generated by death among the Wiru, the first known as *kioli*, the second *kange*. The former is obligatory, the latter optional. At a death, kinsfolk go into mourning much as in Hagen (they are said to be in *tumai yapu*, the house of death). Again, women are prominent in crying and singing: new laments are often made. Commemoration of the dead was sharper in the past: men and women wore bones of kin or spouses round their necks; the bones of a baby which died might be hung up in a netbag and kept for some months, wrapped in sweet-smelling grasses, while its mother mourned her loss. Skulls were kept and placed collectively in a hamlet or village-based cult house (*tapa yapu*). The missions again forbade all these customs. Since 1974 almost all the people have been baptised by one or other mission. In 1980 a first move to revive the building of a traditional long-house for a pig-kill, with associated rituals towards ghosts, has been made by a single outlying group. It seems probable that *kange* was associated in the past with both warfare and a keener pursuit of prestige by men, and to this the people may also now be returning. During 1980 big-men began increasingly to discuss such *kange* gifts. *Kioli* payments, however, have never lapsed. Moreover they must be prepared very shortly after the death, while the initial phase of mourning is still in swing. In one case I saw in 1967, the father of a young child which died while still at the breast began preparing items of wealth as soon as he realised that its life was over, and proceeded with the collection of payments the next day, almost as though to do so could assuage, or draw his thoughts away from, the death itself.

The child here was Apuka, son of Pendena, of Angaliri clan, and he died late on Saturday, December 2nd 1967. After a day's mourning he was buried on the Sunday. Throughout that day Angaliri men gave helping gifts to Pendena: I recorded 6 pearl shells and a salt pack presented in this way, and Pendena sorted them out. Crying and singing continued on the next day, and on the 5th Pendena gave the *kioli* proper (Table 1). He received two pigs also in help from affines (one from his ZH, one from a W classif. MB).

The groups from which the recipients came were:

1. M's local lineage and congeners (Koliri of Kerepali village) — 10 recipients;
2. MM's local lineage (Epea of Tunda and Tarini villages) — 3;
3. MMM's local lineage and congeners (Pakiri of Tunda) — 4;
4. FM's kin, FZ, FZH (but also belonging to category 2) — 3;
5. Co-resident — 1 (this may appear simply because I did not elucidate the relevant relationship, however).

From this list the true predominance of payments to matrilateral kin is apparent, as is also the fact of continuing to make payments to MM's and MMM's people when these are also co-resident in the village or nearby villages belonging to the same political confederation (in this case Peri of Tunda). This is not to say that the gifts have any direct political significance, since they are patently made to a network of kinsfolk who are chosen because they are also neighbours and are relied on for help in other activities as well.

The laments sung for Apuka remind us that he was very young, too young to talk, when he died:

TABLE 1

Kioli for Apuka, child of Pendena (December 5th 1967)

Recipient	Relationship to Apuka	Items given
1. Poya	MB	1 large pig; 1 small pig (for return); 1 bailer shell
2. Yapai	MFBS (= classif. MB)	1 small pig; 1 pearl shell
3. Nakwaima	MFBSS (= classif. cross-cousin)	1 pearl shell
4. Kuluwa (son of 2)	MFBSS (= classif. cross-cousin)	1 pearl shell
5. Kunukuna	MFBS (= classif. MB)	1 pearl shell
6. Tepi	FZH (also classif. MMBS)	1 pig
7. Kepambo	MeZ	1 pearl shell; $4.
8. "Wife of Tata"	MMZ	1 pearl shell; 1 pack of salt; $2.
9. Taguna (son of 5)	MFBSS (= classif. cross-cousin)	1 pearl shell, 1 nassa headband
10. "Mother of Waki"	MMM lineage member	$2
11. Timini (son of 5)	MFBSS (classif. cross-cousin)	1 red bird of paradise plume; $1.
12. Yanda	MM lineage member	$2.
13. Kupi	MMM lineage member	1 pearl shell; 1 nassa headband (in return for a gift received before)
14. Ayopo	Co-resident (Windiperi clan)	$2 (in return for an axe)
15. Andia	FM classif. BS (= father's classif. cross-cousin)	1 axe; 1 pearl shell
16. Wipai	Married to MMM people	1 axe; $2
17. Yokame (wife of 6)	FZ	1 axe (in return for small pig brought and given to 1)
18. Akena	MMM lineage member	1 axe (in return for an axe)
19. Liriame (daughter of 8)	MMZD (married to Angaliri)	$4

TABLE 1 (continued)

Recipient	Relationship to Apuka	Items given
20. Pengene	MF people (classif.) (married to Angaliri)	$2
21. "Wife of Poya"	MBW	$1

Totals: 4 pigs; 9 pearl shells; 5 other valuables; 4 axes; $22

Notes

1. The descriptions of kin-relationships here follow the explanations I was given at the time, though I have in some instances made them precise by checking in genealogies separately recorded.

2. Except where otherwise recorded, the gifts were made for no subsequent return. The explanation given was that if Apuka had lived he would have made payments to these kinfolk, and so his father made them now. It is notable in that almost everything went to people living in the general Tunda village area (excluding only 7 and 15). In some instances the payments were in direct return for items received earlier by Pendena, who acted as sole donor, though helped in discussion by senior men of his group, the Angaliri.

3. The large pig presented first to Poya (no. 1) had already been nominally allocated to Apuka, and was therefore, in accordance with custom, given for no return to his MB.

4. The MMZ (no. 8), a somewhat querulous lady, complained about the small amounts of wealth being paid, claiming that she had helped to look after the child while its father was away working on contract labour at coastal plantations, hence she should be given more now (cf. Brown, P., 1961: 90). In the event she and other women were told to go away and get food from their gardens to sell to the government officer, whose patrol was to visit the village the next day, and by this means she was quietened.

5. Women appear as recipients in 7 cases. Of no. 7 I was told that she would pass the shell on to her husband, who would then give it to his own mother's kin. In this way goods continue to travel on matrilateral circuits, and the overall extent to which marriages tend to be contracted in a given local area determines, at least in part, the curvature of the flows of wealth.

6. In cases 13 and 18 it is notable that the gifts were repayments. It seems likely that Pendena exchanges with these as relatively distant kin because they are also neighbours. No. 16 may have received because he was also a well-known ritual expert.

7. Pendena's relations with his wife's father's group were complicated by the fact that he had spent much of his own time away from Tunda. His father died of sorcery, Longai (a senior man) told me, and the mother then re-married a Koliri man of a nearby Maupini village. When Pendena grew up he himself married Peame, a Koliri girl, of a different lineage, at Kerepali village, and went to live there. Later his WyB died of sorcery, and his Tunda kinsfolk said that Pendena himself might be accused of causing the death. They therefore gave a *kioli* to the wife's people to enable him to return: two pigs and a large pack of indigenous salt. The fact that this *kioli* had been made for himself may have increased Pendena's alacrity in making a "return" *kioli* for his dead son, especially as there had been suspicion of sorcery earlier.

8. On September 11th 1980 I asked Pendena and his wife if they would mind recounting to me the items he had given for Apuka's *kioli*. Beginning with the pig he had presented to the MB, Poya, as a *kamo kai* (pig to wipe off the mourning clay), Pendena showed an exact recall of the payments he had made to the close maternal kin, and also those to "his own side" (nos 6 and 15 in the Table). He left out all items given to women and to more distant matrilateral kinsfolk. His wife was also clearly most anxious that the items given to the men of her lineage should be accurately stated. This is an interesting example of selective memory, which emphasises the prime importance of the mother's brother and his lineage.

Dearest child, Apuka,
What did you do, my son?
My son, I am sorry for you,
My good child Apuka,
What has happened to you?

Tomorrow they will build a house
For you to sleep in alone,
Opossum-child of the Molea stream.

My son, I bore you and I am sorry now,
Oh my mother, oh my child,
What did you do, why did you die?
Dear child, Apuka mine,
You said no words to us.

Given this, the amounts of wealth paid out by his father were by Wiru standards quite considerable, and certainly greater than those a Hagen father would expect to pay to mother's kin at the death of a young child. The explanation is contained in the direct statement made by my assistant, Kapu, who is himself of the MM group (Epea), that Pendena was paying because Apuka himself would have paid his mother's people had he lived. In other words, the expectation that gifts will flow to the mother's people is so strong that a father has to make up for the loss of these in case the anger of the maternal kin is again directed towards him. Therein lies an apparent contradiction: if mother's kin expect payments, why should they show malevolence and destroy a source of such payments? There was no suggestion in this case that the child died because of the *awa*'s (MB's) curse, yet it is plain that such a fear exists, and no other explanation of Apuka's death was offered either. The matter was in fact left as a mystery, expressed in the songs by the repeated phrase "What did you do?". Apuka's paternally derived individuality, expressed by reference to his long, handsome nose like that of the Kareo opossum living by a stream in Angaliri territory, was also briefly celebrated. Had he lived, this individuality, or "nose" (*timini*), might have given him prominence as an adult. Meanwhile the promise of his "body" (*tingine*) was given as soon as he was born from his mother, and to the string of those groups from which "mothering" was derived (M, MM, MMM) payments had to be made.

The example indicates, with much poignancy, how strongly the "life track" of the individual is anticipated by the Wiru. The contrast with Hagen culture, and its stress on status and achievement, is striking;

but the domain of *kange* payments does provide scope for achievement in Wiru also.

Not all men make *kange*. My survey in Tunda village in 1967 also came at an "unusual" time, since it was done five years after pacification, when a hiatus had developed in exchange relations, and big-manship, such as it had been, was definitely at a low ebb. Some men who would ordinarily have begun their own *kange* had therefore held back, because of mission disapproval of all "pagan" ceremonies. Despite this, I recorded in 1967 the *kange* made by 36 men, of middle-age or older, and it was clear that the practice, like Hagen *moka*, is not the prerogative of big-men; although it is certain that big-men had given more *kange* than others. As an example I cite those made by Kumbea, a recognised big-man in the Angaliri group in Tunda, with three wives and an established reputation in pig-killing at festivals (Table 2).

Kange in the past was conducted with considerable ceremony, and might be made either at a concerted, group level as a compensation for deaths sustained by allies or individually as an extension of *kioli* payments made earlier. That prestige was gained by holding a *kange* is clear from remarks that if a group made many *kange* others around would be envious and kill them by sorcery — a statement which would make no sense if applied to the performance of *kioli*. *Kange* payments to allies were in any case a necessity, for otherwise they would withdraw their support. I have not witnessed a payment in the old style, with full decorations, so quote instead a description by Longai, an old man with an excellent, clear memory, who himself had made five *kange* (A. J. Strathern, 1978: 101). His account applies to the context of ally payments:

When they were planning to make a *kange* for a man, they would hold up two pearl shells and say "This man will not stay in the ground, I will make *kange* for him". This would be for someone from an ally group of us Peri, someone from Weriko or Maupini. The men who called on him to help them fight would say "Let us plant a cordyline for this man". The two sides would then first exchange pigs, or a pig would be exchanged against two shells, given to "break the pig's head". Then I, or another man, would kill one of the pigs and all the Tunda men would contribute pearl shells to me in return for eating small parts of the meat. When the shells were prepared, I would put on a cassowary feather head-dress (this is the *kange*), I painted white circles round my eyes so that I resembled the *kolokolai* bird, and I rubbed charcoal all over my skin. Others did the same and we stalked up and down like ghosts before paying the *kange*. Later when the recipients themselves killed pigs they would return to us ribcages and sides of pork.

Such payments in Hagen have proliferated and grown into full-blown *moka* prestations, but in Wiru this has not happened; instead,

TABLE 2
Kange made by Kumbea-Kaiama, up to 1967

	Recipient and relationship to donor	Occasion of payment	Items given	Assistance from others	Items received in return
1.	Kelea, WB	After deaths of two of his children	40 pearl shells	3 shells, 1 in return for a pig	"Some" ribcages of pork; 1 live pig
2.	Lawa, FBWBS (= MBS)	After death of the FB, Yoke	40 pearl shells	5 shells	1 live pig
3.	Pia, MBS (who gave them to his FM people)	After death of the MB, Mandi	(a) 4 shells and a pig (b) 40 pearl shells	—	1 live pig

Notes

1. Kumbea stressed that he had given most of the items in *kange* for little or no return, and also that the bulk of the items were supplied by himself with little help from others. Other cases show that it is quite usual to expect pork in return for shells and to receive aid from kinsfolk in raising the shells needed. Kumbea's reluctance to make more *kange* than this is probably related to his perception that little is returned; indeed he said that he would no longer exchange with his MM's people because of the poor returns he received from the second-stage recipients of 3.

2. In 1980 Kumbea's co-resident lineage mates and others of Angaliri who saw themselves as his followers combined to help him make a substantial further *kange* to his cross-cousins, particularly to Pendepo. There were protracted arguments about whether to add a live pig to the gift, as was customary, even though very few returns would be made for the pearl shells. One of his daughters brought him a pig for this purpose, and was discomfited when her father was inclined to keep it rather than passing it on. She argued that she had brought it because this *kange* was instead of making a prestation after he died, and so it should not be withheld from her father's maternal kin.

only the individual, uncoordinated *kange* have continued, a return to the interpersonal network of ties which also informs the *kioli* payments. As I have noted, interest in new *kange* payments quickened during 1980 and they became a dominant topic of conversation in Tunda village.

5

Differences between the precise patterns of death-payments in Melpa and Wiru are clear, and follow the stress laid on personal achievement in the former society, as against matrilaterally derived "body" in the latter. But one feature definitely links the two together, and in terms common to many, if not all, the societies of Melanesia: death is seen primarily as an occasion for regenerating exchange ties. Much more emphasis is placed on the acts of payment and exchange which follow hard on the funeral than on the interment of the dead person or the construction of memorials for him or her. In both societies there are ideas about places that dead ghosts travel to and about the influence they can exercise over living kinsfolk. But there is little or no idea that the way the body is laid in its grave can influence the security of the ghost, or that the dead person's spirit can use any treasures of the living world in its subsequent existence. For these reasons, the burial of valuable shells with the bodies of the deceased would make no cultural sense. Rather, it is the gift which is also the sacrifice to, and for, the dead. In Hagen when pigs are killed and their flesh presented to the mother's kin and many other groups around, the occasion is also overtly one of sacrifice, at which the ghosts from all the various groups are expected to participate. In Wiru, there is no special pig-killing of this kind, but the swift and earnest presentation of wealth items to the "ones who bore" the dead person bears the unmistakeable mark of an offering too. In both cases, too, we find an equation between "wealth" and "the person". Just as the person in life dispenses wealth to kinsfolk and partners and thus achieves social identity, so when the person dies a last recognition, or else a re-creation of those "parts" which he or she demonstrated while active, must be put in hand. In Hagen, indeed, the person can be replicated and magnified after death through the extension of exchanges which can follow death itself; a war-hero's death may be paid for over and over again, to echo in the speeches of men for generations. That type of continuity is not aimed at in Wiru, where the memory of a leader may, however, be perpetuated in the form of names succeeded to in a patrilineal group; and where, on the other hand, personal individuality is always being returned to the folds of matrilateral kinship (cf. A. L. Epstein, 1979: 201, on the significance of the Tolai *tambu* currency, which has to be saved in life and then disbursed at death, in order to enable the soul to enter the place of the dead).

Since the person is seen in this way as creating an identity through exchange activities, it clearly makes sense that if the aim of funeral activities is partially to recreate such an identity, lost by the person's death, then exchanges are the roads along which the recreation, or replacement, can take place. The Wiru matrilateral payments might, indeed, be seen as "paying off" rather than renewing ties, but the extension of payments beyond the mother's immediate local lineage to MM's and MMM's groups indicates that this is not what in fact happens. Indeed the rubric of matrilateral payments is employed to select out congenial recipients of gifts within the wider local community.

My interpretation here is related to a passage in Marie Reay's study of the Kuma, who live just to the east of the Melpa; and also to Roy Wagner's account of the Daribi, eastern neighbours of the Wiru. Here is Reay, on the death of a big-man:

He himself has inherited no great number of valuables from his father. When a man of great wealth dies, his maternal cross-cousins lie with his wives and slaughter some of his pigs, reducing the herd his sons will inherit to the number owned by one of little wealth. Some of the dead man's plumes and shells decorate the body when mourners are due to arrive, and these valuables are left in the charnel house or the grave. The sons themselves break up many of their father's shell ornaments and pile the fragments on top of his body. If the dead man's wealth were not destroyed, his heirs would be suspected of causing his death by witchcraft. The valuables they give his maternal relatives as compensation for his death have been collected largely from other members of his sub-subclan . . .

Reay, 1959: 97

The body of a big-man is decorated, then; but in denial of any desire to inherit his wealth his sons destroy valuables and pile them on the body itself: a pattern not, to my knowledge, found in Hagen, but indicating by inversion the same rule that I find inscribed in Hagen death exchanges, that wealth is not for the dead to carry away intact. The Kuma sons, in denying the smashed shell to their exchange partners, also deny it entirely by breaking it to pieces. Shells are *exchange* objects; the alternative to giving them away is not hoarding or burying them, but destroying them.

This feature of the angry destruction of wealth and other resources at death is matched by accounts from the Daribi (and indeed the Kuma themselves, Reay, 1959: 69) of how maternal kin may threaten to break up the settlement of agnatic kinsfolk on the death of their sister's child:

Their attitude is traditionally one of bitter reproach toward the clan mates of the deceased, who are accused of negligence in allowing him to die. Customarily they vent their anger by cutting down food-bearing trees, especially bananas . . . They may also chop at the house with their axes, break their own bows or walking sticks upon entering, or attack members of the deceased's immediate family. People are often beaten with sticks . . .

Wagner, 1972: 146

Here there is a sense of violent rupture, and a wish to take revenge on those to whom the maternally derived body of the person has been entrusted. Again, there is no exact parallel with the Wiru, but the feeling of "ownership" on the part of the maternal kin is expressed powerfully in the Daribi custom. The Daribi also make payments to such kin throughout life, as do Wiru, ending with a payment known as *puiabo*, of between 10 and 20 "units" of wealth, paid by co-clansmen for a man, and by husband to wife's father and brothers for a woman (these then pass it to her maternal kin in turn) (Wagner, op.cit.: 52–53). Wagner also writes:

The definition of social units . . . involves the substitution of relatively "permanent" items of wealth for rights in human beings. These items include . . . shell ornaments, axes, bush knives, and Australian currency, as well as meat, represented by live pigs, pork, smoked marsupials, chicken or tinned meat.

ibid.: 49

The rupture of death can be mended, then, only by renewing the flows of these items. Conversely, a death may be required to stimulate that flow. The former proposition underlies Hagen and Wiru death payments; the latter is characteristic of the logic of certain cargo cults, themselves perhaps in part influenced by Christian ideas of "redemption". Burridge has formulated this point as follows:

Since existence in community, a moral order, necessarily entails existence within a network of obligations, redemption itself can only be realised at or after that appropriate death which brings to an end an appropriate mode of discharging one's obligations.

Burridge, 1969: 6

However, in Melanesia, these obligations are discharged in such a way as in fact to create new obligations; so that, while redemption does not properly occur, neither is cargo found nor do social relations come to an end.

The contexts in which this renewal of obligations occur are two: first, as I have repeatedly stressed, by gifts to maternal kin; and second, through sacrifices to the spirits of the dead, seen as agencies which transcend the rotting of maternally created flesh and blood. It is here that we see the significance of the classic opposition between bone and blood, the former usually identified with paternal procreation. It is bone which endures and remains in the ground after flesh has been reabsorbed. Indeed, in Hagen, this distinction is employed to express the difference between enduring claims to land and transient claims to the use of the land's surface for purposes of gardening. The former is *möi ombil*, "the bone of the land"; while food-plants are said to grow on its "grease", *möi kopong* (cf. Goldman, 1980: 217). The anger of maternal kin at the loss of their sister's children through death may be interpreted, then, as anger that the part which is theirs will rot most speedily, and moreover its "grease" will go down into another group's land. Hence they must be paid for this. Nor do they ordinarily expect to claim the bones, which remain as a locus of supernatural power for those who retain them. Sacrifice to the "heads" of dead big-men, in particular, is the means of access to such power, and invocation of their names recapitulates those groups and individuals who claim access.

In familiar fashion, then, exchange relations are set up, not only between the paternal and maternal kin of the deceased, but also between the living kin and the spirits of the dead themselves. This again shows that death does not mean the ending of obligations, but their renewal and sometimes even their amplification.

If we now return to the starting point of this paper, which was the contrast between Goody's treatment of "income and outlay" in his analysis of LoDagaa funerals, and the "total" emphasis on exchange relations and their reproduction which seems necessary in the analysis of Melanesian funeral practices, we may ask further if there are particular material and ideological factors involved in such a contrast. To assess the former of these factors would require a complete re-examination of the data, which I cannot do here, though it is worthwhile to refer to Barnes's brief but seminal observations in his "African models in the New Guinea Highlands" article (Barnes, 1962: 6). In terms of ideology, however, what stands out is the clarity with which the social person in Melanesia is conceived of as a product of paternal and maternal procreation, and it is this division which is also taken as the model for wider structural relations. In such a schema it is the person who is the prime form of "movable property" and not any material property which he or she "owns" and others inherit. The indigenous model of society is one of reproduction not inheritance, and death generates a separation of the paternal and maternal forces brought together at the time of birth. Further, even this separation contributes to the replenishment of life itself, since wealth is used to repay maternal kin for their contribution of flesh and the same wealth can be used to obtain an equal amount of life-giving female fertility; while the bones remain with the paternal kin, as a sign of a continuing male procreative presence, which has to be activated through the sacrifice of pigs, the nearest complete equivalent to people.

References

BARNES, J. A. (1962). African models in the New Guinea Highlands. *Man*, **62**, 5–9.

BROWN, P. (1961). Chimbu death payments. *Journal of the Royal Anthropological Institute*, **91**, 77–97.

BURRIDGE, K. O. L. (1969). "New Heaven, New Earth: a Study of Millenarian Activities". Basil Blackwell, Oxford.

EPSTEIN, A. L. (1979). Tambu. The shell-money of the Tolai. *In* "Fantasy and Symbol: Essays Presented to G. Devereux" (R. Hook, ed.), pp. 149–205. Academic Press, London and New York.

GOLDMAN, L. R. (1980). Speech categories and the study of disputes: a New Guinea example. *Oceania*, **50**, 209–27.

GOODY, J. R. (1962). "Death, Property and the Ancestors". Tavistock, London.

REAY, M. O. (1959). "The Kuma: Freedom and Conformity in the New Guinea Highlands". Melbourne University Press, Melbourne.

STRATHERN, A. J. (1970). Wiru penthonyms. *Bijdragen tot de taal-, land- en volkenkunde*, **126**, 59–74.

STRATHERN, A. J. (1971), "The Rope of Moka". Cambridge University Press, Cambridge.

STRATHERN, A. J. (1978). "Finance and production" revisited: in pursuit of a comparison. *In* "Research in Economic Anthropology" (G. Dalton, ed.) vol. I, pp. 73–104. JAI Press Inc., Greenwich, Connecticut.

STRATHERN, A. J. (1979). "Ongka". Duckworth, London.

STRATHERN, A. J. (1980). The central and the contingent: bridewealth among the Melpa and Wiru. *In* "The Meaning of Marriage Payments" (J. Comaroff, ed.), pp. 49–66. Academic Press, London and New York.

STRATHERN, M. (n.d.) Culture in a netbag: the manufacture of a subdiscipline in anthropology. Malinowski Memorial lecture, delivered March 11th, 1980.

WAGNER, R. (1967). "The Curse of Souw". University of Chicago Press, Chicago.

WAGNER, R. (1972). "Habu: the Innovation of Meaning in Daribi Religion". University of Chicago Press, Chicago.

WEINER, A. (1980). Reproduction: a replacement for reciprocity. *American Ethnologist*, **7**, 71–85.

Chagga "Customary" Law and the Property of the Dead

SALLY FALK MOORE

> When the phenomena of primitive societies emerge into light, it
> seems impossible to dispute . . . that Intestate Inheritance is a
> more ancient institution than Testamentary Succession.
>
> <div align="right">Maine, 1861: 195; <i>see also</i> ibid.: 177</div>

The situation may have been a good deal more complicated and varied than Sir Henry Maine ever imagined. Typologically there are many intermediate forms that lie between intestate succession and testamentary allocation, and there are curious combinations of the two. In certain systems, such as that of the Chagga of Kilimanjaro in the early 1900s, though everyone died technically intestate, and there were rules designating preferred heirs, there remained an important element of contingency. Final disposition of property after death was in the discretion of a body of kin, and they had the choice of *not* following the rules of preference where they thought it appropriate.

Paradoxically, for the kin group, the declared wishes of the decedent could be among the most important considerations they had to take into account. To the extent that it was believed that the dead were aware of the activities of the living and had power over their well-being, any disregard of the expressed preferences of the dead could carry perils. But the possibility of being done in by some dissatisfied spirit was always uncertain, and the lust for wealth might leave the living willing to take the risk. A man who wanted a more reliable means of control over his affairs could take this-worldly measures before he died. Not only could he make transfers *inter vivos*, but, as far as *post mortem* disposition goes, he could make his desires regarding allocations and disinheritance widely known, and could exact specific public promises regarding these. But if there were a particular person he wanted to disinherit, even more extreme measures were available. He could take the precaution of making a particular heir with a claim to priority completely disreputable, arranging the disqualification of the heir through witchcraft and other accusations. Moreover, for good measure, he could publicly put a curse on anyone who might disobey him. If the "intestate" decedent were sufficiently determined to structure the situation so that his wishes would be followed, the allocating body could be left with little choice.

That is a kind of intestacy all right, but with a difference: it was manipulable by prearrangement, and/or modifiable *post mortem* by an allocating body. The existence of this kind of systematic combination of apparently fixed rules of intestate succession and an institutionalised mode of discretionary application, permits a great deal of adaptability to the exigencies of special cases. It also allows for the accommodation of historical change without necessarily appearing to do so. Since, in theory, the transfer of property from one generation to the next is one classic means by which the reproduction of a stable social order is thought to be effected, any transformation either in the contexts of inheritance or in its practices is of the greatest sociological interest. It is one way to get at the particular cultural route by which macro-economic changes travel to the micro-level, sometimes without appearing to be effecting any change at all. The Chagga of Kilimanjaro present an interesting instance of such a situation.[1]

For most of this century, the Chagga have seen themselves as applying the traditional legal rules of inheritance by means of an indigenous procedure. But the context in which this "traditional" process takes place has changed radically. The hand that once held a spear now holds a transistor radio, and the plot that once produced mostly bananas is now full of coffee bushes. There is a voluminous record of Chagga law made by the missionary Bruno Gutmann in the earliest decades of this century but published in 1926. To a great extent what he described was a system of rules. Many of the selfsame rules are cited by Chagga today to explain who happens to have what property in a patrilineage.

Because Gutmann's work is the baseline from which historical inquiry into Chagga law proceeds, one is confronted with the problem of trying to understand how the lineage rules of property law he described actually operated in practice a hundred years ago, without having available for that period the kind of behavioural field material that is accessible now. This question is especially acute where particular rules seem to continue to be as they were. Customary law, however often reiterated, is not a fixed and unchanging body of rules detached from their historical milieu. This problem has led me to try to develop some approaches to the contextualisation of legal rules of which two will be presented in this paper. One consists of patching together some demographic and economic information to suggest the impact of changed material conditions over time. The other consists of looking at particular case histories of the exercise of discretionary decision. What emerges about Chagga lineage structure is that the social location of discretion over certain allocations of property, and over certain decisions, has on the whole remained, as far as one can tell, substantially unchanged since Gutmann wrote. However, the conditions that have to be taken into account in the making of discretionary decisions have changed considerably.

There is nothing mysterious about the reason why some of the law associated with the Chagga kinship property complex has survived, albeit in a transformed state. Today, as a hundred years ago, each Chagga household lives permanently in the midst of its banana grove. Most households also plant annual crops on secondary plots, but they live in the banana grove. In the older areas of settlement, most of these individually held groves are in patrilineal clusters of anything from half-a-dozen households to more than a hundred.[2] (There are also some scattered households, "isolated" from the point of view of localised patrilineage attachment, but in the older areas of settlement these are in a minority.) For most men in those areas, the localised patrilineage remains their principal social resource, and their avenue to land.

Today, everyone is involved in the cash economy. Coffee is grown in the banana gardens all over the mountain. Land has long been bought and sold. Rich lineage brothers are employed, or do business, as well as having banana/coffee groves. Poor brothers are farmers only. Employment or small businesses are the principal bases of modern economic stratification, with multiple-plot landholding an adjunctive and compounding condition. However, despite the cash economy, socialism, and the Tanzanian villagisation programme, as agnatic control of access to some land has continued, the localised patrilineages go on having considerable vitality in certain areas. Some of the core of Chagga lineage law seems to have survived from the period of independent chiefdoms, through the German colonial rule, from 1916 to 1961, and has continued in being through nearly twenty years of independence. In those areas where lineages have a localised centre, the lineage is hanging on through thick and thin.

Yet the lineage is certainly not what it was. It was once corporate. It not only had an internal organisation dominated by the senior men, but it had an external spokesman, a representative, gifted in oratory, who dealt with the Chief and with other outsiders when collective interests were at issue (Gutmann, 1926: 14–15). There was ultimate collective liability to outsiders for certain offences of members, particularly in the payment of blood-wealth. And there was some collective responsibility for tribute to the Chief and for the fulfilment of punitive *corvée* labour obligations (ibid.: 382, 377). Formerly, the lineage had significant collective external relations with the public political domain. It has none of these any longer.

Internally, while it would be misleading to say that there was collectively owned property, it would be more faithful to the facts to say that the lineage controlled the allocation of unused, unclaimed meadow lands in the general territory where it was settled. It could also assign the properties of members who died leaving no close genealogical heirs. In a sense, this could be called a reversionary right, but that would seem to make a special case of the death of a man without male issue and close kin, when in fact the lineage dealt with the properties of *all* decedents who died in its territory, including the property of wives. When a person died, there was a meeting four days after death, now called the *matanga*, at which a disposition of the properties, claims, and debts of the deceased was made (ibid.: 34). If the deceased were a man, the inheritance of widows and the guardianship of minor children was also arranged at that time. The *matanga* was part of the general administration by the lineage of certain affairs of members. The lineage holds no collective property today and, as indicated earlier, probably held none a hundred years ago. But the *matanga* survives, as do various other aspects of lineage administration of the intra-lineage affairs of its members. Obviously where there is discretion to allocate property (and other rights) there is concomitantly the capacity to impose the sanction of withholding such rights. Among the Chagga, the transfer of property from one generation to the next, both *inter vivos*, and from the dead to survivors, constitutes a typical instance of the use of a system of benefits as a system of punishments.

Central to any understanding of the Chagga patrilineage (including its legal rules of property and inheritance) is the realisation that the benefits of membership can (and could in the past) be denied or withdrawn. Men could be expelled from the lineage (Gutmann, 1926: 19, 235). Fathers could refuse to provide bridewealth for a marriage of which they did not approve. Fathers could also discriminate against sons they regarded as unworthy, or give preferential treatment to favourites in matters of property. The normative rules that specify who shall hold what property were always subject to some degree of discretionary application, usually on the part of seniors in relation to juniors, the group in relation to individual members. For every normative rule about property, there is a dark side, the withholding of property instead of its bestowal, deliberate delays and hard bargains, and in the background, unfavourable decisions, the possibility of disinheritance, expulsion and other extreme measures. In the late nineteenth and early twentieth centuries, lineage members who felt unjustly dealt with had the option of appealing to outside authorities, the district head, the Chief, and later on, in British colonial times, to the Primary Court, the District Officer, the local missionary; today, they can appeal to the various Party officials and courts. An angry person might also move away and start elsewhere. But although such alternatives were and are there in theory, they surely are not always attractive or practical.

The pre-colonial society and its rules of property and inheritance

The way the lineage has fitted into its political environment over the years, and bonded itself to a variety of new overarching political structures, is too long a story to describe in detail here. But a few background comments are in order. The political structure of pre-colonial times is easily outlined. A local cluster of patrilineages formed a district, or *mtaa*. Several such districts comprised a chiefdom. It is a simple, three-layer organisation: patrilineages, districts, chiefdom. This was cross-cut by an age-grade system. The Chief's authority rested in substantial part on the military grade, which was at his beck and call.

There were many chiefdoms on Kilimanjaro. Some were more powerful than others. Some were allies, some enemies. The history of the area is a long sequence of small-scale wars and raids for cattle, for slaves, for the control of trade and trade routes. The many chiefdoms fought each other, settled their differences and fought again.

The Chagga were directly involved in a regional economy in the nineteenth century, and probably much earlier. There were three major geographical zones involved, all larger than any chiefdom. The first was Kilimanjaro itself, because the chiefdoms not only fought, but also had peaceful economic relations among themselves. There were many women's markets on the mountain, and women from ordinary households went from one chiefdom to another to trade. There were

other connections. When men placed their surplus cattle in the herds or
households of other men, they frequently did so in chiefdoms other
than their own, and regularly travelled to check on their well-being.
The second zone was the area immediately surrounding the mountain.
Kilimanjaro was inextricably tied to the plain around it and to the
nearby Pare mountains, because Kilimanjaro has no iron, virtually no
clay, and no salt. The trade for those products of the plain and nearby
areas is very ancient, and for pots at least may go back 2000 years. The
third zone of trade, trade with the coast, probably explains a great deal
about nineteenth-century Chagga warfare and about the centralised
organisation of Chagga chiefdoms. Not only were the Chagga in the
ivory and slave trades, but the chiefdoms also did a big business in the
provisioning of caravans, with their hundreds of porters. Items from
the domestic economy, cattle and food, were also important in the
trade economy.

As the century progressed, many cattle were needed to exchange for
elephant tusks, or for slaves, or to ransom captives, and to feast guests
and provision their parties. Competing chiefdoms tried to capture the
trade, one from another. They raided each other repeatedly for cattle,
and for whatever else came to hand, and to establish relationships of
tribute and alliance. The connection between warfare and the caravan
traffic is not far to seek. Nor is it difficult to see how chiefs with external
military powers were able to use force internally, inside the chiefdom,
as an enhancement of personal authority.

When the Germans arrived and settled in, the business in ivory,
slaves and caravan provisioning faded out. Warfare was stopped. The
military age-grade was abolished. Coffee, cash and Christianity came
in. The colonial administrators reorganised the chiefship, and imposed
cash taxes, hut by hut. Settlers appeared. The structure of trade
changed. Churches and schools and clinics opened. New information
and new ideas spread quickly. Later, under British administration, a
coffee cooperative was organised. Chagga coffee competed with settler
coffee. Over the decades the Chagga prospered. They became among
the most educated, the most modern, and the most well-to-do of the
peoples in what is now Tanzania.

But most of the local economy on Kilimanjaro was still founded on
the land. Even employed men counted both on their coffee income and
on the subsistence foods from the groves. The coffee trees were planted
among the bananas, in the home plots of the members of the
patrilineages. The law of the banana gardens easily became the law of
the coffee groves.

What does Gutmann say about that law? The most striking thing to the modern eye about Chagga rules of succession to property and of inheritance is that they had a combined version of primogeniture and ultimogeniture (Gutmann on inheritance, 1926: 27–68). In matters of family property the eldest son and the youngest were favoured. Middle sons got a diminished share, when they received anything.

Also fundamental to the system was the notion that women received property, not from their fathers, but from their husbands. In a proper marriage, which was virilocal, a woman was given a house, a cow, and a banana garden to tend and to use. The cow was for central heating, milk, manure, and above all, for calves. The garden was for vegetables as well as bananas. The gardens, being manured, were continuously cultivated, and permanently occupied. Other plots on which annual crops were grown were held for a year at a time. Fallowing was a factor in the difference in tenure. All households used lands under both types of tenure, permanent and temporary.

In some circumstances, a husband could reassign the cow he bestowed on his wife, but the house and garden were normally hers for the duration of the marriage, and beyond, into her widowhood, and at her death passed to her youngest son. A polygynous man had to provide each wife with a separate hut and banana garden and, if possible, her own beasts. Thus, to marry, a young man had to have access to land and to livestock as well. But sons did not have to wait around for their fathers to die in order to be able to marry. It was a paternal obligation to provide the firstborn son with a developed banana grove at the time of the son's marriage. The youngest son had almost as easy a time. The father kept the youngest by his side, in his own *kihamba*, his banana grove, for life. It was the obligation of the youngest son to look after his father and mother in old age. And it was the youngest who eventually inherited the paternal hut and grove, when both parents had died. Unlike their favoured elder and younger brothers, middle sons were supposed to start new gardens for themselves in the bush.

Once a man developed a banana grove, it became his property to leave to descendants or, failing male heirs, to kinsmen, subject to a life interest in his widow. A man also had the right, if there were no objection from the lineage, to give away a grove he had developed himself (Gutmann, 1926: 304). The customary return payment for such a garden, bestowed on a non-kinsman, was said to be a cow and a goat. To be valid, any transfer to an outsider had to be arranged in a ceremony before witnesses, including a representative of the owner's lineage, as well as the children of the seller and buyer. Milk and beer were poured against the bananas, and the owner declared that he and his heirs waived all claims to the land forever. The minor son of the owner also was sometimes asked to transfer a banana shoot to the new owner as a symbol of his relinquishment of interest. Despite all these formal precautions, it sometimes proved difficult to alienate cultivated banana land to an outsider in such a way as to preclude all subsequent lineage challenges. The major ground on which transfer might later be questioned was that either the lineage or the potential heirs had not consented properly. Certainly, if no kinsman of the owner had been present at the ceremony of transfer, the agnates could bring their case to the Chief, and he could invalidate the transaction.

From this and other evidence, it is clear that the lineage had a kind of residual interest in the developed banana groves of agnates which it could assert if it chose, to prevent alienation to outsiders. This potentially assertable lineage interest is in keeping with the general system of contingent inheritance. If a man died without male issue, a brother could claim his banana grove. Failing a brother, another agnatic kinsman could claim it. And there were various rules which established which brother and which agnate had the prior right. The lineage made the official allocation. Presumably alienation to an outsider was blocked only when someone in the lineage wanted the grove in question, or when the lineage did not want a stranger resident in a particular site. Though there must have been more or less desirable locations, there was no general shortage of land in pre-colonial times, nor reason to have more banana groves than a man and his family could look after. Some groves were even abandoned. But from maps of present lineage holdings made during field work, there seems no doubt that efforts must have been made to keep intact the kinship integrity of the core lands occupied by a cluster of agnates, the heart of patrilineage territory. The peripheral holdings, or the property of households that hived off and settled away from the main lineage cluster, were not as important. At the edges of lineage territory, or at a slight remove, room could always be made for a non-kinsman.

The legal rules about conditional alienability of land, proximate administrative rights in the lineage, and ultimate administrative rights in the Chief, have to be seen in terms of another factor in the nineteenth-century context. Not only was there plenty of land, but migration seems not to have been unusual. At that time reversionary rights in land were probably seldom a controversial issue. Litigation about cattle is mentioned far more frequently by Gutmann than disputes about land. When he speaks of the wealthy of pre-colonial times, he speaks of lineages wealthy in cattle.

As for cattle, inherited by sons from fathers, the same general forms of preferred position for eldest and youngest existed as were followed in relation to land. On their father's death, sons inherited the cattle stalled in the maternal house. If there were few animals, these were divided between eldest and youngest sons of that mother. Middle sons had to live on promises. A not-yet-born calf was owed them at some indefinite future time. If there were many animals, and sometimes men had quite a number of beasts stalled in the households of others, the largest number of those "outside" cows went to the eldest, a slightly smaller number to the youngest, and only a beast or two to the middle sons.

Gutmann describes a particular quarrel among three brothers regarding the division of the agistment cattle of their deceased father that was adjudicated in the early years of this century (Gutmann, 1926: 36). The father, Kirumbujo Mate, had been hanged by the Germans with his Chief in 1900. He left 38 head of "outside" cattle. The court decided that his eldest son should receive 20, the youngest 16, and the middle son a mere 2 animals.

As with the land, not all transfers of livestock from fathers to sons were made at death. Some beasts were given to sons by a father during his lifetime. Not only was he supposed to provide all sons with bridewealth for marriage, but he might also give them animals at other times. He could, for example, assign the anticipated bridewealth of a particular daughter to a particular son. Obviously, a father could use his power over *inter vivos* transfers of property to try to control his sons. If they quarrelled with him, he could infer that they wished him dead, and he could curse them, or try to arrange that they acquire a bad reputation in the eyes of the lineage, and he might try to have them disinherited.

The lineage decided who received what after a man died. They took into account the allocations he had made in life, the intentions he might have indicated, the usual normative rules, and lineage ideas about what was suitable in the particular situation. In pre-colonial times, normally the major unallocated property that remained to be distributed after death were the paternal cattle stalled in non-kinsmen's households, and some personal possessions (Gutmann, 1926: 38). Unused land such as meadow, fallow and deserted groves normally passed to the eldest son as his father's successor as head of the family. From time to time the particular division of allocated animals stalled in the maternal hut must also have been an issue, as were questions of debt: bridewealth debts, guardianship debts, agistment debts and the like, owed to or owed by the decedent (usually in livestock). On the fourth day after a death, when the localised lineage got together to settle these matters, affines, neighbours, creditors and debtors were also called to attend. Anyone with any property claims on the decedent was to declare them at that time, at what is now called the *matanga*. Those assembled, led by the senior men of the lineage, then held a palaver and allocated the unassigned property.[3] As mentioned earlier, they also arranged for the care of widows and minor children and made claims and met obligations. Widows were inherited, but had the option of refusing a particular partner. But agnatic guardianship over household property and minor children was mandatory.

When a man with a number of sons died, the senior son, being the positional successor of the father as family head, was supposed to administer his larger share of inherited wealth as his father would have done, not only for his own benefit but also to provide assistance to his younger brothers as they might need it. He was supposed to help with bridewealth for unmarried brothers, and to give the unoccupied lands he administered to them if they needed a plot.

In pre-colonial times challenges to the decision of the lineage at the death palaver, the *matanga*, could be heard by the Chief. But he was usually amenable to listening to a case only if he were paid the large fee of a cow and a goat. That was expensive and risky. There was considerable pressure, economic and social, to try to settle most intra-lineage matters "at home".

Some of the same structural relations that pertained to land and cattle were reflected in the patrilineage rules regarding the slaughtering of beasts and the sharing of meat (Gutmann, 1926: 40, 44–49). Slaughtering feasts were celebrations of agnatic kinship, in which the men of a minimal segment of a localised patriline got together, killed an animal, divided the meat, cooked and ate a small portion of it on the spot, consumed a good deal of beer, and then took home their various uncooked shares. Father and first-born son received the most important cuts. At the feast, seniority was the major principle of distribution. And, lest the dead withhold their blessings on seeing their descendants gorging themselves, a sliver of every man's share was also offered to the ancestors, as well as a libation of beer.

Such feasts took place in connection with every wedding, every birth, after a man's death, and on every other imaginable occasion when someone who could afford to be host found reason to invite his agnates to share a beast with him. Gutmann says wealthy men slaughtered about five times a year. Some of the feasting seems to have been rather secular in general ambience. But, when something was wrong in the lineage, when there was an illness, or some other misfortune threatened, the sacrificial element of the slaughtering feast became its central rationale. Otherwise it was often a more joyful celebration, to bring ancestral blessing to the house and meat to the stomach.

Few slaughtering feasts involved the whole of the localised patriline. Most were held for small sub-segments, the male descendants of one grandfather, or one great-grandfather. And within any single minimal lineage segment there existed a system of slaughtering partnerships. It was one of the rules of the game that no man ever slaughtered one of his own beasts. The host's slaughtering partner always did that office for him, killed the animal, butchered it, and distributed the meat. Brothers who were slaughtering partners were supposed to have the closest possible relationship of mutual aid in all matters, not just in exchange feasting.

The ideal way for slaughtering partnerships to be divided was supposed to be as follows: if there were several sons, the first and the last were slaughtering partners. If there were an even number of middle sons, these were paired, eldest and youngest, and in between. If there were an odd number of sons, or of middle sons, the left-over man had to find a half-brother or other less closely related kinsman to be his partner. Depending upon the configuration of the family, age-distributions, and so on, there was a range of alternatives that could be followed or improvised. The ideal pairing rules covered only a few of the possibilities, and could scarcely have ensured durability over time, since partners might die.

From the point of view of law, what matters about all of this butchering is that slaughtering partners were preferred mutual heirs if either died without male issue. The first and the last sons were mutual heirs, and a pair of middle sons could be mutual heirs. Depending on whether there were an even number of sons, what the sequence of deaths might be, and any number of other contingencies, these rules were subject to adjustment. But it is especially interesting to note the ideal pairing of the eldest and the youngest, and the dramatic reiteration of their special relationship in the slaughtering rituals, and the separation from them of middle brothers. The inheritance of widows and the guardianship over them, and over the land, cattle and minor children of their house, conventionally followed the same lines, unless one of the parties had some objection, or the lineage chose to designate someone else at the *matanga*.

The slaughtering feasts continue to this day, and the pairing of eldest and youngest sons, and the allocation by fathers of property to their sons, favouring eldest and youngest, as well as the assignment of widows and minor children to the care of agnatic guardians. But the circumstances in which this happens have utterly changed.

The significance of demographic change

Once a changing demographic background is taken into account, the significance of seemingly stable legal rules of inheritance must be understood to be changing concomitantly. Let us start with the rules favouring first and last sons, which put middle sons at a distinct disadvantage. These rules presuppose a family with three or more sons. Only then are they applicable. How often are such families likely to occur in a stable population? Very rarely, one would think.[4] Polygyny might improve a man's chances of producing more than one son, but a hundred years ago how many would have survived to adulthood, and married? Chiefs and their favoured henchmen probably had many more children than other men, having more wives. And the rules concerning families having many male heirs may have had more pertinence to them than to most others.

Like many African peoples, the Chagga had customs putting the preferred spacing of children at about three-year intervals (Raum, 1940: 88; Griffiths Report, 1930: 13). There is no way to know for certain whether the population was rising rapidly in the nineteenth century. It seems unlikely. But the population explosion of the twentieth century is well documented, and current genealogies show an amazing number of three-son families that are not chiefly families. In 1913, the Germans estimated the Kilimanjaro population to be slightly under 110 000 persons (Iliffe, 1979: 144). Sixty years later there were more than 400 000 and that figure does not include the thousands of emigrants who left to settle elsewhere.

In his land tenure report on the Moshi District in 1930, Griffiths, the District Officer, compared some of his figures on the number of surviving children with figures collected by Sir Charles Dundas nine years earlier (Griffiths, 1930). In 1921, thirty-four chiefs with 285 wives among them produced only 1·38 surviving children per wife, though each woman had borne an average of 2·45 children. In the period preceding 1920, infant mortality was obviously very high. But matters were improving. Griffiths' information of 1930 pertained to 34 Christian husbands and their 34 wives. Among them 6·09 children per woman survived out of 6·88 born. Infant mortality had gone down substantially, at least in the Christian community, and in monogamous marriages the women were having more than twice the number of children. Griffiths estimated that the time necessary for a doubling of population would be about 30 years. He was right. The population has continued to rise with the same speed since 1930. In a census of 100 households made by this writer in 1969, there were 745 persons, of whom 426 were under 18, more than half. The population explosion continues.

When one comes to look at the genealogies of men alive today, to see how many men in recent generations have had three sons, it is no surprise that there are a remarkable number. The genealogies are all pyramidal in the usual manner, starting with an apical ancestor and spreading out with each subsequent generation. They are confined to males, and often males who did not have male offspring are dropped from memory. The ones I have collected commonly go back only six generations or so. What they show is consistent with the population trends collected from other sources. If one looks for three-son families in one of the Mosha lineages of Kilema, of 13 men of the grandfather generation who had sons, 8 had three or more. Of the Nguma lineage, also of Kilema, of 7 men of the grandfather generation who had sons who grew to adulthood, 3 had three or more sons. In short, of these minilineages, almost half of the men of the grandfather generation who have sons at all have had at least three. Other lineages for which genealogies were collected show the same tendency.

What the population explosion has meant is that virtually every cultivable inch of Kilimanjaro is now occupied, and wherever possible is under coffee and bananas. The open meadows and spaces between the core territories of localised lineages of the nineteenth century no longer exist. Every banana grove is right next to another one. Many lineages still manifest clustering in the old areas, but they are all inter-digitated with others, at least at their borders, and some individual members are scattered. The population explosion has driven some people from the central banana belt. Some have moved up the mountain and others downward, to lands that were not occupied formerly. In the areas of relatively new settlement (1950s on) one seldom finds the kind of lineage clustering that exists in the older areas. But it is just as crowded. There is no more bush land for middle sons to cultivate, just when there are many middle sons.

This means that fathers have tended to change their practices, and now frequently subdivide whatever they have in the way of land among all their sons. Wealthy men, meaning those with salaried jobs, are always on the lookout for land to buy, hoping to obtain extra plots to give to their progeny later on. There are no fathers who can supply their sons with plots of the size that were commonly available at the turn of the century.

Not only have the plots become much smaller through subdivision, but, as more and more of the land has come to be under coffee rather than being committed to bananas and other vegetables, the capacity for food production per acre in the groves has gone down. The food produced on secondary plots has become essential, and some food is imported into the area and bought with coffee cash. Though livestock are kept, there are far fewer beasts than formerly because it is impossible to feed them. More people keep goats than cows, and few have animals placed with others. Small amounts of meat for ordinary meals can be bought at the butchers' shops by those who can afford it. That meat comes from Maasai cattle. But the few Chagga cows and goats that are stalled at home are still the only acceptable meat for bridewealth and for lineage feasting, and are reserved for that purpose. Livestock are obviously valued, but they do not compare in material importance with banana/coffee gardens, a small business, or a job. No one could buy a banana/coffee grove for a cow and a goat today. Any Chagga would laugh at the suggestion.

What is the general consequence of this situation for fathers of several sons, and for brothers *vis-à-vis* each other? The discretion of fathers over the allocation of land to sons involves the sons in a bitter competition. Paternal influence over them, which one might expect to be attenuated by all the many aspects of modernisation that are present, still seems very intense. The interest of brothers in each other's health, sickness, sex of offspring, sterility of wives, guardianship of widows, and the like, is very deep, because as far as obtaining land is concerned, a very sick brother without male heirs could turn out to be the best brother of all. When a man has no son, or endures a long illness, or a child dies, suspicion of witchcraft is usual.

Where there are three sons or more such suspicion may readily fall on middle brothers. Because, according to customary law, they are not entitled to paternal land as a matter of right, but are given it as a matter of paternal generosity, they are vulnerable to dislike for diminishing the shares of their brothers. This unfavourable circumstance predisposes them to be blamed for any trouble that arises. Middle brothers can sometimes overcome the structural tendency to make them the scapegoats for the land hunger and fear of disease of their brothers, but the pressures are frequently far too great.

Men other than middle sons can find themselves in similarly damaging disputes for very similar reasons. For example, if a man with two sons subdivides his grove between them, he is thereby diminishing the share of the younger, who would have received the whole thing under customary law rules. It is assumed that the younger will resent this. Consequently, any misfortune that befalls the elder of his sons may lead to suspicions of witchcraft on the part of the younger, and to a variety of disputes. The same is true of mutual heirs. The expectations that might have been met under customary law can thus be used as an explanation for the location of resentment or enviousness, that can lead to witchcraft. This occurs now, even in a time when the specific allocations to eldest and youngest prescribed by customary law are often not followed. Yet, however frequently land is subdivided, such subdivision is seen not as a change in the customary rules but as an exception to them, permissible because of the exigencies of land pressure.

An extended case history

Against this background we can now inspect an extended case history that stretched over an eight-year period. It illustrates the present situation. Other cases like it are easy to come by on the mountain. It is a Chagga soap opera, which shows the bitterness of the competition for land and the atmosphere in which claims are made under the banner of customary law. It is a case of man who tried to sell his land in lineage territory to an outsider, a neighbour, member of another lineage. It is also a case of witchcraft and violence. What it shows is the way in which the *matanga*, the meeting to dispose of the property of the dead, can be used punitively.

The story begins in the 1950s. The father of our main character was twice married, and had two plots in lineage territory, one for each of his two wives. The father had three sons, two with the first wife, one with the other. Our anti-hero is the younger son in the two-son family. To provide these two sons with land, the father subdivided their mother's plot in two, giving half to his elder son when that son married, and leaving the younger son with the mother on the remainder. In the late 1950s, the father went off to Mombasa to work and never returned. Nor was he heard from. As the years passed, it was generally assumed that he had died. In time, all three sons married and had children.

After some years, the son in the one-son family became violently mad, and eventually attacked a lineage member with a panga and was carted off to an institution, where, the family says, he is incarcerated for life. Eldest son was appointed guardian of the madman's wife, child and property by the lineage, just as if the mad half-brother were dead. As guardian, the eldest son took the coffee from his wards' land and sold it, in theory for their benefit. It is true that he paid some of the child's school fees, and gave some shillings occasionally to his mad brother's wife, but there was never any accounting of a formal nature. Being a guardian can be very profitable. The wicked uncle as guardian is not an unfamiliar figure in Chagga families.

Once the father had decamped for Mombasa, the full responsibility for looking after his first wife fell on the younger son. Her house was in his portion of the father's banana grove, and as youngest this was his traditional role. He picked and sold the coffee from their half of the plot. It is this son who is the centre of our story. When I first heard about him in 1968, he was in debt. He had borrowed money from a man outside the lineage. His agnates said that he spent his money in the *pombe* shop on beer, and was otherwise lazy and improvident. Worse, he did not take proper care of his mother, who by then was blind. Her house had collapsed in the bad rains that year, and he had no cash with which to repair it, or rather to replace it, which was what was needed. The mother moved in ''next door'' with her elder son, on his half of the paternal plot. The elder son complained repeatedly to his agnates about the irresponsibility of the younger son toward the mother.

Meanwhile, the younger son was being harried by his creditor, who threatened to sue. Since land was the debtor's only property, this might have meant a forced sale. A senior lineage cousin (Cousin I) stepped into the breach and paid the debt. The cousin was wealthy by local standards since he had a salaried job as an attendant in a nearby clinic. To his kinsmen, the cousin made something of a point of how generous he was to help his irresponsible relative. But he not only took care to make an arrangement to be repaid, he also hoped to buy the land himself. The agreement between the cousin and the debtor was that the debtor was to pledge all of his coffee money for the number of years necessary to clear the debt. Any such arrangement would be sure to put such a man right back into debt, since some cash income is indispensable to a Chagga family.

The debtor began to think about selling his plot of land, as indeed his kinsmen rather expected. Not only did Cousin I hope by paying the debt to be a preferred buyer, but another employed cousin, Cousin II, also asked the debtor secretly to please sell the land to him instead. The debtor kept his own counsel and, thinking he would get a better price from an outsider, negotiated with a neighbour, an affluent man who owned a pick-up truck, and who was in the business of transporting produce and goods.

The neighbour made the debtor an offer of 5000 shillings, and said he wanted to go to a lawyer in town the very next day to draw up documents regarding the sale. The debtor accepted. A down-payment of 800 shillings was made. In Chagga law, no right to land passes until the full purchase price has been paid. The seller can always change his mind in the meanwhile and nullify the deal by returning such monies as have been paid him. The seller always continues to retain possession until the full price has changed hands.

No sooner had the wife of the debtor seen money pass from the truck owner to her husband than she made up her mind to tattle to his kinsmen. From her point of view, such a sale would do her son out of his eventual inheritance. While buyer and seller were in town with the lawyer, she went to Cousin I and told him what was going on. The debtor soon heard from Cousin I who reminded him of his moral obligations, pointing out that he had no right to sell without the consent of his agnates. But Cousin I did not trust the debtor. He tried other means of blocking the sale as well.

Cousin I sought out the debtor's wife and mother and persuaded the two of them to go to the Divisional Executive Officer to beg him to stop the sale of this land. Their argument was that the debtor's father might still be alive and might return from Mombasa. In short, they were arguing that the debtor was trying to sell land that was not his, but his father's. The Executive Officer agreed, and prohibited any immediate sale from taking place. The buyer was soon heard grumbling about his 800 shillings and wondering whether he would ever see his money again.

Time passed. The father did not return. Government was reorganised and the role of the Divisional Executive Officer passed out of existence. The man with the pick-up truck resumed his payments and by 1973, he had paid in full. But being nervous because of the lineage opposition, and because of Tanzanian legislation nationalising land, he thought he would insure his right to possession by improving the land in some way. Today in Tanzania the land belongs to those who "put their sweat into it". No fool he, he started to construct a small house with the complicity of the debtor.

This led to the next effort of the old blind mother (at the instigation of the various men of the lineage) to mobilise the authorities. She went first to the local Primary Court to try to assign the plot by "will" to her grandson, the debtor's son. But she had no standing to do so, and the Primary Court advised her to take her case to the Court of Arbitration, or Reconciliation, a layman's court of local TANU Party appointees, who hear cases informally and are supposed to try to effect a settlement satisfactory to both parties. Her case was to come up in October, 1973.

Meanwhile a disaster brought to an end whatever reserves of sympathy the debtor might have had in the lineage. His elder brother, living on the other half of the paternal grove, fell ill. The illness went on for some months and did not go away. At home, he called a *mganga*, a local healer and diviner, and he still did not improve. He went to the hospital and they were not able to cure him. He returned home expecting to die. Sick elder brother told everyone who came to see him that it was his younger brother who was killing him, and that younger brother must not be allowed to have anything to do with his corpse, or his family, or his property after his death. Indeed, from a genealogical point of view (and a customary law point of view), younger brother would have been the obvious candidate to become the trustee of his elder brother's estate and guardian of his widow and of his only, very young son, a position of some material advantage. And had he become, as he would have, the only sane survivor of the three brothers, he also normally would have been made trustee of the mad half-brother's land and guardian of his wife and children as well.

There were more troubles to come. Getting into the act, another cousin, Cousin III, an immediate neighbour of the debtor, with a contiguous banana garden, told everyone that several of his goats had died and he knew who was responsible. He alleged that chickens from the debtor's *kihamba* had repeatedly wandered on to his land scratching in the soil. Cousin III said he had complained to the debtor's wife, and told her to keep her chickens at home. The implication was that the chickens were somehow transferring witchcraft substance from one place to the other. The chickens did not get the message, and continued to roam. Cousin III took matters into his own hands. He went to the *kihamba* garden of the debtor when the debtor was away and beat his wife until she was unable to move. She sent her young son to fetch the police ten or more miles away. They came and took her to the hospital, arrested Cousin III and booked him for assault. Rich Cousin II bailed out Cousin III, and a date was set for the hearing on the assault.

The debtor reported at the court on the appointed day. In fact he walked the many hot miles to the court several times to testify in the criminal proceedings against his lineage brother. But every time he appeared at the court, the case was postponed, or the clerk told him he had come on the wrong day. Then he was told the case had been dismissed because of his absence. Another cousin told me the clerk of the court had been bribed. Since the debtor was illiterate and the situation was being manipulated by clever wealthy Cousin II, he could easily have been outwitted, with or without a bribe. But even if the debtor had persisted, he might have lost the case for lack of evidence. As another cousin said to me, "After all, there were no witnesses except for the wife herself. There cannot be a case. Who will believe her?"

Then October 1973 came, and the case brought by the old blind mother to halt construction of the house (by the buyer of the land) was heard by the Arbitration Tribunal. They heard testimony and then ordered construction suspended until they would have an opportunity to inspect the premises and hear the testimony of the sick brother and neighbours. As it happened, the debtor's luck continued to be bad. His sick elder brother died on the very day the court came to inspect the land. The court withdrew and the proceeding was never continued.

The story ends with the *matanga* of the dead brother. The debtor went to the beer-drinking-of-mourning of his brother, but not to the *matanga*. It had been made clear to him that his kin were against him and that he dared not show his face again. At the palaver on the fourth day after the death, the lineage decided that the debtor was to be prohibited from having anything to do with his deceased elder brother's estate or family, that he would not be made trustee or guardian and, worse, that no one in the lineage should have any further contact with him, including his three sisters.

Not surprisingly, when I returned in 1979, the debtor had left the area in disgrace with his wife and children. The man with the pick-up truck had possession of the land, having finally acquired it 8 years after his first down-payment.

Conclusions

There are at least three complexes of legal obligation involved in this case history: that surrounding kinship, that of cash, and that of the property law of the state. The three nexi are contemporaneous and interlock in practice, but they dominate different arenas of allocation, negotiation and disputation. The relations among the three legal complexes have by no means been fully worked out by the Tanzanian courts, so it becomes catch-as-catch-can for interested parties.

On one level, this long story is nothing but a tale of the competition between salaried men of two different lineages for the plot of an illiterate impoverished debtor who was being forced to sell. The kinsmen of the debtor argued on customary law grounds that they should have priority as buyers. The man with the pick-up truck succeeded in obtaining the land on the ground that it was simply a modern market transaction. Though it has the rhetorical appearance of a quarrel between traditionalists and modernists, that is not what this conflict concerned. The roles and rhetoric could easily have been reversed had the lineage memberships been the other way around. The deep split exemplified is not between tradition and modernity, but is that which lies between the financially and socially competent, and the financially and socially disabled. Yet the case history shows that in present conditions it is not always possible for the salaried men to buy out their least-well-off kinsmen smoothly and quietly. The poor may be recalcitrant, and the competition among the salaried men can be fierce.

On another level, the significance of this case history is organisational. It shows the remaining capacity of the localised lineage to administer and enforce certain elements of Chagga law. Although the lineage has obviously lost direct control over the right of members to sell to outsiders, it has not lost all control over the allocation of the assets and obligations of the dead, particularly when there is a question of trusteeship and guardianship. Nor has it lost control over the punishment of ostracism. For locally resident members, the lineage is still a body with which to contend.

But what normative regularities does the lineage seek to enforce, and by what principles of adjustment does it amend those when it sees fit? What is left of the customary laws that Gutmann described? Though the rules regarding the transfer and inheritance of property continue to be stated more or less as Gutmann rendered them, it is clear that in practice many other things can and do happen. There have been fundamental changes in every aspect of the socio-economic context. The place of the localised lineage in the society has changed. The demographic situation has been radically altered. The kind of property involved is not the same. From a pre-colonial emphasis on the scarcity of cattle, with banana lands valuable but plentiful, there has been a shift to land scarcity and to cash-cropping and work for cash as the central features of economic life on Kilimanjaro. The economic importance of the guardianship of widows is not new. But formerly, apart from providing the guardian with a wife, with access to her child-bearing capacities and to her labour, its greatest economic value was in endowing the guardian with discretion over the disposition of household livestock and over the marriage of wards. The land question was secondary. Now the guardian has no sexual rights, and livestock are negligible in numbers and importance, but the guardian has access to a valuable coffee-cash income, and in some situations can influence the allocation of scarce land. The land and coffee questions have become primary. Thus today, to the extent that traditional rules are being invoked to legitimise the administration of a widow's property, they are being applied to a different kind of property. Elements of the organisational structure of the past are visible in the social relations that surround a lineage member's assets, but this does not mean that the old rules are applied.

What can be seen in the case history are at least three instances in which the customary rules were *not* applied literally as Gutmann described them. But with respect to two of these "customary" rules, it is noteworthy that the social location of discretion over allocation remained in its traditional place. Exceptions to the rules were being made by the same agencies that could have made exceptions in earlier times.

First, the customary rule that a woman's youngest son inherits her banana grove was not observed here. The father who went to Mombasa divided his wife's grove between her sons. As many other men have done before and since, the father exercised discretion and made adjustments to the normal rules to fit the circumstances of land shortage.

Second, the customary requirement that the consent of the localised lineage be obtained before land is alienated to an outsider has now been informally translated into a demand by affluent kinsmen that they be offered first refusal. And this requirement turned out to be unenforceable. Because the salaried men are the modern pillars of the lineage, they can sometimes mobilise it for their own purposes. But they cannot always engage public agencies in their cause, certainly not on the ground of some traditional control that the lineage might once have had over members' property. The fact that the lineage no longer has any official political existence, that it has no standing in court, and no right, reversionary or any other, in land, prevented them from pressing in public the customary rules that they advanced in private.

Third, the normal customary rules which would have made a surviving brother the most appropriate trustee and guardian of his elder brother's estate and family were not applied by the lineage at the *matanga*. Whether the people at the *matanga* were punishing the debtor for witchcraft, or for trying to sell to an outsider, or for neglecting his mother, or for fiscal irresponsibility, or for all four, is hard to say. Their motives cannot be fully known. What is clear is that they had the discretionary power to make the decision, just as they would have had a hundred years ago. The localised lineage of the Chagga continues to have some capacity to administer the affairs of its members.

This case history involves two deaths, and with respect to both there is much more to be taken into account than a simple contrast between intestate succession and wills. The presumable intention of the first (putative) decedent, the father who decamped for Mombasa, was to divide his land among his sons. Had his death been ascertained years earlier and a *matanga* held at the time, the kin assembled would undoubtedly have felt bound by his *inter vivos* allocation. There had been no will in any technical sense, but an intention had been made manifest in action, through the division of land. The kin would have been unlikely to defeat so clear and fair an intention by strictly applying the traditional rules of preferred intestate succession. It was only because no *matanga* had ever occurred that when the lineage brothers saw that they were not going to be given first refusal on a sale, they began reinterpreting the absent man's intentions. As for the second death, that of the elder brother who thought he had been bewitched by his younger brother, the dead man's accusations and wishes were given full effect. Whether this would have been true even if the facts of the case had not made the decedent's views congruent with the interests of the prosperous surviving kinsmen, one can only guess. The assets involved were both material and human, and the debtor was cut off from both. His brother's death proved to be the occasion for his deprivation and banishment.

It is evident that the kin at the *matanga* had many choices and considerable power in the mid-1970s. They could treat orally (or otherwise) expressed wishes or intentions of decedents as equivalent to testamentary dispositions even when these were expressed indirectly and not necessarily made in anticipation of death. Or they could apply the rules of intestate succession. Or they could invoke a variety of other standards of fairness as they saw fit. There is no way to know exactly how often in the deep past the lineage simply affirmed the stated customary rules of succession and inheritance, or instead how often it may have exercised a more active discretionary role, and/or may have taken decedents' wishes into account. That the discretionary power was there and was used from time to time seems not to be in doubt.

And there is no doubt either that the discretionary power of the lineage has been exercised over a century during which the contextual meaning of the customary law has changed continuously. Customary law is deeply misunderstood when it is depicted as "traditional" by definition, preserved intact, rule by rule. That statements of rules persist is no sign that their significance is unchanging.

As for the future, as long as a body of Chagga agnates are informally interposed in this way between a decedent and the potential heirs of his property, and as long as rights to land are involved, the importance of localised kinship groups on Kilimanjaro is certain to continue. They "administer" some of the affairs of their members. Such discretionary powers over valuable assets and privileges inside a bounded group provide an opportunity for the exercise of social discipline. The threat of potential sanctions imbedded in these quasi-administrative arrangements is a dimension of ongoing social relations, even though the necessity for actual allocations occurs only intermittently, when there has been a death. Where normatively prescribed arrangements about property and persons can be legitimately altered or benefits can be justifiably withheld, the social site of discretionary allocation is as important a part of the law as the "normal" rules themselves. The place of "customary" rules must be understood in a somewhat different way from the way it has often been considered in the past.

Situations of explicit dispute are not the only revealing ones that bear on conflicts of interest and on law. Quasi-administrative decisions, negotiations and allocations can be just as telling. As has long been apparent, an understanding of the complex and changing arrangements involved in the disposition of heritable rights and obligations makes it possible to understand a great deal about the living, not only about the dead.

Notes

1. Fieldwork on which this article is based was carried out over the period 1968–79 during five visits to Kilimanjaro, all but the last of several months' duration. The author wishes to acknowledge with gratitude the hospitality of the University of Dar es Salaam where she was a Research Associate during her various periods of study, particularly that of the Law School which has repeatedly been hospitable and helpful. The work in Tanzania was financed by grants from the Social Science Research Council of New York, and by the National Science Foundation, Washington, D.C., for which the author is duly grateful.

2. In one set of 300 households surveyed in this research, all in one sub-*mtaa*, there were 40 "clans" represented. But actually 12 lineages or "clans" comprised 259 of the households, grouped in clusters of 6 or more households. One of these 12, an ex-chiefly lineage, had 57 member households. The next largest lineage had only 31. As is evident, there is a wide range of localised lineage sizes.

3. Attendance is variable. I attended one at which there were about 60 people (a woman's *matanga*), another where there were so many I could not count them, and I would judge that there had been between one and two hundred people present at one time or another. Other *matangas* may involve only a handful of kin. But usually, everyone who has any property interest at all, and is on the mountain, and can attend, does so. Many come without material interest.

4. In Jack Goody's paper "Strategies of heirship" there is a table on family size and on the likelihood of a male child predeceasing his father in pre-industrial conditions. It indicates that in the circumstances, there is a 2/3 chance that a son will die before his father. And, as for numbers of sons, it says that there is a 7·2% chance of having two or more sons where

the average number of children is 2·5. The chances of having two or more sons goes up to a 28·3% chance where the average number of children goes up to 6·0 (Goody, 1973: 17–18).

References

GOODY, J. (1973). Strategies of heirship. *Comparative Studies in Society and History*, **15**, 3–20.

GRIFFITHS, A. W. M. (1930). "Land Tenure, Moshi District". Unpublished typed report. Copy in Rhodes House Library, Oxford. MSS.Afr.s.1001.

GUTMANN, B. (1926). "Das Recht der Dschagga". Beck, Munich.

ILIFFE, J. (1979). "A Modern History of Tanganyika". Cambridge University Press, Cambridge.

MAINE, SIR HENRY (1861). "Ancient Law". John Murray, London. Page references to 1894 edition.

RAUM, O. F. (1940). "Chaga Childhood". Oxford University Press, London.

Death and the Demographic Transition: a note on English evidence on death 1500–1750

ALAN MACFARLANE

> It is very naive to claim to understand men without knowing what sort of health they enjoyed. But in this field the state of the evidence, and still more the inadequacy of our methods of research, are inhibitive. Infant mortality was undoubtedly very high in feudal Europe and tended to make people somewhat callous towards bereavements that were almost a normal occurrence.
>
> Marc Bloch, 1962: 72

Bloch's statement succinctly raised the three questions which will be briefly discussed in this paper: What is the "state of the evidence"? What are the "methods of research"? What is the relationship between mortality rates and sentiment? These are very large topics upon which much has been written. But for those who are experts in other disciplines or other periods it may be useful to draw attention to some recent developments in the attempts to answer these questions.

It is widely accepted that one of the major transformations in world history has been the rapid reduction in infant, child and adult mortality during the so-called "demographic transition" of the last one hundred and fifty years. Most human societies for most of history, it is argued, experienced high mortality, either perennial or in the shape of crises, which kept their population in long-term equilibrium. Thus most of the societies investigated by historians, archaeologists or physical anthropologists have experienced crude death rates of over thirty per thousand

and had an expectation of life at birth of between twenty-five and thirty-five years. Infant mortality rates have often been above two hundred per thousand, marriages have lasted on average for about ten years before being broken by death, most of a person's close relatives have died by the time he or she reaches the age of twenty. A "modern" western society is now in a completely different situation. Crude death rates of about ten per thousand prevail, with expectation of life at birth of up to seventy years, infant mortality rates of under twenty-five per thousand, marriages lasting up to thirty years unless broken by divorce or separation, and most of a person's close relatives remaining alive until he or she is in later middle age. Death has very radically altered its face. Although, in the long term, we all die, death appears to be less unpredictable, more controlled. The potential consequences of a change from a "death-logged", to modify Victor Turner's phrase, to a relatively "death-free" society are immense. We may briefly outline just one of them.

A widespread and superficially attractive theory is that alterations in mortality patterns will change the whole intellectual and emotional structure of a society. Thus it is sometimes argued that the decline of interest in the after-life and in established religion in nineteenth-century Europe, the movement towards a secular atheism, was related to the rising control of mortality. Furthermore, it has been argued that whenever there is a great change in the demographic infrastructure, then human character and personality will change. We may expand this argument in relation to the treatment of close relatives.

The French historian Ariès (1962: 38–39) provided one version of an alleged direct connection when he stated:

People could not allow themselves to become too attached to something that was regarded as a probable loss. This is the reason for certain remarks which shock our present-day sensibility . . . Nobody thought, as we ordinarily think today, that every child already contained a man's personality. Too many of them died.

The theory was given more precise expression by the demographer David Heer (1968: 454):

There is also a possible connection between the level of mortality and the amount of emotional energy that parents invest in each of their children . . . Where mortality levels are high, one might expect parents, in the interest of self-protection, to develop relatively little emotional involvement in any one child.

This is an argument which has been developed and expanded by recent historians of the family. A feedback loop has been added to the original thesis. High infant mortality led to a lack of emotional involvement.

The consequent lack of care increases the infant mortality still further. Another extension of the argument is to other human relationships. Husbands and wives dared not invest strongly in their emotional relationships because of the threat of death. The subsequent callousness led to further mortality and insecurity. Even more widely, the callousness within the family arising from demographic insecurity led to whole societies in the past being inhabited by cold and aggressive individuals, incapable of love and affection. The birth of affection, joy, spontaneity is dependent on the demographic revolution.

This is a thesis which was developed specifically in relation to the history of north-western Europe from the medieval period. But if it is true there, it clearly has implications for all peoples who exist on the wrong side of the revolution in mortality. It is strongly implied that the relations between parents and children in all "pre-transition" populations will be cold and lacking in affection or even interest. Although there is not an absolute and easy correlation, Stone (1977: 82) argues:

It is fairly clear that the relative lack of concern for small infants was closely tied to their poor expectation of survival and that there is on the average a rough secular correlation between high mortality and low gradient affect. The high gradient affect characteristic of modern Western societies is unlikely to develop on a mass scale before child and young adult mortality have declined and before child numbers have been reduced by contraception.

The second part of the argument was anticipated by a United Nations publication in 1953 which suggested that increased emotional concentration on children would be one of the beneficial effects of contraception (1953: 80).

There are a number of assumptions in this argument which it would be worth testing. Firstly, it assumes that the high mortality of "stage one" of the demographic transition theory is universal in "pre-modern" societies. Secondly, it assumes that "modern" societies exhibit a uniformly loving and tender attitude towards, and treatment of, children. Thirdly, it assumes that those societies studied by anthropologists in the Third World, or by historians and archaeologists throughout the world before the nineteenth century, exhibited a basically identical set of attitudes towards children. This evolutionary view is vigorously demonstrated in the remark of Lloyd de Mause (1974: 1):

The history of childhood is a nightmare from which we have only recently begun to awaken. The further back in history one goes, the lower the level of child care, and the more likely children are to be killed, abandoned, beaten, terrorized, and sexually abused.

It is not within the scope of this brief paper to do more than draw attention, within the context of part of the history of one country, to some of the sources and methods we might use in order to approach an answer to some of the very large questions raised here. As a social anthropologist I am suspicious of such demographic reductionism which dismisses the vast effects of religion, ideology, social relations, economic and political forces, and assumes a direct and easily ascertained relationship between a specific demographic feature, mortality, and individual human psychology. Since there is a very considerable amount of description of the incidence of and reactions to death in non-western societies, it would be very possible to test the above propositions against anthropological findings. Here we will pursue a different path, inspecting some of the ways in which one could test theories which are becoming part of the established wisdom of many demographers and social historians.

I have chosen England during the period 1500–1750 because it provides an ideal intersection between a society which by all accounts was still "pre-modern" in its mortality characteristics, yet which was highly literate and whose records have survived in more variety and quantity than any other European country. The evidence which has survived may be divided for convenience into that bearing on two levels: reactions to and perceptions of death, in other words the "normative" level, and the actual incidence of death, the "statistical" level. Within the general category of "normative", the material may again be divided into sources which deal with death in general and those which describe reactions to the deaths of specific individuals. Each of these sources of evidence has associated problems of interpretation to which we can do no more than allude.

In answer to the question, "What did people feel about death in this period and in what way did the feelings change?", an obvious source of evidence is the poetry of the period. The famous sonnets of Shakespeare and Donne are only the most notable examples of a vast literature devoted to analysing, distancing, humbling or accepting the fact of death. Changes in the absorption with death can be charted. Yet every poem and every line has to be carefully weighed in order to discover the stylistic and traditional constraints on the expression of thought and emotion. The interpretation of the treatment of death in the golden age of English drama, in the Elizabethan, Jacobean and Restoration tragedies and comedies, is equally difficult. Every emotion from horror to ridicule is expressed and quotations supporting almost any interpretation of the attitudes to death could be assembled. The third major artistic representation of death is in the painting and sculpture of the period, in the superb funeral monuments and in the paintings such as the one which depicts in one scene the whole life and the ritual treatment of the death of Sir Henry Unton, now in the National Portrait Gallery. Clearly it needs erudition and a deep understanding of symbolism in order to deal with such representations. Yet they cannot be neglected if a proper study of death and its repercussions is to be made.

Apparently more straightforward are the direct statements concerning mortality made by contemporaries. Philosophers constantly mused on the topic and there are numerous speculations to be found in the works of men like Raleigh, Bacon, Burton, Hobbes. There was also a vast pamphlet literature in England during this period in which writers like John More and George Strode provided "A lively Anatomie of Death" (1596), "The Anatomie of Mortalitie" (1618) and many other analyses. Shorter versions of this didactic literature appeared in the numerous printed sermons of the period. General remarks on the treatment of death in different societies of a kind which are of particular interest to anthropologists were made by those who travelled, noting for example that the English and the Highland Scottish treatment of death was very different. To ignore the speculations of the many great men who wrote in this sophisticated and literate civilisation is artificially to delimit our understanding.

Yet it is well known that the general theories and general perceptions of a phenomenon may be very different from the reactions in specific cases. For the latter we may turn to equally voluminous evidence. An obvious source is the class of diaries and autobiographies. Many of these contain exquisite accounts of the reactions of individuals to the death of others or their own imminent death. To quote just one reaction, when the nonconformist clergyman Oliver Heywood (1882: 177) lost his wife in 1661 he wrote: "I want her at every turn, every where, and in every work. Methinks I am but half my self without her." Equally rewarding are contemporary letters mourning, commiserating, or describing households in mourning. The wishes of individuals concerning what should happen to their bodies after their death, and their hopes and fears concerning resurrection, can be investigated through the preambles to wills. Again it is necessary to be cautious since it is known that the introductory words often followed a standard formula, or that the wording was suggested by the scribe rather than the testator.

England in the period under review was a highly centralised and bureaucratised nation with a complex system of overlapping secular and ecclesiastical jurisdictions. Death and its consequences were of major concern to many of these authorities. Thus we find a vast amount of evidence concerning the treatment of death in the various administrative and judicial records. For instance the ecclesiastical courts were deeply concerned with death in many ways. To quote just one example, an Essex man was presented in 1605 "for his unreverent lewd and most wicked demeanour" because "at what time their vicar came with the dead corpse accompanied with the neighbours to bury", the accused "had with shovels put in the earth and so filled up the grave so as neither their vicar could further proceed in the prayer, or the dead be buried accordingly, to the great offence of all the beholders and the more for that the party to be buried died in childbirth and could not without great offence many ways remain long above the earth . . ."[1] One aspect of death which aroused especial interest was sudden or "unnatural" death. As well as the coroner's inquests which were to be held on every sudden death and the trial records in cases of suspected homicide, there were numerous pamphlet and ballad accounts of particularly brutal or tragic deaths.

I have only touched on a few of the more obvious classes of evidence which give a clue to feelings and attitudes. For the anthropologist there is a great deal in the contemporary folklore sources, the almanacs, herbals and other collections which provide intriguing insights into the popular treatment of death. Then there are numerous special sources which cannot easily be classified. Three of these may be mentioned as instances: a collection of the lives and dying remarks of many later seventeenth-century Quakers; a catalogue of all the people whom a certain Richard Smyth of London had known in his life and the manner of their dying; an unusual set of parish books for Aldgate in London from 1558 to 1625 which gives many details concerning the deaths of those mentioned (Tomkins and Field, 1721; Ellis, 1849; Forbes, 1971). Another revealing class of material is that of medical handbooks, both the general guides to health and disease, and specific works on subjects such as midwifery.

For anyone interested in the social perception of death and its ritual treatment there is a life's work in such sources. Many of the questions posed by anthropologists concerning the function of ritual, the interpretation of suffering and death, the relations between the world of the living and the dead, could profitably be explored using such material. Some of these questions have not been asked by historians before, but the methods to be used in the analysis of the material are familiar. Here as elsewhere great care is needed in evaluating silences in the sources, the reasons why a document was written, the implicit biases in the writer's mind, the sources of his or her ideas. But there are particular difficulties with both the period and the topic. The evidence is much wider than that for any period before 1500 and indeed better than that for most other nations in the world before 1800. It enables us to ask the kind of questions a social anthropologist would ask of a living society. Yet many of the ways in which an anthropologist would gather information and test his preliminary theories are closed to the historian.

Until the studies have been made, it is impossible to generalise with confidence. But even a preliminary and superficial reading of the sources which have been outlined above would show to a sympathetic anthropologist that the picture of a brutalised society, insecure and obsessed with mortality, along the lines of the argument suggested earlier, is not correct. Clearly there are differences in the attitude to death and there are major swings through the period. But anyone who has read the literary, legal and autobiographical evidence with a relatively open mind will find an immense amount of material to suggest affection, love, spontaneity and a deep and tragic grief. The feelings are as strong and poignant as any we find today, the tenderness as marked. To dismiss the society as cold and brutal is a facile distortion of the material. Thus the first part of the hypothesis concerning the link between mortality and human emotion and thought does not fit well. In relation to the second half, namely the nature of mortality itself, we need to turn to different evidence.

One advantage of a historian is that he can survey a period of two hundred and fifty years, or even more, whereas most anthropologists are limited to the ethnographic present. Another advantage is that the historian usually has a considerable amount of material at the level of observed behaviour, the statistical level. At this level the questions change, for we turn our attention to the incidence of death. Is it possible to discern patterns in the age, temporal, sexual or other distribution of mortality? We may distinguish two major approaches. These may be called single-source and multi-source or, as they are called in relation to parish registers, aggregative and reconstitution studies.

The single-source approach consists of finding a type of record which directly or indirectly records a death and in placing this death in relation to other information in the same source. This method was pioneered in England in the 1950s by Hoskins (1957, 1964) and other local historians, who counted up the totals of burials in parish registers. Where the registers are missing, it has also been possible to count totals of registered wills (Fisher, F. J., 1965). Medievalists, who lack direct records of burials, are forced to use indirect evidence or more socially restricted documents such as *inquisitions post mortem*, manorial transfers, heriots or coroner's inquests (Hollingsworth, 1969). Even in the period after 1538, when parish registers had been introduced, documents are lost or missing for certain periods, so it is important to be able to establish how accurate an impression one would gain of mortality from various types of source. Aggregative or single-source analysis assumes a calculable relation between the incidence of reported and actual deaths in the population under investigation.

Single-source analysis, the totalling of deaths from one source, is a rough tool. It does not allow, for example, age- and sex-specific rates. In order to move beyond these figures, the method of linking records, particularly birth or baptism records with burials, was devised in France and then developed in England and elsewhere (Wrigley, 1966). This has given us a new understanding of mortality in early modern Europe and is currently helping us to recover the precise shape of the demographic changes of the last three hundred years. Yet there are limitations even in this approach. Firstly, there is the question of the extent to which those people who are recorded in both burial and baptism records in a specific parish are representative of the whole population. By definition they come from the least mobile part of the population who may be different in other ways. Secondly, there are further questions concerning mortality, especially concerning the relationship it bears to class, status, mobility, family patterns and economic fluctuations, which cannot adequately be answered merely from records of births and deaths. What is needed is a method of setting the deaths within the context of all the other records bearing on the same period. This is the basis of a method which my colleagues and I have been developing in relation to two English parishes over the period 1500 to 1750, namely Kirkby Lonsdale in Westmorland and Earls Colne in Essex.[2]

The two parishes were chosen partly because they each contain especially good records, a listing of inhabitants in 1695 for Kirkby and a diary for Colne. They also have good runs of parish registers, manorial records and the other sources used by local historians. Furthermore, they provide a good contrast to each other. The parish of Kirkby Lonsdale is an upland, pastoral one near the northern border of England while Earls Colne is a lowland, mixed arable and livestock parish, near London. The combined population of the two parishes was about three thousand persons during the period of study. All the accessible and surviving records of the two parishes are being assembled and indexed. The method of indexing the records by hand has already been explained elsewhere in some detail (Macfarlane *et al.*, 1977). Basically it consists of creating cross-references by name, place and subject. This makes it possible to "reconstitute" the lives of thousands of individuals, not just their births and deaths, but also the social and economic context of these events.

On the basis of such hand reconstitution it is possible, given enough time, to work out many features of the mortality pattern in the selected parishes (Wrigley, 1968). Some of the evidence used in these studies has been used by historians for some time; other material, particularly listings of inhabitants and the records of ecclesiastical and manorial courts, has hardly been used by historians until the last few years. The methodology for bringing such sources together and evaluating their meaning is just being worked out. It is hoped that these developments will go some way towards overcoming Bloch's objections concerning the weak state of the evidence and the inadequacy of the methods of research.

There are certain limitations in the present hand methods of analysis. It requires an enormous amount of labour and time to reconstitute a parish fully in this way when the records are full. Another limitation is the slowness of certain types of search through the hand indexes. It may take a very long time to discover the universe within which an event occurred, for example how many children aged less than five there were still present in the parish, from a certain socio-economic level, who were "at risk" of dying but did not in fact do so. We therefore decided to attempt a simultaneous computerised analysis of the data. We have been designing a system by which it is possible to put in uncoded and unstructured historical data of all kinds, in its original form and word order. By adding syntactic marks which can at any time be altered or removed without affecting the original historical records, we are able to provide a structure for the computer. The material from the parish records in this form is stored within a relational database which has been designed for the project. It can be interrogated by way of a high-level query language (Harrison *et al.*, 1979). At present we are designing ways of linking together references to the same historical individual, for example the same names in a baptism and a burial, partly by machine and partly by hand.

The results of this intensive local study will have to await further publication. It will be possible to establish the characteristics of many of those who died, their age, family position, residence, wealth. By integrating this material with more general studies and with the sources already briefly surveyed we will be in a position of which Marc Bloch could only dream.

Notes

1. The case is in an act book of the Bishop of London's Commissary in Essex and Hertfordshire, under the date 7 March 1605, now deposited in the Guildhall Library, London.
2. This project is financed by the Social Science Research Council. I am grateful to them; and to my colleagues Sara Harrison, Charles Jardine, Jessica King and Tim King, members of the project, for their suggestions.

References

ARIÈS, P. (1962). "Centuries of Childhood" (trans. R. Baldick). Knopf, New York.

BLOCH, M. (1962). "Feudal Society" (trans. L. A. Manyon). Vol. 1. Routledge and Kegan Paul, London.

ELLIS, SIR HENRY, (1849). "The Obituary of Richard Smyth". Camden Society Publications, No. 44. Camden Society, London.

FISHER, F. J. (1965). Influenza and inflation in Tudor England. *Economic History Review*, 2nd series, **18**, 120–129.

FORBES, T. R. (1971). "Chronicle from Aldgate". Yale University Press, New Haven.

HARRISON, S., JARDINE, C., KING, J., KING, T., and MACFARLANE, A. (1979). Reconstructing historical communities with a computer. *Current Anthropology*, **20**, 808–9.

HEER, D. (1968). Economic development and the fertility transition. *Daedalus*, **9**, 447–462.

HEYWOOD, O. (1882). "Autobiography, Diaries, Anecdote and Event Books", vol. I. A. B. Bayes, Brighouse.

HOLLINGSWORTH, T. H. (1969). "Historical Demography". The Sources of History Ltd., in association with Hodder and Stoughton, London.

HOSKINS, W. G. (1957). "The Midland Peasant". Macmillan, London.

HOSKINS, W. G. (1964). "Provincial England". Macmillan, London.

MACFARLANE, A., HARRISON, S., and JARDINE, C. (1977). "Reconstructing Historical Communities". Cambridge University Press, Cambridge.

MAUSE, L. DE (ed.) (1974). "The History of Childhood". Psychohistory Press, New York.

MORE, J. (1596). "A lively Anatomie of Death". London.

STONE, L. (1977). "The Family, Sex and Marriage in England 1500–1800". Weidenfeld and Nicholson, London.

STRODE, G. (1618). "The Anatomie of Mortalitie". London.

TOMKINS, J. and FIELD, J. (1721). "Piety Promoted". Dublin.

UNITED NATIONS (1953). "The Determinants and Consequences of Population Trends". U.N. Department of Economic and Social Affairs, New York.

WRIGLEY, E.A. (ed.) (1966). "An Introduction to England Historical Demography from the Sixteenth to the Nineteenth Century". Weidenfeld and Nicholson, London.

WRIGLEY, E. A. (1968). Mortality in pre-industrial England: the example of Colyton, Devon, over three centuries. *Daedalus*, **97**, 546–80.

Death and Time

S. C. HUMPHREYS

My grandfather's clock was too tall for the shelf
So it stood ninety years on the floor.
It was taller by far than the old man himself
Though it weighed not a penny-weight more.
It was bought on the morn of the day that he was born,
And was always his treasure and pride;
But it stopped short, never to go again,
When the old man died.

I want to look at the relation between death and time from three different angles which are relatively independent, although not totally unconnected:

1. What is the "right time" to die?
2. What is the temporal structure of death as a *rite de passage* by which a person is transformed from being one of the living to being one of the dead?
3. What kind of time, or timelessness, characterises the world of the dead?

I am asking these questions on a comparative basis, but can only draw on limited material, mostly from ancient Greece and modern western societies, in suggesting the range of possible answers.

The good death

First, then, what is the right time to die? The question, obviously, is not one to be answered merely from demographic statistics. The cultural model of a good death is not necessarily the kind of death which is statistically most frequent, although demographic patterns certainly have to be taken into account. The *kalos thanatos*, good death, for archaic Greeks was that of a young warrior in battle, but this need not imply that death in battle was commoner than the death of the elderly—still less that it was commoner than the death of infants. In Victorian novels, the good death is that of a virtuous and preferably innocent person; hence the impressive death-bed scenes in Victorian fiction are often those of children or young women.[1] It is *after* the "demographic transition", when they are becoming less frequent, that such deaths acquire especial cultural significance.

The ideal of the "good death" is related, obviously, to conceptions of virtue, but also to conceptions of the overall shape of man's existence —life and after-life. When Croesus asked Solon whom he considered the most blessed of men, he refused to grant the title to anyone still living: a life could only be judged when completed by its death (Herodotus I. 30–32.) The first place went to Tellos of Athens who died in battle and received the honour of public burial on the battlefield, when he had already produced sons and grandsons; the second place went to Cleobis and Biton, two Argive youths who died in the sanctuary of Hera after displaying heroic strength and exemplary piety by hauling their mother six miles in an ox-cart to a religious festival. They were commemorated by statues at Delphi; to have a permanent monument, tomb-mound or statue, was an important element in the "good death".

Tellos was a grandfather—to leave sons behind to inherit was important. But Tyrtaios states firmly that it is shameful for old men to die in battle rather than young ones (Fragment 10, West, 1972), and he is making an aesthetic point as well as a moral one. The hero who died well had to look well in death; and in the archaic period old age seems to have been seen as a kind of decay which was more to be dreaded than death. Mimnermus refers to Tithonus' everlasting old age as a fate worse than death (frag. 4, ibid.) and speaks of the brevity of youth in terms later used for the brevity of life as a whole (frag. 1); for him old age is more or less equivalent to death, and the fates offer man a choice between the two, of which death, he implies, is preferable (frag. 2). The same motif of choice appears in the *Iliad*, where Achilles has a choice between a heroic death at Troy and eternal glory (*kleos aphthiton*) or old age without fame (*Iliad* IX. 410–416). Just as the good Christian death is one which transports the dead to heaven before he or she has become too much contaminated by the world, so the good Greek death is one which translates the dead into heroic immortality (embodied in sculpture or verse) while he is at the height of his strength and beauty.

Such conceptions — depending in the one instance on the concept of the hero's death and in the other on a marked devaluation of this life in comparison with the next — may be rare. But it seems likely that many cultures have some idea of the "right" shape for a satisfactory life, and make judgments that some deaths are untimely while other people have lived too long. Apart from the intrinsic interest of such ideas about the shape of a living career,[2] they also have a bearing on my next topic, the temporal structure of the process of becoming one of the dead, which begins with the decision that someone is dying.

Becoming dead

The process of dying, in its widest sense, stretches from the decision that a person is "dying" (as opposed to being temporarily unconscious, or seriously ill, but with chances of recovery) to the complete cessation of all social actions directed towards their remains, tomb, monument or other relics representing them. Besides the beginning and end of this process, I shall pay particular attention to the transition from dying to being dead, the rituals surrounding removal of the corpse from the immediate proximity of the living (burial or other forms of disposal), and the transformation of the decaying cadaver into a stable material representation of the dead (mummy, skeleton, ashes, tomb, monument, ancestral tablet, etc.).

In this process we can analytically distinguish at least four separate levels of transformation and reorganisation which do not necessarily harmonise with each other. Social relationships have to be reorganised and rights over property and persons reallocated to fill the gap left by the deceased. Mourners have to adjust psychologically to their bereavement. The process of bodily decay has to be dealt with. And, in the beliefs of most peoples, some insubstantial part of the deceased leaves the body and starts on a new career. All these processes "take time" and demand different kinds of attention from the bereaved. All of them, needless to say, may be influenced by the social status of the deceased.

Dying

David Sudnow (1967) has pointed out the problematic nature of the decision that someone is to be classified as dying, and has shown that in the modern hospital the decision may be markedly affected by the age, social status and perceived moral character of the patient. More strenuous efforts in treatment are made with young or well-to-do patients than with the old, the poor, alcoholics or addicts.

In the county hospital where Sudnow did his research, to be classed as dying meant a decrease in attention from hospital staff, and often from kin as well. In other circumstances, however, a sick person may claim to be dying in order to attract greater attention; it would be interesting to have information on the situations in which such claims can be effectively made. (In our culture, of course, they are associated with rich persons who have competing heirs.) How long can the process of dying (real or feigned) be prolonged? Bourdieu (1977: 166) was told by an old Kabyle women that, in the old days, "death came slowly, it could take a night and a day or two nights and a day. Death 'always struck them through their speech': first they became dumb. Everyone had time to see them one last time; the relatives were given time to assemble and prepare the burial." This remark makes several valuable points. The rituals of dying and of burial have their appropriate *dramatis personae* who have to be brought together; the time required to collect together kin widely scattered (or to transport the corpse back to its kin) appears to have been one of the main motives for the development in the USA, first of airtight coffins with lids partially made of glass and then of embalming (Habenstein and Lamers, 1962; ice was also extensively used). The fact that among the Kabyle silence is a sign of approaching death shows one way in which the status of dying person may be claimed and the status of living social actor renounced.[3] There are presumably many other ways in which this is done. The dying Jew, at the end, turns to the wall, away from the living, to pray. The ancient Greek summoned kin and trustees to hear his last will and testament (even if the will had been written, it should preferably be confirmed by being read aloud at the death bed) and instructions for the payment of all his debts and for his burial (see Humphreys, 1980, for references). The death of Socrates as reported by Plato in the *Crito*, regarded as a voluntary suicide rather than a public execution, became the model for philosophical displays of calmness in the face of death, professions of faith concerning the after-life and a new version of the heroic death under the Roman Empire, that of the secular martyr for freedom (Tacitus, *Annals* XVI: 34–35, cf. XI: 3; Pliny, *Letters* III: 16; Wirszubski, 1950: 142). The Christian rites of dying, as practised in earlier centuries (Ariès, 1975, 1977), combine reconciliation to make a peaceful conclusion to all social relationships, confession and absolution from all worldly sin, and a profession of faith in the after-life which may be influenced by the tradition of the Christian martyrs. In nineteenth-century fiction one often meets the idea that the dead have a vision of the after-life in their last moments—frequently in the form of a vision of dead kin waiting to greet them "on the other side".

The ethnography of dying is extremely poor, no doubt because ethnographers have been inhibited by their own taboos from studying it; yet it is clear that in many societies dying is far from being a private matter, that the rearrangement of rights and roles occasioned by death may well begin during the process of dying, and that the rituals carried out and the roles in them of kin of different statuses or of specialists can provide important insights into cultural values.

Death

It is common in English to speak of "the moment of death": death is thought of as an easily recognisable natural event which happens suddenly and rapidly. Cases in which the brain ceases to function while the heart and other organs do not, so that social death precedes "natural" death, are extremely disturbing and have provoked attempts to legalise the acceleration of organic death in order to close the gap — either by legalising euthanasia or by redefining "death" in terms of brain functioning. But this conception of the sharp distinction between a period of "dying" and the subsequent stage in which the dead person is "laid out" for final rites before being removed from the social context of the living does not necessarily exist in all cultures. W. H. R. Rivers (1926) asserted that on Eddystone Island the words usually translated "living" (*toa*) and "dead" (*mate*) in fact formulated a different opposition, between a person who was in a lively and healthy state and one who was seriously ill, old and weak, or dead. Consequently the decision to classify a person as *mate* could set preparations for burial in train immediately, and the burial was not necessarily delayed until all movement and vocalisation had ceased. Something of a similar kind occurs both in the "ritual murder" of divine kings (Huntington and Metcalf, 1979) and in the discreet measures to avoid prolonging the process of dying practised in modern hospitals (Sudnow, 1967). Even the suicides of Roman senators who preferred death to exile from political life can be seen as a way of harmonising social and physical death; the whole subject of the ways in which the dying can exercise control over the timing of their own death, and the conditions in which they might wish either to accelerate or to delay it, requires study.

Assuming the more common situation in which an event called "death" must be recognised before the body becomes a corpse, there are still at least three important processes which may take place either during the process of dying or after death: the farewell greetings from kin and friends, the redistribution of roles and property rights and, in society where this is a normal part of dealing with all deaths, the determination of the cause of death. All of these are of more interest to the living than to the dead—but may well be of interest to the moribund. In our society the rights of the dead to have their wishes carried out (and, if necessary, their deaths investigated and avenged) are protected by a specialised legal apparatus. Without this, the dying person may have to mobilise public opinion to support his authority: preparations for death, in relation to the transfer of property, may be made well in advance—or, conversely, the culture may attribute a charismatic authority to the words of a dying man which is difficult to overrule (cf. the papers by Strathern and Moore in this volume).,

There are, in any case, some temporal constraints on the duration of the early stages of "becoming dead", both social and technical. The start of the process is difficult to predict, and it therefore has to run its course in competition with other activities already planned, and this may generate pressures to curtail it; and secondly, once organic death has occurred, the decay of the cadaver has to be taken into account. The ideal funerals of the *Iliad*, in which the gods magically embalm the bodies of Patroclus, Hector and Achilles to preserve them untouched for nine and even, in Achilles' case, seventeen days of ritual lamentation before their cremation, well illustrate the operation of these conflicting pressures in Greek thought: for society to suspend its operations for as long a period as possible added to the honour of the dead, yet physical decay profaned it. In the sumptuary legislation of Solon at Athens *c.* 590 B.C. on funerals, and in the funerary regulations of other Greek cities, the period during which the dead were exposed for ceremonial "viewing" was limited by law. Even in the *Iliad*, another form of cultural control over the length of the "viewing" period is hinted at in Achilles' dream that Patroclus comes to him and asks for speedy burial so that his soul may depart for Hades. The *Iliad* is also interesting for its combination of (supernaturally accomplished) embalming and cremation: it seems more usual for these two processes to be regarded as alternative means of avoiding the problems of physical decay, either by indefinitely postponing or by forestalling it. At present, it seems, the Americans embalm but rarely cremate; the British cremate but rarely embalm. Herodotus' report that Egyptian embalmers were suspected of practising necrophily with young and beautiful female bodies (II. 89) perhaps suggests that the Greeks subconsciously felt preservation by mummification to be almost too much of a good thing.[4]

The period immediately preceding and following death is that which faces the bereaved with the most conflicting demands. On the one hand they are expected to share in some sense in the journey of the dead away from society; on the other hand they are involved in an intense social activity of reaffirming relationships, mobilising resources for the entertainment of guests or the destruction of wealth, legitimating an altered social order. Contact with the corpse is often considered polluting and the mourners, whether for this reason or others, are often required to segregate themselves from normal social intercourse. Granet (1922) says of Chinese mourning: "De même que la mort retranche le défunt de la vie familiale, le deuil supprime, dans le courant des jours, les rapports entre parents. Chacun, strictement isolé, est contraint à la vie la plus ralentie qui soit, et, dans ce néant, ne doit point avoir plus de sentiments actifs que le mort lui-même." It is perhaps not surprising, in view of these conflicting demands, that many societies assign to women the roles which involve the closest contact with the corpse and the most marked detachment from the rhythms of everyday life, while leaving men to deal with the more public aspects of the funeral. But the situation here is far from simple. The less intense participation of women in public social life which functionally justifies associating them with the dead, rather than the living, when a division of labour along these lines is required, may often itself be ideologically justified by ascribing to women qualities for the manifestation of which death offers exceptional opportunities. In ancient Greece, the opposition between men and women was associated with the distinction between emotional control and unrestrained emotional displays (Just, 1975); emotion was not only non-social, it was antisocial, and its uninhibited release in funerals was dangerous and disturbing: funerary laws restricted the public participation of women in funerary processions to close kin and those over the age of sixty. Even so, a funeral was one of the few occasions (the others being also ritual) on which a young man could see an unrelated girl and fall in love with her (Lysias I. 8; Terence, *Phormio*, 91–116). Bloch (in preparation) suggests other reasons why women may be given a prominent role in death rituals.

One would expect *a priori*—the expectation seems to be more or less borne out by the ethnographic data I have been able to consult, but the subject requires further discussion—that societies in which power is personal and labile will show a more intense interaction between the living on the occasion of death (as in Andrew Strathern's Melanesian material) whereas those in which it is solidly anchored in corporate groups may focus their attention more on the care of the dead. This is a point which needs to be discussed.

Burial and reburial, monuments, commemoration

Robert Hertz' famous "Contribution à une étude sur la représentation collective de la mort" (1907) presents us with a model of primary and secondary disposal of the remains of the dead in which the process of decay of the corpse, the mourning regulations imposed on the bereaved and the supposed experiences of the spirit of the dead move in parallel: when decay is finished and secondary burial accomplished, mourning comes to an end and the spirit of the dead is definitively established in its new existence. There is no reason to expect, however, that in all societies the correspondence will be as neat as it is in the model (cf. Huntington and Metcalf, 1979). Seen in a wider context, both the collection of bones for secondary burial after the flesh has decayed and the belief that at death a spiritual part of the person leaves the body to become established in some new form of existence form part of the tendency to try to transform what was a living person and is now a decaying cadaver into something permanent and stable—mummy, monument or memory, ash, ancestor or angel. Broadly speaking, there seem to be three main ways of accomplishing this. The deceased may become identified with some stable material object, usually a part of, receptacle for or representation of his or her own body; he or she may be reincorporated into society as an ancestor or by reincarnation; or he or she may start a new life in the world of the dead. These alternatives are not by any means mutually exclusive; they frequently coexist in a somewhat loose and apparently inconsistent articulation (cf.Cunha, this volume).

I shall not spend time here on discussion of primary and secondary burial, of which good accounts are available (Hertz, op.cit.; Huntington and Metcalf, 1979; Bloch, 1971), except to remark that secondary rituals obviously increase the room for manoeuvre in those aspects of funerary rites which are concerned with renewing, reorganising and re-legitimising relations between the living. There is a great deal of variation in the interval between primary and secondary disposal both within and between societies (Miles, 1965). Even when the time of secondary burial is supposed to be related to the duration of the decaying of the corpse, this process can take very different lengths of time within a single society, depending on differences in soil (Ariès, 1977), and widely divergent culturally standardised intervals are cited: the Balinese permit secondary disposal (cremation) after 42 days (Huntington and Metcalf, 1979: 85–86), while the Chinese village studied by Emily Ahern (1973) allowed six to seven years for the corpse to become clean.

As I have already said, allowing the bones of the dead to become separated from the flesh which once encased them is only one of a number of ways of representing the separation of a part of the person which is capable of achieving immortality from the parts which are subject to destruction by time. In ancient Greece, what it was important to preserve was the memory of the deeds of the dead, embodied either in immortal words or in stone (cf. Svenbro, 1976; Vernant, 1978). The inscribed slab, relief sculpture or statue which stood over a Greek tomb was the product of the convergence of two different ideas: the *sema* or sign which indicated the burial place of a hero — which might be simply an earth mound, but might also have some object fixed in it to signify the status of the deceased in life, as Elpenor in the *Odyssey* asks to have his oar set up over his grave — and the *kolossos*, a stone substitute for the deceased, either aniconic or anthropomorphic, which symbolised the fixity of the dead: it could be used to pin down troublesome ghosts (Vernant,1965b, 1976, 1977, 1978) and, as the use of anthropomorphic statues developed, was also used to create a perpetual relationship between a deity and the worshipper whose statue was dedicated in his or her shrine (cf.Ducat, 1976). Vernant's work on the category of the "double" in Greek thought, as represented by the *kolossos*, has been strikingly confirmed recently by D. Lanza's discussion of Aristotle's views on death (1980): Aristotle states roundly that a corpse is no more a human being than a statue or painting is: both lack the characteristics of a functioning living organism which are essential to the concept of man, and are therefore called "man" only by homonymy.[5] The statue, like the corpse, both is and is not the deceased. Through the inscriptions engraved on its base, it has a voice: it hails the passer-by, explains whose monument it is, and asks for a tribute of mourning (cf.Humphreys, 1980):

Man, as you go on your way thinking of other things, stand and pity, seeing the *sema* of Thrason.

I.G. I² 971 = I³ 1204

Sema of Phrasikleia. I shall be called maiden for ever,
For the gods allotted me this name in place of marriage.

I² 1014 = I³ 1261

It is particularly clear in the case of the second inscription that Phrasikleia is fixed eternally in the form of a beautiful maiden through the setting up of the monument (cf.Vernant, 1978).

Maurice Freedman (1958: 84) made a distinction between ancestor-worship and memorialism which seems to me more appropriate to the ancient Greek data than for the contrast between domestic "remembrance" of the deceased who were personally known and structurally significant ancestor-worship to which it was originally applied. What the Greeks hoped to achieve for the dead was perpetual remembrance, by strangers as well as kin. The dead did not become ancestors (they had no effect on the lives of their descendants and were not reincorporated into society to serve as focal points in the genealogical definition of social relationships): they became *monuments*.

I have discussed elsewhere (1980) the individualising character of archaic Attic funerary sculpture and inscriptions. Family solidarity was apparently manifested before Solon's legislation at funerals, when the participants after interring the newly dead would make a round of other graves — presumably of members of the same family — making offerings, probably, lamenting and praising their occupants. But the fact that Solon forbade this practice shows that he considered it one of the ways in which the living flaunted their prestige in a provocative and factious manner, rather than a pious obligation to the dead. The evidence for the grouping of tombs in a single enclosure or under a single mound, in the archaic period, is far from clear; but if family solidarity *was* manifested in this way, it was not made explicit in inscriptions or sculpture. It is significant that the majority of monuments were set up by parents to children, especially to youths who died a hero's death in battle.

There is a hiatus in the inscriptional and sculptural evidence from *c.*500 to 430 B.C. — funerary monuments being forbidden by law — and in the late fifth and the fourth century the situation is different. Funerary reliefs often show a family group of two or more persons (see Clairmont, 1970), inscribed *stelai* may carry a number of names, and funerary enclosures group the tombs of members of the same family. Nevertheless, large groupings are rare. The largest yet found is an enclosure which contained monuments to 18 members of a single family, spread over six generations; one stone listed 11 of these together. It is not irrelevant that two of the men were professional diviners (*manteis*). Out of a sample of *c.*600 tomb inscriptions of *c.*430–317 B.C. surveyed, only 37 grouped together persons who were neither spouses, parent and child, or siblings (Humphreys, op.cit.). The aim of the grouping of kin on tombstones and in tomb enclosures seems to be to perpetuate eternally a closeness which existed in life and was to be renewed in the grave — not to make a statement about family continuity.

The texts on which Fustel de Coulanges based his belief that the Greek son had a sacred duty to make offerings regularly at his father's tomb, and that to be deprived of such offerings was the worst of fates, occur in fourth-century law court speeches dealing with situations which arise out of adoptions. The speakers of course appeal to feelings which seem "natural" to their audience—the desire to see one's identity perpetuated in an heir, the desire to "keep property in the family", the lack of proper feeling of an heir whose first act was to grub up and sell for firewood the olive trees which had been the pride of the estate ([Demosthenes] 43.69). From the time of Homer and Hesiod, it had been considered a tragedy for a man to leave no sons, so that his estate was divided among his kindred (cherôstai). The customs of adopting a young kinsman, if one had no children, or of passing the estate to a daughter's son through uxorilocal marriage to her next-of-kin if there were daughters only, had developed as ways of avoiding this fate. But it must be remembered that the man with more than one son had to divide his estate equally between them: the continuity of the stem family which Fustel had in mind (Humphreys and Momigliano, 1980) was lost if there was more than one heir, and there is little sign that it was important for most Athenians to be able to point to a continuous succession of generations in the tomb. This is confirmed by the form of the endowments for funerary cult set up in the late fourth century and later; although the fund set up to provide income for the cult is sometimes vested in a family group to which future descendants are to be recruited in perpetuity, the cult is to be offered only to the nuclear family of the founder, who become more or less assimilated to divinities. Their descendants are to officiate, not to share in the cult when their turn comes to die. And there was no feeling that the cult had to be restricted to descendants. Those who could afford it would leave property to endow a commemorative festival for the whole city, administered by its magistrates (Schmitt, in press).

The medieval Christian who arranged to be buried in or close to a church, and donated property to pay for perpetual masses for his soul, used the same mechanism of the funerary endowment (already employed by Hittite kings), but with a different end in view. Whereas the pagan looked for continuity of existence in men's thoughts, and in his tomb or statue as a focus for these, the Christian was concerned about the fate of his soul in a future existence.

The Christian theory that the actions of the living can affect the fate of the souls of the dead in the separate world into which they have passed is, as far as my knowledge goes, uncommon. It is much more usual, where behaviour oriented towards the dead continues after the definitive disposal of the corpse, for it to be based on the belief or hope that the dead have a continued interest in the affairs of the living. Chinese ancestors are informed of all important events in the family (Ahern, 1973); less benign ancestral spirits may have to be placated regularly, and especially when things go wrong (Freedman, 1967). They are reincorporated into the time which governs events among the living; and they may also be subject to the effects of time in that they move further away from the living as newly dead ancestors are interposed between themselves and their living descendants.[6] This is not true for the Malagasy Merina, who mix up all their ancestors together in the tomb (Bloch, 1971), but it is likely to be true for those systems in which a single genealogical map structures the relationships of both the living and the dead.

It would be interesting to collect comparative material on the representation of ancestors. The Romans kept masks of their ancestors at home and their descendants wore them, with the insignia of the highest honours achieved by each in his lifetime, at family funerals (Polybius VI.53 ff.). The West African Kadara have masks in which they impersonate ancestral spirits to frighten women and children. In the latter case, however, the "spirits" have a non-human appearance, and it seems possible that there might be an inverse relation between the reincorporation of the dead into society as ancestors—a different kind of being from people—and their figured representation in monuments.

Monuments, as Panofsky (1964) has pointed out, can be classed as either prospective or retrospective. Prospective monuments represent the dead in his or her future existence: Egyptian tomb sculptures, late medieval skeletons and depictions of bodily decay, nineteenth-century angels. Retrospective monuments try to recreate the living as an anchor for memory—whether this is the eternal memory that the Greeks considered the deserts of the hero, or the personal memory of the mourners on which the nineteenth-century European and American tomb-cult centred, and which now has new resources of technology to draw on. Sculptured tomb-monuments are now rare (see, however, Jean-Didier Urbain, 1979), but other means of preserving memories of the dead have developed. A study of the use of photographs by mourners is badly needed[7]; and a Boston undertaker recently advertised a tomb which would incorporate film and tape-recordings of the deceased, along with "a 20-foot scroll containing his writings" (specially aimed at academics? *Boston Globe*, Feb. 1974, cited by Vermeule, 1979: 211). The custom of dispersing the ashes of the cremated dead in some place chosen by the family, rather than depositing them in a crematorium—which has sometimes been taken to show the end of all concern for the physical remains of the dead—is a way of strengthening the association of the dead with personal memories of places significant in their lifetime. (I have heard a woman say that she wanted to be cremated because her son had been cremated.) Embalming seems to be another way of providing an acceptable memory-image of the dead to cancel out the sight of them after death; embalmers make efforts to recreate the appearance of the living person, and use photographs to help them in their work. (Cf. the anticipations of modern practice quoted by Ariès, 1977: 501.) If the custom of making commemorative visits to the tomb is on the decrease in western civilisation, as it appears to be, then — discounting the possible effects of increased spatial mobility — one of the probable reasons seems to me to be the reluctance to associate commemorative thought with anything as clearly linked to the idea of death as a tomb or cemetery. The attempt to avoid or deny the existence of death by no means implies a lack of concern with the dead.

Formal mourning is also increasingly rejected as being a reminder of death which interferes with the process of turning the dead into ''memories'' — the only form in which they can continue to exist in this society which no longer believes in an after-life. Formal mourning was a way of signalling the assumption of a role which required correlative behaviour from others in the process of restructuring social roles made necessary by death. In modern society this process is fragmented: those whose death is felt to be significant to a community wider than that of their personal intimates are commemorated by memorial services at which their career is summed up and given a place in the history of the community, by biographies which perform a similar function, perhaps by memorial funds which go to endow a facility for the community to be personally associated with the name of the deceased. Here we are not so far from the ancient Greek funerary foundation. But in other cases the process of personal psychological adjustment to grief, rather than the readjustment of a wider society, is considered now to be the most significant of the processes set in motion by death. Grief is seen as a kind of illness (Marris, 1974) and the tempo of recovery from illnesses is governed by the patient's own estimate of his or her capacities or, in serious cases, that of an expert therapist. Furthermore, significant points in the period of grief may be marked by psychic phenomena which occur at unpredictable times — particularly poignant feelings of loss, hallucinations or dreams of the dead which may be either distressing or consoling (Marris, op.cit.; Gorer, 1965). The modern literature on mourning gives a distinct impression that its time-structure is not fully subject to control by the living — hence, partly, the sociological nostalgia for *les deuils d'antan*.

Hence, too, perhaps, the popularity of spiritualist techniques for producing and controlling the renewed contact with the dead which the bereaved in one way or another seek. It would be useful to have material on the contents of these conversations with the dead: whether the bereaved want references to the shared past or assurances of a shared future, what form these take and what general theories of the nature of life and after-life underlie them. It would also be useful to have comparative material on contacts with the dead through dreams, visions or spirit mediumship in other societies (cf. Cunha, this volume).

The world of the dead

It will be clear by now that it is difficult in most cultures to locate the dead unambiguously in one place. They are simultaneously in the remains of their bodies, in their commemorative monuments and in some other place to which their spirits go. What I want to ask, in this section of the paper, is how the absence of the dead from the social time to which they belonged while living is represented in the temporal structure of the world of the dead.

For a start, the cessation of time may be reflected in the monument itself, not merely in the sense that any inorganic representation conveys a sense of immobility, but through the representation of the deceased as dead or sleeping. The idea that the dead are asleep occurs in ancient Egypt (Morenz, 1973) and is hinted at in early Greek thought by the idea that Death and Sleep are twin brothers, children of Night, and by Homer's reference to profound sleep as "sleep like death" (*Odyssey* xiii. 79; Vermeule, 1979: 145–154). The boon granted by Hera to Cleobis and Biton was to fall asleep in her sanctuary at Argos and never re-awaken; the idea that it is best not to be aware of one's own death is not prominent in antiquity, but recurs in Aristotle (Lanza, 1980). I know no Greek representations of the dead as sleeping, but the Etruscan dead are normally shown in a recumbent position on their monuments —usually reclining on one elbow as at a banquet, a motif which also occurs in Greece, but sometimes asleep (Panofsky, 1964). References to the sleep of the dead occur in literary sources of the Hellenistic and Roman Republican periods (Callimachus, Lucretius, Catullus . . .; references are collected in Lattimore, 1942, and Ogle, 1933); they are commoner in Latin than in Greek. Christians took over the motif and gave it a new sense; whereas for pagan philosophers sleep implied freedom from the cares of life, for Christians it was a peaceful way of waiting for the Resurrection (Ferrua, 1962; Stuiber, 1957).

The timelessness of the existence of the dead is also symbolised in Greek mythical thought by their lack of memory—they drink of the waters of Lethe, oblivion (Detienne, 1967; Vernant, 1959, 1960). Their existence has no history in it; they do not produce. In the islands of the Blest harvests occur three times a year (an indication of perpetual spontaneous abundance rather than of the presence of a plant cycle even here) and agricultural labour is absent, as in the Golden Age. The torments of Hades consist of never-ending repetitive torture or toil: Ixion revolves on a wheel, Tantalus gazes on food and drink he cannot reach, Sisyphus rolls uphill a stone which perpetually rolls down again, the Danaids try to fill a leaking vessel with water, Oknos plaits a rope which is eaten by a donkey as fast as it is produced.[8] The association of work with time is confirmed by Hesiod's myth of the five races of men: the Gold and Silver races neither work nor grow old, nor do they die; the Bronze race and the Heroes grow to maturity, fight and die before they grow old; only in the Iron race do men work and age. It is also confirmed by Hesiod's view of work, in the *Works and Days*, as historical in the sense that it produces irreversible effects: if you work you will be able to buy another man's *kleros*, if you fail to work you may have to sell your own.

Other cultures have different views. In the Egyptian after-life men have to work, unless they have been provided with *ushabti*-figures to take their place when they are called on to do so. In Eddystone Island, according to Rivers (1926), it is believed that the dead go to another island where they lead a life which seems an exact copy of that of the living: they farm, fish, fight and even die. What the society of the dead never seems able to do, as pointed out in Manuela Carneiro de Cunha's paper, is reproduce itself through procreation.

Other theories may contrast the time-structure of the world of the living with another kind of time, natural rather than social. Plato in his later works said that the dead shared in the unchanging movements of the stars in the existence "outside time" which they led between successive incarnations (Burkert, 1972: 365–367). For the Egyptians, the daily reincarnation of the sun was a guarantee of the reawakening of the dead in the afterworld (Morenz, 1973). The movements of sidereal bodies seem both temporal and eternal.

A similar conception of an eternal, cyclical "natural" time is shown in Wordsworth's

> Rolled round in earth's diurnal course
> With rocks, and stones, and trees.

But the history of the idea of the relation between Death and Nature, from the Romantics onward, is far from simple and does not seem to have been adequately studied (Van Tieghem, 1921, is the only useful reference I have so far found). It is a long way from Wordsworth's lines written on a girl he perhaps anyway saw as a part of nature rather than society (he says nothing like this in epitaphs on friends) to the frankness of

> The daisies in the dell
> Will give out a better smell,
> Because poor Judd is underneath the ground.
> *Oklahoma*

With the shift in attitudes which turns thinking about death from an unpleasant but salutary moral exercise — the more unpleasant, the more salutary — to a comfortable and comforting kind of melancholy, a natural setting becomes the appropriate one in which to do it (van Tieghem, op.cit.; Ariès, 1977; French, 1974). Plants provide a vivid though unclear metaphor for the triumph of life over death. (The analogy is unsatisfactory if pursued to its logical conclusion; in ancient Greece, to compare human life to that of the leaves on the trees was a bitter thought, not a consoling one.) The romantic lover may identify the scent of the roses growing on the grave with the breath of the beloved (Desbordes-Valmore, "L'Élégie", 1822, in Bertrand, 1973: 68). In the nineteenth century, especially its second half, flowers replace black drapery in the decor of burial rites (Habenstein and Lamers, 1962). But I do not know how this vaguely formulated association between the dead and the self-renewing life of plants developed into the association between death and fertility which we find in nineteenth-century anthropology, and into the conception of the dead as potential manure which seems now quite common.[9] (Huntington and Metcalf, 1979: 89–92, say that the Mambai of Timor believe that the bodies of the dead help to renew the black earth which feeds plants, which in their turn feed humans: they point out, following M. J. Adams, 1977, that a study of the place of the rotting process and rotting substances in the material culture of different societies could provide insights into their attitudes to corpses.) I suspect that the association between death and fertility in anthropological writings may be an instance of the projection onto "savages" of a train of thought which was already implicit in the anthropologists' own culture but would have been unacceptable if openly voiced. If this is so, we should regard it with particular caution.

In a loose kind of way, the myth of Persephone seems to provide a link in ancient Greek culture between the cycle of plant death and rebirth and the fate of the dead. Some of the mystery religions may have exploited this suggestion, but we know too little of their cosmologies to be at all certain of this — and the more closely one looks at the evidence, the more problematic the whole situation becomes. In the earliest version we have of the Persephone myth, the probably seventh-century *Hymn to Demeter* from Eleusis, one of the main centres for mystery cult and perhaps the earliest (Richardson, 1974), what the story does is to explain why plants die and agriculture is necessary. Hades snatches Persephone away to the underworld; Demeter, heartbroken, puts a stop to the life of plants which have hitherto grown spontaneously, and this threatens the life of men who depend on plants and thus, indirectly, the supply of sacrifices to the Gods. Zeus is thus motivated to intervene: Persephone is restored to the world of the living for eight months of the year; this division of her time between the living and the dead inaugurates the annual cycle of plant life, and Demeter teaches men the secrets of agriculture. The presupposition of the whole story is that the realm of Hades is already constituted as the land of the dead from which no one returns except by divine intervention, and it seems to be assumed also that men are already mortal before the story begins.

Greek mystery religions, and even the Pythagorean doctrine of reincarnation, seem to be more closely connected to another side of Greek ideas about the after-life which reverses the common idea that death is forgetfulness, *Lethe*, to assert that the privileged dead can attain *A-lethe-ia*, non-*Lethe*, a memory which is knowledge of past, present and future, or of unchanging truth (Vernant, 1959, 1960; Detienne, 1967). Here the timelessness of death is linked to the timeless existence of the gods — who may have a temporal past (Gernet, 1932, suggested that they acquired biographies, by association, from heroes), but are not expected to have a temporal future, although they may be able to foresee the future of men. In this they resemble the dead. To associate the gods with atemporality implies a negative judgment on time: an existence in time is imperfect, incomplete, overshadowed by coming decay. In this line of thought, life may be equated with death and death with life: for Plato, the body is a tomb, *soma* equals *sema* (Courcelle, 1966). The true Pythagorean sage can remember all his previous incarnations but the ordinary man forgets these, and the timeless periods of existence between them, each time he enters a new body. Reincarnation here — as perhaps elsewhere, except where it is restricted within a single descent group so that the reincarnated spirit is assured of the same social status in its next existence — is predominantly negative in its implications, a form of punishment or at best a stage in a slow process of purification. For Greek philosophers, truth and reality are timeless and unchanging. Similarly, in Christian thought, Purgatory is a protraction of the timebound existence of the living which prepares them for the timeless bliss of Heaven.

Some questions in place of a conclusion

The number of possible oppositions between time and timelessness, decay and permanence, memory and oblivion, movement and stillness, activity and its suspension, incompleteness and completion, is very great, and the possibilities of manipulating these oppositions in fresh combinations increase with developments in material culture and social complexity (the "memory" attained by the Greek initiate in the after-life could not exist without the *lethe* of the non-initiate with which it is contrasted). What are the implications of this perspective on death for future research, both anthropological and archaeological? What questions does it suggest, to which we could, but at present do not, know the answers?

1. One area which is obviously under-researched is dying. Far too many ethnographic reports treat the constation that someone is dying or dead as non-problematic and begin their analysis of funerary institutions with the announcement of death. The recognition of approaching death, the management of "false alarms" and the rites of dying and their duration all need study.
2. More attention should be paid to the differential treatment of the dead at different ages, to ideas about the age at which the "good death" occurs and their implications for conceptions of the shape of life, to the forms of memorial and after-life considered appropriate for young and old, those with children and the childless.
3. We have far too little precise information, archaeological, historical or ethnographic, about the length of time for which commemorative rituals continue and ancestors are still individually honoured. Both historians and anthropologists have been too often inclined to accept normative statements about the perenneity of tomb cults and ancestor-worship, without going into precise details. The demographic probability of the direct line of descent dying out within a limited number of generations, at least in a society such as that of ancient Greece where marriage was monogamous and no value was placed on having a large number of children, should also be considered (cf. Goody, 1973).
4. I have suggested at various points in the paper that death presents problems of time-management: restructuring of relationships within

the family and with outsiders, the psychological adjustment of the bereaved, the preparation of the material equipment and the summoning of the personnel needed for funeral rites, the process of decay undergone by the corpse and the experiences ascribed to the spirit of the dead do not necessarily all harmonise easily on a temporal scale. The unpredictability of death raises interesting questions about the difference between societies in which funerals are the most important form of ritual and those in which a fixed calendar of rites to honour the gods has a more central position. (Secondary burials are sometimes assigned a place in a fixed calendar, as are commemorative rites.) Lavish exchange or destruction of wealth at funerals raises questions about the institutions through which it is mobilised and about the relations between the alliance structures involved in funerals, marriages, vendettas and other reciprocal ceremonial exchanges. (Here again, as pointed out by Miles, 1965, secondary burials allow more time for mobilisation and more latitude in fixing a date.)

5. I have also suggested that the temporal structure of the after-life — where the dead live in a world of their own and are not reincorporated as ancestors — would repay more systematic study. Since the activities of the dead are usually only a selection from those carried out by the living, it is interesting to see which of the activities of the living are considered too closely associated with the processes of growth, reproduction and decay which characterise life to be carried over into the world of the dead (cf. Cunha, this volume).

In general, the study of the position of death in social and cultural systems has been far too narrowly conceived. It needs to be expanded to take in all the ways in which people may prepare for death — from constructing their own tombs to conferring property rights on their heirs *inter vivos* — and all the ways in which memory of the dead may be preserved. Funerals and cemeteries are not the only occasions and places in which death can be studied.

Notes

1. Beth in L. M. Alcott's "Good Wives"; Humphrey in Florence Montgomery's "Misunderstood"; Theodore, a mentally retarded teenager, in C. M. Yonge's "The Pillars of the House". Despite Luke XV.7, the deaths of repentant sinners occupy a much less central position.

2. It should not be forgotten that there are careers ending in particular types

of death which are exemplary for their badness as well as those which are exemplary for their heroism. The oldness and ugliness of the typical English witch is an obvious example.

3. This association between loss of speech and the onset of death is also made, as Helen King pointed out to me, in the Hippocratic corpus, in *Epidemics* III.5-6 and III.17.13-15; cf. *Epidemics* III.1.2, *On the Sacred Disease* 10.

4. The theme of necrophily occurs also in the story of Periander of Corinth (Herodotus, V.92), in the myth of Achilles' love for the dead Penthesilea and in Admetus' promise to the dying Alcestis that he will sleep with a statue and with dreams of her (Euripides, *Alcestis*, 348-356; cf. Aeschylus, *Agamemnon*, 414 ff. with the comments of Vernant, 1976). A graffito of Roman imperial period from Egypt, in which a Greek boy claims that his ashes smell better than Egyptian mummies, preserves echoes of the cultural rivalry between cremators and mummifiers (Perdrizet, 1934).

5. In fact Aristotle (*Meteor*, 389b 31 ff., *De gen. an.* 734b 25 ff., *De part. an.* 640b 35 ff., *De an.* 412b 10 ff.) does not directly refer to statues but to "flesh made of stone or wood", "a hand made of bronze or wood", "a painted doctor" (evidently a common philosophical example), "a wooden or painted eye". It may be significant that he is more reluctant to say that a statue is not a man than to say that a corpse is not a man.

6. Ancestors who have achieved special fame in life keep their prominence for the living longer than the undistinguished (Freedman, 1958: 84). In any society in which prestige counts for something, alongside status in a kinship system, it may continue to affect status after death as well as in life.

7. Note the examples of tomb monuments incorporating photographs, sometimes in combination with sculpture, illustrated by Urbain (1979) and Rahtz (this volume).

8. See Keuls (1974) for the argument that these "sinners" are undergoing purification through toil rather than eternal punishment. The more fortunate Greek dead play draughts (Pindar frr. 129, 130; cf. Herodotus II.122), another non-productive activity. I owe these references to Robert Garland.

9. "Lorsque je serai de retour dans ma patrie, je veux, dans le petit champ que me laissera mon père, creuser moi-même le lieu de ma sépulture . . . Comme ce lieu sera cher [à nos enfants] s'ils ont nos goûts, s'ils ont mon âme, souvent ils baiseront après ma mort les arbres voisins: c'est sous leur écorce qu'aura filtré la matière qui composait mon corps." (Amaury Duval, 1801, quoted by Ariès, 1977: 504.) But the essays for the Institut competition of 1801 were in some respects ahead of the thought of their time, and others had different ideas for making use of the physical remains of the dead: Pierre Giraud proposed to vitrify them and turn them into commemorative plaques (Ariès, op.cit.: 506-509).

References

ADAMS, M. J. (1977). Style in southeast Asian materials processing: some implications for ritual and art. *In* "Material Culture: Studies, Organization and Dynamics" (H. Lechtman and R. Merrill, eds), pp. 21–52. West, St Paul.

AHERN, E. (1973). "The Cult of the Dead in a Chinese Village". Stanford University Press, Stanford.

ARIÈS, Ph. (1975). "Essais sur l'histoire de la mort en occident du Moyen Âge à nos jours". Seuil, Paris.

ARIÈS, Ph. (1977). "L'homme devant la mort". Seuil, Paris.

BERTRAND, M. (1973). "Marceline Desbordes-Valmore: les oeuvres poetiques". Presses Universitaires, Grenoble.

BLOCH, M. (1971). "Placing the Dead: tombs, ancestral villages and kinship organization in Madagascar". Seminar Press, London and New York.

BLOCH, M. (in press). Death, women and power. *In* "Death and the Regeneration of Life" (J. Parry and M. Bloch, eds). University Press, Cambridge.

BOURDIEU, P. (1977). "Outline of a Theory of Practice". Cambridge University Press, Cambridge. (Original French edition, Droz, Geneva, 1972).

BURKERT, W. (1972). "Lore and Science in Early Pythagoreanism". Harvard University Press, Cambridge, Mass. (Revised and translated version of "Weisheit und Wissenschaft", Nürnberg 1962).

CLAIRMONT, C. (1970). "Gravestone and Epigram". Von Zabern, Mainz.

COURCELLE, P. (1966). Le corps-tombeau. *Revue des études anciennes*, **68**, 101–122.

DETIENNE, M. (1967). "Les Maîtres de la vérité dans la Grèce ancienne". Maspero, Paris.

DUCAT, J. (1976). Fonctions de la statue dans la Grèce archaïque: *kouros* et *kolossos*. *Bulletin de correspondance hellénique*, **100**, 239–251.

DUVAL, AMAURY (1801). "Des Sépultures". Panckoucke, Paris.

FERRUA, A. (1962). Paralipomeni di Giona. *Rivista di archeologia cristiana*, **38**, 7–69.

FREEDMAN, M. (1958). "Lineage Organization in Southeastern China". Athlone Press, London.

FREEDMAN, M. (1966). "Chinese Lineage and Society: Fukien and Kwangtung". Athlone Press, London.

FREEDMAN, M. (1967). Ancestor worship: two facets of the Chinese case. *In* "Social Organization. Essays Presented to Raymond Firth" (M. Freedman, ed.), pp. 85–103. Cass, London.

FRENCH, S. (1974). The cemetery as cultural institution: the establishment of Mount Auburn and the "Rural Cemetery" movement. *In* "Death in America" (D. Stannard, ed.), pp. 69–91. University of Pennsylvania, Philadelphia.

GERNET, L. (1932). "La Génie grec dans la religion". La Renaissance du Livre (A. Michel), Paris.

GOODY, J. (1973). Strategies of heirship. *Comparative Studies in Society and History*, **15**, 3-20.

GORER, G. (1965). "Death, Grief and Mourning in Contemporary Britain". Cresset Press, London.

GRANET, M. (1922). Le langage de la douleur d'après le rituel funéraire de la Chine classique. *Journal de psychologie*, **19**, 97-118. (Reprinted *in* Granet, "Études sociologiques sur la Chine", pp. 221-242. P.U.F., Paris, 1953.)

HABENSTEIN, R. W. and LAMERS, W. M. (1962). "The History of American Funeral Directing", revised ed. (original ed. 1955). Bulfin Printers, Milwaukee.

HERTZ, R. (1907). Contribution à une étude sur la représentation collective de la mort. *L'Année sociologique*, **10**, 48-137.

HUMPHREYS, S. C. (1980). Family tombs and tomb cult in ancient Athens: tradition or traditionalism? *Journal of Hellenic Studies*, **100**, 96-126.

HUMPHREYS, S. C. and MOMIGLIANO, A. D. (1980). Foreword. *In* N. D. Fustel de Coulanges, "The Ancient City" pp. ix-xxiii. Johns Hopkins University Press, Baltimore.

HUNTINGTON, R. and METCALF, P. (1979). "Celebrations of Death. The Anthropology of Mortuary Ritual". Cambridge University Press, Cambridge.

I. G. "Inscriptiones Graecae".

JUST, R. (1975). Conceptions of women in classical Athens. *Journal of the Anthropological Society of Oxford*, **6** (3), 153-170.

KEULS, E. (1974). "The Water-carriers in Hades. A Study of Catharsis through Toil in Classical Antiquity". Hakkert, Amsterdam.

LANZA, D. (1980). La morte esclusa. *Quaderni di storia*, **11**, 157-172.

LATTIMORE, R. (1942). "Themes in Greek and Roman Epitaphs". University of Illinois, Urbana.

MARRIS, P. (1974). "Loss and Change". Routledge and Kegan Paul, London.

MILES, D. (1965). Socio-economic aspects of secondary burial. *Oceania*, **35**, 161-174.

MORENZ, S. (1973). "Egyptian Religion". Methuen, London. (German edition 1960.)

OGLE, M. B. (1933). The Sleep of Death. *Memoirs of the American Academy in Rome*, **11**, 81-117.

PANOFSKY, E. (1964). "Tomb Sculpture". Thames and Hudson, London.

PERDRIZET, P. (1934). Le mort qui sentait bon. *In* "Melanges Bidez" (*Annuaire de l'Institut de Philologie et d'Histoire*), vol. II, 719-727.

RICHARDSON, N. J. (1974). "The Homeric Hymn to Demeter". Clarendon Press, Oxford.

RIVERS, W. H. R. (1926). The primitive conception of death. *In* "Psychology and Ethnology" (Rivers), pp. 36-50. Kegan Paul, London.

SCHMITT, P. (in press). Evergétisme et mémoire du mort: à propos des fondations de banquets publics dans les cités grecques à l'époque hellénistique et romaine. *In* "L'Idéologie funéraire. La mort et les morts dans les sociétés anciennes" (J.-P. Vernant, ed.). Cambridge University Press, Cambridge.

STUIBER, A. (1957). "Refrigerium Interim". Hanstein, Bonn.

SUDNOW, D. (1967). "Passing on: the Social Organization of Dying". Prentice-Hall, Englewood Cliffs, N.J.

SVENBRO, J. (1976). "La Parole et le marbre. Aux origines de la poétique grecque". Studentliteratur, Lund.

URBAIN, J.-D. (1979). "La Société de conservation". Payot, Paris.

VAN TIEGHEM, PAUL (1921). "La poésie de la nuit et des tombeaux en Europe au 18e siècle". *Memoires de l'Académie Royale de Belgique* (Lettres et sciences morales), ser. 2. 16.

VERMEULE, E. (1979). "Aspects of Death in Early Greek Art and Poetry". University of California, Berkeley.

VERNANT, J.-P. (1959). Aspects mythiques de la mémoire. *Journal de psychologie*, **56**, 1–29. (Reprinted *in* Vernant, 1965a, pp. 51–78).

VERNANT, J.-P. (1960). Le fleuve "Amélès" et la "Mélété Thanatou". *Revue philosophique* **85**, 163–179. (Also Vernant, 1965a, pp. 79–94.)

VERNANT, J.-P. (1965a). "Mythe et pensée chez les Grecs". Maspero, Paris.

VERNANT, J.-P. (1965b). Figuration de l'invisible et catégorie psychologique du double: le colossos. *In* Vernant 1965a, pp. 251–264.

VERNANT, J.-P. (1976). Étude comparée des religions antiques. *Annuaire du Collège de France*, **76**, 367–376.

VERNANT, J.-P. (1977). Étude comparée des religions antiques. *Annuaire du Collège de France*, **77**, 423–443.

VERNANT, J.-P. (1978). Étude comparée des religions antiques. *Annuaire du College de France*, **78**, 451–466.

WEST, M. L. (1972). "Iambi et Elegi Graeci", vol. II, Clarendon Press, Oxford.

WIRSZUBSKI, Ch. (1950). "Libertas as a Political Idea at Rome". Cambridge University Press, Cambridge.

Death with Two Faces

J.-P. VERNANT (translated by J. LLOYD)

As portrayed in epic, where it occupies a central position, Greek death appears disconcerting. It has two contrary faces. The first face is a glorious one: death shines out as the ideal to which the true hero devotes his existence. With its second face, death embodies the unsayable, the unbearable; it manifests itself as a terrifying horror.

The purpose of the following discussion is to bring out the meaning of this double aspect more clearly and to indicate the necessary complementarity of the two opposed images in archaic Greek thought.

I.1   As we have shown elsewhere, there is a parallelism or continuity between Greek funeral rituals and epic verse. Both are directed to the same end, but the epic goes a step further than the funeral ritual. The funeral rites aim to procure for the person who has lost his life access to a new state of social existence, to transform the absence of the lost person into a more or less stable positive social status, that of ''one of the dead''. Epic goes further: through glorifying praise, indefinitely repeated, it ensures for a small minority of the chosen — who thus stand out from the ordinary mass of the deceased, defined as the crowd of ''nameless ones'' — the permanence of their name, their fame, and the exploits they have accomplished. In this way it completes and crowns the process that the funeral rites have already set in motion: the transformation of an individual who has ceased to be into a figure whose presence, as one of the dead, is forever a part of the existence of the group.

I.2   In comparison with other civilisations, the strategy of the Greeks with regard to death comprises two characteristic and intimately connected features. One concerns certain aspects of the personality in death, the other the various forms of social commemoration.

285

In his status as one of the dead, the hero is not envisaged as the representative of a family line, as a link in a continuous chain of generations, nor — for those at the summit of the social hierarchy — as the holder of a royal office or a religious priesthood. In the verses that celebrate his glory, and on the stele which marks his tomb, he is commemorated as an individual defined in personal terms by his valiant deeds; in death, he is still identified with the career which was his in life and which, in his prime, at the peak of his vitality, found its fulfilment in the "fine death" of the warrior.

For the Greeks, to exist "as an individual" meant to make oneself, and to remain, "memorable": the "individual" has escaped from anonymity, from oblivion, from being wiped out — and so from death — by means of death itself, a death which *by* allowing him access to glorification in song has made him even more present to the community, in his status as a dead hero, than the living are to one another. It is epic verse, as oral poetry, that is chiefly instrumental in maintaining his continuous presence within the group. By celebrating the exploits of the heroes of years gone by it performs, throughout the Greek world, the function of a collective memory.

I.3   Firstly through commemoration in song, repeated for all to hear, and secondly through the funerary memorial set up for all to see, a relationship is established between a dead individual and a community of living people. This is not simply a family community, nor is it limited to the boundaries of a particular social group. In wresting the hero from oblivion, commemoration by the same token strips him of his purely private characteristics; it establishes him within the public domain, it makes him into one of the elements that form the common culture of the Greeks. In and through the epic poem, the heroes represent "the men of years gone by"; for the group as a whole they constitute its "past". They thus form the roots of the cultural tradition which binds together the entire Greek people and in which they recognise themselves and each other, because it is only through the exploits of these departed figures that their own social existence acquires meaning, value and continuity.

I.4   The individuality of the dead man is not connected with his psychological characteristics or with the personal aspect of him as a unique and irreplaceable being. Through his exploits, his brief life and his heroic destiny, the dead man embodies certain "values": beauty, youth, virility and courage. But the rigorous nature of the course of his life, his rejection of all compromise, the radical nature of his commitment and the extreme compulsion that makes him choose death in order to win glory make him a model of "excellence" for the living and lend that excellence a lustre, power and lasting quality that no ordinary life can have. Through the exemplary nature of the figure of the hero, as he is described in epic and depicted on the stele, the vital "worldly" values of strength, beauty, youth and ardour in combat acquire a consistency, stability and permanence which enable them to elude the inexorable decline that is the stamp of all human things. By wresting the names of its heroes from oblivion, the social memory is really attempting to root a whole system of values in the absolute, in order to preserve it from precariousness, instability and destruction: in short, to shelter it from time and from death.

In the relationship that is established, through the various forms of collective commemoration, between the individual with his heroic biography and the public, the Greek experience of death is transposed onto an aesthetic and ethical plane (with a "metaphysical" dimension). Just as they elaborated in mathematics the concept of space as an idea, one could also say of the Greeks that they constructed the concept of death as an idea or, to be more precise, that they undertook to socialise and civilise death — that is to say to neutralise it — by turning it into an "ideal type" of life.

II.1   However, epic did not simply give the face of death the dazzling glory of the ultimate degree of existence, the brilliance of life — a life which, in order to fulfil and sublimate itself must first be lost, which in order to assert its worth in perpetuity must disappear from the visible world and be transmuted into glory in commemorative poetry. In a number of ways, epic also denied the very idealisation that its song had the function of establishing in its verses.

When the epic text is content to counterpose the fine death of the young warrior who has fallen as a hero in the heat of battle, in the flower of his youth, and the dreadful death of an old man slaughtered defencelessly like a beast, or when, in contrast with the wonderful corpse of the hero stretched out on the field of battle where "all is beauty", it describes a body abused and unrecognisable, disfigured, mutilated, cut into pieces, a piece of carrion left for the wild animals or rotting in the open, then the denial does not really pose any problem: two contrary forms of death lend each other confirmation and reinforcement by their mutual exclusiveness. But there are some cases where the denial, as if operating from within, calls into question the very thing that epic is celebrating in the fine death, namely the glorious destiny of the hero. At times it presents death in general and the fear that it inspires in every human being in a picture so horrible and terrifying in its realism that the price to be paid for "commemoration" seems a very high one and the ideal of "imperishable glory" is in danger of appearing a very poor bargain.

II.2   Let us begin with the most general aspect of the problem. If death did not appear in epic as the ultimate horror, if it did not assume the monstrous mask of Gorgo so as to embody all that is beyond humanity, the unsayable, the unthinkable, all that is radically other, then there would be no heroic ideal. There would be no merit in the hero confronting death, choosing it and making it his own. There can be no heroes if there are no monsters to fight and overcome. Establishing an ideal concept of death does not mean ignoring or denying its dreadful reality. On the contrary, the ideal can only be constructed to the extent that the ''real'' is clearly defined as being opposed to it. (The construction of an abstract and perfect mathematical space presupposes, as its condition,the depreciation of perceptible space.) Far from underestimating the reality of death, its ''idealising'' takes this reality as its point of departure, depends upon it, just as it is, and aims to pass beyond it by reversing the perspective and inverting the terms of the problem. How is it that life is destroyed and sinks into death? That is the common question. To this question epic adds another: how is it that certain of the dead remain forever present in the life of the living? The first question presents death as the irremediable human evil; the second presents the heroic death as the condition for glorious survival in the memory of other men. Both questions, however, concern only the living. Whether it be dreadful or glorious, real or ideal, death is always the exclusive concern of those who are alive. It is the impossibility of conceiving death from the point of view of the dead that constitutes its horror, its radical strangeness, its complete otherness and that at the same time makes it possible for the living to bypass it by instituting within their social existence a constant commemoration of certain types of death. From the point of view of its function as a collective memory, epic is not composed for the dead; when it speaks of them or of death it is always to the living that it is addressed. About death as such or about the dead among the dead there is nothing to say. They exist on the other side of a threshold that nobody can cross without disappearing, that no word can reach without losing all meaning: in a world of night where the indiscernible reigns, a world both of silence and indistinguishable sound.

II.3   In Book xi of the *Odyssey*, Odysseus, having passed through the land of the Cimmerians, enveloped in night, crosses the waters of the River Ocean, the frontier of the world, and lands on the shores of Hades. Here the living hero meets the shade of the dead Achilles. This encounter brings together on the one hand the champion of endurance whose ideal, in the teeth of winds and tides, is to return safe and sound to his home and, on the other, the ''best of the Achaeans'', the model of the heroic warrior whose memory the entire *Iliad* is devoted to exalting because he chose a brief life and through his fine death managed to achieve imperishable glory. What words do they exchange? No doubt at all is involved where Odysseus, the living man, is concerned. Having learned from the trials and endless misfortunes that he has endured, one after another, in this life, Odysseus salutes Achilles as "the happiest" of beings, the one who was honoured as a god by everyone on earth and who continues, in Hades where he towers high above the others, to know nothing of misery, the common lot of all mortals. But Achilles' reply seems, at a stroke, to demolish the entire edifice the *Iliad* constructs to justify, celebrate and exalt the fine death of the hero. What Achilles says to Odysseus is: "Don't come and sing the praises of death to me in order to console me; I would rather live as the least of the servants of a poor peasant than reign as master over the innumerable masses of the dead."

Even allowing for the extent to which the *Odyssey* might stand in polemical contrast to the *Iliad* and for the way in which the characters of Odysseus and Achilles in the two works stand in opposition to one another, the fact remains that this episode truly appears to introduce within epic writing itself the most radical denial of that heroic death which the bard's poem presents as a survival in imperishable glory. But is there really any contradiction here? There would be if this glorious survival was localised in the kingdom of the dead for the Greeks, if the reward for a heroic death was entering Paradise rather than continuing to live on in the memory of living men. In the land of shadows, the shade of Achilles has no ear for the song of praise celebrating his exploits, no recollection to evoke and preserve the memory of himself. Achilles can only recover his senses, mind and consciousness — his identity — during the brief moment when, having drunk the blood of the victim sacrificed by Odysseus to call up the dead, he re-establishes a kind of fleeting contact with the world of the living. Before being lost, dissolving once more into the indistinct crowd of the dead, he has just enough time, having for a moment become once again Achilles, to rejoice at the news that, among the living, his son is of the same heroic cast as his father.

The glorious survival for which Achilles gave his life and chose death is the thing that haunts the memory of Odysseus and his companions, who are convinced that there is no destiny happier than his; it haunts Neoptolemus, so anxious to equal his father; it haunts all the living — Homer's audience — who can only conceptualise their own existence, their own identity, by reference to the heroic example. But in Hades there can be no glorious survival; Hades is the land of Oblivion. How can the dead remember? Why should they? Recollection can only take place within time. The dead do not live within time, not in the fleeting time of perishable living creatures nor in the constant time of the eternal gods. For the dead, with their empty heads, without energy and swathed in shadows, there is nothing to recollect.

II.4. The episode of the *Nekuia*, one moment of which we have described here, ends with Odysseus' precipitous departure for his ships. All of a sudden the hero was seized with "green fear" at the idea that Persephone could send up to him from the depths of Hades "the Gorgon head of the terrifying monster" (xi. 633–635). This head, a glimpse of which changes a man to stone, marks the limit between the dead and the living; it stands guard over the threshold, forbidding entrance to those who still belong to this world of light, this world of clear, articulated speech and recollection where every being, with its own form (its *eidos*), remains itself at least as long as it has not tipped the balance over into the other kingdom, the place of darkness, oblivion, confusion, that no words can describe.

This dreadful terror that the mask of Gorgo inspires is one that Odysseus has already experienced right at the beginning of the *Nekuia* and he expressed it then in exactly the same terms: "green fear clutches me" (xi. 43). What then overwhelmed him with alarm was not the mask of Gorgo but the monstrous otherness that can be glimpsed through it. What Odysseus was afraid to see — on the other side of the threshold, so to speak — was the dead gathering together in their own land, the swarming, indistinct mass of them, the innumerable crowd of shades who are no longer anybody and whose huge, confused, inaudible clamour has no longer anything human about it.

To call forth the dead, as Odysseus undertakes to do to question the shade of Tiresias, is to introduce order and number into their formless magma, to distinguish individuals by compelling them to fall into line, one behind the other, each one stepping forward in turn, on his own, to speak in his own name and remember.

Odysseus, the hero faithful to life, by executing a ritual of evocation which for a brief moment reintroduces the illustrious dead into the universe of the living, accomplishes the same task as the bard: when the poet, inspired by Memory, begins his song of recollection he admits that he is incapable of telling the names and exploits of the entire obscure crowd of warriors who fell beneath the walls of Troy. From among this anonymous faceless mass he selects and concentrates upon the exemplary figures of a small number of the chosen. In the same way Odysseus, wielding his sword, wards off the immense crowd of insubstantial shades from the blood of the victim and only allows it to be drunk by those whom he recognises because their names, saved from oblivion, have survived in epic tradition.

The episode of the *Nekuia* does not contradict the ideal of the heroic death, the fine death. It strengthens and completes it. The terrifying world of death is a world of confusion, chaos, unintelligibility, where nothing and nobody can exist any more. The only values that exist are the values of life, the only reality that of the living. If Achilles chooses to die young it is not because he values death above life. On the contrary, he cannot accept sinking, like just anybody, into the obscurity of oblivion, merging into the indistinct mass of "nameless ones". He wants to continue for ever in the world of the living, to survive in their midst, within them, and remain there as himself, distinct from any other, through the indestructible memory of his name and his renown.

The Greek ideal concept of death is this heroic attempt to push away as far as possible, beyond that uncrossable threshold, the horror of chaos, the horror of what has no form and no meaning, and to affirm in the face of and despite everything, the social permanence of this human individuality which must, by its very nature, be destroyed and disappear.

Death and the Hero

ROMILA THAPAR

Scattered across the Indian sub-continent are large numbers of memorial stones dedicated to men who have died in an act of heroism such as defending a village against raiders by land or by sea, or cattle against cattle-lifters, or who have died on the battle-field. Such stones have come to be called hero-stones and have quite recently attracted the attention of historians, archaeologists and anthropologists. Associated with them are the sati-stones, memorials commemorating the wives who have immolated themselves either on the funeral pyres of their husbands or on hearing of the death of their husbands in battle. Both these categories of memorial are in origin associated with the cult of the hero and date back to times when society was suffused with the ethics of the heroic age.

These stones are of more than archaeological interest since the concept underlying the monument not only relates to the changing perception of the death of a hero, but also indicates an important variant of what is generally described as "the Indian" view of death and the after-life. The latter derives from the high culture of brahmanical texts and practice, whereas the cult of the hero-stone is clearly a substratum cult, but with a widely distributed following. That historians and archaeologists have until recently tended to ignore this cult may also be partially explained by its being culturally a substratum cult and by the fact that it contradicts the neat generalisations culled from the classical Sanskrit texts.

The location of the hero-stones is neither geographically uniform nor arbitrary. They are found in larger numbers in western India (Rajasthan, Gujerat and Maharashtra), central India (Madhya Pradesh and the southern edges of the Ganges valley) and in south

India (Andhra Pradesh, Karnataka, Kerala and Tamil Nadu). Northern and eastern India generally register fewer examples.Topographically and ecologically there is a frequency of such memorials in upland areas, in the vicinity of passes across hills, and in areas regarded traditionally as frontier zones which often included primarily pastoral regions, the outskirts of forests and the edges of what have come to be called the ''tribal areas of central India''. Hero-stones are relatively infrequent in the large agricultural tracts of the Indus and Ganges valleys and in the agriculturally rich delta areas of the peninsula.

The origin of the hero-stones remains obscure. They may possible derive from the menhirs of the megalithic cultures in India of the first millennium B.C. (Srinivasan, 1946; Sontheimer, 1976). Their geographical distribution in the Indian peninsula seems to coincide with that of megalithic settlements, but the latter extend further into other areas as well. The closest correlation of the geographical distribution of hero-stones with archaeological cultures would be with the Black-and-red ware culture of the second and first millennia B.C., a ceramic industry which is also associated in some areas with the megalithic culture. India is a country of startling cultural survivals: the single menhir of stone or wood is still erected as a memorial (not necessarily over a grave) among the Marias of central India and the Khasis of the north-eastern hills. Another megalithic association is suggested by the occurrence of hero-stones in groups, rather like a graveyard, on the edges of settlements. However, the single stone can be located anywhere. The megalithic necropolis would suggest burials linked perhaps through kinship and possibly associated further by common claims to clan rights and land ownership.

The form of the hero-stone changed through time and the change was related to the status of the hero as well as to the action performed by him. The simplest stone was a flat slab on which was depicted the hero armed with a bow and arrow or a sword. The hero of higher status rode a horse and the trappings of the horse indicate status (Fig. 1).

FIG. 1. Hero stone of an early variety from Chanal (Bellary District) in Karnataka. (Courtesy: Director, Institute of Indian Art History, Karnataka University, Dharwar.)

The association of cattle or a wild animal such as a tiger would point to the hero dying in a cattle raid or mauled by a tiger (Fig. 2). Some stones also depict one or two objects which it is thought had a role in religious ritual, and on occasion a brief inscription is added containing the minimum information on the hero. Such simple stones have been dated to the mid-first millennium A.D. and continue into later centuries.

Towards the end of the first millennium A.D. the style of the hero-stone in many areas changed and became far more elaborate. The stone could now be either a slab, as before, or else a square column up to two metres in height with panels sculptured on all four sides. The shape of the stone came to resemble a small shrine with a decorative design on the top (Mate and Gokhale, 1971; Sontheimer, 1976). The three or more sculptured panels had a recognisable theme. The sun and the moon were sculpted at the top signifying the eternal character

FIG. 2. Hero stone showing hero grappling with a wild animal. From Pala, North Kanara District in Karnataka. (Courtesy: Director, Institute of Indian Art History, Karnataka University, Dharwar.)

of the memorial and the act (Fig. 3). Inscriptions of this period recording grants of land often state that the grant would last "as long as the sun and the moon endure", a phrase which signified that the grant could not be revoked. The symbolism would also relate to timelessness, a condition which the hero, when deified, would share with the gods. The highest panel carried the symbols of the religious sect to which the hero belonged: thus the *lingam* and the *yoni*, indicating phallic worship, were the symbols of the Śaivite sect to which sometimes the bull vehicle of Śiva was added (Fig. 4); the standing or seated figure of Mahavira would indicate a Jaina devotee. The hero might even be shown worshipping at the shrine. The second panel depicted the veneration of the hero, or else the hero being carried in a palanquin by celestial maidens (*apsaras*), presumably towards heaven. The lower panels provide the narrative of the incident. The hero is shown fighting either

FIG. 3. Hero stones from Wadhwan in Saurashtra (Gujerat). The sun and the moon are symbols of eternity. The mounted hero. (Courtesy: Director General, Archaeological Survey of India, New Delhi (Photo No 845/61).)

on foot or on horseback duly armed with a bow and arrow or a sword and spear and shield. He is frequently surrounded by enemies, some of whom he has killed (Fig. 5). In other cases the panels show stampeding cattle. In the coastal areas along the west coast sea battles with ships are more frequent. Except in rare cases of lengthy eulogies, where inscriptions occur on such stones they provide a minimum of information giving the name of the hero, perhaps mentioning the king of the region and a brief word of praise for the action.

The names in the earlier inscriptions suggest persons of low status, soldiers and guardians of the village, who died fighting against cattle-

FIG. 4. Hero stone from Banavasi (North Kanara District) in Karnataka. Lowest panel: the hero in action. Middle panel: the hero being transported to heaven in a palanquin. Top panel: the worship of a Śiva *lingam* in a shrine of an early architectural style. The hero is seated to the left and the bull Nandi, the vehicle of Śiva, is depicted on the right. (Courtesy: Director, Institute of Indian Art History, Karnataka University, Dharwar.)

lifters, marauders or invading armies on the rampage in the country-side (Vanamamalai, 1975). Many of the earlier stones from Tamil-Nadu come from North Arcot District which is known to have been at that time an area of livestock breeding where cattle-raiding would be one method of increasing wealth. The change in the style of the hero-stone seems to reflect a change in the status of the hero being

FIG. 5. Hero stone (in the Government Museum, Bangalore). Lowest panel: the hero fighting against cattle raiders. Middle panel: the hero being taken to heaven. Top panel: the hero deified. (Courtesy: Directorate of Archaeology and Museums in Karnataka, Mysore.)

Fig. 6.

memorialised. The elaborate stones commemorated heroes who claimed to belong to the upper caste groups, often claiming *ksatriya* status — it being the function of the *ksatriya* in the caste hierarchy to protect the other sections of the society. The indication of the hero's religious sect (Fig. 6) may have been due to the influence of the *bhakti* (devotional religion) sects which were popular at this time. The hero travelling to heaven was an essential element in the cult of the hero from the earliest times.

The earliest descriptions of hero-stones in literary sources come from the Tamil Śangam literature, generally ascribed to the period between 300 B.C. and A.D. 200 but possibly including interpolations of a later period. The *vīra-kal* or *Vīra-k-kal* is , literally, hero-stone, and is also referred to as *naḍukal*, the planted stone (Subrahmanian, 1966b). The stone, it is stated, commemorates a hero who has been killed in battle. The disembodied soul is regarded as powerful and could use its power for good or ill. It had a tendency to return to its kinsfolk unless it was appeased with rituals and the setting up of a stone, and these in turn were the means by which the power of the soul was appropriated by the kinsfolk. The cutting of a specially selected stone, which was believed to embody the soul of the hero, was begun on an auspicious day (Vanamamalai, 1975). When cut it was erected under a shady tree, bathed and purified and then inscribed. It now became an object of worship and the hero was immortalised both in the stone and in the songs and ballads composed about him. The stone was decorated with flowers and peacock feathers. The hero's spear and shield were placed close to it and the whole enclosed in a canopy of cloth. At regular intervals food specially cooked for the purpose was offered at the stone. Those going into battle sought the blessings of the hero by worshipping at the stone.

The symbolism of the objects associated with the ritual suggests various other links. The spear associated with the hero is also the symbol of the god Murugan whose priests carried a spear (Subrahmanian, 1966a). Murugan as Kārtikeya was worshipped as the god of war who killed the *asuras* (demons), was the lover and abductor of Valli and was the god of the hill-top.[1] His vehicle was the peacock which was

Fig. 6. Hero stone from Kaikini (North Kanara District) in Karnataka. The form is now far more complex with greater detail in the event shown. Lowest two panels: the hero in action. Middle two panels: the hero being deified and his eulogy being sung. Top-most panel: the hero worshipping at a Jaina shrine. The *kīrtimukha* mask at the top and other embellishments would link this stone chronologically with the temple architecture of the early medieval period. (Courtesy: Director, Institute of Indian Art History, Karnataka University, Dharwar.)

sometimes depicted on his banner, as was the cock. There are two major legends regarding his origin. The *Mahābharata* (III.213 ff.) narrates that the gods required a hero to lead them in the war against the demon Taraka and for this purpose Skanda was born as the son of the great god Śiva and his wife Pārvatī (Bhattacharya, 1970). Skanda was also known by the names of Kumāra, Mahāsena and Kārtikeya. His vehicle was the peacock. Another version of the story links his birth to those who are associated with the worship of the ancestors. It is said that Agni, the god of fire, dropped his seed on the banks of the Ganges and the six sisters known as the Kṛittikas nurtured it and Kārtikeya was born with six heads. The Kṛittikas are connected with fertility and the month of Kārtik is both the time of the harvest and the time of worshipping ancestors with the lighting of lamps. The ritual period of the *śrāddha*, when ceremonies are performed for the ancestors and for those recently dead, and specially prepared food is fed to selected brahmans, precedes the month of Kārtik. Rituals related to the worship of ancestors and the feeding of brahmans at the time of the *śrāddha* would also involve a display of wealth and of redistributive activities, this being one of the auspicious occasions for making gifts to worthy brahmans, who in turn ensured the well-being of departed souls.

Whereas in south India the references to hero-stones in literary sources seem to be earlier than their archaeological counterparts, in other areas of the country the archaeological finds predate the references in literature which are generally fairly late. Hero-stones in western Rajasthan referred to as *kīrti-stambha*—literally, pillars of fame—go back to the seventh century A.D. but a larger number are of the eleventh century and later (Agrawala, 1963). Many depict cattle raids and cleverly use a well-known legend to symbolise the protection of cattle.[2]

The hero-stones from Saurashtra and other parts of Gujerat are called *pāliya*, the etymology of the word being perhaps connected with *pāla*, the protector or guardian. The *pāliya-bhumi*, the place where several hero-stones are placed together, is often on the outskirts of the village and preferably on the bank of a river (Fischer and Shah, 1970; cf. Fig. 7). Those linked to the local ruling family may have their stones in the courtyard of the temple. The sculptured side generally faces east. The stones are worshipped annually at the time of Dipāvali, the festival when lamps are lit and which marks the autumn harvest and the start of the winter, which falls in the month of Kārtik. Those who claim descent from the hero also worship the stone on other occasions such as the period of the *śrāddha* and at the time of a marriage in the family. In the ritual connected with the setting up of a hero-stone, peacock feathers are important but the spear is absent.

Associated with the hero-stone are other memorial stones which may be regarded as complementary in some cases and subsidiary in others. Memorials to wives who have immolated themselves on the death of their husbands or have become *satis* (virtuous ones) are complementary to the hero-stone and sometimes the two memorials are combined in one. Occasionally in one of the panels of the hero-stone, there is a representation of both husband and wife on the funeral pyre (Sontheimer, 1976). However, the sati-stone is generally an independent memorial.

FIG. 7. A group of hero stones from Bedekini (North Kanara District) in Karnataka. Courtesy: Director, Institute of Indian Art History, Karnataka University, Dharwar.)

Saṅgam literature refers to *sati* as the condition of literally falling into flames; it is associated generally with the wife of the warrior, although on occasion other women are also said to have undergone the ritual of self-immolation (Subrahmanian, 1966b). The memorial is referred to as the *sati-kal* (sati-stone) or the *mā-sati-k-kal* and appears to have been the counterpart of the *vīra-k-kal* of the hero or the chief. The explanation for both kinds of memorials is that they symbolise loyalty to a person, the hero to his chief and the wife to her husband, and the preservation of honour. That it was also considered the normal ritual for the wife of the dead hero is apparent from a different source, the epic *Mahābhārata* in northern India where the wives of some of the heroes are said to have immolated themselves on the death of their husbands (Kane, 1941: 623 ff). A later source refers to all the widows of the Yādava clansmen becoming *satis*. Texts of the second millennium A.D.

debated whether such an act should be regarded as suicide, and therefore condemned, or as an act of merit, and therefore recommended.

The sati-stone depicted the right arm of a woman, bent at the elbow at a right angle with an open hand whose palm faced out. The arm could be shown tied to a post or free. The forearm is covered with bangles and occasionally a lime is held in the hand. The sun and the moon are depicted on either side and signify eternity as in the case of the hero-stone. Sometimes an auspicious symbol such as the *svastika* is also added (Figs 8 and 9). A brief inscription may mention the date and the names of the woman and of her husband. The right arm indicates purity and the condition of *sati*. It has also been suggested that it represents one of the high castes since in some rare cases the left arm replaces the right (Sontheimer, 1976). The post probably does not point to the woman having been tied to the post before immolation because the ritual demanded that she sit on the pyre with her dead husband's head in her lap. The post may well signify the act of sacrifice since in the Vedic sacrificial ritual the sacrificial offering was tied to the post (*yūpa*). The open hand and the lime symbolise the absence of evil and tradition has it that they both scare away the demons. A woman normally has to break her bangles on the death of her husband and a widow is recognised by this. The prominence given to the bangles in the sati-stone emphasises that the *sati* is not to be regarded as a widow since she remains a wife to her husband, having following him in death. Sati-stones were also frequently worshipped, the *sati* being regarded as a deity. She was required to bless the assembly before stepping onto the funeral pyre and her curse was greatly feared. In some cases sati-stones have come to be the centre for the sanctum of large temples such as the one of Jhunjhunu in Rajasthan.

As in the case of the hero-stones, the frequency of sati-stones also dates to the period after the mid-first millennium A.D. Among the earliest epigraphical references to a *sati* is that to the wife of a chief, Goparaja, who died in battle in the early sixth century A.D. (Fleet, 1970). The inscription appears on what seems to be an elaborate hero-stone memorial in the form of a *lingam* (phallus) indicating Śaivite associations. Sati-stones increase in number towards the end of the millennium. The largest archaeological finds date to more recent centuries. Where castes are mentioned, the majority claim *kṣatriya* status, and they therefore belong to the land-owning castes who linked themselves to the best known lineages of earlier times.

Subsidiary memorials, not unrelated to the hero-stone, are those which are meant to appease the spirit of the dead. The setting up of these stones or wooden memorials follows a pattern similar to that of

FIG. 8. Sati stone from Wadhwan in Saurashtra (Gujerat). The right arm of a woman with bangles intact and an open hand with a lime. The *svastika* symbol indicates an auspicious event and the sun and the moon symbol for eternity are prominent. (Courtesy: Director General, Archaeological Survey of India, New Delhi (Photo No. 842/61).)

the hero-stones.[3] The significance of these memorials for this discussion lies in the method of their being made and erected for much the same ritual was probably carried out for the hero-stone and the sati-stone. The ritual is performed by the *bhagat* or local cult priest and not by a brahman, thus emphasising the substratum nature of the cult. The role of the *bhagat* is important since it links the action to the Little Tradition. None of the texts refer to the brahman performing the ritual for erecting the hero-stone or the sati-stone. Doubtless the more elaborate rituals of the high caste *kṣatriya* immortalised in a hero-stone may well have been performed by brahmans but this may not have applied to the more primitive hero-stone.[4]

Echoes of the hero-stone ritual can also be observed in the worship of cult deities such as Iyenar (Whitehead, 1921). As the guardian of the village Iyenar rides a horse and is sometimes represented only by a clay image of a horse, but is invariably surrounded by clay images of the heroes who assist him. The ensemble is placed on the outskirts of a village under a large tree. Offerings of food are made by the villagers to the heroes, the food being eventually eaten by the cult priest who is usually not a brahman. Sheep, goats and fowls are also offered and after the sacrifice the priest keeps the head whilst the body is taken by the worshipper. At the annual festival the image is washed in a liquid paste made from a number of ingredients and the figure draped in red cloth. The ritual at this time is in imitation of the worship of images in the temples dedicated to various Hindu deities of the Great Tradition.

The differentiation between the hero-stone and the memorial to the spirit of a dead man has its counterpart in the death rituals of what may be called the Great Tradition in Hinduism. The early texts on domestic rituals mention two categories of rituals for the dead (Ap.D.S. II.7.16.1–3; Apte, 1954). The lesser category relates to the *pretas*, those recently dead whose spirits may still be hovering among the living and who have to be appeased and set to rest by a series of ceremonies. The more important rituals are dedicated to the *pitṛis*, the ancestors in the patrilineage for whom rites are performed, particularly during the annual calendrical period of the *śrāddha* when food is offered to the ancestors to nourish them and when brahmans are fed. Whereas the first category of ritual grows out of a fear of the *preta* and the need to propitiate him and convert him into a friendly ancestor, the second is essentially born out of the need to nurture the souls of the ancestors and to maintain a tradition of remembrance. It is assumed that the ancestors are living in heaven, for the dead are nourished in heaven by the food given at the *śrāddha*. Such a concept would seem to conflict with that of a cycle of rebirth and reincarnation. Some texts seek to

FIG. 9. Sati stone from Bedekini (North Kanara District) in Karnataka. In addition to the usual features of the sati stone, it depicts the hero and the sati seated together. (Courtesy: Director, Institute of Indian Art History, Karnataka University, Dharwar.)

explain this contradiction by arguing that the food reaches the ancestor whether he be identified with the gods or reborn in some other form. Such rituals seem to reflect an early and continuing belief in heaven and hell which is interwoven into the concept of reincarnation.

Implicit in the notion of the hero-stone is also the interweaving of various customs regarding the disposal of the dead. Both the Vedic texts and the Śaṅgam literature assume the coexistence of a variety of methods. The dead can be cremated, buried, cast away or exposed. Gradually cremation became the norm in the high culture. The *asuras*, opposed to the practices of the *āryas* in many instances, were known to bury their dead in stone structures beneath the earth (*Ṛgveda* X.18; *Atharvaveda* XVII.2.34; *Śatapatha Brāhmana* XIII.8. 1–4). This may be a reference to megalithic burials in stone cists. The range suggests the continuance of earlier forms of burial together with cremation. The memorials, to the extent that they symbolise a grave, are suggestive of the notion of burial even when the actual disposal may have been cremation.

The firm faith in the belief that the hero lived in heaven after he died suggests the popularity of an alternative to the belief in reincarnation. This is particularly striking in the centuries A.D. when the doctrine of reincarnation was widely accepted. Living in heaven was in a sense the termination of a cycle of lives, although this is not stated. Heaven was essential in any case if the hero was to be deified, which seems to have been a recognised tradition. The grammarian Pāṇini, composing his grammar in the fifth century B.C., states that distinguished *kṣatriya* heroes become the objects of religious devotion (IV.3.99). Deification is perhaps most evident in the concept of the *pañca-vīraḥ* or five heroes of the Vṛṣṇis, a sub-clan of the Yādavas.[5] The pre-eminent family among the Vṛṣṇis was that of Vasudeva, and three generations of his descendants —sons, grandson and great-grandson—are deified as the five Vṛṣṇi heroes. Among them one, Kṛṣṇa Vāsudeva, was to be identified as the *avatāra* or incarnation of the god Viṣṇu. Tradition maintains that Kṛṣṇa Vāsudeva has a pastoral association, his early life being spent among the cattle keepers of Mathura. It was also around the cult of the *pañca-vīraḥ* and Kṛṣṇa Vāsudeva that there developed the *bhakti* movement of devotional religion which has come to be called Bhagvatism. There appears to be a curious intertwining of the cult of the hero with pastoralism and with the emergence of the devotional sects.

The transformation of a hero-stone into a deity can be seen in the cult of Viṭhobā at Paṇḍharpur (in Maharashtra), in the suggestion that the image now worshipped was in origin a hero-stone and the hero was gradually changed into a deity and given a new iconography, in keeping with his incorporation into the cult of Kṛṣṇa Vāsudeva (Deleury, 1960; Tulpule, 1977–8). Paṇḍharpur was located in the pastoral zone of the western Deccan and the pastoral appeal of the Kṛṣṇa cult would have attracted to it the local people. The evolution of the hero-cult, with strong pastoral overtones, into a cult of devotional religion occurred in this area as well, perhaps through the impact of the migration of pastoralists and of religious ideas. By the twelfth century Paṇḍharpur became the centre of the *bhakti* or devotional cult in which devotion was directed to Kṛṣṇa as the cult deity and he was said to have taken the form of Viṭhoba. This deity and the territory in which he was worshipped became crucial in the self-perception of the Marathas when they set up a state in the seventeenth century. The original hero of the hero-stone had undergone a transformation and was now in a world far removed from that of the heroes.

The world of the heroes was steeped in the notion of status by birth, this status being reinforced through the heroic act (*vīrya*) which brought the hero fame (*kīrti, yaśa*) (Kailasapathy, 1968: 229ff). In a society given to competitiveness, the heroic act was also an act of individual self-assertion and the hero-stone captured the moment of self-assertion for eternity. For the hero's wife to become a *sati* would be in keeping with the values of the heroic cult where the woman was also required to demonstrate an almost aggressive self-assertion through a heroic act, thereby ensuring herself both fame and deification. Together with the stone the ballads and the epics were the means of conveying the renown to later generations. The hero-stone commemorated in form what the epic commemorated in words.

That this changed somewhat in later centuries is suggested by the function of the hero-stone and the *sati*-stone in the second millennium A.D. The heroic act became an avenue to status and status in itself required the association with a heroic act. Those of high status were eulogised through hero-stones until finally the mere fact of belonging to a ruling family entitled one to a hero-stone, as for example in the *chhatris* of some Rajput royal families. In the same way the act of self-immolation was no longer a voluntary act of heroic dimensions but was on occasion the sordid detail of a royal funeral or, as some have suspected, the ritual removal of a legitimate heir to an inheritance.

The hero-stone in the earlier periods was the focus of gatherings of kinsmen and a form of ancestor worship, since it was generally the patrilineages which maintained the worship of the stone. This helped to strengthen lineage ties as well as the historical memory of the village and the locality. The rituals emphasised the aggregation of the hero to the community rather than his separation, despite his deification. The memorials provided a different type of continuity from the *śrāddha* ceremonies: it was a political and social continuity, relating to territory and descent groups. In the folk culture the hero-stone replaced the historical text and the tending of the hero-stone was almost synonymous with recording the past. The frequency of hero-stones is greater in areas where the oral tradition was the custodian of history. The incidental echoes of the *śrāddha* rituals would have served to foster communication between those of the Great and the Little Tradition, for the hero-stone represented a substratum cult. Those lacking a sufficiently high status perhaps used the hero as an ancestor and, latching on to his lineage, may well have used this to claim *kṣatriya* status. The hero entered the collective memory and became an ideal. The symbols associated with him raise him, as it were, above the context of family, time and place.

The hero-stone cult had an extensive distribution in India; nevertheless, it manifests local styles and has distinct regional forms. Yet in substance it is similar and much of the symbolism seems to derive from the same sources. Did the cult originate in the widely diffused Yādava clans who, as cattle-herders and early agriculturalists in many regions, carried it with them in their extensive migrations and who continued with the cult even when some of their lineages rose to the status of dynasties (Thapar, 1978: 240 ff)? Or did it have its origins in a "heroic age" which venerated its heroes in a near-identical fashion in many parts of the sub-continent? The association with Kārtikeya and later the assimilation of the Kṛṣṇa Vāsudeva cult were common features over a wide geographical area. Admittedly both can easily be explained since the first is the deity of war, so essential to a hero cult, and the other, being the pastoral god *par excellence*, would be the natural deity in cattle-keeping areas. The elaboration of the cult in its second and later phase does suggest the rise in status of groups lower in the social scale as well as the mingling of local cults with those of what might be called the classical culture.

An impressionistic assessment of the geographical distribution of these memorials (in the absence of careful mapping) suggests that they tend to be concentrated in what have been called "frontier zones" — the peripheral areas of kingdoms and the intersection of ecological zones, particularly where pastoralism separated areas of intensive cultivation or lay close to forested areas. Frontier zones were often maintained as buffer regions where political security was transient and where royal armies did not necessarily guarantee protection to the local inhabitants. They would therefore inevitably have recourse to their own arrangements for protection, in which the village hero or the local chief played a major role. If the "hero" happened to be a member of the local elite his family may well have emulated the life-style of the royal court and the hero would stake his claim to status by protecting the villagers. In the absence of royal troops this would give considerable credibility to the hero, particularly when the protection may have necessitated defending the village from the pillage of royal armies campaigning in the vicinity. This would suggest a differentiation of military functions in a decentralised political system. The core areas of powerful kingdoms would have had less use for what they would have regarded as upstart heroes. The hero cult therefore also acts as a marker separating those societies in which the significance of the clan and the heroic ideal remain strong from those in which such things are regarded as memories of the past. Peasant protest arising from an inability to pay revenue demands often took the form not of revolts but of migrations. Such peasant groups would tend to settle in the frontier zones in an effort to bring fresh land under cultivation and this would bring them into conflict with the existing population. Alternatively, protesting peasant groups if they failed to find fresh land would take to brigandage, and raiding a village was a relatively easy means of acquiring a minimum livelihood.

The period from the late first millennium A.D. was characterised by shifting political boundaries in which small states were frequently founded, survived for brief periods and then were either incorporated into a larger state or were readjusted in new alliances. This brought frontier zones into importance either in their earlier role as buffers or alternatively as areas to be settled and developed. The western Deccan around Paṇḍharpur was a clear example of such an area. The gradual conversion of the hero-stone into Viṭhobā and its links with the Kṛṣṇa cult not only demonstrates the process of the mutual assimilation of cults and rituals of the Great and the Little Tradition, but also marks the acculturation of the frontier zone. Not surprisingly such cults play a significant role in state formation.

But above all the hero-stone gave a different meaning to death. Death is in any case a change in status and the deification of the hero was a distinctive change. That it was not an ordinary death is reflected in the fact that although the death rites may have been restricted to the polluting space of the cremation ground, the event was commemorated in the precincts of the temple or in an area which acquired sanctity because of the presence of the hero-stone. The setting up of the hero-stone echoes the burial practices of earlier times and yet it does not mark the place of relics from the cremation. To this extent it differs from the tradition of building tumuli to the dead in which their relics were enshrined as in some of the *stūpas* and *caityas* adopted in Buddhist ritual.

The heroic act ensured the hero an abode in heaven. The promise of heaven, explicit in the early hero-stones, continued in the later phase as well. Not only did the hero not have to suffer the cycle of rebirth but his reward was immediate in his being taken to heaven. In the absence of an eschatology requiring a judgment day, this was a condition of eternal, timeless bliss. But the ultimate appeal transcended heaven and lay in the fact of deification. In a culture where the bestowal of divinity on animate and inanimate entities is common, deification was in itself perhaps not startling, but that it meant a different level of status for the hero was in effect the prize which made the heroic action worthwhile and placed a premium on a hero's death.

Notes

1. In the *tinai* concept, as evident from Śaṅgam literature, the hill region is associated with the Kuriñci flower which in turn was the symbol of Murugan. It is also connected with love in the Akam part of the literature and with cattle raiding in the Puram sections. There is therefore an inter-linking of many ideas (K. Sivathamby, 1974).
2. Among the legends related of the cowherd god Kṛṣṇa Gopāla set in the region of Mathura (on the Yamuna south of Delhi) there is one which states that the power of Kṛṣṇa was challenged by the god Indra who poured down torrents of rain to flood the land and terrorise both men and cattle. Kṛṣṇa, undaunted, lifted the mountain Govardhana on his finger and the cattle took shelter beneath it and survived the wrath of Indra. The use of this imagery of cattle sheltering beneath a mountain is frequent in these hero-stones where it replaces the depiction of the hero protecting cattle and such stones are therefore called *Govardhana-kīrti-stambha.*
3. The memorial is dedicated to one who has died suddenly or violently and whose spirit is thought to haunt and possibly harass his living kinsmen. The ritual is performed by the *bhagat*, the priest of the local cult, who is not a brahman. In a version of the ritual prevalent in Gujerat the memorial is cut from a log of teak wood taken after due libations to the tree in the forest and in the presence of family members accompanied by musicians. The assembly travels to the forest in a cart. The carving of the log takes a few days and although women are not permitted on the premises, others can watch the process and feed at the expense of the family whilst doing so. A small stone is taken from the property of the deceased and is said to represent the soul of the person who has died. This is buried either on the property of the deceased or along a road leading to his village.

The memorial is placed on the ground above the stone, a ceremony which leads to much festivity. The ritual performed by the *bhagat* requires him to go into a trance and request the spirit of the deceased not to haunt and harass the living. A chicken is beheaded and its blood mixed with alcohol, some of which is sprinkled on the memorial and the remainder drunk by the *bhagat*. The feathers of the chicken are placed on the memorial and its flesh and the alcohol are given to those present. The memorial has a flat surface and is generally of wood. Since stone is expensive, stone memorials are a sign of status. The top is shaped and the symbols of the sun and the moon are shown, with scenes depicted beneath them in horizontal panels. There is usually a bird, generally a peacock or a parrot, a man or a rider with an attendant, a cartful of musicians perhaps representing the ritual of cutting the log, and possibly some indication of the situation in which death has occurred, as for example the depiction of a snake or a crocodile. The memorial becomes the permanent resting place of the spirit of the deceased and is named after him. It is worshipped annually by the entire family (Fischer and Shah, 1973).

4. An interesting dichotomy is observed in some cases. In the village of Bedsa (near Poona in Maharashtra) a clear distinction is maintained between the hero-stone depicting a single hero crudely cut in stone worshipped by the Mahar untouchable community with goat sacrifices and alcohol being part of the ritual conducted by Mahar priests, and the elaborately sculpted square columns of the heroes of high status which stand in a row beside the Śiva temple and are worshipped with offerings of coconut and *sindhur* (vermilion powder) by the brahmans of the village. The former is now described as the guardian of the village by the Mahars and even if it was once a hero-stone it is now serving the function of a cult deity as well. The high status heroes are remembered more precisely as persons who repeatedly defended the village from invaders.

5. The term *pañca-vīrah* is reminiscent of the Tamil term *aimperumvelir*, also meaning the five great heroes or chiefs and who are also said to be of the Yādava clan (Subrahmanian, 1966a: 110). The five heroes were worshipped as a group and by the early centuries A.D. images of the five are also referred to (The Mora Inscription, "Epigraphia Indica" XXIV: 194; the Ghosundi inscription, *ibid.* XXII: 204). For the persistence of the pattern of five heroes, see Thapar (1979).

References

AGRAWALA, R. C. (1963). "Pascami Rājasthan ke kuch Prārambika Smṛiti Stambha". *Varadā*, April 1963, 68ff.

AP. D. S. = Āpastamba Dharma Sūtra: "The Sacred Books of the East" (M. Müller, ed.), vol. 2, translated by G. Bühler (1879). Clarendon Press, Oxford.

APTE, V. M. (1954). "Social and Religious Life in the Grihya Sutras". Popular Book Depot, Bombay.

ATHARVAVEDA-SAMHITA, translated by W. D. Whitney (1971). Motilal Banarsidass, Delhi.

BHATTACHARYA, S. (1970). "The Indian Theogony". Cambridge University Press, Cambridge.

DELEURY, G. A. (1960). "The Cult of Viṭhoba". Deccan College, Poona.

"EPIGRAPHIA INDICA" (1892). Burgess, J., and Hultzch, E., eds. Archaeological Survey of India, Departments of State and Public Institutions, Calcutta.

FISCHER, E. and SHAH, H. (1970) "Rural Craftsmen and Their Work". National Institute of Design, Ahmedabad.

FISCHER, E. and SHAH, H. (1973). "Vetra ne Khambha — memorials for the dead". Gujarat Vidyapeeth, Ahmedabad.

FLEET, J. F. (ed.) (1970). "Corpus Inscriptionum Indicarum", vol. III. Indological Book House, Varanasi.

KAILASAPATHY, K. (1968). "Tamil Heroic Poetry". Clarendon Press, Oxford.

KANE, P. V. (1941). "History of Dharmaśāstra", vol.II, part 1. Bhandarkar Oriental Research Institute, Poona.

MATE, M. S. and GOKHALE, S. (1971). Aihole: an interpretation. In "Studies in Indian History and Culture" (S. Ritti and B. R. Gopal, eds), pp. 501–504. Karnatak University, Dharwar.

RGVEDA, "The Hymns of the Ṛgveda", translated by R. T. H. Griffith (1963 reprint). Chowkhamba Sanskrit Series, Varanasi.

ŚATAPATHA BRĀHMANA, "The Sacred Books of the East" (M. Müller, ed.), vol. 12, translated by J. Eggerling (1882). Clarendon Press, Oxford.

SIVATHAMBY, K. (1974). Early South Indian society and economy: the Tinai concept. Social Scientist, 29 (vol. 3, no. 5), 20–37.

SONTHEIMER, G. D. (1976). Some memorial monuments of western India. In "German Scholars on India" (Cultural Department of the Embassy of the Federal Republic of Germany, ed.), vol. II, pp. 264 ff. Nachiketa Publications, Bombay.

SRINIVASAN, K. (1946). The megalithic burials and urnfields of South India. Ancient India, 2, 9–16.

SUBRAHMANIAN, N. (1966a). "Pre-Pallavan Tamil Index". University of Madras, Madras.

SUBRAHMANIAN, N. (1966b). "Śaṅgam Polity". Asia Publishing House, Madras.

THAPAR, R. (1978). Puranic lineages and archaeological cultures. In Thapar, "Ancient Indian Social History: some interpretations", pp. 240–267. Orient Longman, New Delhi.

THAPAR, R. (1979). The historian and the epic. Annals of the Bhandarkar Oriental Research Institute, 60, 199–213.

TULPULE, S. G. (1977-8). The origin of Viṭṭhala: a new interpretation. Annals of the Bhandarkar Oriental Research Institute, 58–59, 1009–15.

VANAMAMALAI, N. (1975). Hero-stone worship in ancient South India. *Social Scientist*, **34** (vol. 3, no. 10), 40–46.

WHITEHEAD, H. (1921). "The Village Gods of South India" (2nd edition). Association Press and Oxford University Press, Calcutta.

The Death of the Gods

ELENA CASSIN (translated by S. C. HUMPHREYS)

The topic I have chosen to discuss is the meaning of the concept of "death" as applied to a god, i.e. in the culture with which I am concerned, a being characterised as immortal. As far as I know, the problem has never been discussed except in studies of the gods who die and are reborn: Tammuz-Adonis (Gurney, 1962) or alternatively Marduk (von Soden, 1955, 1957).

The first point to be stated is that in ancient Mesopotamia even the death of men and animals is not presented simply as a given fact present from the beginning of time. No text on the creation of man clearly alludes to it. It is nowhere stated that this animated doll which the gods produce out of a cleverly worked mixture of clay and blood (*Atraḫâsis*, Lambert, W. G. and Millard, 1969: 56 ff.) or from a scrap of clay (*Theodicy* XXVI ll. 276–279, Labat *et al.*, 1970: 327; *Gilgamesh* Tablet II, ll. 33–34, Labat *et al.*, 1970: 151) or, alternatively, from coagulated blood (*Enûma-elish*, Tablet VI, ll. 5–6, Labat *et al.*, 1970: 59) is destined to die, i.e. to distintegrate after a longer or shorter period of life.

In Genesis Elohim does not fix the duration of the life of Adam; the only allusion to the matter occurs in Genesis IV when Elohim chases Adam and Eve out of the garden of Eden for fear that, having eaten the fruit of the tree of knowledge, they should also taste that of the tree of life and so become immortal. The first human death is that of Abel, and it is a death by violence. Other indications also suggest that the idea of death as a natural phenomenon establishes itself on earth only with difficulty. The life-span attributed to the descendants of Adam and Eve in the Bible is very long, and it is only after the Flood that human life contracts to a shorter duration. In Babylonia too there is a possible allusion in the poem *Atraḫâsis* to a fixing of the term of human

317

life after the Deluge.[1] The oldest, and only, explicit reference is that in *Gilgamesh* which clearly states the problem of the opposition between death as the lot of mankind and immortality as the lot of the gods (*Gilgamesh* Tablet X, MIII ll. 2–5: Labat *et al.*, 1970: 205).

But if, as the wise Siduri said to Gilgamesh, the gods have allocated death to mankind while reserving life for themselves, this does not exclude the possibility that the gods in certain circumstances can themselves be put to death. Situations of this type already appear in Sumerian myths. Nevertheless, in the myth of the creation of the universe and of man narrated in the *Enûma-elish* the theme takes on a more precise significance from the fact that a succession of murders committed against the primordial gods is recorded.

The first to suffer is Apsû. This god, from whom "the gods are born" forms with Tiamat, "who shall bring them all to birth", the primordial couple, "when the sky above had not yet been named and the earth below still lacked a name". The first gods were born from the union of Tiamat, the salt waters, and Apsû, the sweet waters which come from below ground. Evolution to more developed divine forms proceeds gradually as new gods are born; and the autonomy which the young gods manifest leads to generational conflict. Apsû decides to exterminate them, but Ea's wide-ranging knowledge enables him to realise what Apsû is planning and frustrate the plot: he looses on Apsû a spell which paralyses him. Apsû loses his attributes of sovereignty, the diadem (*agû*) and shining light (*melammu*), allows himself to be bound, and is put to death (Tablet I, l. 69: Labat *et al.*, 1970: 40). From this moment Apsû becomes the dwelling-place of his conqueror, Ea, ruler of the element of water.

The struggle between Marduk and Tiamat, who remained a widow after the murder of Apsû, is far more instructive. It brings into conflict two deities whose opposed character is stressed by the texts. One of them, Tiamat—the waters of the sea, sometimes calm, sometimes uncontrolled—constitutes with Apsû the origin of all things, but she produces them in a way which is, literally, anarchic—following no pre-established plan. The pairs of gods who are born from them are all prototypes: Laḫmu and Laḫamu, Anshar, the totality of Things-Above; and Kishar, the totality of Things-Below. Anshar and Kishar introduce a mutation because they produce a son, Anu, who is their equal and resembles his father. Anu in his turn produces a son "who is his replica and his image", Nudimmud, the god Ea.

Tiamat is slow to react to her husband's murder and is only roused from her passivity by pressure to avenge Apsû's death from a group of deities opposed to the actions of the younger gods. Her whole behaviour is characterised by indecision and the absence of a consistent line of conduct.

By contrast, Marduk, who is one of the youngest gods, represents a fully "acculturated" type of divinity. His exceptional vitality appears from the moment of his birth; it is proved by the halo round his head, but this is not his only original trait. In opposition to Tiamat, whose power and ruling status come from the fact that she is the primordial goddess and also the widow of Apsû, Marduk demands to be *elected* champion of the gods by the assembly (*puḫru*). Thus two totally different types of sovereignty are represented and contrasted in the personalities of Tiamat[2] and Marduk.

In the face of Tiamat and her followers, monsters whom she has transformed into gods purely by wishing it, Marduk is the incarnation of legitimacy and order. This key distinction between them can be discerned in all fields, even in the choice of the arms Marduk uses against his adversary. Marduk fights from a chariot — a vehicle which at this period (second half of the second millennium) is the typical attribute of royalty. As for his weapons in the stricter sense, while the bow (*qašhtu*) and club (*miṭṭu*) are used in Mesopotamia both in war and in hunting, the same cannot be said of the net (*saparru* or *shushkallu*) which is reserved for hunting alone. In the hands of the gods, the net is used to entrap in its meshes humans whom they wish to chastise.[3] The fact that the net appears among the arms used by Marduk against Tiamat thus has a precise meaning: the primordial goddess is seen here as a wild animal to be hunted rather than as an equal to be met in combat. The net has an important role to play in the fighting. Marduk succeeds in spreading it out and enveloping Tiamat, on whom he then looses the storm-wind which gets into her throat and forces her to keep her mouth wide open. The text describes how Marduk's arrows seam the interior of Tiamat's body, distended by the wind, until the moment when he literally finishes her off: puts an end to her life and stands upright on her corpse.

Other traits too present Tiamat as a formless, savage creature. "Her speech is full of lies, like those on the lips of a *lullû*." The *lullû* is the living creature which the goddess of childbirth, Bêlêt-ilî or Aruru, makes with her hands out of a scrap of clay.[4]

All humans share the nature of being *lullû*, yet for some this is only the point of departure for a further evolution, whereas for others it is their definitive state. The opposition between Tiamat, the Lie, and Marduk, the Truth, in reality only expresses one aspect of the idea which runs right through the poem, that of legitimacy. Yet there is something more. When Marduk approaches Tiamat's corpse, which he is going to split in two ''like a fish for drying'' (Tablet IV, l. 136, Labat *et al.*, 1970: 54), the remains of the goddess are referred to by the term *kûbu*, abortion.[5] Alive, Tiamat was a *lullû*, a creature which had not yet achieved cultural maturity; dead, she is no more than a *kûbu*, an embryo which has not yet reached physical maturity. Alive or dead, she is no more than a potentiality. It is out of this potentiality that Marduk, architect of the universe, will create according to a pre-established plan beautiful and perfect things (*niklāti*), that is, the heavens and the earth.[6]

The third god to be put to death was to be Kingu, whom Tiamat had married after Apsû's death, concurrently passing on to him the sovereign power, without having her choice ratified by the assembly of the gods. Marduk reproaches her with this high-handed act as he launches his attack on her: ''You named Kingu as your mate, you established him on a dais of sovereignty to which he had no right.''[7] Furthermore, Tiamat had handed over to Kingu the ''tablets of destiny'' which made the holder's words irrevocable. Despite this power, Kingu passively allows himself to be bound. When Marduk, having created heaven and earth, decides to create man in order to relieve the gods from their daily labours and permit them to rest, it is Kingu — according to a very early motif — who will be sacrificed for his guilt in having incited Tiamat to rebel against her children; his coagulated blood will be used to build a framework of bones in order to construct the living being named ''man'' (Tablet VI, ll. 5–6; Labat *et al.*, 1970: 59).

The violent actions to which these three gods are subjected end in death. In the two former cases the same verb *nâru(m)* is used to express the action of killing (for Apsû, Tablet I, l. 69, Labat *et al.*, 1970: 40; for Tiamat, Tablet IV, l. 105, *ibid.*: 53). Kingu however is ''bloodied'' — literally, ''they opened his blood'' (Tablet VI, l. 32, *ibid.*: 60). The verb *nâru(m)*, which in Hebrew and Arabic means ''pierce'', is used in Akkadian for ''killing'' a man or a god, but never an animal.[8] However, the action of *nâru(m)*, ''killing'', can be directed against cedar trees (*erênu*), which always have a special significance in myth and history (Cassin, 1968: 62–64).

Neither the word *mûtu*, ''dead'', nor the verb *mâtu*, ''to die'', is used with reference to any of the three slain gods. In fact, though they are killed, none of them *dies*. To die is to disintegrate, disappear, revert to nothing, to the primal clay. The three gods, on the contrary, acquire a new form and structure by being put to death: this is so not only for Tiamat whose carcass is used to create heaven and earth, and for Kingu whose blood forms the skeleton of man, but equally for Apsû who becomes the container (i.e. something fixed, with precise limits) of the god Ea. This transformation, which is also an evolution into more complex and higher forms, implies that the vital force of the gods is inexhaustible. There is therefore no contradiction between the events described above and the passage of *Gilgamesh* mentioned earlier. To be killed is not, really, to die.

This brings me to reflect on the meaning, at the level of mankind, of the concept of "natural death". In the Bible, to die old and full of years, like the patriarchs, has a different significance from dying young. The Old Testament prophets — Hosea, for example — when they heap curses on the infidelity of the people of Israel to Yahweh, comparing it to prostitution, establish a connection between the nation's immoral conduct and the sterility[9] with which adulterous women are afflicted, or the ephemeral life[10] of any children which they may somehow bring to birth. It appears that both abortion or losing a child at an early age — or at any rate before it reaches adulthood — may be a sign that the child was the result of an irregular union. Furthermore, when someone dies young, there is always a *reserve of life* which remains unused, and which may represent a danger for the living: energy no longer linked to its original purpose. The young dead person, unhappy and unsatisfied, becomes as a result virtually a demon.

A group of texts studied a few years ago by Sylvie Lackenbacher (1971), throw a remarkable light on this problem. Some concern the young man (*eṭlu*) who has missed out on everything in his brief life. They represent a sort of lament of the unlucky man (Cassin, 1968: 93–94) which lists the setbacks which have punctuated the life of a being persecuted by fate. His mother brought him into the world in the street, with cries of pain;[11] his life was passed in anguish and prostration. He never enjoyed the pleasures and delights of youth: he did not marry, he did not sire a child, "he did not touch the genitals of his wife, nor lift aside her clothing from her loins"; in any case, his marriage was not consummated, because he was expelled from his father-in-law's house (Lackenbacher, 1971: 124, ll. 15–22). In these conditions the *eṭlu*, once dead, cannot but become a menace to the living, an evil *eṭemmu* or a demon, for example a *lilû*. In spells against the demon *Ardat-lilî* (Lackenbacher, 1971: 131–141) we find a whole series of activities appropriate to those whose life has been cut short by death. She is "the girl who did not get her share of luck". She has been deprived of the same joys and pleasures as the *eṭlu*, but in reverse (*ibid.* 136, 140; ll. 9 ff.):[12] "The young girl who, unlike a normal girl, has never been impregnated by a man, the young girl who, unlike a normal girl, has never been deflowered by a man; the young girl who has never touched her husband's genitals, the young girl who has never lifted aside the garment from her husband's loins, the young girl whose fibula has never been opened by a handsome man, the young girl whose breasts have never filled with milk . . . the young girl who has never been called by the name of mother, who has never named (a child), the young girl who does not run with the (other) young girls in the streets and lanes."[13]

It is possible that conceptions of a similar nature come into play also in the practices documented in Mesopotamia, in Israel and in the Semitic world in general for the treatment of enemy populations in war. The way in which the corpses of enemy warriors are treated is worthy of note, even though other elements must clearly be taken into account here. For example, the emasculation of dead warriors is evidently prompted by several motives. It is not only as a proof of his own valour that a warrior cuts off the genitals of the enemy he has killed (Widengren, 1953). By mutilating the dead of the parts which served, while he was alive, as the source of future lives, the Assyrians,[14] for example, operate symbolically on the future of the nation they have temporarily vanquished. Yet in addition it is necessary to destroy this reserve of life, as if the warrior was not really dead until the parts in which his vital force was concentrated have been destroyed. To rip open the bellies of pregnant women[15] and to slaughter all married women (the ḥerem)[16] testify to the same urge to destroy all potential for life which might be dangerous to the conquerors. As the bones of the dead enemy are scattered or ground to powder, the seed is squeezed out from the testicles of the still-fresh corpse like "seeds of ripe cucumber", and the wombs of the women are emptied of the embryos they contained.[17] In order to eliminate the enemy, the tree must be deprived both of its roots and of its buds.

In other words, it seems that even at the human level a violent interruption of life does not completely cut off biological continuity. It is this which makes it necessary to proceed to additional operations whose effect is not purely symbolic.

It follows equally that in the case of the death of a kinsman or friend the reverse behaviour is found: every effort is made to preserve the corpse integrally and save the reserve of life which it still contains. In the case of a young man or woman who dies unfulfilled, an appropriate ritual (e.g. of marriage) may be performed to offer him or her a compensation for what was missed in life, in order to prevent this unused energy from turning into a malign force.

Notes

1. According to a restoration recently proposed by W. G. Lambert (1980: 57-58), the myth of Atraḫâsis contains a reference to a limit set on human life by the goddess Nintu, advised by the god Enki, after the Flood (cf. Lambert and Millard, 1969: 103).
2. On the first type of sovereignty, see Cassin, 1969: 144 ff.
3. The net is an attribute of warrior gods of the type of Ninurta (Ningirsu is represented on the Stele of the Vultures encircling the enemies of Lagash in his net) and also of gods of justice like Shamash. For the net of Yahweh see Hosea VII: 12; Ezekiel XII: 13; XVII: 19-20, XXXII: 3; Job XIX: 6 and *passim*.
4. In the myth of the creation of mankind it is Bêlêt-ilî — also called Nintu or Mami — who has to make *lullû* to relieve the labouring gods of their burden; in *Gilgamesh* it is the goddess Aruru who makes the *lullû* Enkidu.
5. This term must be taken literally and not translated "monster" as e.g. Labat does (Labat *et al.*, 1970: 54).
6. *Enûma-elish*, Tablet IV l. 136: "He splits the abortion, he wishes to make beautiful things". Cf. Labat *et al.*, 1970: 54.
7. Tablet IV ll. 81 ff., Labat *et al.*, 1970: 53. The contrast between Marduk and Kingu, the general of Tiamat's army, is further heightened by the ardour of the former and the inactivity of the latter, who takes no part in the fighting, in which only Tiamat and Marduk are involved. The impression is always given that the sovereignty which Kingu acquires "through the marriage-bed" is to be contrasted, in its effeminate and feeble character, with the sovereignty of Marduk, legitimised by the assembly of the gods (cf. Cassin, 1969).
8. On the contrary, the verb *dâku*, which also means "kill", is used of humans, of animals, and of a tall plant (a palm-tree or reeds, for example) which is left to die.
9. Hosea IV: 10, IX: 14. The relation between adultery and sterility also appears in Genesis XX: 17, where the wives of Abimelech become sterile after the "adultery" of Abimelech with Sarah, and in Numbers V, where a woman undergoing the ordeal by bitter water will be able to bear a child if she is innocent, while if she is guilty her belly will swell but she will remain sterile.
10. Hosea IX: 16b, "And if they bear children, I will kill the darlings of their womb", and earlier, chapter 12, "And if they rear sons, I will take these from them before they come to manhood". Cf. also Wisdom III: 16, "But children of adulterers, these shall have no future, the offspring of an unlawful bed must vanish."
11. Lackenbacher, 1971: 124 ll. 7-8. To be born in the street can have a number of connotations. The street represents open space in opposition to the closed space of the house. To be born in the street may be due to a chance circumstance and in this case it is an omen; but it may equally indicate the social status of the mother. See in this connection the

significance of the street (*sûqu*) in certain legal documents of fraternal adoption (Cassin,1968: 87 n.26). Proper names mark those who bear them as coming "from the street" (Sûqâja and Sûqâjtu). In the present case, however, the birth of the *eṭlu* in the street suggests that he has failed to achieve a proper entry into life, just as the young woman who after her death becomes an *ardat-lilî* (see below) fails to achieve a proper end to it.

12. Several lines on the obverse of the tablet (Lackenbacher, 1971: 131) also mention the frustrations and setbacks which have marked the short life of the future *ardat-lilî*: among other things, she has "mismanaged" her death by not giving up her *eṭemmu*, spirit, through her mouth (Lackenbacher, 1971: 131, 139, ll. 8–9, column I of the obverse).

13. With regard to the "amusements" shared with companions (a reference to age-classes?), which the *ardat-lilî* has missed, it is worth recalling that Ereshkigal, the Lady of the Great Earth, the goddess of the lower world, also complains of having been deprived of the pleasures of other young women — the dance, the revels of young girls. Another young woman destined to die before having fully lived, the daughter of Jephthah (Judges XI: 37) although she is resigned to the fate awaiting her, asks her father, "let me be free for two months. I shall go and wander in the mountains, and with my companions bewail my virginity", before being sacrificed to fulfil the vow made by Jephthah to Yahweh.

    For a different interpretation of the passage concerning the *ardat-lilî* see Finkelstein (1966).

14. Luckenbill, 1924, 46, vol. VI. ll. 10–12. For discussion of this passage see Cassin, 1968: 128 n. 43.

15. 2 Kings VIII: 12, XV: 16, Amos I: 13 (cf. Hosea X: 14), Hosea XIV: 1.

16. Numbers XXXI: 17, 18, 35; Judges XXI: 11–12.

17. This is the meaning of the constant curse in Akkadian inscriptions, "May the gods tear out his roots and destroy his seed", on which see Cassin (in press), n.47.

References

Cassin, E. (1968). "Le Splendeur divine". Mouton, Paris and La Haye.

Cassin, E. (1969). Pouvoirs de la femme et structures familiales. *Revue d'assyriologie*, **63**, 121–148.

Cassin, E. (in press). "Le mort — valeur et représentation". In "L'Idéologie funéraire" (J.-P. Vernant, ed.). Cambridge University Press, Cambridge.

Finkelstein, J. J. (1966). Sex offenses in Sumerian laws. *Journal of the American Oriental Society*, **86**, 355–372.

Gurney, O. R. (1962). Tammuz reconsidered. *Journal of Semitic Studies*, **7**, 147–160.

Labat, R. Caquot, A., Sznycer, M. and Vieyra, M. (1970). "Les Religions du proche-orient asiatique". Fayard/Denoel, Paris.

LACKENBACHER, S. (1971). Note sur l'*ardat-lilî*. *Revue d'assyriologie*, **65**, 119–154.

LAMBERT, W. G. (1980). The theology of death. *In* "Death in Mesopotamia" (B. Alster, ed.), pp. 53–66. Akademisk Forlag, Copenhagen.

LAMBERT, W. G. and MILLARD, A. R. (1969). "Atra-ḫāsis". Clarendon Press, Oxford.

LUCKENBILL, D. D. (1924). "The Annals of Sennacherib". Oriental Institute Publications No. 2. University of Chicago Press, Chicago, Illinois.

SODEN, W. VON (1955). Gibt es ein Zeugnis dafür, dass die Babylonier an die Wiederauferstehung Marduks geglaubt haben? *Zeitschrift für Assyriologie*, **51**, 130–166.

SODEN, W. VON (1957). Ein neues Bruchstück des assyrischen Kommentars zum Marduk-Ordal. *Zeitschrift für Assyriologie* **52**, 224–234.

WIDENGREN, G. (1953). Quelques remarques sur l'émasculation rituelle chez les peuples sémitiques. *In* "Studia Orientalia Ioanni Pedersen", pp. 377–384. Munksgaard, Copenhagen.

Index of Personal Names

A

Abel, 317
Achilles, 266, 280, 288f., 291
Ackerknecht, E. H., 39, 53
Adam and Eve, 317
Adams, M. J., 276, 281
Adams, W. Y., 35, 49f., 53
Admetus, 280
Aeschylus, 280
Agrawala, R. C., 302, 313
Ahern, E., 268, 271, 281
Aird, I., 68, 74
Alcestis, 280
Alcott, L. M., 279
Alexander VII, Pope, 122, 124
Allison, A. C., 68, 74
Almeida, M. B. de, 161
Anderson, R. M., 74, 77
Angel, J. L., 49, 53, 79, 84, 87ff., 92, 98
Apsû, 318ff.
Apte, V. M., 306, 314
Apuka, son of Pendena, 213–216
Ariès, Ph., 250, 258, 264, 268, 273, 276, 280f.
Aristotle, 269, 274, 280
Armelagos, G. J., 35f., 39, 42, 49f., 53–57

B

Bacon, F., 253
Bakhtine, M., 173
Baré, J. F., 144, 146
Barley, N., 1, 10, 150, 159
Barnes, J. A., 222f.
Barnstaple, E. A., 75
Barraud, C., 175
Barton, T. S., 56
Bassett, E. J., 47f., 54
Batrawi, A. M., 34, 54
Battiscombe, C. F., 117, 135
Beare, A. S., 78
Bêlêt-Ilî (Aruru), 319, 323
Bellamy, D., 61, 74
Bennet, G., 141, 147
Bennett, J. H., 73f.
Bentall, H. H., 74
Bentham, J., 125
Bernhard, W., 68, 74
Bernini, G. L., 121f., 124
Bernini, L., 78
Berry, A. C., 25, 30, 35, 54
Berry, R. J., 1, 7, 11, 25, 30, 35, 54, 61, 66, 70f., 73ff.
Bersu, G., 28, 30
Bertrand, M., 276, 281
Bhattacharya, S., 302, 314

Subject Index

335